W9-BDZ-143

MUSKINGUM UNIVERSITY LIBRARY
NEW CONCORD, OHIO 43762

Harvard Historical Studies · 177

Published under the auspices
of the Department of History
from the income of the
Paul Revere Frothingham Bequest
Robert Louis Stroock Fund
Henry Warren Torrey Fund

Reimagining Europe

Kievan Rus'
in the Medieval World

Christian Raffensperger

Harvard University Press
Cambridge, Massachusetts
London, England
2012

Copyright © 2012 by the President and Fellows of Harvard College
All rights reserved
Printed in the United States of America

Library of Congress Cataloging-in-Publication Data

Raffensperger, Christian.
    Reimagining Europe : Kievan Rus' in the medieval world / Christian Raffensperger.
        p. cm.
    Includes bibliographical references and index.
    ISBN 978-0-674-06384-6 (alkaline paper)
    1. Kievan Rus—History—862–1237.   2. Kievan Rus—Civilization—Byzantine
influences.   3. Kievan Rus—Relations—Europe.   4. Europe—Relations— Kievan
Rus.   5. Christianity— Kievan Rus.   I. Title.
    DK73.R24 2012
    947′.02—dc23   2011039243

For Cara

Contents

Reimagining Europe

Introduction

Rethinking Rus'

Students of history often begin by seeking "the facts," a set of concrete pieces that will create an edifice of "truth" and thus an explanation. This is difficult to accomplish even for something as recent as World War II, much less an arena of study dealing with events that took place a thousand years ago. Simon Franklin, one of the most distinguished scholars of medieval Rus', aptly states the problem for those of us working in Rusian history:

> Historians of Kievan culture spend much of their time trying to find plausible ways to fill the gaps *between* the sparse fragments of real evidence, contemplating the unknown and the unknowable. Any connected account of Kievan culture is an agglomeration of hypotheses. Worse than that: virtually any reading of any word in a Kievan text is hypothetical. The manuscripts are late, the variants are prolific. Either we retreat behind raw data, or else we accept that choices have to be made but that certainty is unattainable, that there is an implicit "perhaps" in every statement.[1]

It may seem odd to begin a book that seeks to prove, or disprove, as the case may be, a vision of medieval Rus' and Europe with a quotation illustrating that everything is in flux; however, this is a requirement for understanding the arguments within this book, as well as much of Kievan history. While I am firm in my commitment to the facts, arguments, and hypotheses presented here, much of what I say contains "an implicit 'perhaps.'" Following the German historian Gerd Althoff I believe that "it is better to admit ignorance on specific issues than to manufacture apparent certainties that create more problems than they resolve."[2]

1

With these caveats understood, the work presented here attempts to overturn the historical misperception that Rus' in the tenth, eleventh, and twelfth centuries was part of a Byzantine Commonwealth, and thus separate from Europe, substituting instead a broader picture in which Rus' was a functioning part of the larger medieval European community alongside its neighbors, such as Sweden, Poland, the German Empire, and Hungary. This perspective and the framework for the argument that is laid out here challenge the conventional wisdom in regard to the place of Rus' in Europe with the aim of creating a wider medieval Europe and a broader historiography in which Rusian scholars can draw on European materials, and vice versa, to show the interrelationship of the various European societies, Rus' included.[3] Such a change in the scholarship would lead to a better understanding of all the parties involved and would build on the framework of a European Rus' that has been created in this book.

The idea of "Europe" itself can be interpreted in many ways. Europe is a continent, though one with no firm eastern border, but also an idea. Latin has traditionally been used to define "Europe" for medievalists. The language of the Roman Empire, appropriated by the Roman Church, has seemed coterminous with the boundaries of medieval Europe.[4] However, this presents a variety of problems, to note only two: One, the majority of the European (however defined) elite were illiterate in this period,[5] while two, Latin was clearly a language of religion for the Roman Church, but not for all Christianity and not for one single political entity. The plurality of political entities leaves space for the viability of other languages, and the existence of multiple languages for Christianity allows them all to participate in a larger Christian *oikoumene*. Thus if one speaks of "Christendom," this should include all Christian political entities, at least in the period before serious schism between the Constantinopolitan- and Roman-based churches.[6] This problem is not the focus of this book, and is much larger than it, but for the purposes of argument here, Europe will be a geographical construct, as well as what Timothy Champion has called "a culturally constituted entity."[7] The participation of Rus' in broader European affairs, religion, marriage, culture, and so forth inherently includes Rus' in a single culturally constituted entity, for which we will use the identifier *Europe*.

The scholarship that has focused on Rus' over the past two centuries has rarely used the formulation "medieval Rus'," which I use here. The reason for this exemplifies the problem that this book hopes to solve. Those writing about the Middle Ages, or medieval Europe, rarely include Rus' except for an almost obligatory mention of the Vikings, the conversion to Christianity (with emphasis on the "Byzantine" portion of the conversion), or the Mongols, depending on the book's subject or time period.[8] Those writing about Rus' write about *Drevniaia Rus'*, using the Russian formulation of "ancient Rus'," and focus almost exclusively on Rus' itself, Rus' as progenitor of the Russian or Ukrainian state, the traditional Rusian–Byzantine ties, or sometimes Rusian–Scandinavian ties[9] (though usually only early Viking-era relations such as the Normanist controversy, which I view as resolved).[10] The two scholarships have been divided somewhere along the eastern border of Germany, and their lack of interaction has left enormous lacunae in the historiography. Hidden in those lacunae are the connections between Rus' and the rest of Europe in the medieval period. This book is an attempt to draw out those connections in a few key areas, specifically dynastic marriages and religious and trade connections, to show the engagement of Rus' with Europe and remedy the division in medieval European scholarship.

This book also strives to revise the idea of the Byzantine Commonwealth codified in the writings of Dimitri Obolensky in his book of the same name.[11] This idea has played into the common perception, advocated originally by Muscovite theoreticians to create a closer tie with Byzantium's legacy, that the conversion of Rus' to Christianity through the mediation of Byzantine priests placed Rus' in the orbit of the Byzantine emperor. Following the publication of Obolensky's classic work, this idea became interwoven into the minds of historians working on all aspects of medieval history, including Byzantium, medieval Europe, and Drevniaia Rus'. The problem is that Obolensky's formulations, though well researched and formulated, create a flawed picture by focusing almost exclusively on the Slavs, and so a major theoretical portion of this book has been devoted to revising his idea. The Byzantine Ideal, advanced in Chapter 1, lays out the idea that Byzantium was the *magistra Europae,* and not just the master of the Slavs, due to its continuity with the Roman Empire. In addition, Rus' (and other Slavic-based political entities) did not copy from Byzantium or have Byzantine ideas/titles/

and so on imposed upon them—rather, they were appropriating Byzantium, as were other peoples of Europe, because of Byzantium's grandeur and its imperial legacy. This change in formulation results in a changed medieval world in which Byzantine influence is not an either/or proposition, but rather a sliding scale. Rus' was not a satellite of Byzantium, but one of many European kingdoms appropriating Byzantine titulature, art, architecture, coinage, and so on to reinforce their own legitimacy.

This book as a whole lays out a new framework for medieval Rusian history, one in which Rus' is part and parcel of medieval Europe. The topics and ideas advanced here could each be dealt with in a book, or books, of their own, by specialists in history, art history, linguistics, and numismatics. This book truly is a framework, a base, upon which to build future research for myself and other scholars. But it is also a brief window into Rusian history from the end of the tenth through the mid-twelfth century. After the middle of the twelfth century, politics and religion began to change in both Rus' and the West. The advent of the crusading ideal in Europe hardened perceptions of the divide between Latin and Orthodox Christianity and pushed those attitudes from the religious into the political sphere. This was cemented by actions such as the 1204 sack of Constantinople, and multiple crusades against Rus' by Swedes, Rigans, Teutonic Knights, and others. The disintegration of central control in Rus' in 1146, which marks the ending point for this book, combined with the Mongol invasion and subjugation of Rus' a century later provided further blows for Rusian integration into Europe. The picture presented here attempts to accurately reflect the image of Rus' in medieval Europe for a brief two hundred years with the understanding that after that period, the picture slowly but completely changed.

Transliteration and Foreign Names

The transliteration in this book has followed the accepted practice in use in the historical discipline in American universities, thus the use of -ii instead of the European -ij for the endings of some Russian words. Similarly, the Rusian royal family is here spelled *Riurikid* rather than the more common *Rurikid*. Transliteration of Greek has followed similar guidelines in the few places that Greek has been transliterated rather than translated.

Foreign names abound throughout this book, and every attempt has been made to express correctly each name in regard to its original language while following modern American conventions. However, due to the plethora of accepted spellings for many foreign names, consistency was the key for the majority of such names—for example, the use of *Knud,* rather than *Canute, Cnut,* or *Knut.* Names of Rusians are often expressed in the first instance with the Russian convention of name and patronymic, such as *Vladimir Sviatoslavich.* The modern *-ovna* and *-ovich* endings have been used when appropriate, though the *-ov-* addition occurred after the medieval period. Similarly, patronymics as shorthand for a large family group have also been used, such that in multiple places there is discussion of the struggles between the *Iziaslavichi* (sons of Iziaslav) and the *Vsevolodovichi* (sons of Vsevolod).

One of the most complex issues in regard to translation was the titulature used, in addition to modern territorial appellations. Part of the bedrock of this book is that the territory under discussion is Rus', not Russia. This is to correctly express the historically accurate terminology and to avoid the modern political and ethnic entanglements used by reading Russian or Ukrainian history back into this period, when there was no linguistic, or other, differentiation. Despite this sentiment, I have used anachronistic terminology for Sweden where the kingdom was not unified into one until the middle of this period. Before that time there were two relatively independent kingdoms of the Svear and the Götar, which have been falsely unified in my text.[12] Similarly I have used the idea of a "German Empire" to avoid the more anachronistic "Holy Roman Empire," which did not appear until the early modern period.[13] The rulers of the German territory very rarely referred to themselves as *rex Teutonicorum* or *rex Germanorum,* much preferring to associate themselves with the Roman heritage and ties with the Roman Empire via the title *rex Romanorum.* However, "German Empire" and "emperor" are more accurate than either "Holy Roman" or "Roman," and lead the reader to the correct conclusions in regard to territorial holdings and placement in Europe. All of these problems are underlain by one not discussed here at all and better left to other places, which is the nature of the medieval state itself as an entity with a concretely defined center and ruling family, but with porous boundaries that are often handed back and forth between centers with little fanfare.[14]

The actual titulature was a problem as well, the most significant issue being what to call Rusian rulers. This problem, I am afraid, awaits a longer survey.[15] In the Old East Slavic chronicles the ruler was called *kniaz'*, which has been translated into English most recently as prince, though it was commonly translated as duke from the sixteenth through the early twentieth century. In Latin, however, the Rusian ruler was almost without exception called *rex*, which is always translated into English as king. I have spoken at length elsewhere regarding the correct modern English translation, which should be king,[16] but this book is not the place for such an elaborate argument, and so the Rusian title, kniaz', is often simply left as "ruler," with other qualifiers as necessary.[17]

Sources

To return to my opening quotation and the problem expressed by Simon Franklin, a few words must be said about the main source base for Rusian history, the *Povest' vremennykh let* (henceforth, *PVL*), and the Rusian chronicles in general. Chronicle writing began in Rus' in the second half of the eleventh century, as far as historians and linguists can determine.[18] It is at this time that references in the *PVL* (compiled roughly 1116) begin to be expanded, as if the chronicler had more information, was dealing with personal informants, or was simply more familiar with events. Exact dates become more common, and celestial observations such as comets are mentioned and are readily datable. Unfortunately, the earliest extant redaction of the *PVL* is the Laurentian, dating from the later fourteenth century and named for its copyist, the monk Lavrentii who worked for Dmitrii Konstantinovich of Suzdal'.[19] This version has been the most commonly used, until quite recently. The Hypatian redaction, the extant version of which is dated to the mid-fifteenth century, is the other common version of the *PVL* and represents an alternate chronicle tradition from the Laurentian.[20] As one can imagine, the problems associated with using fourteenth- and fifteenth-century redactions to discuss events of the tenth, eleventh, and twelfth centuries is problematic, to say the least. For years scholars have debated the question of the reliability of the *PVL* as a source for early Rus'. There is an immense amount of scholarship on the provenance of the chronicle, from classic work like that of A. A. Shakhmatov (whose *Razyskannia o russkikh letopisiakh* has recently been reprinted) to more modern commentaries by Donald Ostrowski and Omeljan Pritsak, among others, all of which deal in some way with the relevance of the chronicle to the period it is written about.[21] I will direct the reader to this scholarship, rather than attempt to summarize and duplicate it here. Following these authors, the majority of historians believe that, in general, the *PVL* presents an accurate picture of the time under discussion, rather than simply reflecting the period of the extant redaction. The situation for the historian is, however, still complicated by the fact that the chronicles were created for a political purpose, by rulers seeking to portray their own rule and that of their close kin in a favorable light; and thus with the text accepted as relevant, the issue of bias comes to the fore. With the spread of the Riurikid family and the growing association of particular kin-groups of Riurikids with specific towns or areas, there developed a regional chronicle tradition in the twelfth century, picking up from the *PVL*, such that each town of any size had its own chronicle. Many of these chronicles are extant today, though also from later redactions. For this book, I have used Donald Ostrowski's interlinear collation of the major extant copies of the *PVL*, for the period through the early twelfth century as the main Russian primary source.[22] This version contains all of the relevant chronicle traditions, as well as providing a paradosis, representing the best reading of the various chronicle editions. This allows the reader to see not only the best possible reconstruction of the text, but to check that information with the extant sources to determine why and how the choice of reading was made. It is the best way that historians have to work through the major source problems of dealing with the few Rusian sources for the history of medieval Rus'.

I have used a variety of sources beyond the Russian chronicles, including ecclesiastical sources[23] and foreign (non-Rusian) materials including royal and monastic chronicles, saints' lives, charters, and histories.[24] This allows me to compare and contrast the material with the Rusian chronicles to attempt to evaluate the validity of their presentation. It also allows me to work on the larger goal of this book of integrating Rus' more broadly into medieval Europe. The medieval European sources mention Rus' quite often and in a straightforward fashion indicative of regular contact and the expected understanding of the readers. European sources tell a tale about Rus' that is different from that told in most histories, and those sources deserve inclusion in any work on medieval Rusian history.

One significant source problem remains, and that is the authorship of the Rusian chronicles. The authors, as was common of chronicles throughout Europe in the Middle Ages, were monks. Immediately this creates a problem, as the worldview of the church was not always the worldview of the people the monk was writing about. This problem surfaces in every chapter of this book, in particular in regard to the growing schism between the Latin and Orthodox churches, which the monastic authors of the Rusian chronicles are much more concerned about than the rulers of Rus' seem to be from their various actions. The monks also, I believe, deliberately avoided mention of the West and Western contacts of Rus', either because of anti-Latin feeling (as seen in the numerous anti-Latin polemics included in the *PVL*) or because of a narrow parochial attitude focused on church affairs and local Rusian affairs, probably in that order.[25] This being said, the chroniclers do *not* go out of their way to explicitly denounce those Rusians who spend time or marry in the Latin West. Those travels and/or marriages might not be mentioned with specificity, or referred to at all, but it does not seem to prejudice the chronicler against those individuals.[26] Source bias is a difficult problem, but one every historian must deal with. One of the most common ways to work around such problems is, as I have done, to use multiple types of sources. The Latin chronicles, Greek sources, Scandinavian sagas, and other sources all come with their own biases, but by working with all of them, the information from the Rusian sources can be integrated into a more complete whole that displays the historical actors and their actions more accurately.

The aim of this book is to create a picture of a Rusian kingdom that was part of medieval Europe during this period. To do that I have laid out a theoretical challenge to the prevailing wisdom on the place of Rus' in Europe, revising the concept of a Byzantine Commonwealth toward that of a Byzantine Ideal. The Byzantine Ideal was emulated not only by the Rusians and other Slavs but by all of Europe because of the legacy of Rome preserved in Byzantium, thus placing Rus' in an equal position with the other kingdoms of Europe and not uniquely indebted to

Byzantium. I have also attempted to discuss the religious question, one of the strongest arguments for creating a medieval Rus' separate from Latin Europe. I show that Rus' did convert under the auspices of the Byzantine Church but attempted to steer a path between Orthodox and Latin Christianity, maintaining ties with both, and accepting saints, saints' lives, and other religious accoutrements from both sides of the supposed ecclesiastical divide to create their own micro-Christendom. Rus' also existed in an economic world in which they participated in various "exchange zones," and not simply along the north–south axis, the route from the Varangians to the Greeks. The Russian trading connections, centered in many ways on Kiev, made Rus' a centerpoint of trade not only in Europe, but for Western Eurasia. The main connection that Rus' had with the rest of Europe, however, was a political connection, expressed through the plethora of dynastic marriages arranged between the Riurikids and the royal families of Europe in the tenth through mid-twelfth centuries. These marriages, their political role, and the vastly understated position of the women involved in them are discussed at some length in this book to show their role in connecting Rus' into the web of medieval European politics and in placing Rus' firmly in medieval Europe. It is my hope that this book, which only scratches the surface of many of these important topics, not only will create a new picture of a European Rus' in the mind of the reader, but also will lay the groundwork for future scholarly studies in which Rus' is integrated into medieval Europe and the details of Rus' can be examined alongside those of England, France, Germany, and Poland without special comment as to the appropriateness of the Rusian example.

— 1 —

The Byzantine Ideal

Much historiography has placed Rus' and the other Slavic lands under the sway of a theoretical Byzantine Commonwealth. But as this book will endeavor to show, this is not entirely correct. The paradigm of a Byzantine Commonwealth as codified by Dmitri Obolensky gives the impression that there was a measure of central control exercised by the Byzantine emperor over the territory of the commonwealth.[1] Although this is incorrect, Obolensky is correct in his assertion that Byzantium had a strong influence on the Slavic lands.[2] This is most clearly seen in the lands of the South Slavs (Bulgaria and Serbia), where there were kingdoms occasionally politically subordinate to Byzantium and that spawned rivals for the title of emperor of the Romans. The emendation to this assertion is that it was not just the Slavic lands that were influenced by Byzantium, but also all of Europe.[3] While modern historians persist in using the name Byzantium (begun by German historians of the sixteenth century), the medieval world on all sides of that empire knew it as Rome. It was, especially in their iconography and self-conception, the continuation of the Roman Empire begun by Julius Caesar in the first century B.C.E., and because of that it was the longest-lasting empire in western Eurasia in the Middle Ages. The importance of this realization lies in the understanding of the medieval mindset. In the words of D. M. Nicol, "The Byzantine Empire was not, like the kingdoms or principalities of antiquity, a temporary phenomenon which would one day come to an end. It was 'a realm foreseen in the plan of the Creator, anchored in Christian eschatology, organically involved in the age-old history of mankind and destined to endure until the Second Coming.'"[4]

The ruler of a "barbarian" kingdom in late antiquity usually looked to the Roman Empire for validation and was tied to the emperor in some manner.[5] This tradition did not end with late antiquity and the fall of the Western Roman Empire. Rulers in the early medieval and medieval periods still felt a historical lack in their own dynastic histories and they attempted to tie themselves to the Roman legacy. The easiest way to do that was with a tie to Byzantium.[6] This idea will be discussed in depth later with regard to marriage (Chapters 2 and 3), but that was not the only way a country could tie itself to the Roman legacy. Examined in this chapter are a variety of ways kings and kingdoms could create a physical tie with Roman antiquity that would legitimate their own rule. These numerous methods included stylistic appropriation of Byzantine and Roman titulature and rulership, seals and coins, and perhaps most visibly, art. These techniques for increasing a kingdom's ties with Roman antiquity are all part of a Byzantine Ideal in medieval Europe. The majority of this chapter will deal with Europe outside of Rus'. Rus' appears in this chapter to discuss, briefly, specific instances of influence from Byzantium and Rusian reaction to them, but while the amount of Byzantine influence on Rus' has been well documented, the interpretation of the image of Byzantium, specifically their Roman heritage, is slightly different from that in western Europe.

What is the Byzantine Ideal? The Byzantine Ideal is a concept designed to revise the idea of the Byzantine Commonwealth. Dmitri Obolensky's *The Byzantine Commonwealth* is an impressive work of scholarship that documents pervasive Byzantine influence on the Slavic states of Eastern Europe.[7] However, it focuses almost solely on those Slavs, excluding other regions that were influenced by Byzantium for geographic reasons, and implying through the use of the term *commonwealth* some measure of central control that did not exist.[8] The existence in Byzantine imperial ideology of a "family hierarchy" headed by the Byzantine emperor reflected Byzantine belief, but not necessarily political reality, though most honored Byzantium's cultural heritage and position as the continuation of the Roman Empire.[9] The essence of the Byzantine Ideal is that Byzantium, as the last vestige of the Roman Empire, exerted an ideological or cultural force on the kingdoms of medieval Europe as they were establishing themselves and their dynasties, and those kingdoms then endeavored to connect themselves in some way to Byzantium and through Byzantium to Rome in order to enhance their own legitimacy.[10] The rulers and elites of these European kingdoms subscribed to the Byzantine Ideal by using Byzantine titulature, imagery, and art to enhance their own status both with their peers and with their people. These rulers did not create their own legitimating devices; instead, after converting to Christianity, they needed a new source for the legitimacy of their rulership as they could no longer claim descent from a god or gods, as had previously been common. A new type of legitimacy was required, and Rome was the model of worldwide empire that was most often chosen. After the fall of Rome in the west, this did not mean the end of Roman legitimacy, for Rome continued in Constantinople, still exerting an influence on Europe.[11] Henry III, for example, was one of the most powerful medieval German rulers—he was crowned emperor, held a vast empire in central Europe, and placed three popes in Rome—and yet he also "took pride" in his Byzantine heritage and imitated the Byzantines "in dress and deportment."[12] Like Henry III, the rulers and elites of various European kingdoms, including the German Empire, France, Anglo-Saxon England, and Norman England, sought to enhance their own status and prestige through a connection with the Rome that we know as Byzantium.

The terms *Byzantine* and *Roman* must be discussed as well because there is a certain amount of understandable confusion. In the medieval period the Roman Empire never fully collapsed. The Roman Empire fell at Rome, but continued in Constantinople until 1453, which is to say that for many medieval peoples, the empire based at Constantinople was always, at least to some extent, the Roman Empire. The modern term *Byzantium* was popularized in the nineteenth century for the Eastern Roman Empire after the fall of Rome in the west. The term was a reference to the city that became Constantinople in the fourth century, and has been used by some as a way to reserve the "Roman" legacy for the city of Rome and western Europe in the Middle Ages.[13] However, despite some disparaging terminology of the western medieval peoples toward the Byzantines as "Greeks," or worse, "Greeklings," they often referred to them as Romans. Liudprand of Cremona, a fluent Greek speaker himself,[14] provides a fascinating example as he uses the term "Roman" disparagingly to refer to the town and the people living there, while he uses "Greek" as a both positive and negative descriptor of the Byzantines, depending upon the piece of work.[15] To avoid a confusion of terminology throughout this chapter (and through-out this book), I will refer to the Eastern Roman Empire as Byzantium and its inhabitants as Byzantine, but it is essential to remember that for the purposes of medieval peoples, Byzantium continued the majesty of Rome and the idea of empire that it symbolized.[16]

Also of importance in this discussion is the question, Whose image is being appropriated? The simple answer is Rome, but which one? The first Rome (Rome) or the second Rome (Constantinople)? In her in-sightful book, *Europe after Rome,* Julia Smith discusses a few of the appropriations that will be discussed in this chapter, and applies them to attempts to imitate the first Rome.[17] However, while her examples are excellent and her argument persuasive, I have interpreted the evi-dence slightly differently and with a slightly different focus—Byzantium. The Carolingians, Ottonians, and others whom she discusses as using that "rhetoric of Romanness" were in fact appropriating Byzantine im-agery and titulature to do it. It was Byzantium that preserved the Roman art and architecture, the Roman titles and symbols that were then reintro-duced into western Europe, in the manner of the Renaissance, hundreds of years later. Paul Magdalino demonstrates particular reasons for the fo-cus on the second Rome, rather than the first:

The most eloquent testimony to the wealth of Byzantium in the late twelfth century comes from the observation of an Anglo-Norman writer, Gerald of Wales, that the revenues of the German and English monarchies were as nothing compared with those of the kingdoms of Sicily and the Greek empire before these were destroyed 'by the Lat-ins'; the yearly income from Palermo alone (a smaller city than Con-stantinople) exceeded that from the whole of England.

The pull of Constantinople was due not only to its role as the admin-istrative capital, but also to its status as the 'reigning city' of New Rome, an unrivalled showcase of holy relics, glittering treasures, an-cient public monuments and magnificent buildings, a megalopolis with a population somewhere between 200,000 and 400,000.[18]

To take another example, even in the early Middle Ages coinage was being copied from Byzantium, rather than from Rome proper. This is clearly indicated by the appropriately falsified mint marks on the coins in Gaul and elsewhere that used "CON" or some variation of it to purport to being minted in Constantinople.[19] It might have been easier to use a Roman mint mark, but it was the Byzantine one that was chosen, indicating the focus of their interest, and of the prevailing influence in Europe.[20]

The purpose of the Byzantine Ideal is to unite smaller individual studies of incidents of influence. This phenomenon is Europe-wide and thus needs to be understood in a larger context than can be provided by a series of smaller studies on history, art history, numismatics, and archaeology. The Byzantine Ideal brings together the data provided by these individual studies within the framework of a Europe looking toward Byzantium for legitimacy; from rulers seeking stability in coinage, or grandeur of titulature, to rulers and elites looking to model their own art on Byzantium to show their level of culture, Europe looked to define itself using Byzantine imagery and terms in an attempt to carry on the Roman legacy. The very fact of this appropriation inherently changed what was appropriated, so that while showing the importance of Byzantium to them, they also used the appropriated thing for their own purposes. The kingdoms of medieval Europe that appropriated titulature, art, architecture, and the rest from Byzantium were not part of a Byzantine commonwealth, but all held Byzantium in a place of honor, and used its creations for their own purposes to enhance their own legitimacy through a link with the last remnant of the Roman Empire.

The importance of the existence of the Byzantine Ideal to the image of Rus' in medieval Europe is obvious. In the contemporary picture, Rus' and most medieval Slavic states are adjuncts to Byzantium and Byzantine history because of their borrowings from Byzantium. However, once one examines the history of Byzantine influence on medieval Europe, the picture changes. Krijnie Ciggaar has been a driving force behind the new studies on Byzantine influence in Europe (which do not include Rus') but has taken her position too far in a certain direction: "Western Europe was original in its willingness to accept foreign elements and foreign ideas. By its consciousness of its own identity it could open its frontiers to foreign influences and drink from the Byzantine fount of life and learning."[21] Instead of Byzantium being all-powerful, western Europe was a bastion of originality in its desire to learn from Byzantium, once again leaving out central and eastern Europe. When

Rusian appropriation of Byzantine style is discussed, it is a clear case of cultural hegemony, or a case of Rus' simply being in the Byzantine orbit, or commonwealth.[22] When the same occurs in western Europe, they are considered original for their decision to appropriate from Byzantium. However, this all changes with the Byzantine Ideal under which Rus' was just one among many in Europe who appropriated from Byzantium, none of which were ruled or controlled by, but rather were influenced by and enamored of, Byzantium. This places Rus' firmly among such western European stalwarts as the German Empire, Anglo-Saxon England, and Normandy. The inclusion of Rus' in such a group goes a long way toward advancing the proposition that Rus' was part of medieval Europe in this period and not a member of a Slavic Byzantinophile fringe, and it leads to a re-envisioning of the place of Byzantium in the cultural *Weltanschauung* of Europe.

Another of the problems in dealing with this topic is the idea of influence. "The process of influencing and of being influenced, of actively copying elements of other cultures or rejecting them, is complex and complicated."[23] Ciggaar is not wrong in stating that this is a complex problem. For many years the idea of cultural influence has operated under the precept of what Peter Brown has called "cultural hydraulics," which is to say that culture moves from a high-pressure area to a low-pressure area.[24] This idea is evident in works like *The Byzantine Commonwealth* and Robert Bartlett's *Making of Europe,* where there is clearly one dominant culture (the Byzantines and the Franks, respectively) and all other areas inevitably come to exhibit characteristics of that culture purely based on reaction to high- and low-pressure zones.[25] When one examines this picture in any depth, it is clearly incorrect—cultures do not behave like water, seeking to become level across boundaries. A different language must be used—we should be discussing appropriation, as Kathleen Ashley and Véronique Plesch write: "Contrary to the notions of 'origin' or 'influence,' 'appropriation' emphasizes the act of taking; it is understood to be 'active, subjective, and motivated.'"[26] This seems to be a better definition for our purposes. Constructive borrowing might be another, perhaps more wordy way to say the same thing, though borrowing has the unnecessary implication of a repayment.[27] Medieval Europe was not destined to absorb aspects of Byzantine culture because it existed in a cultural low-pressure zone. Instead, each kingdom *chose* to appropriate certain elements from Byzantine culture because it wanted those elements for itself, to use for its own purposes—not coincidentally like the root for appropriate, *appropriare* (to make one's own).[28] A good example of this is Byzantine products that were used in the West, though not for their intended purpose, such as a Byzantine chrysobull that was so beautiful it was used as an altar frontal in Goslar Cathedral.[29] Byzantium was a cultural power in the Middle Ages, but that did not mean that Western and Slavic cultural appropriations were inevitable. Instead, Byzantium was honored as the surviving remnant of the great Roman Empire. Appropriating its symbols, terminology, and art, among other things, was seen as a way to take for one's own kingdom a part of that heritage and the veneer of legitimacy that came with it.

As mentioned above, there are numerous disciplines that have contributions to make to the Byzantine Ideal. This book is written from the perspective of a historian, not a numismatist, archaeologist, or art historian. Though experts in those areas have been cited copiously here to provide some of the evidence for the Byzantine Ideal, it was impossible to read or cite everything in all of those disciplines. Like other topics in this book, the Byzantine Ideal is a framework for a larger discussion, one that specialists in many disciplines can begin or continue. For instance, the art historical discussion regarding the influence of Byzantine art in Europe has been ongoing for quite some time, notably launching the first issue of the Dumbarton Oaks Papers in 1941.[30] I do not claim that these are all unique elements that are being presented in this book; many of the same examples can be seen in topical studies in various disciplines or in the works of Krijnie Ciggaar, Julia Smith, and others (all of whose fine work I am indebted to). Rather this chapter seeks to bring together disparate materials from different specialties and unite them under what is new: a common idea, the Byzantine Ideal, which ultimately aids in the creation of the idea of Rus' as a European kingdom as well as changing the way Byzantium is viewed in the medieval European world.

Titulature and Rulership

The Byzantine emperor offered an example of what it meant to be a supreme ruler for other leaders of the Middle Ages. Because of this, which stemmed in part from his descent from the Roman Empire, medieval rulers looked for ways in which they could appropriate some of that imperial grandeur and power for themselves.[31] One of the ways that medieval rulers did this was by adopting Byzantine imperial titulature. They used Byzantine titles to lend themselves and their courts an aura of Roman respectability. Though this section is primarily concerned with titulature, medieval rulers also adopted Byzantine ceremonials and/or law as aspects of rulership; titulature and rulership, then, are ways of connecting one's rule with Byzantium, and through it with the Roman heritage of Europe.

One of the best-known of the Byzantine connections with medieval western Europe is the rule of the German Ottonian emperors. Otto I endeavored to obtain a Byzantine *porphyrogenite* bride for his son Otto II. This marriage did not occur, but Otto was able to arrange a marriage with a non-porphyrogenite Byzantine princess, Theophano. This marriage was designed to increase the legitimacy of Ottonian imperial rule, as a marriage with a Byzantine princess connected the kingdom directly to Byzantine nobility.[32] One of the children of this marriage was Otto III, who became German emperor and was largely raised by his mother, as his father died when he was still young. Otto III had a penchant for things Byzantine, and when he began to rule on his own he began a program that has been referred to as a *renovatio imperii*.[33] This term comes from Otto's first lead seal,[34] which read *"Renovatio imperii Romanorum"* and was dated 998.[35] The seal had an armed figure of Roma on the verso and on the recto a bearded figure copied from a seal of Charlemagne. The idea of renovatio imperii, first articulated by P. E. Schramm, is that Otto was attempting to revive elements of the Roman Empire, specifically the "authority and rule of the emperor."[36] It was only natural for Otto to use both Byzantine and Carolingian techniques in doing this, as Charlemagne himself had appropriated Roman/Byzantine imagery and titulature for himself in his attempt to rebirth the Roman Empire in the west.[37] Otto III also had a deep fascination with Charlemagne and Roman antiquity. He went so far as to open Charlemagne's tomb at Aachen to associate himself and his rule with that ruler. Also essential to an understanding of his nature were his frequent visits to and stays in Rome, meant to garner for himself Roman authority.[38] Otto III, then, was drawing on these two sources to identify himself and his kingdom with Roman imperial power. Gerbert of Aurillac (later Pope Sylvester II), who was a tutor of Otto III described him as "Greek by birth, Roman by Empire, as if by hereditary right [he] seeks to recapture for himself the treasure of Greek and Roman wisdom."[39]

Though he used Charlemagne's head on his coins, the majority of techniques used to identify Otto's rule with Rome were in fact Byzantine. In large part this is because Otto also borrowed from both Charlemagne and the papacy, both heavily influenced themselves by Byzantine titulature and ceremony.[40] "For a family with pretensions to being the *beata stirps* ('blessed family')," such as the Ottonians, "readily recognizable emblems of long-established authority were of inestimable value."[41] Though Otto never used the words "renovatio imperii" except on the seal, his political actions seemed to indicate that he was attempting to appropriate Byzantine styles to do just that, and that those symbols were understood by the political elite with whom he was dealing.[42] This observation is not just a modern one, as some might have it.[43] In the eleventh century, Thietmar of Merseburg wrote that Otto "wished to renew the ancient custom of the Romans."[44] One of the most interesting of Otto's Byzantine initiatives for the Slavic world is his creation of the archbishopric of Gniezno in the year 1000.[45] It has been said that at this meeting Otto also crowned Bolesław as king of the Poles.[46] Though the source for this coronation, Gallus Anonymous, was writing over one hundred years after the events and with the aim of honoring Bolesław's descendants, a much more contemporary German source alludes to something similar. Thietmar of Merseburg, who kept abreast of German imperial affairs, especially those having to do with Poland, records that Otto III raised Bolesław from a *tributarius* into a *dominus,* perhaps implying his ascension to king.[47] The whole episode is indicative of Otto's attempt to create a Byzantine-style empire for himself.[48] The Byzantine emperor was the head of the church as well as of the state for most purposes, and though Ottonian rulers had had the ability to appoint bishops, Otto's wholesale reorganization of the eastern elements under the new archbishop of Gniezno overstepped those older abilities, and was more like the act of an emperor with ecclesiastical authority.[49] This is compounded by Otto's raising of Bolesław to the level of king. An emperor, on the Byzantine/Roman model, had tributary kings serving under him, and this was what Otto made Bolesław, as indicated perhaps by the extensive gifts given to Otto after the Gniezno visit.[50] The affair with Poland is only confirmed by Otto's relations with Hungary, where he was also involved in the creation of an independent archbishopric and the coronation of King Stephen.[51] The same is true of Venice, where he did not explicitly grant independence to the doge but stood as godfather to the son of the doge, thereby creating an implicit subordinate relationship.[52] That this would happen once might be odd, but these three occurrences indicate that Otto was attempting to create subordinate kingdoms to bolster his imperial title. This is confirmed by a miniature from the gospel book of Otto III.[53] This miniature depicts four women paying homage with gifts to the emperor. The emperor is clearly Otto III, and the four women are labeled Sclavinia, Germania, Gallia, and Roma (from farthest to closest to Otto III). The women clearly represent what Otto considered to be the four provinces of his empire, and not coincidentally are ordered in a fashion indicating the importance of Rome, and of the Roman heritage. The inclusion of Sclavinia in this miniature shows that Otto did intend for Bolesław, as a representative Slavic leader, to bear a subordinate role in his empire.

As was seen with his seal discussed above, titulature was also a concern of Otto's. In 998 he began to change titles at his court to reflect imperial eminence. The titles were almost uniformly Byzantine in style, but did not reflect the political reality of Otto's court. For instance, the *praefectus navalis,* who would ostensibly be Otto's head admiral, had no ships under his command.[54] Gerd Althoff, whose excellent biography and review of the scholarship on Otto III informs much of this section, believes that this is because the titles accreted over time rather than being assigned en masse, but this does not answer the question of why there was no weight to the titles.[55] Perhaps the answer lies at the heart of the issue of titulature itself: image. The reason to create impressive-sounding titles or to use titles reminiscent of Rome or Byzantium was to create the image of continuity or the image of a link between Byzantium and Ottonian Germany. Otto's use of Byzantine titles at court created the image to those coming to court of Byzantine grand ceremonial. This is also the reason he wanted to centralize his empire with a capital at Rome.[56] The vast majority of medieval rulers were itinerant, following an earlier model of rulership in which the leader needed to be in close contact with his people to keep their loyalty, did not have the infrastructure to command from a central location, and did not have the ability to feed a court at a central location.[57] All of these things did not speak to the greatness of an empire. The majesty of Rome, or new Rome (Constantinople), was made whole in the capital city. In Constantinople the emperor could, and did, command the entire realm with a network of bureaucrats and a tax-gathering apparatus that nothing else in the European world could rival. This image of a settled, sedentary ruler was the image of empire that Otto and others wished to create for themselves, both as a symbol for their people and to enhance their own prestige as rulers.[58] As Karl Leyser put it, the Ottonian dynasty had taken from Byzantium "the visual representation of emperorship."[59] So, for Otto, it was important to re-create himself in the image of the Roman Empire he knew, Byzantium, so that he could have his own empire both in his eyes and in his people's.

Titulature is an important way for rulers to identify themselves to their people and to hearken to something or someone else. In an interesting example of this, the German emperors rarely referred to themselves as "German" (note, as well, Germania's tertiary position in Otto III's gospel book). There are in fact only two instances of the title *rex Teutonicorum* in this period.[60] Instead the ruler often took the title *rex Romanorum,* king of the Romans.[61] Though Rome and much of northern Italy was controlled by the German emperors, their heartland was still north of the Alps. The title was not intended to evoke the central point of their regime, but to invoke the ghost of the Roman Empire. They saw rex Romanorum as equivalent to the title *basileus Romanorum*—used by the Byzantine emperor, in his own view—the one true emperor of the Romans.[62] However, even Ottonian-sponsored writers clearly delineated between German "kings" and Byzantine "emperors," causing further complications in a modern quest to understand titulature.[63]

The Germans were not the only ones to be fascinated by imperial titles.[64] The rulers of Anglo-Saxon England also styled themselves as emperors, though in an interesting historical note they are never referred to as such in modern historiography. Beginning at least with Offa of Mercia in the eighth century, the ruler called himself "emperor of Britain."[65] This continued for quite some time, and there are extant seals and letters from other rulers, such as Edward the Confessor (r. 1042–1066), who called himself *Anglorum basileus*.[66] This was not all—in his writings, Edgar (r. 959–975), who also used the title *basileus*, used words such as *imperium* and *imperator* to describe his land and himself.[67] Ciggaar, who has made an extensive study of this, does not believe that the Anglo-Saxon rulers had any imperial pretensions,[68] but I must disagree. The use of imperial titulature by itself is enough to imply that Anglo-Saxon rulers were consciously imitating Byzantium, and Walter de Gray Birch, whose titulature study informs this article and Ciggaar's book, says, "England . . . was not only a kingdom, but an empire." When this is combined with the Anglo-Saxon rulers' appropriation of Byzantine seals and art, the pattern becomes crystal clear. The Anglo-Saxon rulers, like their contemporaries on the continent, looked to the glory of Rome preserved in Byzantium and wanted some of that glory for themselves.

The appropriation of Byzantine titulature did not end along with the Anglo-Saxon rule of England in 1066. William "the Conqueror" himself, after claiming the throne of England, used the title *basileus*.[69] This was not the only appropriation of Byzantine style that William engaged in. The very tactics he used to engineer his conquest of England seem to have been adapted from Byzantium.[70] These came from the Normans operating in the Mediterranean who learned tactics, such as building boats to carry large numbers of horses, fighting both for and against the Byzantines, who brought those ideas back to Normandy.[71] After the conquest, William continued his Byzantine appropriation—apart from using the title *basileus*, which was already a practice of English kings, William planned for himself a Byzantine-style coronation, complete with a Byzantine-style crown and a simultaneous coronation of his wife, something typically Byzantine.[72] He topped it all off with the appropriation of a coin of his contemporary, Isaac Comnenus.[73] It seems likely that William was not acting blindly in these instances, but had set out to methodically appropriate Byzantine imagery to enhance his own rule. He would now rule Britain as well as sizable territory on the continent, making him a very powerful ruler in Europe. To define that power he chose to use the titulature and imagery of Byzantium.

Having strayed slightly, it is time to return to the specific topic of titulature in regard to some of the least well-known but most Byzantine-influenced of European peoples—the Slavs. Medieval Rus' did not share the picture of Byzantium that much of western Europe had. In general it seems that Rusians did not view Byzantium as the continuation of Rome and her majesty, which represents a deviation from the larger pattern of the Byzantine Ideal, but they did recognize its political and cultural importance to medieval Europe.[74] To that end, as will be discussed later in this chapter, they appropriated some measure of Byzantine imagery, chiefly artistic. In the area of titulature, the Rusian case is different from that seen already, as, unlike the Anglo-Saxons or the Germans, the Rusians never adopted an imperial title for their ruler. The Rusian title, *tsar'*, which was the rendering of "Caesar," was used on rare occasions for a deceased Rusian ruler, but never for a living one.[75] Simon Franklin has argued, following Vladimir Vodoff, that *tsar'* was used by the Rusians as more of a moral title than a political one, indicating a ruler who had lived a good and faithful life. This is not the equivalent of *basileus,* as some have argued, though it did become that. It was only after the final collapse of the Byzantine state that a Rusian ruler, by then Muscovite, took the title *tsar'*, though even then he never appropriated the appellation *Romanorum.*[76] Various Rusian rulers did occasionally refer to themselves as *archon* on coins and seals.[77] This Byzantine title was applied in the *De cerimoniis aulae Byzantinae* in the feminine form to the Regent Ol'ga when she made her famous journey to Constantinople,[78] though this may have nothing to do with the trend of Rusian rulers being called archon.[79] This title was a common Byzantine one for tribal rulers, including the leader of the Hungarians[80] and the leaders of various steppe tribes,[81] and perhaps indicated their perception of the Rusians.[82] That the Rusians embraced the title, to some degree at any rate, shows their regard for the place of Byzantium in the medieval world. Similarly, the Anglo-Saxons, though using a variety of other titles, also used *archon,* though rarely, and Gray Birch considers it to be equivalent to *rex,* in their perception, lending another view on both the perception of the title and its use in Europe.[83] Finally, it seems that even though the Rusians did not adopt the Byzantine perception of their Roman inheritance, they did honor Byzantium (most likely as a *Christian* empire, rather than a Roman one), and appropriated from the Byzantines to enhance their own kingdom.[84]

The South Slavs represent another side to this story. They were geographically much closer to the Byzantines than anyone else in Europe, and perhaps because of this proximity they were more interested in appropriating Byzantine imagery and even in attempting to take over Byzantium.[85] The Bulgarians demonstrated from very early on in their history that they wanted to be the equal of Byzantium, and an early ruler, Symeon (r. 893–927), unsuccessfully attempted to capture Constantinople several times.[86] During his lifetime he did claim the title *emperor*, which he rendered as *tsar'* in Slavonic and *basileus* in Latin.[87] Interestingly for our analysis of titulature, in a particular concession the Byzantines even allowed Symeon the title *basileus,* having him crowned in the Blachernae Palace by Patriarch Nicholas Mysticus in 913.[88] Perhaps even more interesting is the fact that Symeon combined his titles and called himself "Emperor of the Romans and the Bulgarians."[89] Symeon's son Peter (r. 927–969) received official recognition from Byzantium for his title of *emperor,* though only *basileus Boulgaron,* in 927 when he married a daughter of the Byzantine emperor Romanus Lecapenus (920–944).[90] It seems clear from the determination with which the Bulgarians pursued the imperial title that they deliberately intended to appropriate for themselves a visible sign of Byzantium.[91]

The Serbs and Croats also maintained an intimate relationship with Byzantium. At times this involved a designation or devolution of Byzantine titles to the local rulers. For instance, in the early eleventh century the Byzantine emperors assigned the Serbian ruler Ljutovit the titles "*prōtospatharios* of the Chrysotriklinos," and "*hypatos* and *stratēgos* of Serbia and Zahumlje."[92] These titles, assigned by Byzantium as part of a political move, were the beginning of more widespread use of these titles in the Balkans. In the much later medieval world, the Serbs also began to adopt Byzantine titulature to enhance their own prestige. In 1343 Stefan Dušan (r. 1331–1355), "king of Serbia, Albania and the coast," added "king of the Romans" to his official title. Two years later he went even further and named himself tsar', which interestingly was rendered as "emperor of the Serbs and Greeks" in Serbian, and as "emperor of the Serbs and Romans" in Greek.[93] Dušan's intent was clear; he believed that co-opting the imperial titulature would enhance his own status and lend credence to his attempt to control parts of the Byzantine Empire.

These South Slavic examples illustrate more clearly than examples from Rus' or anywhere else in Europe the desire to appropriate Byzantine imagery to the fullest extent. Both the Bulgarians and the Serbs were close neighbors of the Byzantines and desired not only to imitate them but to become them. Their experience represents a qualitative difference from that of other European appropriators, who were attempting to generally enhance their own legitimacy rather than to become Byzantium. The South Slavic states were perhaps the closest of those discussed to attaining the Byzantine Ideal.

It is acknowledged that the "barbarian" kingdoms of late antiquity participated in the imperium of Byzantium and acknowledged a relationship with the Roman emperor because it lent them an air of majesty and respectability.[94] However, after the ascension of Charlemagne and the creation of his "Roman" Empire in 800, the view is that this acknowledgment generally stopped, as the West had come of age.[95] Instead it appears, given the numerous examples discussed above, that the lure of Byzantium for rulers seeking legitimacy had not ended.

A further series of examples of this from the eleventh century are embassies to Byzantium announcing a new ruler's ascension. Upon his ascension to the throne in 1043, Edward the Confessor sent an embassy announcing his coronation to the Byzantine emperor along with gifts to garner his good will.[96] In return, Byzantine silks were sent to Edward as a coronation gift. Interestingly, those silks perfectly match ones from the grave of Pope Clement II, who died in 1047.[97] Clement II ascended to the papal throne in 1046, and the suggestion that both sets of silks may have been coronation presents from the Byzantine emperor is not out of the realm of probability. We find corroboration for this type of behavior in the *Chronicon* of Thietmar of Merseburg, which tells of Bolesław Chrobry's taking of Kiev in 1018. After he had completed his pacification of the city, Bolesław sent an embassy to the Byzantine emperor, Basil II.[98] The embassy asked Basil only for peace and friendship, but its existence has been read by modern historians to place Rus' further into the sphere of Byzantine influence, intimating that such placement could only be the reason Bolesław would inform the Byzantine emperor of his taking Kiev. In light of the evidence provided by Ciggaar about possible English and papal embassies to Byzantium announcing coronations, it seems more likely that Bolesław was just following the accepted practice of the time.[99] In fact, it seems likely that even the Ottonian emperors followed this practice, as Werner Ohnsorge cites a letter sent to Otto I from Byzantium upon Otto's assumption of the throne.[100] This letter, which may have been solicited by an earlier announcement of Otto's ascent to the throne, also adds to the discussion of titulature, because it gives Otto the title "great king *(megas rex)* of the Franks and Saxons," rather than giving him either of the imperial titles, *basileus* or *imperator*. These embassies served to announce accepted fact to Byzantium, but also initiated a gift response in which the newly crowned ruler would receive presents from the Byzantine emperor, presents that would also gift the new ruler with some of the prestige and legitimacy of the Roman Empire. For the Byzantine emperor the embassy also established that ruler as part of the imperial hierarchy, thus reinforcing his perception of himself as universal emperor, and reinforcing the place of Byzantium/Rome in the minds of Europe's elite.

In the late tenth century, Hugh Capet of France wrote a letter to the Byzantine emperors asking for a marriage between a Byzantine princess and his son Robert.[101] The importance of this marriage for the Capetian dynasty is made clear by A. A. Vasiliev, who argues that the marriage would have increased their prestige at home and "would have meant for him the recognition by Constantinople of the legitimacy of his ascension to the French throne."[102] Rulers of territories both large and small prized recognition by Constantinople in their quest for prestige and legitimacy. The archaeologist Wladislaw Duczko makes the argument that the Byzantine artifacts found in Viking-age Sweden are indicative of the high level of prestige in which Byzantium was held in the Viking world. The artifacts themselves are "proofs of the interest of the ruling groups in using symbols from the powerful Empire."[103] Later in Scandinavia the same held true. After participating in the Crusades, Norwegian King Sigurd "the Crusader" returned home via Constantinople, where he traded his ships for horses to return overland.[104] There is no extant Byzantine record of the visit, but for the Norwegian ruler "the official reception by the Emperor was conceived as a token of international diplomatic recognition."[105] This visit was recorded in Scandinavian sources, if not in Byzantine, because while the visit was routine for the Byzantine emperor, it was not for the Scandinavian rulers. The city of Constantinople was awe-inspiring to foreign observers and the majesty of the emperor was unmatched by other European rulers.[106] Recognition of a ruler's ascension or his accomplishments by the emperor of

Byzantium did not mean he was subject to the emperor (despite what the emperor may have thought), but it did enhance his prestige and his legitimacy in the medieval European mindset.

One of the traditional ways in which the South Slavs in particular have been grouped with the Byzantine Empire is through their use of Byzantine law. Both the Bulgarians and the Serbs adopted Byzantine legal formulas, specifically church law, as their own.[107] The Rusians adopted Byzantine ecclesiastical law, but kept a Scandinavian-style law code for secular use until the thirteenth century.[108] The use of Byzantine law by the Slavs has allowed modern historians to group them as part of a Byzantine commonwealth; however, they were not the only ones who adopted Byzantine legal codes or practices. Frederick Barbarossa, no friend to Byzantium in general, adopted the Byzantine versions of the Justinianic Laws.[109] Though those were clearly different from ecclesiastical laws, his goal was to give himself the image of ruler as lawgiver and simultaneously associate himself with the Roman Empire. This was becoming more common in the eleventh century, as the Justinianic Laws made their reappearance throughout Europe.[110] Roger II of Sicily compiled his *assizes* at least half from Justinianic law.[111] Hubert Houben says in reference to Roger, "Roger's recourse to the example of the Roman emperors is indicative of how ambitious his intentions were."[112] The same could certainly be said for Frederick.

One of the more Byzantine punishments, blinding, gives evidence of other kingdoms adopting Byzantine legal customs.[113] Blinding was a rare punishment outside of Byzantium, but it began to crop up in other places in Europe in the late tenth through early twelfth century. Otto III ordered blinding for one of his counts because he was "oppressing the bishopric and the *pauperes* of Rimini."[114] This was not only a unique punishment in the German Empire, as Althoff mentions, but also a unique use of the punishment, which was generally used for getting rid of potential rivals or claimants to a throne.[115] Only a few years after this, Bolesław Chrobry intervened in the dispute for the Bohemian crown and blinded one of the claimants.[116] Whether he learned this technique from Byzantium or from his associate (and possibly emperor) Otto III cannot be known, but he, at least, used blinding for its main purpose, and this suggests knowledge of the practice. The Bohemians, recently exposed to this punishment by Bolesław, made use of it right away as

Jaromír (successor to the blinded Boleslav III) was blinded by his brother Oldřich.[117] Across the channel a few years later, William the Conqueror also introduced the punishment of blinding into English law, perhaps another of his borrowings from Byzantium.[118] In the late eleventh century there is a story from the *Povest' vremennykh let* (henceforth, *PVL*) that is commonly known as the "Blinding of Vasil'ko." Vasil'ko was a minor rebellious ruler who got in the way of the ruler of Kiev, who reputedly ordered him blinded.[119] This blinding also does not conform to the pattern of blinding potential rivals for a throne, and some have suggested that the tale is a later interpolation or at worst an outright fabrication.[120] It is the only example of a blinding in Kievan Rus' (and was considered unusual at the time)[121] and the only one in all of Rusian history, and the only one in Russian history until 1436.[122] In the twelfth century, there are multiple blindings as part of a civil war in Bohemia,[123] and the Byzantine chronicler John Kinnamos suggested that the punishment was known in Hungary for exactly the purpose that the Byzantines put it to.[124] What is especially interesting about this evidence is that something considered uniquely Byzantine came to be used in various parts of Europe over the course of the tenth century forward. This shows not only the spread of Byzantine influence during this period, but also its particular distribution to areas influenced by Byzantium. One might also be able to overlap uses of blinding with amount of Byzantinification in those areas; that is, areas that use blinding "correctly" are more Byzantinized than areas that do not. The results of this might be quite interesting, as we see blinding as a punishment for usurpers or to prevent someone from ruling (the "correct" use), used in Bohemia, Poland, Hungary, and England, but not in Rus' or the German Empire, a correlation that does not match the traditional understanding of patterns of Byzantine influence in Europe.

Coinage and Sigillography

The areas in which deliberate appropriation of imagery is most visible, coinage and sigillography, exemplify the importance Byzantium had in the medieval world. Until the mid-eleventh century, the Byzantines had run the most stable currency in Eurasia, not changing for hundreds of years.[125] The weight of the Byzantine nomisma became the standard weight of coins throughout Europe. This was a basic, but essential, appropriation as kingdoms attempted to reinforce the authority of their own coinage, and chose the obvious example to base it upon.[126] However, though the weight of the material involved did not change, the style of the coins did. As each new emperor or group of emperors took the throne, they issued their own coinage, complete with their image and sometimes their own patron saint or an image of Jesus Christ.[127] These coins traveled throughout the European world, and because they were Byzantine they were prized not only for their precious metal content but for their images. Just as many nations in the modern era once named their money after the American dollar, many medieval kingdoms wanted their own nomisma.[128] The appropriation of the images on those coins was an effective way for rulers to enhance their prestige with their people and make their monetary issue popular and/or easily acceptable. Though they could not always match the gold content or stability, they could replicate (to a certain extent) the exterior, appropriating the image of a stable currency, if not the stability itself. Certainly, not every coin style throughout Europe was appropriated from Byzantium,[129] but enough are to make the case for a continuation of the idea of the Byzantine Ideal in the fields of coinage and sigillography.

One of the issues in studying numismatics and sigillography is common with historical action in any other discipline—agency. Discussed in this chapter are changes made to seals and coins, changes that I, and others, have interpreted as consciously originating from the ruler. For instance, in her discussion of the ideology of rulership in Bohemia, Lisa Wolverton notes the same problem and acknowledges that although the "dies were cut and coins stamped by mint-masters . . . they surely operated, and chose their designs, at the duke's orders."[130] There is a contrary school of thought advanced by the eminent numismatist Philip Grierson, who attributes decisions on what type of coinage to make to be entirely up to the discretion of the various moneyers.[131] So, when a new coin is introduced, the agent for change is a moneyer taken with a new style, rather than a ruler. Because there are no sources on this issue apart from the coinage itself, there can be no easy resolution. However, there is a solid scholarship on rulership being composed of equal parts power and image,[132] therefore something as important as the image of the ruler provided on something that many people, and especially the powerful people, in the kingdom will see, such as coinage, would most likely not have been left to the discretion of a moneyer. A ruler, whatever the title, had to protect his or her image, and the image on coinage was vital to the perception of the ruler by the kingdom.

In the case of Byzantine sigillography,[133] not only the imagery but also the style was copied by medieval rulers. Charlemagne himself adopted the Byzantine lead seal, moving away from the wax seals that were common in the West.[134] This was an obvious appropriation of Byzantine style, as they were the only ones using lead seals at the time. It was also a clear case of appropriation—Charlemagne did not blindly copy the current Byzantine sigillography, but adopted an early Byzantine profile type for his own new lead seals.[135] The same elements are noted in a significant seal of Otto III. In 998 Otto III issued his first lead seal—up to this point all of the seals of the Ottonian rulers had been wax.[136] The Ottonian Empire claimed to be the descendant of Charlemagne's "Roman" Empire, but it had not used lead seals for nearly two hundred years. For Otto, the seal evoked Byzantium as well as Charlemagne, enhancing his connection with both empires. This is especially true as the seal portrait imitated by Otto is the profile used by Charlemagne, originally taken from early Byzantine seals.[137] Byzantium provided the technology, and the imagery, for two generations of Western empires, two hundred years apart, to appropriate, enhancing their reputation as the preserver of the Roman legacy.

Another generation of German emperors also appropriated Byzantine imagery for their own seals. The Hohenstaufen king Conrad III (r. 1138–1152) appropriated the style of his contemporary Manuel Comnenus (r. 1143–1180) for his own seals.[138] This was theoretically the result not only of an appreciation for Byzantium, but of a personal appreciation for a fellow ruler. Conrad's new seal was very Byzantine in style, showing him "wearing the Byzantine *kamelaukion,* the crown with pendilia worn by the Comnenian emperors in their portraits in Hagia Sophia."[139] Crowns with pendilia are classic features of Byzantine coins and seals and as such are immediately recognizable, perhaps making that image an immediate target for appropriation. Even Conrad III's successor, Frederick Barbarossa (r. 1152–1190), adopted similar Byzantine-style seals.[140] Despite the disagreements he may have had with Byzantium, the style meant imperial power, and that was what he desired.

Constant appropriators of Byzantium, the Norman kings of Sicily, also used Byzantine imagery on their seals. Robert Guiscard began the tradition using the Byzantine title *nobelissimos,* as part of a Greek inscription on his seal in the Byzantine imperial style.[141] His children used Greek inscriptions on their seals as well, even going so far as to use gold seals, as only the Byzantine emperors would.[142] Roger II (r. 1130–1154), on his golden bull, portrayed himself "wearing the traditional ceremonial costume of a Byzantine emperor, with crown and *pendilia,* orb and cross in the right hand and *labarum* in the left." The reverse shows Christ enthroned, and all inscriptions are in Greek.[143] The same is true of Roger's ducal seals and money, which, though often lacking images of Roger himself, had Greek inscriptions and imagery. Though he rarely used an imperial title, Roger's depiction of himself on seals, coins, and mosaics used the full power of Byzantine imperial imagery to reinforce the legitimacy of his rule.[144]

In the region of Europe farthest from Byzantium, numerous Byzantine-inspired coins from the eleventh century have been found. Scandinavia and northern Europe (Sweden, Denmark, Norway, and England) all used Byzantine coins as the basis for some of their own coinage at this time. One of the most common coins found in the north is a *miliaresion* of Basil II (r. 976–1025) and Constantine VIII (r. 976–1028) struck between circa 977 and 989.[145] This coin shows busts of the two coemperors facing each other with prependilia dangling from their crowns.[146] Perhaps because it was plentiful in the north, this coin was copied by many different rulers, but its imagery makes it an interesting subject for discussion. The first known copy of the coin comes from Sweden, where around the year 1000, Olof Skötkonnung (r. 995–1021/1022) had dies cast to strike such coins in Sigtuna.[147] The coin is next found in Denmark under the reign of Harthacnut (r. 1035–1042), where it "shows two facing, tiara-crowned busts on either side of a cross potent."[148] The peak of Byzantine influence on Scandinavian coinage came under one of the successors of Harthacnut,[149] Sven Estridsson (r. 1047–1074), who also struck coins showing busts of two emperors facing with pendilia.[150] The most startling thing about the widespread use of this model of coin in Scandinavia is that in the kingdoms it was used in there were never two rulers sharing power. The purpose of the miliaresion of Basil II and Constantine VIII was to show the brothers as coemperors. The kings who copied this coin in Scandinavia did not choose it to convey such a message, so what were they trying to communicate? The message they were conveying was their desire to link themselves with the monetary and political stability of Byzantium.[151] They wanted to appropriate for themselves the image of stability and rulership portrayed by the coinage.[152]

The miliaresion of Basil II and Constantine VIII was not the only coin copied in the north. Even before the first miliaresion was copied in Sweden, Danish rulers in the 980s were copying Byzantine coins. Some of their coins showed a "cross crosslet with steps" in imitation of the Byzantine design of a cross crosslet.[153] Later in Danish history, Harthacnut, who struck a coin based on the miliaresion discussed above, also struck another Byzantine-style coin. This one was a copy of a "coin of John Tzimiskes (r. 969–975) with a horizontal legend on the obverse and the Emperor's head in the centre of the cross on the reverse."[154] Though from an earlier time than the miliaresion, it was also a likely coin to be found in Scandinavia. Sven Estridsson also struck a Byzantine coin, this one of much greater rarity: a gold histamenon nomisma struck in the name of Byzantine Emperor Michael (r. 1034–1041) from the mid-eleventh century.[155] Sven Estridsson's version is a silver penny whose reverse shows the exact replica of the Byzantine coin. His successors copied this coin and others from Byzantium, but their copies were much less distinct, and the specific coins they used as models often cannot be determined.[156] Harald "Hein" (r. 1075–1080) and King St. Knud (r. 1080–1086) issued coins that show the standing figure of a saint with a cross or crozier—both coin types that seem faintly Byzantine.[157] Contemporary with these Danish coins are some Norwegian coins that were very similar and are thought to have been copied from the Danish model, rather than from an original Byzantine coin.[158] Byzantine coins were the gold standard of objects of appropriation, especially in the late tenth and eleventh centuries in Scandinavia.

One of the interesting things that happened when Byzantine coins were copied is that although the design was often perfect, the lettering was often not. The copyists, it seems, were not familiar with either the Greek language or the significance of the Greek lettering on the coinage, but they knew that it possessed significance and thus could not be done away with entirely.[159] However, in copying it they often got the letters wrong, and the resulting coins look like Byzantine coins except that the Greek is gibberish.[160] There are many examples of this from these coins copied in the north, but the same also happened in Rus'. In Scandinavia, the miliaresion copied by Olof Skötkonnung had a meaningless Greek inscription,[161] while Grierson describes a Danish coin of the later eleventh century that has four lines of text on the obverse that are largely undecipherable, though he was able to determine that the coin was based on a miliaresion of Constantine IX (r. 1042–1055).[162] It becomes clear that the requirement for coinage was not that the inscription be meaningful to the users of the money, who were largely illiterate, but simply that the inscription was present. Once again we see how important image was for rulers, in this case the appropriated image of Byzantium.

One of the most interesting and Byzantine-connected figures in eleventh-century Scandinavia was the Norwegian king Harald Hardraada (r. ca. 1044–1066). Harald was ejected from Norway at a young age and served in various military capacities in Rus' and then in Byzantium before returning to Norway and becoming king.[163] His time spent in the Byzantine Empire has been used to account for many things in Norwegian and broader Scandinavian history.[164] For example, numismatists have often used it to account for the number of Byzantine coins in Scandinavia in the eleventh century.[165] This is, however, not the whole story. Yes, some of the coins exist in Scandinavia only because Harald brought them back. Michael Hendy offers an excellent description of one such coin of Michael IV, discussed above, that Sven Estridsson copied and that may have been a gift from Harald.[166] However, Byzantine coins were present in Scandinavia before the return of Harald from Byzantium and were the result of a long-distance trading system utilizing the east European river systems (discussed in more depth in Chapter 4).

Though he may not have brought back all of the Byzantine coins in Scandinavia, Harald did bring back substantial Byzantine influence. He had coins struck that imitated, not specific Byzantine coins, but Byzantine coins in general, showing him as a facing bust with pendilia.[167] This, along with his economic plans, indicates that he was one of the more knowledgeable appropriators of the image of empire in medieval Europe. More than simply the style of the coins, Harald also seems to have brought back *ideas* about coinage. As mentioned, Byzantine currency, specifically the nomisma, had been stable for hundreds of years until the eleventh century. When the Byzantine emperors began to debase the coinage, Harald was most likely present to observe the effects.[168] While he was king in Norway, Harald reduced the silver content of the coins he struck from 90 percent, the norm at the time, to 20 percent.[169] As part of what seems to be a concerted effort, foreign coins also disappeared from Norway during this time, and the Norwegian coins do not show evidence of pecking or bending to test the content of the metal. The conclusion reached by Brita Malmer is that Harald created the first national monetary system in Scandinavia in which money was issued by the government and accepted by the people on faith that the real value of the coinage was the stated value of the coinage, not its physical value.[170] Harald learned a variety of lessons on his travels, and his appropriation of Byzantine coinage (both imagery and value) helped him solidify his rule and create a more stable kingdom.

The Scandinavians were not the only ones using Byzantine coins, or appropriating their designs. In England, where there were Byzantine tendencies in titulature, Edward the Confessor struck a silver penny, "the obverse type of which is copied from the seated Constantinopolis on a gold solidus of Justin II (r. 565–78)."[171] This is an excellent example of conscious appropriation, as was discussed with the seal of Charlemagne above. Edward chose a particular Byzantine design, from a certain era, depicting a certain image, that was pleasing to him and evocative of what he wanted, and put that on his coinage. His eventual successor, William the Conqueror, did the same. William used a coin of Isaac I Comnenus (r. 1057–1059) as a model for one of his first coins as king of England.[172] The coin is appropriate because it is one of the few Byzantine coins lacking Christian symbolism but instead focused on martial themes. Isaac/William is pictured standing with a sword over his right shoulder wearing a crown, possibly with pendilia. In fact, the continuator of Skylitzes notes that this is due to the fact that Isaac believed his success was due solely to his martial prowess and not to divine will. Though it has been argued that this was not Isaac's intent and was simply a biased reading of the image, the same might be said of William.[173]

The martial image of the ruler was perfect for William, whose sobriquet changed from "the Bastard" to "the Conqueror" after his taking of England in 1066. Across the channel, German rulers also used Byzantine coins as models. In the early eleventh century at mints in the area of Mainz, there were German coins struck on the model of *solidi* of Theophilus (r. 829–842).[174] The use of Byzantine coins as models by rulers does not indicate any sense of political or religious dependence upon Byzantium, but shows the respect which they held for the Byzantine image and currency in the medieval world.[175]

Rusian coinage has both similarities and differences with the discussion thus far. The similarities are in the use of Byzantine imagery for Rusian coins and seals, though, like in the rest of Europe, there is also homegrown imagery, which we will discuss in more detail for Rus' than has been discussed elsewhere here. The differences stem from three factors—first, a better knowledge of Greek language in Rus', which makes a difference in the appropriation and use of inscriptions; second, the use of the vernacular on coins (occasionally alongside Greek); and finally, the simple fact that there are not many extant coins or seals for Rus' from the eleventh and early twelfth centuries, certainly not compared to the number preserved in the kingdoms of western Europe.[176]

Appropriation of Byzantine images for coins begins with the earliest coins struck in Rus', those of Vladimir Sviatoslavich (r. 980–1015). One type of Vladimir's coins contains a direct copy of the image of Christ, from a solidus of Basil II and Constantine VIII. The other face is an interpretation of the same Byzantine coin, showing Vladimir alone (avoiding the unnecessary imagery of dual rulership), but with Byzantine-style crown, including prependilia.[177] Though the image of Christ disappears from Vladimir's other coins and is replaced with the symbol of the Riurikids (discussed below), his image, with Byzantine-style crown, remains.[178] That image, repeated on coins of his successor, Sviatopolk Iaropolchich (r. 1015–1016, 1018), shifts more toward a Rusian design, however. The obverse of the coins show an evolving symbol of the Riurikids, a trident shape originally, that under Sviatopolk grows a cross on one arm and loses the middle tine.[179] The reverse of the coin shows a Rusian image, the ruler seated on his throne, though still dressed in a Byzantine-style crown and perhaps raiment as well.[180] This image, with the inscription "Sviatopolk *na stole*" (Sviatopolk on the throne), is not directly copied from any Byzantine coin or seal, as the emperors rarely appear seated and the inscription is written in Cyrillic.[181] Jonathan Shepard believes that the image has to do with the mechanics of kingship in Germanic lands, where the importance of sitting on the throne is vital to claiming and maintaining power.[182] However, for our purposes it is also important to note the continuing use of Byzantine regalia as part of the Rusian image, a true appropriation.

Such examples of appropriation continue. Oleg Sviatoslavich issued silver coins bearing his baptismal name, Michael, while he ruled in Tmutorokan in the early 1070s.[183] Those coins were modeled on the coins of the Byzantine emperor Michael VII Ducas (r. 1071–1078).[184] Martin Dimnik, who has studied the Sviatoslavichi extensively, believes this appropriation of images was intended to link Oleg to Byzantium in a more concrete manner than seen elsewhere, including Oleg's exile to Byzantium and marriage to a Byzantine woman.[185] Iaroslav Mudryi (r. 1016–1018; joint rule with Mstislav Iaroslavich 1018–1036; r. 1036–1054) also, unsurprisingly perhaps, created coins in a Byzantine style. His Iaroslav Type-III coin is an appropriation of the image of a Byzantine seal, rather than a coin.[186] One side of the coin shows the typical icon image of St. George, which did not appear on Byzantine coinage until the rule of Alexius Comnenus but did appear on earlier seals, with a Greek inscription of the name St. George. The other side shows the Riurikid symbol with the inscription "Iaroslavle serebro" (Iaroslav's silver) in Old East Slavic.[187] So, although Iaroslav used the Byzantine image of St. George (his Christian name), he also used contemporary Rusian imagery and language on the same coin, representing the blending of the Byzantine and Rusian imagery that characterized Rusian coins.

The last note on the imagery of Rusian coinage and sigillography is a technical one. Much as Charlemagne and Otto III switched to lead seals in imitation of Byzantium's use of them, Rusian rulers also used lead seals.[188] Though there are no known wax seals, the use of lead seals, a Byzantine staple, suggests their use in Rus' was imitative of the Byzantine model.

One of the main differences mentioned is language. As was discussed briefly in regard to Scandinavian appropriation of Byzantine coinage, when Greek was used it was usually copied, and poorly. This is not the case in Rus'. Because of the closer linguistic ties Rus' maintained with Byzantium, mostly due to the presence of monks literate in Greek, Rusian coins and seals often carried Greek letters or inscriptions. A seal of Vsevolod Iaroslavich (joint rule with Sviatoslav Iaroslavich 1076–1077; r. 1078–1093) carries a Greek inscription that read "Lord, help your servant Andrei Vsevolodu."[189] The other side of the seal bears the icon image of St. Andrew and the inscription "OAGIOS ANDREI," written in Cyrillic. The use of Greek language with Cyrillic letters shows a clear difference from a simple dumb copying of Greek letters or symbols. Further, the presence of Cyrillic letters sent a different message to the observer, setting it apart visually, even to an illiterate audience. The use of Greek on Rusian coins had a brief heyday in the mid-eleventh century around the reign of Iaroslav "the Wise," potentially due to his appropriation of Byzantine styles, but Slavonic was also there as well, and in the second half of the eleventh century there was a marked decline in Greek and an increase in Slavonic usage.[190] What is interesting is that though the Slavonic claim *na stole* was vital for early rulers, later rulers adopted a Byzantine title for themselves rather than branding their coinage with the Slavonic title *kniaz'*, which never appears. *Archon*, a general Greek term for ruler, begins to appear on Rusian seals in the second half of the eleventh century.[191] The first use of it is attributed to a seal of the Momonakhina, who married Vsevolod Iaroslavich,[192] with the second from her son, Vladimir Monomakh, and becoming more common by the end of the century.[193] The reasoning behind this may simply have been a continuation of the appropriation of Byzantine imagery, specifically by a Byzantine woman, and her descendants. Though Greek fell out of fashion as the language for coins and seals, perhaps the appropriation of the title in Cyrillic lent weight to the stature of Rusian rulers.

Greek and Rusian were not the only languages used on Rusian coinage, however. One coin has been found with a Latin inscription reading "... rator," which Jonathan Shepard believes originally read "imperator."[194] A. V. Solov'ev has stated that the coin belongs to Vladimir Sviatoslavich, and Shepard further explains the Latin inscription by advancing the idea that it was made by a western European moneyer.[195] Latin language chronicles invariably describe the Rusian ruler with the title *rex*, and it is not such a stretch to extend that to *imperator* when the ruler possesses a kingdom stretching from the Baltic Sea to the southern steppe. More recently, Omeljan Pritsak has published a new interpretation of much of Rusian coinage that includes the identification of the Latin title *rex* on coins of Iaropolk Iziaslavich, whose Christian name may have been Peter.[196] Though this title also has been doubted,[197] there is at least the possibility that Latin was used on Rusian coins. There have been numerous finds in Rus' of western coins,[198] and Rusian coins and imitations have been found in places such as Sweden, Norway, the German Empire, and Poland,[199] which shows that Rusians had the opportunity to see and use foreign coinage and that Rusian coinage was seen outside of Rus', allowing the imagery of rulership to travel both ways.

From this analysis we can see that Rusian rulers internalized aspects of the Byzantine imagery, adopting certain general elements, such as the use of Byzantine regalia, the inclusion of saints, and correct Greek, without always following specific coin types. However, as with the rest of Europe there was appropriation from Byzantium, as well as the use of homegrown material to create the image of a successful and powerful rule, ruler, and kingdom.

Art and Artistic Influence

"The history of art offers verifiable and hence valuable evidence for the impact of Byzantium on the West."[200] Even though Anthony Cutler goes on to say that this impact is not visible in other areas, with which I disagree, his point about art, his subject of expertise, is appropriate to our discussion here. Cutler is following in a long line of art historians who have studied the impact of Byzantine art on the West.[201] What they have found has become accepted in the art historical community: Byzantium, especially in the eleventh and twelfth centuries, had a profound influence on Western European art and style.[202] However, like so many studies and realizations, this one has not been effectively used outside its originating discipline (in this case art history) and thus has failed to influence general historians' perception of Byzantine–European relations. This section of the chapter deals with examples of Byzantine influence on art throughout Europe, from Italy to the German Empire and from Iceland to Rus'; these examples show the pervasiveness of

Byzantine influence and the reach of Byzantine art, as well as the priorities of European art procurers and sponsors, all of which informs the idea of the Byzantine Ideal. As has been said, much of this information is well known in certain disciplines, but the purpose of its presentation here is to place it into the context of this theory and also to (re) introduce it to a larger audience.

Probably the most famous example of this phenomenon of Byzantine artistic influence in western Europe is that shown by Monte Cassino in Italy in the eleventh century. At that time the abbot of Monte Cassino was Desiderius (1058–1087, later to become Pope Victor III), who wanted to redo the whole abbey, specifically the main basilica, which he wanted decorated with figural mosaics and new pavement.[203] The style he chose for this was Roman, and thus to do this work he brought in craftsmen from Byzantium and commissioned works of art in Constantinople.[204] Desiderius was able to find many of the materials in Italy, but not the craftsmen, specifically not those who were "experts in the art of laying mosaics and pavements."[205] The problem was that the necessary skills had been lost in Italy,[206] and Desiderius, as others before him, acknowledged that Byzantium was the continuation of Roman majesty and turned to Constantinople for the preserved wisdom. Examples of this type of work are the monumental bronze doors that inspired Desiderius when he visited Amalfi, copies of which he commissioned for Monte Cassino in 1066.[207] Such bronze doors became symbols of Byzantine artistic influence at Monte Cassino and throughout northern Italy, as they spread in the later eleventh century to Venice, Rome, and elsewhere.

Physical decorations transmit one level of influence, but having instructors present increases the potential for influence enormously. To return to Italy some of the artistic skills that he deemed essential, Desiderius sent a group of his monks to Constantinople to apprentice with Byzantine artists. When the monks returned, he began a workshop at Monte Cassino staffed with Byzantine artists and his Byzantine-trained monks.[208] This renovatio[209] made Monte Cassino into the "political and cultural center" of Europe for a few decades in the second half of the eleventh century,[210] and the town was a foothold for the redeployment of Byzantine art in western Europe. According to some art historians, beginning in the eleventh century and spreading north from Italy,[211]

Byzantine art became the source for the European Romanesque style that swept through Europe in the twelfth century.[212]

Byzantine art was prized not only for its artistic beauty and classical heritage, but also for its place as a status symbol, especially in regard to Christianity. Western art patrons, which included both secular and religious rulers of all types, craved Byzantine art for the image it would project about them: that they had the money to afford such art and the taste to choose it, and that they were inexorably linked to the grandeur of Byzantium.[213] Otto Demus, who studied Byzantine art in the West extensively, called Byzantium the artistic *magistra Europae*[214] and singled out one form in particular, saying, "Mosaic, especially, was seen as the imperial art par excellence and was therefore used by secular potentates, such as the kings of Sicily or the doges of Venice, and ecclesiastical ones such as the popes, who wanted to compete in some way with the Byzantine emperors."[215] Desiderius may have continued his role of importing Byzantine art and artists into Italy as pope if his reign had been longer. As it is, there were still many popes interested in the Byzantine arts. Rome was quick to follow in Desiderius's footsteps and by 1070 commissioned a set of bronze doors like those at Amalfi and Monte Cassino.[216] But it was not until Pope Paschal II (1099–1118) that the papacy became deeply involved in importing Byzantine art and artisans to beautify Rome, specifically the Roman churches.[217] Though much of this was the sumptuary arts prized by Crusaders and those following, its importation into Rome was an attempt to reflect the glory of Byzantium and the Rome of old.[218] Besides the papacy, the city-states of Italy, such as Venice, a longtime subject and suitor of Byzantium, were importing Byzantine art and architecture as well.[219] The church of San Marco, the central church of Venice, was constructed in the ninth century on a Byzantine model. When the doge decided to redo the church in the mid-eleventh century, he deliberately chose as the model the Church of the Holy Apostles in Constantinople.[220] This was for the Venetians the model of a glorious Byzantine church that they wanted to appropriate to demonstrate their own rising power. As with Desiderius, for the detail work on the church the doge was required to import Byzantine craftsmen, as the necessary artistic training and skills were not available at that time in Italy.[221]

Perhaps most famous as appropriators of Byzantine imagery are the Normans of Sicily. The Normans, like the Bulgarians, never ceased in their struggles to copy Byzantine majesty while at the same time attempting to make the territory of Byzantium their own. The best example of these rulers is Roger II, who "aspired to emulate the majesty of Byzantine emperors" in art and clothing.[222] Roger II also brought in Byzantine craftsmen to create Byzantine-style art for Sicily and for his court,[223] including the red porphyry tomb that he had constructed for his and for his successors' remains.[224] Moreover, Sicily played a significant role in the introduction of Byzantine style to the rest of western Europe, because it acted as a portal for export to northern countries.[225]

Italian rulers, however, were not the only ones interested in appropriating the visual arts of Byzantium; they were joined by the Ottonian emperors, who, as seen above, were very interested in appearing Byzantine. This was no different in the sphere of art than elsewhere. The Ottonian rulers as well as Henry II presented themselves in their official portraiture as crowned by Christ.[226] This was in deliberate imitation of the Byzantine emperors and was intended as a formal statement that, like the Byzantine emperors, they also were granted a divine right to rule. Their official portraiture was also influenced by the presence of a strong Byzantine princess in the person of Theophano. It has been argued that it is primarily due to her influence that the Byzantine style of royal portraiture, in which husbands and wives are portrayed together, was introduced into the Ottonian dynasty.[227] As with the coronation images, this was designed with the purpose of imitating the Byzantine emperors. As in the Italian examples, the Ottonians both bought Greek art and hired Greek artists.[228] For example, in the early eleventh century the chapel of St. Bartholomew in Paderborn was built by Greek artisans.[229] Additionally, on their miniatures, a field of art in the Ottonian Empire that definitely benefited from contact with Byzantium,[230] they used Greek-language inscriptions.[231] Like some of the inscriptions on coins and seals, the Greek was often incorrect, but this modern realization misses the point of the purpose of the inscription. The inscription was put on the miniature as part of the artwork itself intended to add to the visual signature of the piece, in this case to add to the Byzantine-ness of the miniature. Demus believes that, unlike Desiderius, the Ottonians were more interested in Byzantine art for its Byzantine connection than for its Roman connection.[232] However, this may be a false dichotomy as appropriations from Byzantium were appropriations from the Roman Empire, despite (or even because of) the political rivalry with the current incarnation of the empire.

What was the part of the Slavic lands in all of this? Obolensky makes an argument about cultural imbalance in which the culture of Byzantium spread outward especially into the territories that converted to Orthodox Christianity.[233] Though not expressly identifying art as part of the cultural export package, it is implied as part of the luxury goods the Slavs are quick to acquire.[234] This is the traditional image for the Slavs and specifically for Rus'—a kingdom whose art was heavily influenced by Byzantium, as is illustrated by the appropriation of such Byzantine mainstays as Hagia Sophia and the Golden Gate, both reproduced in Kiev and elsewhere, not to mention mosaics and icon painting.[235] Unlike the traditional image of cultural hydraulics, it seems that Iaroslav the Wise (like Harald Hardrada) was a conscious appropriator of the Byzantine image. According to Elena Boeck, "Iaroslav's patronage reveals sophisticated cultural knowledge of Byzantine ideology, institutions, and symbolism, which he exploited in the service of Rus' international ambitions."[236] Historically, when not contrasted with the Western appropriation, these Byzantine appropriations have placed Rus' more firmly into the Byzantine cultural sphere. However, in his work on Western appropriation of Byzantine art, Otto Demus advanced an interesting idea about Byzantine art in Rus', saying that Byzantium sent "third-rate mosaicists" to Kiev to work on St. Sophia Cathedral.[237] The technical explanation behind the analysis is that "the uncouth figures of the church in Kiev, with their heavy proportions and schematic draperies, look distinctly provincial compared with the elegant, slender saints of the Sicilian churches, true representatives of Constantinopolitan court art."[238] This is an enormous difference from the traditional perspective, best represented here by the opinion of John Meyendorff, who says that the Cathedral of St. Sophia in Kiev preserves some of the finest Byzantine mosaic work of the eleventh century.[239] While Demus acknowledges time could be a factor in the equation, he believes that the greater difference lies in the area of influence. The choice of which artists to send to Rus' and which to send to the West was "due to conscious selection" by the Byzantines, predicated on who could pay the most for their services.[240] To expand and explain Demus's conclusions, there was probably no strong central government exporting art and artisans in Constantinople, regulating to whom and where they would go. Instead we are faced with a simple mercantile equation of supply, demand, transport costs, and price. Transport to the West was cheaper, quicker, and safer, via a sea voyage rather than traversing the steppe north to Kiev, as both Byzantium and Rus' had more prolific trade toward the west than north–south; point one in the favor of the West. The amount the ruler could pay was also greater in the West, where there were long-established luxury markets and more ready cash than in Rus', a second resounding point in favor of the West. Finally, if we can extrapolate from Anna Porphyrogenita's dismay at going to Rus',[241] perhaps the Byzantine artisans were more interested in going west than north. So, despite the religious ties with Rus', the Byzantine artists were more likely to follow the trail of the money and go to the West; thus, the best would go there and others would be hired to make the less profitable and more dangerous journey north to Kiev. This is a different picture from that traditionally expressed—in which the Byzantine emperor dispatched artisans to Kiev to aid in the creation of Russo-Byzantine culture—but it seems more technically correct.[242] Even in the Middle Ages, agency was most likely tempered by economic concerns, so even though Rus' does end up with a heritage of Byzantine art (even more so as the centuries progress),[243] that art does not necessarily measure up to the standards of Byzantine art commissioned in the West in the Middle Ages.

Though not much written about, Byzantine art also found its way to France, first in the 1020s and 1030s when Bishop Gauzlin of Fleury sent envoys to Constantinople to bring back artists and material.[244] Though the source for this is Gauzlin's *Vita*, and thus must be questioned somewhat, the fact that the author decided to include a search for Byzantine artists and supplies to beautify French churches is an important indication of the status given to Byzantium, and it is true that marble imported from Byzantium was used for the abbey church.[245] Much later, Abbot Suger of Saint Denis brought in Byzantine art to decorate his abbey.[246] These examples show the wider influence of Byzantium beyond those areas where rulers were trying to become emperors themselves to areas that wanted to have the finery of imperial style.

One of the most interesting places Byzantine art was found in the European Middle Ages is Scandinavia. Scandinavia was an area far removed from Byzantium, but yet, as we have seen, held many contacts with Byzantium that allowed Byzantine influence to exist there. It is specifically the artwork in some Scandinavian churches that holds a Byzantine style. This particular venue for Byzantine art reflects the Scandinavian perception of Byzantium. Anthony Cutler has said that "they [the Scandinavians] commissioned Orthodox artists to decorate their churches in the manner which, despite doctrinal and liturgical differences, seemed to them most appropriate and impressive."[247] Religious differences aside, the Scandinavians wanted the designs that they had seen in Rus' or Byzantium while working as mercenaries,[248] on Crusade, or on a pilgrimage to the Holy Land, because those designs were beautiful and impressive. They were also believed to be more correct. "Scandinavians of the crusading era regarded Byzantine pictorial tradition as a correct representation of the holy history."[249] Ulla Haastrup's point is an interesting one, and leads us to the preservation of Byzantine- and Mediterranean-style imagery out of context in Scandinavia. For instance, an image in Zealand at Jørlunde Church shows a Byzantine-style Last Supper.[250] In this image, the place of honor reserved for Jesus is at the center of a long table with his disciples on either side of him. This image is out of context for northern viewers, whose lived experience of meals and positioning were much different, and would not have expressed to them what it innately did to a Byzantine or Mediterranean viewer familiar with the cultural context of such a scene. The centrality of Christ's position, the dress of the figures, and even the food consumed were aberrant to northern life, but because of the perception that Byzantium had preserved a closer version, artistically at least, of the time of Christ, that imagery was preserved and even prized.

A vexing question when discussing Byzantine influence on Scandinavian art, and especially religious art, is the role of Rus'. Art historians have taken different opinions on this question, some stating that all Byzantine influence in Scandinavia was mediated through Rus'[251] and some stating that it came directly from Byzantium.[252] Complicating this is the question of whether or not the appropriation of Byzantine religious imagery implies religious contact with Byzantium.[253] As usual, the truth probably lies somewhere in the middle. The majority of Byzantine-style art in Scandinavia seems to have been commissioned from the late eleventh through thirteenth centuries, a time when Byzantine artistic influence was spreading throughout Europe. The artistic growth at Monte Cassino began in the 1060s and spread outward to the rest of Italy and throughout Europe in the later eleventh century. By the end of the eleventh century, crusaders were experiencing Byzantium firsthand, and their numbers only grew in the twelfth century. So it is logical that direct Byzantine influence is possible in many cases. But given the long-standing connections between Scandinavia and Rus', there most certainly would have been Russian influence in many ways. One of the strongest centers of Russian influence was probably on the island of Gotland, where Rus' is known to have had a trading center.[254] The churches at Garda and Källunge on Gotland bear a strong stylistic resemblance to north Russian churches, specifically those at Staraia Ladoga, the first trading settlement of the Rusians.[255] Cutler has theorized that there was a settlement of Rusian artists who worked on those two churches as well as others on Gotland, and that those artists were familiar with styles from areas as disparate in Rus' as Novgorod and Vladimir-Suzdal.[256] The designs in these churches did not stay confined to trading areas, but were populated throughout the island, spreading the Byzantine-style influence.[257] This kind of a Rusian base is important as an extension of Byzantine influence in the north; the Rusian artists were not hired to produce a unique Rusian style, but their version of the Byzantine style. In the church at Källunge there is a steatite Crucifixion, which, although in a church that may have been built by Rusians or on a Rusian model, was definitely a creation made in Byzantium and imported from there.[258] Another direct tie with Byzantium may have been a craftsman who has been named "Byzantios" who worked on Gotland in the twelfth century and created Byzantine-style baptismal fonts.[259] The fonts, along with the various Byzantine-style artworks that have been unearthed on Gotland, provoked the comment from Cutler that "for perhaps a generation Gotland was a remote northern province of Byzantine art."[260]

Gotland, however, was not the only site of Byzantine artistic influence on Scandinavia. In Denmark, twelfth-century paintings in churches at Vä and Måløv show clear Byzantine influences.[261] The paintings at Vä are of a type that can be found in various places in Europe, while at Måløv there are some relatively unique elements including a Byzantine Hodegetria. This icon was famous in Byzantium and in the Orthodox world, but was rare in western Europe at this time; its presence in the church at Måløv seems to indicate a more direct connection.[262] Denmark in general had a strong connection to Byzantium in the twelfth century; besides the churches at Vä and Måløv, there are Byzantine-style wall paintings at Skåne, Sæby, Jørlunde, and elsewhere.[263] These paintings were more than Byzantine in style, many of them also used lapis lazuli for their designs, an expensive material that was available only through trade with Byzantium.[264] Even beyond the wall paintings, "objects like ivories, encolpia, silks, all testify that there was a Byzantine connection."[265]

The farthest reaches of Scandinavia and of Europe bear perhaps the most interesting Byzantine-style artwork yet found. In Iceland, there exists a late eleventh-century Byzantine Last Judgment.[266] The medium used is wood carving instead of wall painting, but in style and imagery it corresponds very closely to the Last Judgment depicted in the Church of San Angelo in Formis in Italy,[267] a church commissioned by Desiderius with the Last Judgment done by commissioned Byzantine artists or the monks trained in Byzantium. This piece of art gives us an excellent concluding example of the reach of Byzantine style throughout the entirety of Europe.

It has become common knowledge that Rus' and the Slavic world were appropriators of Byzantine art and architecture, but this chapter has shown that they were not alone in those appropriations. The German Empire (through multiple dynasties), the Anglo-Saxons, Normans, Scandinavians, Italians, and many others were all interested in appropriation of art, architecture, titulature, coinage, and other images of the Byzantine Empire as a way to connect themselves to the last fragment of Rome, and enhance their own legitimacy. The Byzantine Ideal brings together work in a variety of fields to demonstrate that Byzantium was the cultural magistra Europae, due to its status as the Christian Roman Empire. Viewing medieval history through this lens changes our perceptions of the position of the Slavic world vis-à-vis the rest of Europe.

They were not the recipients of Byzantine cultural dominance, lagging behind Western Europe; instead Byzantium was being appropriated throughout Europe. Kings, dukes, kniazia, and others took what they needed from the image of Byzantium to construct for themselves a framework of legitimacy that tied them into a Byzantine, or Roman, Ideal.

— 2 —

The Ties That Bind

This chapter illustrates one of the main themes of this book, which is that Rus' was part of medieval Europe. The cases used to explore this theme consist of fifty-two known dynastic marriages that took place over the course of nearly two hundred years, 77 percent of them with countries to the west of Rus'.[1] The very existence of so many dynastic marriages with western kingdoms clearly shows the Russian connection with the rest of Europe; however, this belief has not generally been shared by either historians of Rus' or of medieval Europe. This chapter, and the next, remedies this fact by providing a wealth of information on both dynastic marriages in general and the marriages that linked Rus' with the rest of the kingdoms of Europe in specific.

The first section lays the groundwork by addressing the idea of dynastic marriage, therein emphasizing the variety of scholarship on this important topic, much of which has been discussed in medieval history for many years, but which is new to Russian medieval history. This is due, not to a lack of interest or to our not being au courant, but instead to a lack of scholars in the discipline. The reasons for, processes behind, and details of the arrangement of dynastic marriages show the importance of Russian dynastic marriage ties with the rest of Europe. These ties were used to strengthen and enhance political alliances throughout Europe. Examined here are not only Russian examples, but also examples from Byzantium and Western Europe that show the importance of dynastic marriage to the advancement of the medieval political process. "As Henry III of England put it when seeking a wife for his son Edward in 1254, 'Friendship between princes can be obtained in no more fitting manner than by the link of conjugal troth.'"[2] The system of dynastic marriage was the glue that held medieval alliances together and allowed medieval politics to function.

Key to the dynastic marriage system was the introduction of brides from foreign kingdoms. Very often historians of Rus' have followed the tradition of Russian chroniclers, by and large monks in Russian monasteries, and written these women out of Russian history. However, they are a crucial part of the argument that dynastic marriage is what integrated Rus' into Europe, and the lives and workings of these women must be examined in detail. This is why a very important part of the first section of this chapter is devoted to an examination of the power and abilities of royal women in the Middle Ages. To quote Georges Duby, "If we were to believe everything written by men we would be in danger of mistakenly thinking that women had no power whatsoever."[3] There is a large and growing body of scholarship on this issue, and much of it is drawn on to show that queens were not impotent decorations at their husbands' courts, but rather figures of power in their own right who were often able to exercise their own as well as their husbands' power. This shows that Rusian women who left Rus' to marry European royalty were empowered and also influential in their new homes. Key to this argument is the idea developed by John Carmi Parsons that royal daughters were valued by their parents and were reared to be loyal to their families, the idea being that the daughters would then take that loyalty with them when they married and moved away.[4] This loyalty has always been implied when discussing sons, but for daughters it has been assumed that they were chattel to be disposed of, rather than valuable partners. Parsons's idea, which has been discussed by others as well,[5] changes the way a dynastic marriage can be examined, in our example showing that a Rusian woman in a foreign court can maintain and continue to exercise her ties with Rus' to her personal advantage as well as to the advantage of her kingdom and family.

This section will also discuss the thought processes engaged in by the Rusian rulers in conceiving of their dynastic marriages. The majority of marriages were made with kingdoms to their west. This was not a haphazard collection of accidents; rather, these marriages were part of the political processes engaged in by medieval kingdoms. The clear focus of Rusian political and thus marital policy was westward, and this is borne out by the numerous examples discussed.

In the discussion of these marriages, the Rusian women who married out of Rus' have been emphasized because they represent one of the main ways that ties with Europe were fostered and maintained. These women were able to influence events and ideas within their host kingdoms, an idea addressed in great detail in Chapter 3, where specific marriages are illustrated.[6] This lengthy discussion of Rusian dynastic marriages reinforces our understanding of the web of connections that held Europe together from the Atlantic to the Urals and the Baltic to the Black Seas.

One of the many difficulties in a project dealing with medieval dynastic marriage is ascertaining motivation and agency. The identities of the participants can be obtained with a reasonable degree of certainty in many cases, but there is often very little information about who arranged a marriage, or the explicit purpose of said marriage. It is rare to be told very clearly, as Saxo Grammaticus does in the case of Gyða Haroldsdottir, who arranged a particular marriage, though even he leaves out a purpose for the marriage.[7] Generally speaking, what we are left with one thousand years after the fact is conjecture, both as to who arranged the marriage and as to its purpose. I have attempted such conjecture here to explain the system of dynastic marriages undertaken by the Riurikids, and have noted the conjectural nature of the evidence and argumentation where appropriate. As for the agency behind the marriages, that is discussed, equally conjecturally, for each of the marriages. Most often it is assumed that the ruler of Kiev, as *pater familias,* is negotiating the marriage for the good of the Riurikids, and Rus', as a whole. However, with the increasing divisions between families after the usurpation of Sviatoslav Iaroslavich, the Iziaslavichi, Sviatoslavichi, and Vsevolodovichi, among others, all seem to go their own ways. I foreground the conjecture required to discuss these marriages because I believe that such conjecture *is* required, and can be found in a host of studies on medieval women, dynastic marriage, onomastics, and so on. Acknowledging the conjecture required for, and the relevant modifiers in, the text (may be, could have been, possibly, and so forth) does not detract from the utility of the study, or from the validity of the evidence provided.

Past studies of Rus' have primarily focused on political history, leaving out the activities of the women engaged in these dynastic marriages; studies of women in the Middle Ages, while dealing with some queens, have almost completely left Rus' out of their analyses. Because of these lacunae, this chapter and the next blend a major note of political history with minor notes of social and women's history to create a unique perspective on the history of Rusian dynastic marriage, and seek to use all of the available evidence to best discern the history of Rus'.

In total, this chapter shows the enormous importance that dynastic marriages had in the political life of the medieval world, specifically in binding kingdoms together. The numerous Rusian dynastic marriages bound Rus' into a web of alliances that stretched throughout Europe and firmly entrenched them in European politics for this period of the Middle Ages.

The Western Orientation of Rusian Dynastic Marriage

Dynastic marriages happen not through chance, but through careful planning and strategy or through the leveraging of a strategic advantage at an opportune moment. The first Rusian dynastic marriage is well known—it was made between Vladimir Sviatoslavich and Anna *Porphyrogenita*. This was not an accident, but was in fact the result of Rus' leveraging a Byzantine need in order to get its own goal met. The Byzantines needed soldiers to put down a rebellion, while the Rusian goal was entrance into the larger world of state politics.[8] That community, at least the closest pieces of it, was Christian and so conversion was a necessity. By marrying a Byzantine princess, especially a porphyrogenite princess, Rus' would have an immediate advantage in its political position in Christian Europe. A Byzantine imperial daughter born while her father was ruling as emperor was the most sought-after bride in medieval Europe. A porphyrogenita was a symbol of great status, and a dynastic marriage with her was an endorsement of the legitimacy of a kingdom's royal or imperial claims.[9] This marriage also brought with it an important tie with the Byzantine Empire, a key point of importance. Only one time before, in 927, had a porphyrogenite daughter married a foreigner, and in that case she married Peter of Bulgaria (r. 927–969) in order to end a generation of war. Even then, many Byzantines (as well as later historians) thought it may have been too much to give.[10] Over the years, other rulers had sought porphyrogenite princesses for themselves or their sons. The two most notable seekers in the late tenth century were the German Emperor, Otto I (r. 962–973), who attempted to negotiate a marriage between his son Otto II (joint rule with Otto I, 967–973; r. 973–983) and a porphyrogenite princess (possibly Anna herself),[11] and the king of France, Hugh Capet (r. 987–996), who sought a porphyrogenite princess for his son Robert (r. 996–1031).[12] However, where those Christian worthies failed, pagan Vladimir succeeded. And he succeeded because he successfully leveraged his opportunity and offered his own conversion to Christianity, which, while not explicitly stated, was understood to mean that his people would end up converting as well.[13] This dynastic marriage brought Rus' into the world of Christian Europe as a legitimized kingdom with a high-profile tie to the Byzantine Empire, a tie that other kingdoms craved and could not acquire.

After Rus' entered this new political world in such a grand manner, it did not again turn to Byzantium for a marital alliance or any other alliance that is recorded, for more than sixty years. In that time, they concluded approximately twelve known marriages with other kingdoms throughout Europe. Why does this gap exist? In the traditional model of Rusian history, the marriage alliance of Vladimir and Anna Porphyrogenita was the conclusion of long-standing ties between Rus' and Byzantium that had been initiated because of the "route from the Varangians to the Greeks," and was presaged by treaties in 907, 911, and 944. The marriage and the accompanying conversion are perceived to have firmly bound Rus' to Byzantium for the rest of time. This view is one that historians and others have nurtured by beginning with the situation in Muscovy and anachronistically working their way back in history to Rus'. If this view, not developed until Muscovite times, is set aside and the marital policy of Rus' examined carefully, it appears that this first marriage with Byzantium was simply Rus' breaking on to the international political scene in a dramatic way.[14] Moving away from marriages with the Byzantines was most likely simply part of the political-dynastic plan of the Rusian rulers—the best tie possible, with the most prestigious marital partner in the medieval world, was already made. There were certainly other marriage possibilities in Byzantium, as there were always multiple noble families vying for power, not to mention that after the reign of Basil II (r. 976–1025) there was a period of political strife in which his nieces Zoe (r. 1028–1050, with corulers) and Theodora (1042–1055, with corulers; r. 1055–1056) were used as gateways to power for multiple noble families. It was not until the end of this period of strife that Rus' again turned to Byzantium for a marriage tie, approximately sixty-five years after Vladimir and Anna's marriage.[15] With a calculated turn away from Byzantium for more than half a century, the Riurikid princes could also have been trying to avoid what, ironically, was their eventual fate: to be considered solely linked with Byzantium.

The political activities of Rus' involve the Poles most frequently; the Scandinavians, chiefly the Swedes, next; and then the Hungarians and the Germans. At one time or another, Rus' participated in the internal politics of all of these kingdoms through military and marital means.

Again, one is left with the question of why this is. One possible reason is endogamy—a family will attempt to make marriages with other families of similar descent.[16] The Riurikids were of Scandinavian descent, and many of the marriages they made were with Scandinavians. Iaroslav "Mudryi" Vladimirich, who married Ingigerd of Sweden, and his daughter Elisabeth, who married Harald Hardraada of Norway (r. ca. 1044–1066), are the main examples from the eleventh century, but there are multiple instances throughout this period. Even the marriages with the Poles can be ascribed to this theory, because the Poles were also married into Scandinavian and Germanic families.[17] The Rusian marriages with Scandinavia may have been an attempt to stay close to their roots.

The idea of endogamy is similar to advice given by Saxo Grammaticus, the twelfth-century chronicler of Danish history. He said that the Danish royal house ought to marry their neighbors because they shared a culture, and cultural discontinuity in a marriage is too jarring.[18] The life of the Byzantine emperors and that of the Riurikid princes could not have been more different. The Byzantine emperors lived in Constantinople and rarely left. They were surrounded by servants and government bureaucrats.[19] Rus', on the other hand, was still a kingdom, not an empire, and was ruled in the familial manner common in the Middle Ages.[20] The Rusian ruler was often itinerant, a member of a warrior elite who traveled the kingdom with his war band living off the land of his people. He would find much in common with the Scandinavian, Polish, Hungarian, or even German rulers, all of whom lived and ruled in a manner similar to this.[21] The bureaucratic type of government would not take over the majority of Europe until the mid- to late twelfth century. So in marrying his family to the families of the countries to his west, the Riurikid ruler was following the heart of Saxo's dictum by marrying those who were similar to him in order to minimize the difficulties of marriage. As for the idea of "neighbors," Rus' was physically closer to Scandinavia, Poland, the German Empire, and Hungary than it was to far-off Byzantium, from which it was separated by not only the Black Sea but also the often forbidding steppe. All of which is not to mention the Scandinavian origins of the Riurikids, which may have given them a similar cultural base with the larger Germanic world whose inhabitants (France and the German Empire as descendants of the Carolingian empire, Anglo-Saxon England, and of course Denmark, Sweden, and Norway) make up many of the participants in Rusian dynastic marriages.

This physical separation between Rus' and Byzantium may also explain the lack of Byzantine interest in Rus'. Reading the traditional histories of Rus', this statement might come as a surprise, but as Alexander Kazhdan put it, "intermarriages with Kievan princes did not occupy any significant place in the high diplomacy of the Constantinopolitan court of the eleventh and twelfth centuries."[22] Going beyond the soft no "significant place" of Kazhdan, Ruth Macrides, in her analysis of Byzantine marital diplomacy, states that "marital unions with northerners did not cease to be both rare and undesirable."[23] This is a far cry from the view one receives from reading the Rusian chronicles, in which the Byzantine eye seems to be focused ever northward, or from the frequently cited portions of the tenth-century *De administrando imperio* by Constantine Porphyrogenitus dealing with Rus'.[24] Rus' was not a priority for Byzantine politics, or even much of a concern—it receives little mention in the majority of contemporary sources, and no mention in Anna Comnena's famous *Alexiad,* which chronicles the rule of her father, Alexius Comnenus (r. 1081–1118).[25] This example is specifically mentioned because Alexius initiated a period of extensive foreign relations, chiefly through marital relations, and was the instigator for the First Crusade—a venture that Rus' did not participate in, either assisting Alexius versus the Turks in Anatolia, or in the eventual campaigns in the Levant. After Anna Porphyrogenita, none of the few brides who went to Rus' or their marriages are ever mentioned in Byzantine sources, but in that period Byzantine sources record dozens of Byzantine dynastic marriages with other kingdoms of Europe, many in some detail.[26] During the same time, Rus' crops up in many Latin sources from the rest of Europe. Their dynastic marriages were re-corded in local sources, and internal Rusian events made it into some Latin chronicles.[27] Rusian dynastic marriages were overwhelmingly (77 percent of the total number of known marriages) with the kingdoms to their west, for both political and cultural reasons, and that marital orientation reinforced their connection to the larger European world.

Baumgarten and Byzantine Inflation

The last comprehensive work on Rusian dynastic marriages was that of Nicholas de Baumgarten, who in the 1920s compiled a set of genealogical tables covering all of the royal marriages of Rus'.[28] This work was considered exceptional in its time and has been the main source for the little work done on such marriages in the many years since. Unfortunately, Baumgarten includes many marriages with the Byzantines that have since been shown to be false. Alexander Kazhdan reviewed all of the Byzantine-Rusian marriages in 1988 and showed that of the eight marriages Baumgarten listed that fall into the period covered here, only three could be documented.[29]

This reduction emphasizes the point that there were few dynastic contacts between Rus' and Byzantium, but it also requires us to ask, from where did the idea of these marriages come? The initial complication comes from the terminology of the *Povest' vremennykh let (PVL)* itself, where women are rarely referred to by name. Sometimes women are referred to by ethnonym, such as Vsevolod Iaroslavich's "Greek" wife,[30] and other times Greek men and women receive the title *tsarevich* or *tsarevitsa*,[31] respectively. These terms have in the past been logically assumed to refer to a son or daughter of the Byzantine emperor. But Kazhdan surmises that these terms were much more fluid and were likely used in reference to well-placed Greek individuals who were not children of the Byzantine emperor. This naming problem stemming from the *PVL* caused confusion for later chroniclers and historians who attempted to flesh out the history of Rus'.

Many of the marriages that Kazhdan finds to be false can be traced back to sixteenth- and seventeenth-century chronicles that contain narrative accounts added to flesh out earlier chronicles. Others are traceable only to N. M. Karamzin's nineteenth-century opus on Rusian history.[32]

What seems clear from these accounts is that early modern Russians were interested in increasing their historical ties with Byzantium and thus padded their list of dynastic marriages with some extra Byzantine connections. The purpose of this seems to have been to increase the connection between the second Rome and the third, and consequently between the last great Orthodox empire and the next. I would go so far as to postulate that this was not an intentional fabrication of history on the part of these later historians and chroniclers, but rather grew out of their worldview, in which Russia and Byzantium were already closely linked by Orthodoxy and by ties of marriage bookended by Anna Porphyrogenita and Sophia Paleologina, wife of Ivan III (r. 1462–1505).[33] It seems likely that in their minds the relationship already existed, and where there were lacunae in the early chronicles they could be filled in with Byzantine ties, a logical conclusion from the perspective of their worldview.

The Idea of Dynastic Marriage

A genealogical chart is a wonderful tool for examining relationships, but it is also inherently misleading. Look at any genealogical chart and you will find a depiction of marriages, descendants, and even connections between families and countries. But consider instead any one marriage and what is it composed of: two individuals. When this concept is contemplated from a certain angle, it becomes clear how this allowed George Vernadsky to dismiss over a hundred years of Rusian dynastic marriage with a brief treatment.[34] How much difference can one person make? How much influence can be wielded by one person? But the world of dynastic marriage did not just involve one person going to another kingdom. Behind that individual were a family, a political system, a culture, and a religious tradition that she bore with her on her journey. When considered in this light, one person can have a significant influence. This is not to mention the fact that the individuals involved were royalty, and thus more likely able to influence large swathes of society, or that it was never one person going alone. Rather, there was an entourage accompanying the participant in the dynastic marriage so that she was able to bring with her a piece of her homeland and transplant it to her new kingdom. Analyzing the interactions among these underlying forces is one of the aims of this chapter.

In her analysis of Byzantine dynastic marriage, Ruth Macrides concludes that when they work, dynastic marriages unite not only two people, but two families.[35] These families then have obligations to one another because of their marital ties. The most obvious of these obligations is the fulfillment of the original goals of the dynastic marriage. For instance, in the late 1030s and early 1040s, the Riurikids and the Piasts of Poland intermarried twice, both times with the goal of reinforcing the rule of the embattled Casimir (r. ca. 1039–1058) in Poland by battling the Mazovians, who were a threat both to Poland and Rus'.[36] The *PVL* acknowledges this goal by stating that Iaroslav conquered the Mazovians, killed their leader Moislav, and subjected them to Casimir— thus, it seems, fulfilling the primary goal of the dynastic marriage.[37]

But beyond the original political goal, the dynastic marriage can create ties of loyalty between families. Probably the most discussed examples of this in Rusian history are the plentiful ties to the Poles, largely by the Iziaslavichi. These ties allowed exiled Rusian princes to call on the aid of the ruler of Poland, be he father-in-law, uncle, or cousin, to gain assistance in returning to power in Rus'.[38] That these kinds of ties were an essential part of dynastic marriages was acknowledged in Byzantium. John Dukas advised Nicephoras III Botaneiates (r. 1078–1081) to marry Maria of the Alans because she had few relations who might trouble the emperor.[39] However, not only bad things (such as backing for internecine warfare) came of these increasing ties between families. Baldwin III of Jerusalem (r. 1143–1162) was often a mediator for his father-in-law, Manuel I Comnenus (r. 1143–1180), attempting to both keep the peace and placate him.[40] In Rus' there is the example of Sviatosha Davidich, who married Anna Sviatopolkovna. Because of that tie, Sviatosha went against the normal policy of his birth family, the Sviatoslavichi, and on multiple occasions lent his support to his father-in-law, Sviatopolk II Iziaslavich (r. 1093–1113).[41] As can be seen from these examples, when dynastic marriages occurred, not only were two people joined, but also two families. The effect of that joining went beyond the initial political purpose of the dynastic marriage and had repercussions for years to come.

A dynastic marriage was not a simple affair, and rarely was it made quickly. The two parties, generally the parents of those involved, began negotiations well in advance of the marriage.[42] This is nicely illustrated by the example of the marriage of Anna Iaroslavna to Henry I of France (corule with Robert II 1027–1031, r. 1031–1060). In 1049 Henry sent French bishops, either Gauthier of Meaux and Gosselin of Chauny, or alternately Roger of Chalons, depending on the source used, to Rus' to negotiate a marriage agreement with Iaroslav.[43] These bishops were successful in their mission and escorted Anna back to France, where the marriage ceremony was performed in 1051.[44] There is, unfortunately, no record of the negotiations, but the two years between the sending of the embassy and the marriage ceremony were not all travel time, and the negotiations must have been interesting. At stake in a dynastic marriage were not only the wedding and its details, including any dowry, but also the primary purpose of the marriage—to seal an agreement between the parties involved. Duby has said that he believes dynastic marriages were arranged with actual contracts that were negotiated well in advance of the marriage itself.[45] There are multiple examples from elsewhere in Europe, though we have no specific examples from Rus' itself, despite the tantalizing knowledge that French bishops were in Rus' a year, or more, before Anna and Henry's wedding.[46] In both cases of marriages of the sons of German Emperors (Otto II and Otto III) to Byzantine princesses, an embassy was sent from the German Empire to Byzantium to negotiate the potential marriage and the brides traveled to the German Empire only after the negotiations were concluded.[47] What would be negotiated for such a contract varied, depending on the circumstances of the marriage. The well-known marriage of Peter of Bulgaria and Maria Lecapena in 927 ended decades of conflict between Byzantium and Bulgaria and also established an independent patriarchate for the Bulgarians.[48] These marriages were simply capstones on agreements that were concerned with larger factors. The marriages were meant to provide tangible symbols of what had been agreed to as well as to draw the two sides closer together. No physical contract exists for Peter and Maria's marriage, but the act and its immediate repercussions indicate a relationship of cause and effect between the events (peace and the new patriarchate) and the marriage.[49] This is most elegantly illustrated by the history of Byzantine dynastic marriage in which many of the foreign women who married into the Byzantine imperial family changed their names to "Irene," meaning peace.[50]

A dynastic marriage joined two families, but it also sent the female partner off into a foreign land to live at a foreign court and, most likely, to learn to speak a foreign language. Because of her gender and the idea that she was only one person, historians have traditionally down-played the importance of dynastic marriage as a tool for political or cul-tural influence or exchange. This idea has largely disappeared from the discussion of dynastic marriage in Western medieval history and needs to change in regard to Rus' as well. One goal of this chapter, and the next, is to change the perception that Rusian dynastic marriage involved basically the exile of a Rusian princess, never to be seen, heard from, or dealt with again. The correct idea, as some Rusian examples (and many Western and Byzantine examples) indicate, is that a woman who mar-ried into a foreign kingdom did not go alone, did stay in contact with her home, and did sometimes return to her homeland. All of this resulted in increased contact between the two kingdoms involved in the marriage, and inevitably political, cultural, and religious interaction occurred.

Consanguinity

Of enormous importance when discussing medieval marriage in general and dynastic marriage in particular is the concept of consanguinity. According to the doctrine of the Christian Church in this period, people could not marry who were related within a certain consanguineous de-gree, meaning that they shared too much blood to marry and produce children. The medieval period pre-1215 was an especially interesting time in the history of consanguinity legislation because during this era the church stretched consanguinity to seven degrees, an increase from the four that was common in the late Roman world, and the de-grees were calculated in a new manner. Instead of siblings being related in two degrees, as was held previously, the new method of calculation made siblings related in the first degree. This may at first appear to be a small change, but in fact it was enormous. The original method, and the one returned to after the Fourth Lateran Council in 1215, was to count connections between people; thus, for siblings, one degree up to the shared parent, and one degree down to the sibling, for a total of two degrees. For first cousins, a more likely target for marriage than siblings, it was one degree up to your parent, another degree up to your grand-parent, a degree down to your uncle/aunt, and a degree down to your cousin, resulting in a relationship of four degrees.[51]

The new method of calculating consanguinity was based on degrees to a common ancestor, which resulted in a one-degree relationship for siblings (a common ancestor is one generation back) and two degrees for a cousin (a common ancestor is two generations back). When this concept was applied to seven generations of ancestors, it expanded the pool of consanguineous relations to anyone with whom one shared a great-great-great-great-great-grandparent. In the medieval world, in which dynastic marriages had occurred between the royal houses of many kingdoms at least once, this greatly limited potential mates.[52] This is one of the reasons it is exceedingly rare to get multiple marriages between two royal houses in close temporal proximity to one another. The unwieldiness of this consanguinity policy is what eventually led to its downfall and reversal at the Fourth Lateran Council, not to mention that the royal families of Europe were all too related to intermarry by those rules.

For our purposes here, an important issue to address, regarding consanguinity, is enforcement. Enforcement for the medieval church was always a problem, and in the later eleventh century matters began to come to a head with the growth of the reform papacy. Popes beginning with Gregory VII and Urban II attempted to force recalcitrant rulers to follow the religious directives coming from Rome. Consanguinity was a key issue. The case of Philip I of France (r. 1059–1108) and his consanguineous relationship was brought to the fore at Urban II's papal synod at Piacenza in 1095, and numerous other cases pepper the eleventh and twelfth centuries as popes attempted to enforce this doctrine. Another sign that consanguinity was an issue for couples is the use of papal dispensations to allow marriage for couples in consanguineous relationships whose marriages were necessary to their kingdoms, an example of which is the marriage of Bolesław III of Poland (r. 1102–1138) and Sbyslava Sviatopolkovna of Rus'.[53]

The Orthodox Church, like the church in Rome, also maintained a policy against consanguineous marriages. Marriages were also forbidden in the seventh degree, but the Orthodox Church never changed its method of calculating degrees, which created a much smaller pool of consanguineous relations. However, there are no known patriarchal (as opposed to papal) dispensations for Rusian consanguineous marriages in this period, though it seems that Rusians generally observed a policy of avoiding such marriages if at all possible in their marriages within

Rus'.[54] It is difficult to say whether this dialogue informed their foreign marriages to any great extent, as there is only one dispensation involving a Rusian extant from this period (for the marriage mentioned above). The Rusians had multiple marriages with Poles that were consanguineous as defined by both the Orthodox and Roman churches, and had marriages with Danes and Hungarians that were consanguineous as defined by the Roman Church. Whether this reflects participants' lack of knowledge of the consanguinity laws, or a lack of respect for such laws in favor of creating dynastic bonds, or whether the requisite papal dispensation has been lost, is all unknown. But consanguinity was an important feature of medieval dynastic marriage that informed discussion of potential marriage partners and sometimes forced rulers to avoid certain otherwise advantageous marriages.

Medieval Women and Their Place in the Family

There are, at present, at least two competing views of medieval royal brides. The old view is the one mentioned above: despite being royalty, these were still women and thus they had very little ability to act in regard to the arrangement of their marriage or even to act within their marriage. Oddly, royal women still lag behind their religious counterparts as figures of strength and power in the historical imagination, especially in regard to Rus'.[55] This older view has allowed historians and others to virtually ignore royal women in their writing and study of history, making exceptions of only those women who were regents for their sons or who became abbesses. Women were thought, by medieval chroniclers and these historians, to have been allowed to have power over other women in a religious context as long as they were subordinate to the male church or to have power when acting on a son's behalf for a few years as long as there were calmer male heads on the regency council.[56] This view slowly changed with the growth of social and women's history in the later twentieth century.

André Poulet advanced a theory about the powerlessness of medieval women under the aegis of feminist scholarship in the 1990s, deriding the patriarchal power structure that subordinated women to male authority and used them to advance the goals of the patriarchy.[57] Poulet's work joins other modern views of royal women in acknowledging that women were participants in a patriarchal system that was not de-signed to advance their own interests.[58] However, John Carmi Parsons takes Poulet's theory one step further and suggests that women used their place as participants in this patriarchal system to effect change for themselves and to gain power over aspects of their lives.[59] The ability of women to gain power within this system was firmly rooted in the fam-ily structure,[60] which allowed women to gather and retain power in a patriarchal system that in other ways continued to marginalize their roles.[61] As the structure of government largely mirrored the family structure, women's power increased because the royal woman was now fulfilling the role of wife and mother for an increasingly large group of people. Suzanne Fonay Wemple has argued that this trend toward female empowerment increased in the eleventh century with the grow-ing religious and legal emphasis on the marital bond, which allowed a woman to have a say alongside her husband.[62] The increasing power of women can be shown by the increasing number of ruling queens from the eleventh century through the end of the Middle Ages.[63] The posi-tion I have chosen to adopt in this minefield of sensitivity and history is expressed very succinctly by Parsons: "Despite their membership in patriarchal families that traded them in marriage, noblewomen's unique participation in matrimonial politics did afford them opportu-nities to claim power and to achieve some degree of self-realization."[64]

Another aspect of this issue is the appreciation of women by their families. History has long held the view that female children were not desired by their parents and were set aside as disappointments until they could be disposed of in marriage. This view has been propounded recently by Poulet, who emphasizes the patriarchal system and its dis-taste for women in general.[65] Opposing this view is what I consider to be the novel position of Parsons, who advances the notion that female children were prized by their parents, especially by their fathers.[66] This argument is unique and deserves to be described in full. A daughter, in contrast to a son, does not have a claim on any of her father's patri-mony,[67] therefore with the birth of a daughter, the father does not have to worry about finding land for this child or worrying that she will dis-rupt his plans for his firstborn male's succession. Further, a daughter is able to make peace between her brothers, as well as between her broth-ers and their father.[68] Thus, daughters are useful to have as part of a family unit, and are not separated off from the family in some type of ostracized position.[69]

A daughter was a valuable asset because it was through dynastic marriages that alliances were finalized in the Middle Ages, making the mistreatment of a royal daughter illogical. Even more illogical is the idea that daughters were segregated from their families during childhood. The goal of a dynastic marriage was not only to seal an alliance, but to establish a base of power inside another kingdom. The core of that power base was the ruler's daughter. Anything that would prejudice a daughter against the family of her birth, including childhood mistreatment or alienation from her family, would be counterproductive to ensuring her loyalty to them when she was starting a family of her own in a foreign land. The corollary to this statement is that daughters needed to be educated in the use of power so that they could be more effective agents of their home kingdoms and advocates for their father's and, later, brothers' policies.[70] The importance of familial ties to these women is illustrated by a later counterexample. In the early modern period, brides began to be sent to live with the family of their betrothed at a very young age, so as not to develop firm attachments with their birth families.[71] This suggests that the opposite had been true previously, and that families, particularly those receiving brides, were working to counteract the possibility of establishing a center of foreign interest in their court. All of this adds up to a unique picture of medieval daughters that reconceptualizes their place in noble families as well as in dynastic marriage.

A firstborn son was an heir to be prized. A second son was a spare in case something should go wrong. A third son could be a gift to the church and a powerful force in holy orders for the family. More sons than that were dangerous to the succession—as the Rusian example sometimes illustrated. Daughters can now be seen as treasured members of the family, guarantors of potential alliances, and agents of influence in foreign courts. Parsons's argument allows for a reanalysis of medieval family patterns that can now emphasize the role and status of women.

Women in Dynastic Marriage

When a dynastic marriage was arranged, the bride would leave her home and her family and travel to her husband's home to start a family together. Easy as it may have been in the past to overlook what looks like a transfer of a person from one culture and kingdom to another, the marriage was, in fact, a complicated process. The marriage itself took quite some time to arrange, the agreements needed to be finalized, and the entourage needed to be assembled. No royal or noble woman would have been put on a horse and sent off on her own. She would have had a whole troupe of people assisting and serving her in her home country, and these people would be brought with her to serve her as well as to add to her own sphere of influence in her new kingdom.

The most noted company for a woman involved in a dynastic marriage was a personal confessor; because of the woman's rank, this ecclesiastic was usually a bishop. Anna Porphyrogenita brought an entire entourage of churchmen with her to Rus', though they disappear from the records after her arrival.[72] More fleshed-out by the sources is the story of Bishop Reinbern of Kolobrzeg, who accompanied Bolesław Chrobry's daughter when she came to Rus' to marry Sviatopolk Iaropolchich.[73] Reinbern came not only as her personal confessor but also to assist in the conversion of the people of Sviatopolk's realm.[74] This is a clear case of a foreign princess bringing people with her for her own interest and then of those companions having an effect on the people of the host kingdom. It is possible that the lack of concern over particular Christian rite expressed by the eleventh-century Rusian nobility was due to the widespread number of Latin women, and thus probably Latin priests or bishops, living in Rus'.[75]

Another Rusian dynastic marriage provides evidence of a princess's accompaniment in foreign lands. In the late eleventh century, Evpraksia Vsevolodovna was engaged to a German margrave, and her arrival is recorded in a monastic chronicle. She "arrived in this country with much pomp, with camels burdened with precious clothes and stones, and also with countless riches."[76] A woman traveling alone from Kiev to the Saxon Nordmark with a train of camels is more than an impossibility, especially as she was just twelve years old at the time. Not mentioned, but certainly present, was a large entourage, required not only for the maintenance of the princess but also for the hefty maintenance of such a caravan. Not just workers, but companions (soldiers, family members, ladies-in-waiting, and so forth) traveling with the princess to her new home, are mentioned in instances from around Europe (though not Rus'—most likely an issue of sources rather than anything else). Theophano, the much-recorded German empress, was sent with a "splendid entourage" to the German Empire for her marriage to Otto II.[77] Though the members of the entourage are not enumerated, the presence of the entourage is explicitly noted. In a Rusian-connected example, Ingigerd of Sweden brought with her such a party, including her kinsman Ragnvald Úlfsson, who received land and rank in Rus' upon her marriage to Iaroslav the Wise.[78] There are further examples of such parties from throughout Europe, and as a whole they constituted an island of foreign culture in the heart of a kingdom and at the side of the ruler of that kingdom. In the practice of the medieval church, a marriage consisted of one man and one woman, and their consent was all that was needed to make it valid. In the practice of medieval dynastic marriage, a marriage was one man and one woman, envoys and embassies, entourages and baggage trains, and bishops and servants.

Culture was also an important element of these marriages. However, from the historical remove of a thousand years, culture transmitted through marital ties is often difficult to observe and enumerate. One way to show cultural diffusion is through shifts in royal onomastics, which is discussed in Chapter 3. There are clear examples of cultural transmission from other areas of Europe, but examples of this from Rus', well known as an underdocumented area of Europe, especially in regard to the activities of women and medieval secular culture, are nonexistent. It seems, then, that we must run the risk of error and extrapolate these other examples to the Rusian case.

The best example of cultural transmission from this time period is the marriage of Byzantine princess Theophano to the German emperor Otto II.[79] This is one of the most famous marriages in medieval history and has been studied in many books and articles and in its own conference.[80] The reasons for such a study are the obvious importance of the marriage between two European imperial powers and Theophano's enormous impact on the German Empire's politics and culture.[81] The princess introduced Byzantine fashions into the court of the German Empire, brought in Byzantine arts that then influenced German artists, and introduced Byzantine saints into the German calendar, building churches to St. Nicholas, St. Demetrios, and St. Dionysios.[82] Theophano also acted as regent for her son Otto III after her husband's death and helped arrange young Otto's marriage to another Byzantine princess. Admittedly, brides in dynastic marriages did not all have as much power as Theophano, but they did all wield some influence. Ingigerd, another well-represented example, was a keen advisor to her husband, Iaroslav, especially on affairs benefiting her Scandinavian kin.[83] The Byzantine princess Maria, who married Peter of Bulgaria in 927, in a visual sign of power appears on all of the royal seals with him, each of them having one hand on the scepter.[84] The experience of dynastic marriage allowed women to exercise power abroad when they might not have been able to do the same at home, but it also placed an influential person in the heart of a foreign kingdom.

A discussion of the ways in which these women were able to exercise power is important to an understanding of their place in kinship relations, politics, and society, and it also contributes to the refutation of the stereotype of the impotent medieval woman. Lois Huneycutt's work has focused on overcoming this stereotype, not only in modern minds, but also in the reading of medieval sources. She asserts that there is a paradox in that, "while [medieval] theoretical writings on gender attributed qualities such as capriciousness, physical weakness, lust, instability, lack of intelligence, irrationality, and a tendency toward duplicity to the female sex, men of the feudal nobility routinely expected women to occupy positions requiring grave judgment and responsibility."[85] Noble women were expected to take care of the land and tenants, defend property, advance the family's political goals, and raise the children, all while the men were away fighting or crusading for years at a time, and yet were viewed negatively as a sex.[86] This dichotomy existed largely because women were defined by family and kinship structures, and those structures controlled the noble courts and estates and even kingdoms.[87] But it was monks who wrote treatises on the nature of women, and monks lived their lives outside of traditional family and kinship structures, in addition to being constrained by the worldview of the medieval church.

The typical misogyny of medieval chronicles is exacerbated for Rus' by the paucity of sources, so Rusian women almost never appear in the Rusian chronicles, and if they do appear, it is generally as "daughter of," or "wife of," without a name of their own. The worldview of the Rusian monks was informed not only by Christianity, but by the Byzantine

Christian Church. The monks who wrote the Rusian chronicles lived in monasteries run along Byzantine lines, ruled by a Byzantine abbot or at least one Byzantine trained. One possible explanation for the near-total lack of references to European affairs in the Rusian chronicles is the Byzantine focus (even prejudice) of the chroniclers, or their supervisors. Though this explanation has its challengers,[88] and it is true that the chronicles contain both anti-Latin polemics and favorable mentions of notable pro-Latin personages (such as Evpraksia Vsevolodovna),[89] it is difficult to explain away the lack of interest in larger European, or even neighbors', affairs. This situation only complicates the study of Rusian women because they were the ones who married out to the West in large part, and thus were left out of the chronicles twice: once for their gender and once for their marriage.

A queen was a ruler as well as her husband. She was often crowned alongside him and appeared with him and had power of her own. But unlike him she swore no coronation oaths, and thus her power was undefined.[90] The only ritual roles that she was required to fulfill were as royal wife and mother.[91] This made her fertility and her bedroom activities an open topic of conversation in the entire kingdom, for the good of the kingdom depended on her procreative abilities. This situation also led to the creation of a royal imagery of chastity and virginity for queens that belied their procreative function.[92] This royal imagery was vital to preserving the queen's image in light of the intimate nature of her influence. A queen was expected to influence her husband in political matters,[93] and the root of that influence, in the minds of the people, stemmed from the royal couple's connection in the bedroom, rather than from their public relationship. The bedroom, or her suite of rooms, was also where a queen would receive petitioners looking to her for favors or influence.[94] These petitioners acknowledged the power of the queen in her own right, as well as in her ability to influence her husband in matters that she did not directly have power over.[95] Dealing with such petitioners was an ability a woman could have learned from her mother, either actively in training to one day be a queen herself or passively through daily observance of her mother's behavior.[96] There is also the possibility that it was simply expected behavior. Sedulius Scottus's *On Christian Rulers* gives as the ideal model for a queen a woman who was chaste, was skilled in her tasks, ruled her household, and influenced and counseled her husband.[97] Pauline Stafford believes this, especially the part about influencing and counseling the king, to have been a commonly accepted view of proper queens in the Middle Ages.[98] While not addressing widespread acceptance of such views, Parsons believes that there existed an active process of training and that mothers trained their daughters "on the basis of her [the mother's] international experience. . . . A queen could prepare them [her daughters] as disseminators or gatherers of symbolic capital."[99] This training was likely invaluable to the family and thus garnered the king's support because it would create a powerful daughter who would be capable of influencing her husband in her own dynastic marriage.[100] Presumably that influence could be made to work for the benefit of the daughter's natal family in certain cases. This type of training may have also bolstered the loyalty of a daughter to her birth family, something vital when sending her away to be married and live in a foreign land. It should also be noted that there may have been additional training in new ways upon arriving in a foreign kingdom. Leo the Deacon records that Byzantine empresses mentored foreign princesses upon their arrival in Constantinople, in what regard (language, custom, culture, or loyalty) is unknown.[101] Some scholars have suggested that this was a more common practice. S. P. Rozanov believes that Evpraksia Vsevolodovna was sent to the nunnery at Quedlinburg for an education upon her arrival in the German Empire.[102] Whether or not we can extrapolate this example throughout Europe, it seems more than reasonable to suggest that some process of education of these princesses was in the best interests of their families, in order for them to play their political and diplomatic roles to the fullest advantage of their home kingdom.

An overt way in which women could be powerful figures was when they exercised power openly as regents for their sons after the death of their husbands. They were then visibly in power but still technically in a subservient position to a male, in this case their young sons. Queens as regents have been discussed in much of the literature and are thus only briefly mentioned here as one of the ways in which medieval women were able to exercise their power. The only well-known Rusian example of a queen as regent is Anna Iaroslavna, who was regent for her son Philip I of France after her husband Henry I's death.[103] Records indicate that she traveled extensively with her son, and her name joined his on many documents in the short period of her regency.[104] Anna was even noted in two separate diplomas as having her own steward and, presumably, staff who were part of her place in the French familial, and thus governmental, hierarchy.[105] Anna's sister Anastasia may also have acted on behalf of her young son, Salomon, though not technically as regent, as they were ejected from power. They traveled together to the German Emperor and made a plea for aid to another regent, Agnes, regent for the underage emperor Henry IV.[106] Examples of the most powerful and controversial regents are found in the history of the German Empire, where there were multiple powerful female regents and queen-mothers who were able to influence the course of politics.[107] Theophano, as regent for her young son Otto III, for instance, was able to shape his early rule in a much more pro-Byzantine manner than others in court would have liked.[108] Agnes, mother of Henry IV, was also regent for her son, and acted unilaterally to set his agenda, resulting in a coalition of churchmen and nobles bringing an end to her regency.[109] In these instances, female power was not restricted to influencing husbands—these women acted openly for the best interests (in their view) of their families and kingdoms, just one of the ways in which royal women were able to exercise their personal political power in medieval Europe.

Medieval noble and royal women were not powerless figures who were merely exchanged between men in the interests of procreation and treaty making. They were or could be figures of strength, exercising power in conjunction with their husbands or on their own as regents for sons. This image of the medieval woman is an important one that needs to be kept in mind when examining the Rusian dynastic marriage system, in which Rusian women were asked to travel far from home to contract alliances yet were presumed to still be loyal and working in the best interests of their families.

Dynastic marriage provided one kingdom "with a presence at the court of foreign rulers which facilitated cooperation, goodwill and military support."[110] This was an essential feature of the marriage; not only did it seal an agreement, be it a peace treaty or war declaration, it also provided a long-lasting connection between the two kingdoms and provided the bride's home country with a complete embassy in the heart of another realm—an embassy that had particular power as it was centered in a foreign potentate's own household with its leader in his own bedchamber.[111] When viewed in this manner it is almost impossible to imagine that rulers would have neglected their daughters or done anything to divide their loyalties.

In the Byzantine example it is clear that these women retained their loyalties to their own empire. In an examination done by Cecily Hilsdale of Byzantine dynastic marriages we can see that most Byzantine brides who married into other kingdoms returned to Byzantium after the deaths of their husbands rather than making their homes in their host kingdoms.[112] Hilsdale's analysis, which is convincing, is that this shows that Byzantine princesses retained ties with their families and their empire while in their host country, thus reinforcing the idea of a dynastic marriage as an embassy. The same seems to be true elsewhere, to provide just two examples: Astrið of Sweden returns home after the death of her husband, King St. Olaf of Norway;[113] Cunigunda returned to her home in the German Empire following the death of her husband Iaropolk Iziaslavich.[114] Unfortunately, due to the spotty nature of Rusian records of women, there is only one recorded example of a Rusian bride returning home after the end of her dynastic marriage.[115] Evpraksia Vsevolodovna, after siding with the pope against her husband, German emperor Henry IV returned to Rus'.[116] After hearing of Henry's death, she entered a monastery, and upon her death was honored with an elaborate burial in the most holy monastery in Rus' as well as with the erection of her own chapel there.[117] There are no other examples of Rusian women returning home after their dynastic marriages ended,[118] but there are also no other Rusian women who receive the recognition in the *PVL* that Evpraksia does, being mentioned for taking monastic vows as well as for her death,[119] so the evidence is inconclusive. The evidence that women of other kingdoms returned home after their dynastic marriages ended offers up the possibility that Rusian women did as well despite their lack of mention in the Rusian chronicles, as well as reinforcing the familial ties posited above.

Dynastic marriage was an essential part of the medieval political process throughout Europe. It was used to create a physical bond between kingdoms that had made agreements. It was also an institution that drew the kingdoms of Europe closer together as the families involved became intermingled and at times came to view situations through the lens of mutual interest. The women involved were an essential part of the system. In large part this was because the structure of the ruling family was imposed on the government, or more clearly, the ruling family was the government, women and all. Women were thus not possessions to be given or sold, but valued members of the family who exercised power at their home country's court and were participants in dynastic marriages that sealed agreements with foreign powers and led to cultural exchange. Those women then became or had the opportunity to become powers at these new courts, all the while maintaining a loyalty to their home kingdom and using their influence to the advantage of that kingdom. In all of these affairs, Rus' was not an outlier. It did not stand apart from this system, but rather was a part of it. The medieval kingdom of Rus' was a part of medieval Europe, as illustrated by its participation in the dynastic marriage system, consequent marriages with royal families throughout Europe, and the cultural and political similarities briefly mentioned in examples above, and expanded in the next chapter. To understand the position of Rus' in medieval Europe, it is essential to first understand the ideas behind and process of dynastic marriage—a system that functioned as a glue tying the kingdoms of Europe together.

— 3 —

Rusian Dynastic Marriage

An understanding of the theory of dynastic marriage is essential to understanding why Rusian dynastic marriage is such an important part of the integration of Rus' into Europe. With that theory established in Chapter 2, it is necessary to discuss some of the individual marriages that took place between Rus' and the other kingdoms of Europe from the late tenth through mid-twelfth centuries. In that time period there were approximately fifty-two marriages about which enough data has survived to identify both of the participants by family, if not by name.[1] A sampling of these marriages will be discussed in this chapter in order to better elucidate not only the simple fact that Rus' was connected to the rest of Europe, but the various ways in which Rus', via dynastic marriage, participated in broader European affairs.

As yet there has been no English-language study that documents each of the dynastic marriages of the Riurikid princes and princesses from this time period, though there are various books and articles on the genealogy or marriage of one prince or princess or on the marriages of one generation. These writings are largely in Russian, and none focus specifically on the issue of dynastic marriage or the dynastic marriage policy of Rus' as a whole, and certainly none deal with this entire period. This chapter attempts to provide a small part of what is lacking in the scholarship, but does not deal with all of the Rusian dynastic marriages of the time.[2] However, it will provide a cross-section of Rusian marriages to aid in understanding Rusian marital policy of the tenth through mid-twelfth century.

Of the fifty-two known dynastic marriages in this period, forty of them are marriages with European kingdoms to the west of Rus'. As suggested in Chapter 2, much of the emphasis in the descriptions of these marriages is focused on the women. Women were the glue that bound the dynastic marriage system together, and understanding their position is essential to understanding each particular dynastic marriage. This is true not only of Rusian women, but of Western women as well. Of particular importance is the well-recorded and eventful life of Evpraksia Vsevolodovna, about whom a great deal has been written due to the numerous sources that record her life and the important role she played in the battle between the papacy and the German Empire.[3] Her life provides multiple fascinating examples of concepts that can only be assumed in other less well-documented Rusian dynastic marriages. In each of the marriages that follow, women, typically Rusian women, will play a key role.

The first section of this chapter deals with several case studies of Rusian dynastic marriage. The purposes of the marriage are not always clear, though there are some general themes that recur, such as marriages as part of fomenting or resolving a conflict; marriages to create Christianization;[4] marriages that involve speculation (an exiled heir/ruler who may return home); and marriages that are part of large, often Europe-wide, political arrangements. Because we cannot always discern the purpose behind marriages that took place a thousand years ago, the precise purpose of many of these dynastic marriages is unknown, but even with the paucity of sources it is possible to attempt an understanding of the purposes behind the majority of marriages. Although we cannot know everything, the marriages presented here will illustrate a variety of these themes and show the connections that Rusian rulers made with the kingdoms to their west.

The second section of this chapter deals specifically with onomastics and more generally with the influence of Rusian women in their host kingdoms. Although Rusian women are largely left out of the Rusian historical record, especially if they left Rus', in their host countries Rusian queens were able to exercise power and leave a durable mark. Discussed in this section are a few examples of Rusian queens in Europe who were able to introduce new names into the relatively rigid onomastic system used by medieval royalty. In medieval royal families, names were sacred and were essential to the continuity of royal power, thus they were not changed lightly. That the Rusian women were able to change them to reflect and incorporate something of their own culture indicates the level of power they held in their host kingdoms.

Types of Dynastic Marriages

Conflict and Resolution

One of the main reasons for dynastic marriages in the medieval world was conflict—finding or creating allies against a common enemy, mobilizing reinforcements, or making peace to end a battle or a war. This is as common a theme in Rus' as elsewhere, and the marriages of two of the best-known Rusian princes were created for this very purpose. Both Vladimir Sviatoslavich and Iaroslav Vladimirich married with the goal of either giving or receiving military assistance. However, for the purposes of this chapter I will focus on two lower-profile cases, the first of which sought to find allies for a conflict and ends up being two marriages, while the second resolves a conflict (in part).

I would like to begin with the marriage of Dobronega/Maria Vladimirovna (see Figure 1 for a diagram of this marital alliance). The choice of this marriage is dictated by the numerous sources that discuss the marriage, from both Rus' and Poland, which is a rarity, as well as the purpose of the marriage—creating a military alliance between Rus' and Poland for the common purpose of subjecting the Mazovians to Casimir, removing a threat to both kingdoms.

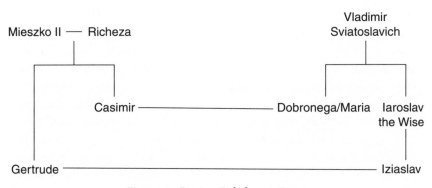

Figure 1. Rusian-Polish marriages

Under the year 1030 the *PVL* records the death of Bolesław Chrobry and a subsequent revolt and period of chaos in Poland.[5] Bolesław Chrobry actually died in 1025, and this entry is referencing the death of his son and heir, Mieszko II, who died in 1034.[6] Such confusions are common in medieval chronicles, especially recounting events before the chronicler's own time. Despite the chronicle having gotten the details wrong, or rather not quite right, this was an important event for Rus'. The heir to the throne was Mieszko's son Casimir, who had fled to Saxony with his mother after Bolesław's death.[7] His mother was Richeza, the niece of German emperor Otto III, and thus her family was quite powerful in the German Empire. In 1039, after an eventful young adulthood in western Europe, including living in Paris and joining the Benedictine order, Casimir decided to reclaim his kingdom and embarked on a plan to retake Poland bit by bit from the groups that had divided it, including breakaway tribes and rebellious nobles.[8]

Rus' at the time preferred a stable, and indebted, Poland on its western border and attempted to aid Casimir in his reconquest. The first recorded instance of Rusian aid to Poland is in 1041, when Iaroslav attacked the Mazovians.[9] The Mazovians occupied a position on the northeastern corner of Poland and had at one point been subject to the Poles. They were also one of Casimir's most significant foes upon his return to Poland.[10] But the question of why Rus' would act in concert with the Poles is not established in the *PVL*. The *Gesta principum Polonorum (Gesta)*, a twelfth-century work of Polish history, records that Casimir was quickly able to bring the majority of Poland, though not Mazovia or Pomerania, under his rule, and after doing so married a Rusian noblewoman[11]—Iaroslav's sister Dobronega/Maria.[12] The thirteenth century Polish *Great Chronicle* records that "*to make peace* in the Polish lands, he [Casimir] married a daughter of the Rusian prince."[13] Only after this did Casimir put down the majority of the rebellions, excepting only the Mazovians. The question of the relative reliability of the two chronicles is an open one, although the *Great Chronicle* has one mark in its favor on this issue, which is its own surprise at the move. The quotation from above begins, "In a surprising move,"[14] which suggests that the Polish chronicler writing from a time of more frequent Rusian–Polish warring was surprised at Casimir's alliance with Rus'. This subtle note may lend enough credibility to the *Great Chronicle* for its interpretation of events—that the marriage to Dobronega occurred before Casimir's reconquest of the Polish tribes, trumping the *Gesta*'s interpretation. Regardless, the marriage to Dobronega occurred prior to the conquest of the Mazovians, the main subject of the Rusian military assistance to Casimir.

This brings us to the issue of the date for this marriage. Both the *Gesta* and the *Great Chronicle* are largely undated, especially in these early sections, and thus cannot be of much assistance in attributing an actual calendar date to these events. The date for the *PVL* entry in which Iaroslav sends his sister to marry Casimir of Poland is 1043, listed after the Rusian attack on Constantinople,[15] but this is already after Iaroslav has made his first attack on the Mazovians in 1041.[16] A generally reliable source from the German Empire, *Annalista Saxo,* records the marriage as taking place in 1039 immediately after Casimir returned to Poland.[17] Lambert of Hersefeld also used this date to record the marriage of Dobronega and Casimir, as well as to determine the birth dates of their children.[18] Thus, the date of the marriage is in controversy in the primary sources, and has only been complicated by the secondary sources.[19] The confusion of the primary sources does not permit certainty, but the evidence of two Latin chronicles for the 1039 date, the 1041 attack on the Mazovians recorded in the *PVL,* and the evidence of the Polish *Great Chronicle* favor the 1039 date for the marriage, a date that is prior to Casimir's reconquest of Poland and certainly prior to the joint attacks on the Mazovians.

This is supported by the likelihood that Iaroslav would not have made the 1041 raid on the Mazovians "by boat,"[20] and thus most likely up the Bug, without either Mazovian provocation or an agreement with the Poles. Mazovian provocation is possible, but unlikely, as Casimir was at that time in Poland and attempting to consolidate his power, which meant diminishing Mazovian power. Iaroslav, in fulfillment of the agreement sealed by the dynastic marriage of his sister to Casimir, could have attacked the Mazovians from the rear in support of an assault of Casimir's. Though the *Gesta* is undated, the next listing after Casimir's marriage is an attack he made on the Mazovians.[21] Unfortunately, after a brief listing of the defeat of the Mazovians and their leader "Miecław" at the hands of Casimir, the *Gesta* moves on to the Pomeranians.[22] This is, however, where the Rusian chronicles are able to fill in some gaps. Various Rusian chronicles list Rusian attacks on the Mazovians in 1041, 1043, and 1047.[23] The *Nikon* and *Tver'* chronicles, unfortunately late chronicles but sometimes reliable, both include the interesting detail that in the 1043 attacks Iaroslav and Casimir fought jointly against the Mazovians and their leader "Moislav',"[24] clearly the same leader described in the *Gesta*. They also record in that same year that Casimir's sister, Gertrude, was married to Iaroslav's son Iziaslav.[25] This is, then, the second dynastic marriage to occur between Rus' and Poland in less than five years, and is related specifically in reference to the joint attacks on the Mazovians, thus reinforcing the ties between the two kingdoms and the importance of their endeavor.

The Mazovian leader, Moislav', is mentioned later in the *PVL* as well, when he is defeated by Iaroslav in 1047 and subjected to Casimir, referred to in the *Tver'* Chronicle as Iaroslav's brother-in-law [*ziat'*].[26] The 1047 attack on Moislav' and the Mazovians is the only instance in the *PVL* in which a Rusian ruler defeats someone and then subjects the loser to another ruler. In history in general this would seem to be a unique experience, and betokens some relationship between the two parties. When the evidence of the *Nikon* and *Tver'* chronicles about the joint 1043 attacks, also against Moislav', are added to the equation alongside the widely acknowledged 1041 attack on the Mazovians, it demonstrates that Iaroslav was working to a purpose against the Mazovians. That purpose—the subjection of the Mazovians to Casimir's rule—seems clearly linked to the dynastic marriage of his sister to Casimir of Poland. As such, a date for the marriage of Dobronega and Casimir must come before the first of Iaroslav's attacks on the Mazovians in order to give the attack purpose.

The marriage of Dobronega and Casimir (see Figure 1) is the first time that the *PVL* records some of the terms of a dynastic marriage, in this case an exchange of property in which Casimir handed over eight hundred people who were taken when Bolesław invaded Rus' on behalf of Sviatopolk Iaropolchich.[27] Though at this point it would be twenty years after Bolesław's attack, some of the people may have been alive or could have had children.[28] More likely, the villages in which the people lived were handed back to Rus'. The other side of this exchange was twofold. First was the already discussed alliance against the Mazovians and the agreement to subject them to Casimir's rule rather than Iaroslav's.

The second factor derives from the *Gesta*'s description of Dobronega as a wealthy woman when she comes into the marriage, implying perhaps that she brought a large dowry, though there are no specifics.[29]

The marriage of Casimir and Dobronega, as well as that of Iziaslav and Gertrude, was created by their families with the purpose of creating a common alliance against a foe, in this case the Mazovians. The Rusians could probably have left the Mazovians alone and prospered for some years until their expansion reached that area, but with the incentive of a marriage agreement they were enticed to deal with their potential problem and Casimir's immediate problem much sooner and in conjunction with Casimir. This alliance of forces illustrated especially in the 1043 entries of the *Nikon* and *Tver'* chronicles can be read as a direct result of the earlier marriage of Dobronega and Casimir. This is emphasized by the 1047 defeat of Moislav' by Iaroslav and his subjection to Casimir, rather than Iaroslav taking the Mazovians over himself. Marriage for the purposes of military alliance was one of the most common and most visible purposes of dynastic marriage in the Middle Ages. But this marriage also seems to illustrate Iaroslav's desire to create binding ties with his neighbors. The subjection of the Mazovians to Casimir, as well as the marriage, put the Poles in his debt and helped set the stage for positive Rusian–Polish relations in the eleventh and twelfth centuries.

The other side of the coin for this type of marriage is the resolution of conflict. There are multiple examples of such marriages in the history of dynastic marriage generally, and Rus' specifically. The many women who married into Byzantium and took the name Irene illustrate the example generally. For specific Rusian purposes, we will use a short example of Rusian marital relations with the Polovtsy. The Polovtsy were one of the many nomadic groups that the Rusians dealt with due to their proximity to the steppe.[30] By the later eleventh century, Rusian rulers began marrying the daughters of Polovtsian rulers, who were required to convert to Christianity, as a way to guarantee a peace, however temporary, between the two sides.[31] Though there are many such marriages (third in number after marriages with the west, and with Byzantium), typically the information about them is very brief, as these alliances produced few records—Rusian chroniclers were only mildly interested in such things, preferring to portray the Polovtsy as a vicious enemy rather than potential ally,[32] and there are no known written records from the Polovtsy (and precious few from other nomadic pastoralists of the Middle Ages).

The first known marriage of Sviatopolk Iziaslavich was with a daughter of Tugorkhan, made in 1094 as part of a peace arrangement with the Polovtsy.[33] The purpose of this dynastic marriage is relatively straightforward to discern, as the chronicle entry lists the peace and the marriage as one unit. However, stating that the peace agreement was with the Polovtsy is a slight exaggeration. Specifically, the peace seems to have been made between Sviatopolk Iziaslavich and the Polovtsy under Tugorkhan. Immediately after listing the peace and marriage, the *PVL* states that Oleg Sviatoslavich attacked the city of Chernigov with Polovtsian allies.[34] This should not be surprising. Though the Polovtsy appeared monolithic to the chroniclers (or were at least portrayed that way), it makes sense, using better-documented nomadic pastoralist societies such as the Xiongnu, to view the Polovtsy as an ever-shifting confederation of groups.[35] Using just the chronicle entry in 1094 it is possible to see that at least one group of Polovtsy was allied with Sviatopolk Iziaslavich and at least one with Oleg Sviatoslavich.

These contesting views of the Polovtsy, though, lead to another question, that of the rite of marriage itself. The Hypatian chronicle says that Sviatopolk "poia zhenu" (took as wife) the daughter of Tugorkhan, and that has been the accepted state of affairs.[36] However, Jan Długosz, in a late medieval history, says that Sviatopolk took her "in consortem,"[37] not in uxorem, or in matrimonium as a wife, but as a "sharer" or "partner," a consort. Długosz's rendering is considerably after the fact, while the *PVL* was, most likely, a living chronicle at the time of the writing and thus should be given precedence; however, the contention should be noted as part of a growing idea of Christian v. non-Christian, and settled v. nomadic dominance issues.

In the case of this marriage, problems arose quite quickly, perhaps because of some of those same issues. In 1096, only two years after the marriage and the peace it was supposed to symbolize, Tugorkhan attacked Pereiaslavl'.[38] During the course of the battle, Tugorkhan was killed, but this led to an interesting development. Even while it was describing the attack, the Rusian chronicle took the time to identify Tugorkhan using kinship terminology as Sviatopolk's "test'" (wife's father,

father-in-law).[39] This is a rare use of such kinship terminology and one of only a very few uses in terms of dynastic marriages in the *PVL*. It seems that Sviatopolk may be behind the reference, or that he also honored and respected the kinship with his father-in-law, as after the battle he brought Tugorkhan's body back to Kiev for a formal burial.[40] It is possible that this was simply honoring a respected enemy, but unlikely as we have no similar events during this period. Instead it appears as if Sviatopolk acknowledged his kin obligations and was treating his father-in-law's body with respect; extending an argument from Chapter 2, this may even have been because of Sviatopolk's wife's, Tugorkhan's daughter's, influence. Despite the fact that this marriage failed to ensure a long-term peace between Rus' and Tugorkhan's Polovtsy, it helped set the precedent for using dynastic marriage to bring peace between Rus' and their nomadic pastoralist neighbors. It also provides a unique insight into kin relations, and potentially an additional example of female empowerment or influence in Rus'.

Grand Coalitions

Some marriages had not one purpose, but many. These marriages advanced the political, military, and/or economic goals of the parties involved in such a way that more than just the two kingdoms providing the bride and groom were affected by the marriage. This type was not common for Rusian marriages, but there are a few examples. This case study focuses on probably the best known of the Rusian dynastic marriages, that of Evpraksia Vsevolodovna and Henry III of Stade, and then later of Evpraksia and German emperor Henry IV. Evpraksia's two marriages were really one alliance that created ties between the German Empire and Rus', specifically the Vsevolodovichi, and that was arranged in part to thwart their joint enemy, the Poles, as well as to deal with issues internal to both kingdoms, and on an even larger scale, affect the history of the papacy.

Evpraksia's early life is a mystery, but she was married at a young age to the Margrave of the Saxon Nordmark, Henry III "the Long" of Stade. When this marriage took place is not known, but the first mention of it is in *Annalista Saxo* under the year 1082. This is the year that Henry of Stade inherited the Nordmark after the death of his father, and his wife is listed as "Evpraksia, daughter of the king of Rus',"[41] though the chronicle was written later and may possibly backdate the marriage to Henry of Stade's inheritance of the mark. The dating is further complicated by issues of the proper age of marriage, whether or not this was observed, and many other details that are specific to the time of the marriage and not generally relevant here for the purposes of discussing the marriage as a whole.[42] Though the exact date of the marriage is not recorded, Evpraksia's arrival in Germany is—as we saw in Chapter 2, a later monastic chronicle records that she "arrived in this country with much pomp, with camels burdened with precious clothes and stones, and also with countless riches," illustrating some of the prestige of a woman embarking on a dynastic marriage.[43]

This marriage did not last long, as Henry of Stade died in 1087. Upon his death, Evpraksia was approximately sixteen years old, a widow with no children and thus no claim on the Nordmark, leaving her brother-in-law to inherit. At this point Evpraksia had multiple possibilities open to her. The most normal would have been for her to return to Rus' and her family. The fact that she does not do this, and instead marries Emperor Henry IV,[44] is important when attempting to understand the reason behind both marriages.

The reason behind these marriages is particularly important, not only for our current discussion of dynastic marriage, but also because of the consequences of the latter marriage to Henry IV. One theory advanced for the first marriage is that it was itself the consequence of a Rusian dynastic marriage. S. P. Rozanov, in an article on Evpraksia, suggests that the marriage may have been arranged by Oda of Stade, a relative of Henry III and his father, Margrave Udo II, and wife of Sviatoslav Iaroslavich.[45] Upon Sviatoslav's death in later 1076 she and her infant son, Iaroslav, returned to the German Empire, and thus may have been in a position to help arrange a suitable marriage between her kinsmen.[46] This offers a tantalizing, and possible, reason for the first marriage, but connections to the second then become quite difficult.[47]

I. S. Robinson in his history of Henry IV put forward the theory, echoing the views of a generation of German historians, that Henry IV married Evpraksia to ally himself more closely with the Saxons.[48] This theory relies on the assumption that Evpraksia was looked upon by the Saxons as one of their own, but this cannot be the case. Evpraksia was a young woman who had lived the majority of her life in Rus', not Saxony, and that was where her familial obligations rested. As she had not had children with Henry of Stade, she had not created a new family of her own in Saxony, and thus was viewed locally, most likely, as an outsider, as witnessed by her brother-in-law's forcing her to leave her deceased husband's home.

The most convincing theory as to the motivations for Evpraksia's marriages has been espoused by multiple authors, but chiefly and most fully by A. V. Nazarenko.[49] Nazarenko suggests that *both* marriages of Evpraksia were part of an attempt by Henry IV to ally himself with Rus'.[50] Nazarenko posits a complex theory in which Henry's goal was to increase the power of his newly elected anti-pope, Clement III, as well as to cause trouble for the Poles (always an interest for the German emperors), while for Vsevolod the alliance was important not only for prestige but to combat problems at home. The Iziaslavichi, perennial rivals, had closely allied themselves with the Poles, both through marriage[51] and through their territorial associations on the western border of Rus'.[52] Throughout Vsevolod's reign, various Iziaslavichi attempted to take back their father's throne and received Polish assistance. An alliance between the German Empire and Rus', specifically with Vsevolod, would put Poland between allies and allow those allies to put pressure on both Poland's eastern and western borders. This alliance would limit the support that the Poles could give to any Rusian usurpers—chiefly the Iziaslavichi. The alliance would also allow Clement III a chance to draw Rus' into his fold, thus increasing his own political/ecclesiastical power.

In the early 1080s, Henry IV was still married and thus could not conclude a marriage for himself. Instead he married the Rusian princess to the young margrave of one of the most powerful marks in Germany, Henry III "the Long" of Stade, margrave of the Saxon Nordmark. The rank and prestige of the margrave of the Saxon Nordmark would have shown Vsevolod that Henry IV was serious about the alliance, and it was kind to Evpraksia, as Henry of Stade was not much older than she. However, when Henry of Stade died, the bond holding the alliance together was in danger, and it was only with the death of the Empress Bertha that Henry IV saw a way to reaffirm the alliance. He would marry Evpraksia himself. This theory proves the most reasonable. It also places the marriages in the context of the European political scheme as a whole and reflects the importance, and even necessity, of dynastic marriages as a key component of politics.

Widely discussed in relation to this marriage is the *Canonical Responses of Metropolitan Ioann II*, written in the second half of the 1080s. In article 13, Ioann II scolds the Rusian princes for marrying their daughters outside of the faith.[53] Though he does not explicitly name the Latins, it is the most common inference and represents a major disconnect between the Rusian rulers and the ecclesiastical elite.[54] Ioann II certainly had knowledge of the German marriages of Evpraksia, as antipope Clement III contacted him, at Henry IV's behest, about a union of the churches under the auspices of Clement III. Ioann II, however, rebuked him in a letter that is extant, and directed Clement III to discuss the matter with Ioann II's superior, the patriarch of Constantinople.[55] One can only speculate what would have happened had a Rusian been directing the Rusian Church at this time rather than a Byzantine. Though the initiative failed, and thus one of the reasons behind Henry IV's desired alliance with the Rus', its attempt shows Rus' as a viable player in the European political situation of the eleventh century.

Henry IV and Evpraksia were married in the summer of 1089 in Cologne by Archbishop Hartwig of Magdeburg. As the chronicler Ekkehard records, "The Emperor celebrated, in Cologne, his wedding, taking to wife the widow of Margrave Udo [Henry III][56] the daughter of the king of Rus'."[57] After the marriage ceremony, Evpraksia Vsevolodovna was crowned Empress of Germany.[58] This was momentous for Rus' as well as for Evpraksia. In the generation before her, Rusian women had been the queens of France, Poland, Hungary, and Norway.[59] However, by the time of her coronation, Evpraksia was the only Rusian queen in Europe and she was not only queen, but empress. This made her the most visible Rusian, male or female, for the majority of Europe.

Despite the political promise of the marriage, Evpraksia and Henry IV soon separated. The story of the separation that is typically told, and originates in the Latin chronicles, is one of marital problems; this story was used to the advantage of Henry's enemies, chiefly Pope Urban II, who worked with Evpraksia to spread these stories to the Latin bishops.[60] But the motivations behind her leaving Henry IV and behind the stories may once again be traced back to broader European politics, and the changing alliances of Rus', representing a move away from German ties (especially after Ioann II's rejection of Clement III's overture), toward Byzantine ties, and strengthening papal connections.[61] After speaking at Pope Urban II's council at Piacenza against Henry IV,[62] Evpraksia returned to Rus' in 1097.[63] The *PVL*, typically silent in regard to women, records Evpraksia's entry into a nunnery in 1106, her death in 1109, and her being accorded the honor of a burial in the Caves Monastery and the erection there of her own chapel, a unique feat for a Russian woman of this period.[64] Though neither of Evpraksia's marriages was a success, maritally speaking, the marriages and her separation from Henry IV served the dynastic interests of the Riurikids, and represent for Rus' successful politics.

Speculation

Speculation may be an odd classification, and it certainly did not exist everywhere in medieval Europe, but performing a dynastic marriage on speculation was an important part of Rusian policy, especially under Iaroslav in the mid-eleventh century. Rus' was a land that over the course of the eleventh century became a home for exiled royalty from throughout Europe. At the time, Rus' was just attempting to make an impression on the European political scene, and by harboring these fugitives it was able to increase its reputation among certain key groups of people. Iaroslav took this a step further, gambling on the eventual return of many of these exiles to their home kingdoms, and married his daughters to some of these exiled princes. If they returned successfully to their home kingdoms, his daughters would then have influential places as queens, and they would establish centers of Rusian culture and virtual embassies at foreign courts. Moreover, Iaroslav and Rus' would be looked upon favorably for aiding the king during his exile. Three of Iaroslav's daughters married such exiles during his rule: Agafia married Edward "the Exile" of England, Anastasia married Andrew of Hungary, and Elisabeth married Harald Hardrada of Norway. The example of Elisabeth will provide the case study for this type of dynastic marriage, as it is well documented and there was significant interaction between Harald and Iaroslav that shows Iaroslav favoring a young exiled royal. It also illustrates the importance of the kinship ties to Harald that were created by the marriage.

One of the most famous characters of the Middle Ages was the Viking, and few Vikings are better known today than the itinerant Harald Hardrada, who became ruler of Norway and then died at Stamford Bridge fighting Harold Godwinsson of England. Harald was the half brother of King St. Olaf of Norway,[65] who himself was brother-in-law to Iaroslav Mudryi.[66] Harald's first recorded visit to Rus' came in 1031, the year after the battle of Stiklestaðir, in which Olaf and his forces were defeated by King Knud "the Great."[67] Rus' would have been an easy option for him, not only because of its proximity, but because there were close ties between his family and the Riurikids. There were marital ties, but also at this time Iaroslav and Ingigerd were raising Magnus, St. Olaf's son and Harald's nephew.[68] Harald developed ties with Iaroslav while in exile, and probably served as a mercenary in Rus'. The Scandinavian sources go so far as to suggest that Harald became head of Iaroslav's bodyguard, perhaps unlikely due to his youth and relative inexperience.[69] More convincingly, they relate that while in Byzantium, Harald sent his money and treasure to Novgorod for Iaroslav to keep safe.[70] This would have been a prudent measure on his part, would have increased his ties with Iaroslav for a future marriage, and could easily have been facilitated by Varangian and Rusian travelers and merchants going to Kiev.[71] In 1042 Harald left Byzantium, to travel back to Rus' as the first stage of returning to Norway, now that his nephew Magnus was ruling there.[72] On the way home he stopped in Rus' to reclaim the wealth that he had had stored with Iaroslav and marry Iaroslav's daughter Elisabeth.[73] Snorre Sturluson quotes a poem that Harald composed on the way home from Byzantium that features Harald in the final line saying, "the gold-ring-Gerth [woman] from / Garthar [Rus'] lets me dangle."[74] *Morkinskinna,* which in this case provides a fuller account, records a series of verses that Harald composed on his way home, each with this as a final line. In that account, it is made explicitly a reference to Elisabeth Iaroslavna, despite accounts of Harald's interest in marrying a royal Byzantine woman named Maria, or Empress Zoe's interest in marrying Harald herself during his time in Constantinople.[75] It is likely that Harald and Elisabeth's marriage was prearranged; both the *Flateyjarbók* and *Morkinskinna* record that Harald in fact asked for Elisabeth's hand while he was living in Kiev as captain of Iaroslav's bodyguard.[76] Iaroslav turned him down, saying that he was well born but had not yet achieved the necessary wealth or fame for Iaroslav to contemplate the marriage, also neatly undermining later placement of Harald as head of the bodyguard. This then provided the impetus for Harald to go to Byzantium, as well as a nice explanation for why he sent his riches to Iaroslav to store for him, as proof of his growing wealth. The story of the relationship between Harald and Elisabeth, though entirely absent from Rusian sources, fits with the picture of Rusian dynastic marriage—Harald was in Rus', specifically at the court of Iaroslav, was at the age when he would be looking to marry, knew Iaroslav's daughters and may have arranged a betrothal (despite their minority), sent his riches to Iaroslav to hold for him, and composed a poem on the way home from Byzantium that indicates a previous association with a Rusian woman.

The marriage between Harald Hardrada and Elisabeth Iaroslavna was certainly a dynastic marriage. Iaroslav was following his policy of wedding his daughters to exiled princes on the chance that they would return home and become kings, and his daughters queens. With Harald, Iaroslav had an excellent chance of his returning home to at least a share of the kingship, as Norway was ruled by Harald's nephew, a man who was also nephew to Ingigerd and Iaroslav and who had been raised partly in Rus'. The marriage was the continuation of a relationship with the Norwegian royal family that had been begun by Iaroslav and Ingigerd with Harald's half-brother St. Olaf over a decade earlier.[77]

This kinship tie represented by Elisabeth was of enormous importance to Harald. This is mentioned in multiple examples; the first is a poem by Stuf the Blind, recorded by Sturluson, on the occasion of the marriage between Harald and Elisabeth. "Kinship won the keen-eyed / king which he had wished, / gold a-plenty as guerdon / gained he, and eke the princess."[78] Harald got the princess, Elisabeth, but it is the kinship itself that leads the poem and ranks with his bride and the wealth he gained through the marriage. Then when Harald left to claim territory from his nephew, Magnus, he met Sven Estridsson, and their respective genealogical relations, through Elisabeth, are discussed to establish a relationship. That kinship relationship established Harald with Sven and through Sven with innumerable other allies in Sweden, which would be used to help Harald's campaign to claim territory in Norway.[79] Kinship was the key to power in this period, especially in Scandinavia, and

Harald's marriage to Elisabeth ensured him a proper start on the path to becoming king of Norway—Iaroslav's speculative dynastic marriage paid off.

Unknown

Due to the nature of the evidence, it is impossible to conclude with any certainty the purpose of some of the known dynastic marriages. In these situations one can advance pure theory or speculation, but only the revelation of new (or new to the author) evidence can alter the analysis. These marriages require no case study as there are few commonalities, but certain marriages can be offered up as clear examples of the unknowns in doing this type of history. The one I have chosen to showcase here is actually quite well known, despite the fact that a reason for it happens to be unknown, though many have been advanced.

In 1043 Iaroslav Mudryi sent an embassy to the German emperor Henry III to discuss a marriage between Henry and one of Iaroslav's daughters.[80] This would have been the ultimate dynastic marriage Iaroslav could have made with the resources available to him. From the beginning of his reign, he had attempted to make an alliance with the German Empire, and now in 1043 he believed he had that chance. The marriage would have bolstered the international prestige of Rus' and created a situation in which Rusian women were the queens of the majority of Europe. Unfortunately for Iaroslav, the proposition was turned down, and his long hoped for alliance with the German emperor would not happen in his lifetime. The reasons the marriage was turned down are not recorded in any records and it has been left to historians to hypothesize. It seems likely that Henry was more interested in securing his western frontier than allying with Rus', and thus arranged a marriage with Agnes of Poitou, the daughter of the Duke of Aquitaine. As there was already a considerable struggle between the various territories of France and the German Empire, this was a more immediate necessity than an alliance with Rus'.

However, Iaroslav's embassy was noticed in Europe, and in 1049 when Henry I of France was again looking to marry, he remembered. Andrew Lewis has said, "Henry I married deliberately and well."[81] His first engagement was to a young daughter of Emperor Conrad II to seal an alliance against Count Odo II of Blois, though she died within a year of the 1033 engagement. Henry continued the alliance by marrying the German princess Mathilda, the niece of Henry III. Mathilda lived long enough to consummate her marriage with Henry (like Conrad II's daughter she had been underage at the time of the initial engagement). She bore him one daughter, who died in infancy before Mathilda herself died in 1044.[82] Henry, however, was still in need of an heir, and thus a bride.

Leaving aside the reasoning behind the marriage for the moment, the process of the marriage is very interesting. In 1049 Henry I sent an embassy to Kiev to negotiate a dynastic marriage with Iaroslav. This embassy was led by French bishops, either Gauthier of Meaux and Gosselin of Chauny, or alternately Roger of Chalons, depending on the source used.[83] Though only the major names were recorded, others were also sent as part of the embassy, most likely a sizable delegation representing the king of France.[84] The purpose of the embassy is clearly stated in all of the records—the negotiation of a marriage between the king of France and one of the daughters of Iaroslav Mudryi (Anna is specifically named in one record).[85] Unfortunately for the modern historian, no record of the negotiations has been preserved, thus the meetings between the bishops and Iaroslav and his representatives or advisors is left to the imagination. They must have been concluded successfully, because Clarius states that they returned with her from Rus' with many gifts.[86] The historian is forced to wonder about what the gifts were, and to whom they were presented. Many of them may have been Anna's to give as she would, or to use to support herself in her new land. Nevertheless, Anna and the French bishops and their entourage returned to France most likely in 1050, and the couple was married in 1051.[87] Anna's interesting life in France included royal influence, discussed later in this chapter, as well as a regency for her son, Philip.[88] However, the details of her life and marriage are outside of our purview here.

The reasoning behind such an influential marriage has been puzzled over by scholars for decades. The difficulties in assigning motive to medieval marriages, and thus in understanding dynastic marriage, can be illustrated with a few of the speculations that have been made. In mid-eleventh-century western Europe the church's revised consanguinity laws were creating an ever-tightening knot around the nobility and royalty of Europe, with fewer and fewer partners eligible for marriage. This was especially true in the case of France. Henry I wanted to marry a woman who had suitably royal blood and to whom he was not related.[89] According to some, this was the only or main reason for Henry's marriage to Anna Iaroslavna—she was royal and they were not related.[90] However, other options have been advanced as well. Two French scholars, R. H. Bautier and André Poulet, have both advanced the notion that this was a dynastic marriage to seal an alliance, as so many were, and not just for the procreation of heirs.[91] The reasoning put forth by both of these authors relies on the established dynastic history of Rus'. Earlier in the eleventh century, Anna's aunt Dobronega/Maria Vladimirovna married Casimir, the king of Poland, and her brother, Iziaslav Iaroslavich, married Casimir's sister Gertrude.[92] Casimir had spent his early life in western Europe, including in Paris and at the Abbey of Cluny in France, and so would have had a base of knowledge about France.[93] In this explanation, Casimir brokered the marriage between Rus' and France with the aim of consolidating an alliance again the German Empire so that, should the empire falter, the two kingdoms on either border might be able to move in and snap up some new territory. Although the rule of Emperor Henry III seemed strong, the empire was actually quite fragile, as became apparent when Henry III died in 1056 and his young son Henry IV became king with a contentious regency council.[94] Jean Dunbabin also points out that power was a personal commodity in the medieval world and thus such a collapse might have been expected by a savvy ruler such as Henry I.[95] The gains for both the Poles and the French are easy to see in this agreement; both would have the potential to capitalize on a possible opportunity in the German Empire. There also would have been a tangible gain for Rus'. Obviously there was the prestige of having a Riurikid princess as queen of France, the farthest kingdom from Kiev a Rusian had yet ruled, but this would also have been a public relations coup for Rus' to get its name and people out into the courts of western Europe and familiarize them with their neighbors to the east. Perhaps more politically important in the immediate present was that Iaroslav was helping his brother-in-law Casimir to focus Poland's attention west, that is, away from Rus'. Though the two were allies in this period, the historical interactions between Rus' and Poland had always included raiding across the border and trading possession of the Cherven towns. Keeping Poland focused west was well worth the investment of a Riurikid princess.

Finding the details of marriages that were arranged and ended a thousand years ago is difficult and relies on a large measure of chance in the preservation of records. It also relies on the will of the chroniclers. The preference of Rusian chroniclers to generally exclude women from the written record removes them almost completely from Rusian history. Only the inclusion of women in Latin sources has allowed the modern historian to find evidence of Rusian women and discern their fates. Taking those records and finding accurate, and plausible, motives for the marriages requires yet another step in this process, one that is fraught with difficulty, as one can see from the speculations above. Even for a marriage as intriguing as that between Anna Iaroslavna and Henry I Capet, we may never know all the reasons for their marriage.

Failed Dynastic Marriages

There is one additional category that needs to be mentioned, if only briefly, and that is marital alliances that do not work out as planned. Evpraksia Vsevolodovna's marriages did not end happily for her, but they do seem to have advanced the cause of Rusian politics, if the supposition advanced here is correct. There are, however, marriages that do not end well either maritally or politically. The example of such failures is the marriage of Evfimiia Vladimirovna to Koloman of Hungary, a marriage with a relatively clear political purpose that simply did not work to the advantage of Rus'.

The marriage of Evfimiia Vladimirovna to Koloman, king of Hungary, has been a subject of intense scrutiny for hundreds of years because of its outcome. The marriage seems to have taken place in 1112, when Evfimiia, who is identified by name in the Hypatian chronicle, is sent to Hungary to marry the king.[96] Though the king is not identified by name, the king at the time was Koloman and the marriage is recognized in numerous other sources.[97] The purpose of the marriage seems clear. With the death of Koloman's first wife earlier that year,[98] Koloman was free to create a new alliance, and Vladimir Monomakh felt himself in need of a connection with Hungary. At this time Sviatopolk Iziaslavich still ruled in Kiev, and the Iziaslavichi held the upper hand in terms of foreign dynastic connections, especially with Poland and Hungary, two dangerous border areas that could shelter them and provide troops as necessary. To remedy that, and counter the marriage of Sviatopolk's daughter Predslava with Koloman's brother, and rival, Almos, Vladimir sent his daughter Evfimiia to marry Koloman.[99] As in all of these cases, there must be reciprocal advantage, and for Koloman it may have been connected to the death of his eldest son Ladislaus that same year.[100] Though he was already old and unwell at the time, perhaps he hoped to sire more sons to protect his lineage from his brother, with whom he often warred.

The marriage lasted less than a year before Koloman repudiated Evfimiia and sent her home to Kiev.[101] At the time, Evfimiia was pregnant, and the assumption has been that she was pregnant with someone else's child. However, multiple contemporary sources identify the son she bore in Kiev, Boris, as the son of Koloman.[102] Interestingly, both Cosmas and Otto would have had better reason to disprove Boris's lineage, as their sponsors were each allied with Boris's foes in Hungary. Thus their testimony in favor of his legitimacy means a great deal. Unfortunately, we are then left with an unanswerable conundrum. Evfimiia, who went to Hungary to seal an alliance, which presumably included producing sons for the king, became pregnant with a son (seemingly by the king), but was repudiated and sent home. The cause of the repudiation is unknown. It is clear from future events that the marriage did not secure its purpose, as would seem obvious from its abrupt end. Indeed, after Koloman's death in 1114 his son Stephen II supported Iaroslav Sviatopolchich against Vladimir Monomakh in Iaroslav's attempts to stay independent.[103]

The fate of Boris was constant warfare to reclaim his birthright. He was raised in Rus', and over the course of his life allied with Bolesław III of Poland and the Comneni emperors of Byzantium to attempt to take the throne of Hungary after the death of his half brother Stephen II.[104] As for Evfimiia, some maintain that she entered a monastery in Rus'.[105] This would certainly have been a common option for a princess in her position, but no reliable primary source records such an event as it was recorded for Evpraksia Vsevolodovna. Her death is recorded in 1138, and she was laid to rest in the Holy Savior's Church.[106] Her burial in a high-status location indicates that the family felt no shame over her failed marriage, but the lack of a response to her curt dismissal from Hungary and the absence of sources on her activities in the intervening years leave a mystery surrounding the dissolution of her marriage. The mystery of Evfimiia's marriage serves as a fitting endpoint for our attempts to discern reason and motivation behind one-thousand-year-old marriages.

Onomastics

Onomastics and Female Power

Female power in the Middle Ages can be difficult to quantify. The vast majority of chroniclers were men, and the majority of literate people were monks—men who participated in a church system that encouraged a subservient role for women. This leaves the modern historian with a written record that depicts men running the government, serving the church, and going to war but that rarely mentions women and more rarely still depicts them positively in situations of power. Many of the depictions of women in the chronicles are negative,[107] which forces modern historians to attempt to read between the lines to determine the true role of women in medieval life. This has resulted in a variety of opinions in the work of historians writing on medieval women, as each has interpreted the texts and their authors' intentions in his or her own way.

But reading between the lines of chronicles is not the only way to attempt to determine the power that royal women may have exercised. Another option is to examine a more personal legacy—their children. The names that parents gave their children were very important in establishing the lineage of their family. "The history of names in this time period—is the history of the struggle for power, the history of alliances and confrontations, the history of divisions and unions."[108] The aristocracy and royalty of Europe were related at many junctures—a broad definition of family could encompass hundreds of people. But parents could differentiate their immediate family from that larger family using naming conventions to show the most important kinship ties.[109] Historians used to think that there was a concrete naming convention for medieval royal families, that children were named after the paternal grandparents, parents, and then the maternal grandparents.[110] In this way the ties to the paternal line were more strongly emphasized. This strict naming convention, however, may not have been as strict as we once thought, or as universal. While families generally maintained naming patterns, which were sometimes quite rigid (see below for a discussion of the naming conventions in eleventh-century France), it is almost impossible to find a pattern for all of Europe that holds true even in any one generation, much less over a considerable amount of time.[111]

This invalidates the idea of pattern, but not the idea expressed within the pattern, that names from the paternal line were favored.[112] Paternal names were used to show that the family was descended in a single line and that the family was an identifiable unit.[113] Indeed, Karl Schmid states that "families and sibs can be recognized by the names which they used particularly frequently, the so-called leading names."[114] In the early Middle Ages, maternal names were occasionally chosen when the woman was of a more prominent lineage than the man. For instance, when the Capetian Hugh "the Great" married Hadvise, sister to Otto I of the German Empire, their second and third sons were named Otto and Henry after Hadvise's brothers to indicate the imperial ties of their family.[115] Another Ottonian example is Otto II, who gave his children names from the paternal line with the exception of a daughter, who was named Sophia in reference to a relative of Otto's wife, Theophano.[116] These were the exceptions, though, and not the rule. Royal names were usually from the immediate paternal family: mother, grandfather, father, brothers, and sisters. As Constance Bouchard puts it, "With rare exceptions, they did not give their sons names held by cousins, by ancestors more distant than their own grandfathers, or by any maternal relatives."[117] Despite the lack of a formal pattern common to all families, there was a normative system of paternal naming that excluded names from the maternal line except in rare cases. This section examines some of the naming conventions of Rusian women who married into other royal families of Europe, looking for these exceptions to European norms.

Before giving the various examples of Rusian onomastic influence, a question must be posed: Who names a child? This question is not easily answered, and there are certainly no sources on this for the medieval period. The traditional assumption is that men named their children. In addition to the assumed medieval male dominance in marriage, this is believed to be shown by the fact that the vast majority of names given to children came from the paternal line.[118] This was true even for daughters, who were often named after their paternal grandmother and aunts. When children received names from the maternal line, it has piqued our interest. Bouchard has posited that in those instances it is often because the mother's family is of higher rank than the father's family, specifically in situations where the women were Carolingians.[119] It is not suggested that the Rusian partner, always a woman in these examples, was considered the more "politically powerful" partner, but that it is often only the politically powerful side that gets to name the children. Also important is an overturning of the traditional idea of dominance in medieval royal marriages. As recent scholarship has shown, and was discussed in Chapter 2, royal women were more empowered than has traditionally been imagined, and this carried over into the realm of naming rights. Timing is part of this issue, as the position of queen solidified in the thirteenth century into our modern view of female intercessor, and not ruler.[120] In the eleventh and twelfth centuries, queens (e.g., Matilda of England)[121] were able to exercise some traditional male royal powers, including naming their own children. Given the fact that "among the high aristocrats of the Carolingian and post-Carolingian world, the naming of children was a serious business—so serious as to be almost immune to fashion and to personal taste,"[122] we must then be dealing with a unique, or series of unique instances when we see a deviation from the expected naming outcome.

The Influence of Riurikid Women on Foreign Onomastics

Over the period discussed in this book, many Riurikid princesses married into the royal houses of Europe, and the majority of them bore children who grew up to rule. This tied the Riurikids firmly into the web of dynastic relations that made nearly all of the royal houses of Europe related to one another in the eleventh and twelfth centuries. This was the time before the power of the queen became confined to a rigid basis as intercessor, and there was still the prospect for and actuality of ruling queens and queens exercising traditionally male powers, such as naming their own children. In regard to naming practices, the Rusian women living outside of Rus' seemed to have an advantage over their foreign sisters. Multiple cases exist of Rusian women seeming to influence or even choose, depending on the interpretation, names from their lineage or tradition for their royal children. Four primary examples of this on male onomastics and three examples from female onomastics are considered here, with attention paid briefly to a few secondary cases of the former.

Anna Iaroslavna and Philip I of France

The best-known instance of Rusian female influence on onomastics is the choice of the name of Philip for the firstborn son of Henry I of France and Anna Iaroslavna (see Figure 2 for naming chart). Anna Iaroslavna was the first wife of Henry to bear children who lived. The choice of his first son's name was vitally important in continuing Capetian dynastic traditions. Henry[123] was the younger son of his father Robert II (r. 996–1031), who was himself the eldest son of Hugh Capet (r. 987–996), in turn the eldest son of Hugh the Great (r. 925–956), whose father was Robert I (r. 923–924), the progenitor of the line.[124] The pattern is clear—for one hundred years the ruler of France had been named either Hugh or Robert. Henry's older brother, Hugh, had died, and so Henry assumed the throne.[125] Henry's firstborn son should have been named either Robert or Hugh. Instead, he was named Philip, and Henry's second and third sons were named Robert and Hugh, respectively. This break with tradition, which seems so incredible when viewed against the backdrop of a hundred years of naming tradition, received no comment from contemporary French chroniclers. For some reason they understood the rationale behind the name and did not voice their opinions on it.[126] When a pattern is broken or changed, it is of interest to the historian. But when the contemporary sources are silent on the change, it becomes an even more interesting mystery.

The choice of the name Philip is intriguing. Dunbabin posits several explanations, but the thread in the most convincing ones is the influence of the queen, Anna Iaroslavna. Philip was not a common name in the West. It was known as a saint's name, and would become important in France later in the Middle Ages, but in the Byzantine tradition Philip was known as the Christianizer of Scythia, the area (and name) the Byzantines identified with Rus'.[127] Anna's grandfather was Vladimir,

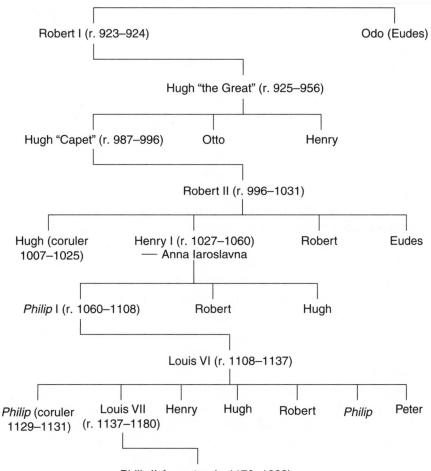

Figure 2. French onomastic history

the Christianizer of Rus', and Anna was a member of the first Rusian generation to be raised Christian. In multiple East Slavic menologies St. Philip is listed under both October 11 and November 14.[128] Unfortunately, Philip's birth date is unknown, but it is believed that he was born between the May 19, 1051, marriage of Henry and Anna and May 23, 1052,[129] which would logically exclude either of the saints' days as listed in the Orthodox calendar. However, Juan Mateos in *Le typicon de la grande église* records another day for a St. Philip, a variant of Philémon, on February 14.[130] This day would fit quite well into the suggested range of birth dates and occurs in a likely window after the marriage of Henry and Anna, making it a probable suggestion. Apart from the evidence of the birth date, which cannot be confirmed, it remains a possibility that Anna's knowledge of the name Philip informed her suggestion of a name for her firstborn son. One fact that can be verified about the name Philip, and what does seem to inform our understanding of the choice, was that after Henry's death, Anna married Raoul de Crépy, count of Valois,[131] and the name Philip began, soon after, to appear in that family as well, suggesting that the introduction of the name into the Capetian line was Anna's influence, not Henry's.[132]

There is also the intriguing possibility that the name was chosen through maternal influence due to the early medieval practice of choosing a name from the higher-ranking lineage. This is dismissed by Dunbabin because it is unlikely that the Capetians would have viewed the Riurikids as a higher-ranking lineage, and in the very few early medieval examples of that practice the names referred to the Carolingian dynasty and none other. Some historians have given as one motive of Henry's marriage to Anna a quest for the "exotic,"[133] and so perhaps the choice of a name from Anna's part of Europe would be simply a part of that urge.

Imperial pretensions may also have given Henry the idea of the name—a Roman emperor named Philip the Arabian (244–249) was widely known in the Middle Ages and was rumored to have been the first Christian emperor.[134] So the attribution of that name, the name of both a Christianizing saint and a Christian Roman emperor, could give the child a strong onomastic background to rule, perhaps more than just France. This cannot be proven; though Philip did display some imperial tendencies in his titulature, this was not unusual among eleventh-century rulers.[135] The choice of a name used by a long-gone Roman emperor and a Christianizing saint may have been pleasing to both Henry and Anna and provided them with a compromise choice in which each got something they wanted.

It cannot be conclusively proven that Anna Iaroslavna dictated the choice of the name Philip to her husband, but the anecdotal evidence suggests that it is a strong possibility that she influenced the naming process. This theory is buttressed by the naming conventions of other

Rusian women in the royal families of Europe. As for Anna's son Philip, he reverted to a traditional tactic of naming his children after paternal relatives, but instead of naming his firstborn son Robert, Hugh, or Henry, he named him Louis (Louis VI, r. 1108–1137), hearkening back to the Carolingian ancestors of the Capetians. There is a maternal onomastic connection for Philip's illegitimate children, as his daughter by Bertrada of Anjou was named Cecilia, the same name as his aunt, Kelikia, the wife of Sviatoslav Iaroslavich.[136] However, in the main line Louis VI was succeeded by his son, Louis VII (r. 1137–1180), who in turn was followed by his son Philip II Augustus (r. 1180–1223). The naming strategies returned to a more traditional pattern, and the Rusian-inspired name of Philip was incorporated into the choice of names of the French royal family.

Two Hungarian Examples

Hungary does not have the plentiful records of eleventh-century France, nor the enormous amount of secondary literature, especially outside of Hungarian. But it is in this time period that four Rusian princesses married into the Hungarian royal line, which was descended from its semilegendary founder, Árpád, and two Hungarian princesses married into the Riurikid line. The first two of these Rusian princesses are discussed here. Though the early history of Hungary lacks as clear-cut an onomastic record as Capetian France, these Rusian women seem to have brought something of their own influence and religious tradition to the naming of their children.

The Hungarian rulers of this time period traced their descent back to Árpád, whose line of descent is more robust than the one-track line that led the Rusians from Riurik to Vladimir.[137] The consistent naming pattern shown during this time period in France or the German Empire did not exist in Hungary. Instead, the rulers had a variety of names, none of which repeated until the mid-eleventh century. Despite the lack of rigid formality, we are still able to note changes in the styles and types of names chosen. Two Rusian women in particular, an unknown Vladimirovna[138] and Anastasia Iaroslavna, married into the Árpád line and introduced names that were inconsistent with earlier Hungarian names (see Figure 3).

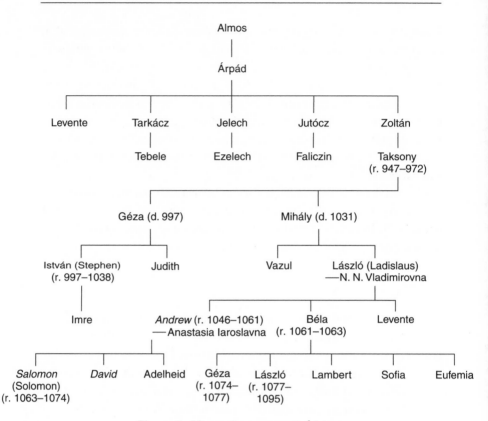

Figure 3. Hungarian onomastic history

N. N. Vladimirovna

This unknown Vladimirovna married Ladislaus of Hungary in the early eleventh century.[139] Ladislaus's contemporary position and title are unknown, but he was the great-great-grandson of Árpád (d. 907), the nephew of Géza (d. 997), the first historical ruler of Hungary, and the first cousin of King St. Stephen (r. 997–1038). He is not known to have ruled, but his children did come into power after the infighting that followed Stephen's death. His marriage to this Vladimirovna resulted in three children, Andrew, Béla, and Levente. "Levente," the name of Ladislaus's third son, was originally the name of the firstborn son of Árpád, but it had not been used since that time as far as we know.

The name of the second son, Béla, had not occurred before in the Hungarian royal line, but it fits the pattern of Magyar names that had been integrated into the nomenclature in the preceding hundred years of the dynasty, and it would be repeated many times in the next two hundred years as well. The firstborn son was named Andrew, a name that had never before appeared in the Árpád line and never would again. The name had not appeared in the Riurikid line either at the approximate time of Andrew's birth in the 1020s, though Vsevolod Iaroslavich, who was born circa 1030, may have been given the Christian name Andrei.[140] Apart from this mention, the name does figure prominently in the *PVL*. One of the first stories recounted in the *PVL* is the legendary journey of St. Andrew, brother of St. Peter, from his base at Sinope through Rus'. The legend recounts that it is on this trip that St. Andrew blessed the eventual site of the city of Kiev.[141] Philip may have Christianized the Scythians, but Andrew was the one who blessed the site of the city of Kiev and actually traveled on the river systems of eastern Europe from Cherson to Novgorod. Andrew was well known in Rus' with his main saint's day on November 30,[142] and there were other minor feast and saints' days for other Andrews in the East Slavic menologies. However, as mentioned, the name had not yet appeared as the name of any ruler known to either the Rusians or the Hungarians.

The birth date of this Vladimirovna is unknown, but it is likely that she was born after the Christianization of Rus' under her father Vladimir, and was thus raised a Christian. It is only conjecture, but she may have learned the story of St. Andrew's trip through Kiev from the priests who came from Cherson. This story could have had a significant influence on her, and it may be why her firstborn son was named Andrew. In the Árpád lineage, no other reason presents itself for the name given to her and Ladislaus's firstborn son, and it certainly does not fit the pattern of names they gave to their two other children. Instead, it is a saint's name that was known in Rus' in the eleventh century[143] and may have been popular because of its association with the city of Kiev, the city Vladimir ruled and most likely where his daughter grew up. Although the evidence is circumstantial, it is a reasonable conjecture, and one that is supported by the other instances discussed in this section.

Anastasia Iaroslavna

Told to flee by his cousin Stephen because of the coming turmoil surrounding Stephen's imminent death, Andrew, son of the unknown Vladimirovna, ended up in Kiev.[144] Andrew then married the daughter of Iaroslav Vladimirich, Anastasia, with whom he returned to rule Hungary in 1046.[145] They had three children, Salomon, David, and Adelheid. To address the last first, Adelheid was a common German name, but one unknown at this point in the Árpád dynasty. Where it comes from is an interesting, but unfortunately open, question, as it can be found in royal families throughout Europe. The two sons, Salomon (Solomon) and David,[146] were given biblical names. The historical Solomon and David[147] were often paired in medieval stories and sermons because of their work building and maintaining peace in the kingdom of Israel. The Sermon on Law and Grace, attributed to Ilarion, mentions the two kings in passing, and, as well as underscoring their importance, makes clear that the Rusians knew of the biblical kings at that time.[148] With the weight of these biblical kings behind their names, it seems clear that Andrew and Anastasia intended for Salomon and/or David to rule as king. Adding weight to the choice of the name David was its growing fame in Rus'. The saints Boris and Gleb, whose Christian names were Roman and David, respectively, were Anastasia's uncles. Their murders and the ensuing drive for their sainthood in the mid-eleventh century led to the popularization of both their Slavic and their Christian names. Shortly after the birth of Anastasia's son David, her brother Igor' named one of his children David, and it became progressively more common in the eleventh century in the Riurikid line.[149]

By the time Andrew came to the throne of Hungary, the line of Géza had died out and the line of Ladislaus was the only remaining Árpád line, of which Andrew was the eldest male. His intention to abrogate the traditional custom of passing the rule from eldest male to eldest male (lateral inheritance), as was also the custom in Rus', was confirmed when he had Salomon crowned at the young age of five.[150] This suggests that the purpose of the name Salomon may have been to imply the divine right to rule held by King Andrew's son.

The question that remains is where Andrew might have come by this intention to suggest divine right via the name, as well as the name itself.

It seems possible that Andrew learned of both either while in Rus' or from Anastasia. By the time of their marriage in 1038 both Rus' and Hungary had experienced internecine warfare over inheritance. The evident problems of lateral inheritance and such strife may have encouraged Andrew to attempt to consolidate control of his realm for his family, and his family alone. Anastasia and Rus' may also have provided the motivation for the naming of his sons. Rus' converted to Christianity at least a decade before Hungary, and its royal family was more thoroughly converted—Andrew's own brother Levente supposedly lapsed into paganism.[151] Anastasia's specific involvement in the naming is not clear, but it can be inferred that she had a powerful effect on the king. On the occasion of the birth of Salomon in 1053, for instance, Andrew founded the monastery of Videgrád. This was an Orthodox monastery intended to honor Anastasia.[152] It seems clear that Andrew paid honor not only to his wife but to her Church and teachings that he learned from both.[153] Further, once Andrew's brother Béla mobilized an army and took Hungary for himself,[154] Anastasia was an important advisor to her young son the king, who was in exile in the German Empire. Salomon was married at a young age to Judith, the daughter of Henry III of the German Empire,[155] helping him regain the throne from first his uncle and then his cousins.[156] Anastasia had influence not only with her young son, but also with her husband, and was able to help both with revolutionary ideas, including a new plan for succession in Hungary.

Ingeborg Mstislavna and Waldemar, Great-Grandson of Vladimir

Sometime in the 1120s, Knud Lavard (the Bread-Giver), the son of Danish King Erik I Ejegod, married Ingeborg, daughter of Mstislav Vladimirich (Figure 4).[157] At the time of his death, Knud Lavard held the titles of Duke of the Danes and King of the Slavs by dint of his having conquered the Abodrite Slavs with the aid of Holsatian troops from Emperor Lothar III, at whose court he had been raised.[158] Prior to his death, he fathered four children with his Rusian wife, and the only son was named Waldemar.[159] The history of the Danish kings has been well recorded, and all of the kings after Harald Bluetooth can be traced without much difficulty. In that list is a collection of Haralds, Knuds, Eriks, Svens, and another name or two, but there had never before been a Waldemar. This name, though, appeared in European sources, in Latin and Old Norse, of the eleventh and twelfth centuries in reference to Rusians named Vladimir, specifically, Vladimir Sviatoslavich or Vladimir Monomakh.[160] It thus seems clear that the first use of this name in Scandinavian onomastic traditions is a reference to a Rusian ruler. Ingeborg Mstislavna was the granddaughter of Vladimir Monomakh, and it is likely that this was the source of the name for her firstborn son. As is well known, Vladimir was an important name in Rus', and one son, usually the firstborn, bore that name in many of the Riurikid lineages.[161] It is not unlikely that Ingeborg followed this tradition in the naming of her own son.

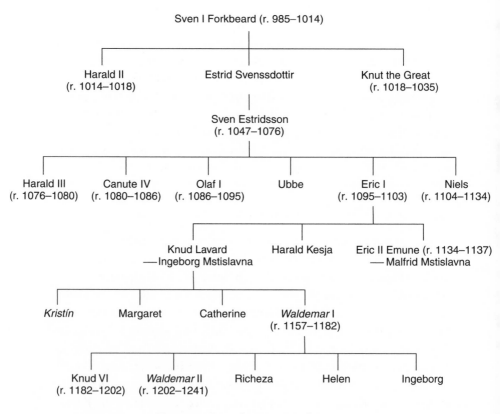

Figure 4. Danish onomastic history

But why? This is the question that must be asked when a new name appears in royal onomastic traditions. Why was this name chosen by these people, and at this particular time? Vladimir was the name of a Slavic rex in the minds of the Latin European world, and thus was a royal name. In 1129 Knud had taken control of the kingdom of the Abodrite Slavs[162] and had been proclaimed "rex Sclavorum," as recorded by twelfth-century chronicler Abbot Wilhelm.[163] This was shortly before the birth of his first son, and he most likely intended for that son to inherit his Abodrite kingdom. A widely recognized Slavic name might have been most helpful in that respect. Whether this completely explains the rationale behind choosing the name is impossible to say, but the most likely source for the name was Ingeborg, the granddaughter of one Vladimir and, as of 1131, sister to another.[164] Interestingly, one thirteenth-century saga written to glorify St. Knud and tell the tale of the Danish kings records that Waldemar was born and raised in Rus', and that is how he came to have a foreign name.[165] Whether this is a type of folk etymology to explain the foreign name of a Danish ruler, or the author of the saga had some precise knowledge, which is possible, we cannot know for certain today. Interestingly, the name became a popular Scandinavian one.[166] Waldemar I became "the Great" and ruled Denmark from 1156 to 1181. He fathered two sons, the first of whom bore Waldemar's father's name, Knud (Knud VI, r. 1182–1202), and the second bore his own, Waldemar (Waldemar II "the Victorious," r. 1202–1241).[167]

As an interesting and more successful parallel to the example of King Andrew of Hungary, Waldemar was both the son of a Rusian princess and later the husband of another Rusian princess.[168] Multiple marriages between families almost always indicate a desire to strengthen ties, as was seen in the marriages between Rus' and Poland. In the case of Waldemar's marriage, a second Rusian marriage may have been the suggestion of Ingeborg.[169] Interestingly enough, the issue of succession was also at stake in Denmark. Succession to the throne of Denmark followed the pattern common to many kingdoms of Europe, including Rus' and Hungary—the eldest male of the blood was able to inherit the throne, and often the leading candidate was chosen by some type of assembly.[170] Waldemar wished his firstborn son to follow him to the throne, so in 1170 he arranged a special ceremony in which the son was crowned king by archbishop Eskil of Lund.[171] At the same ceremony,

Waldemar himself was crowned king, the first ecclesiastical coronation in Denmark. At the same time Waldemar's father Knud Lavard was confirmed as a saint.[172] When Waldemar died and Knud VI succeeded him, it was the first hereditary succession in Danish history.[173] This may have just been an outgrowth of the times—Karl Schmid postulates that around the year 1000, the kingdoms of Europe began to transfer to a patrilineal kinship system. However, it was already the late twelfth century when this occurred in Denmark, and there exists the remarkable coincidence of it happening the exact same way as in Hungary approximately 150 years earlier. The most interesting aspect of which, for our discussion, is that Rusian women were involved in both of these situations as wives and mothers of kings and heirs.

Agafia Iaroslavna

Another brief example of a Rusian princess who may have injected new names into a well-known royal lineage is Agafia Iaroslavna. According to the theory of René Jetté, which has been further developed by Norman Ingham, exiled English prince Edward married the Rusian princess Agafia, the daughter of Iaroslav Mudryi, during Edward's exile in Rus', probably sometime in the 1030s.[174] The couple had three children, Edgar, Margaret, and Christine (Figure 5). Edgar is an Anglo-Saxon name that most likely came from Edward's family, but the names of the daughters were not until that time found in the English onomastic tradition.[175] Christine[176] and Margaret[177] were saints' names known in eleventh-century Rus',[178] and later in the century we have another example of the name Christine being used for a child from a Rusian-Scandinavian marriage.[179] Religious names seemed to be the preference of Rusian women of this generation who lived outside of Rus'. Thus it is possible that Agafia, the Rusian princess, was able to name her daughters after female saints that were known in Rus'. This becomes even more likely when it is known that at the times of their births the family was most likely residing in Hungary at the court of King Andrew and Queen Anastasia. Anastasia, of course, was Agafia's sister and, as we have seen, named her children after biblical figures, Solomon and David.

Both Edgar and Christine died childless, Edgar while working for his cousin Philip I of France harassing the Normans and Christine in a

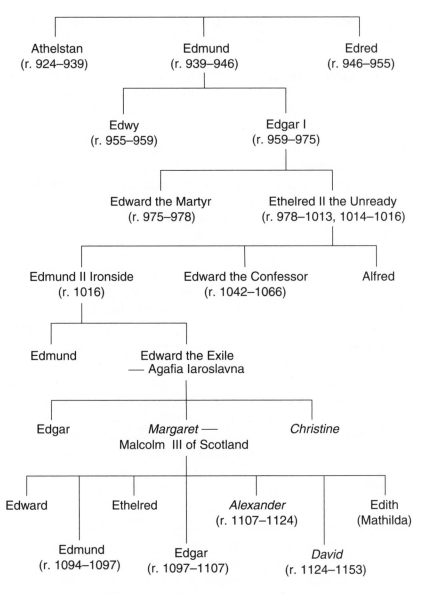

Figure 5. Anglo-Saxon onomastic history

nunnery. Margaret married and had children with Malcolm III, king of Scotland. There is a great deal of literature on Margaret, as she was a very well-known and influential queen.[180] Margaret continued the tradition of introducing new names into royal onomastics and named her two younger sons Alexander and David. David was the name of the cousin in Hungary with whom she had grown up, in addition to being a known Rusian name.[181] As before, both of these names were known and used in the Orthodox Church,[182] and Margaret's well-known piety probably encouraged her use of such names for her children. Her husband, Malcolm III, had sons from his first marriage to a Scandinavian woman named Ingibjorg. Their sons were named Duncan, Donald, and Malcolm, names from Malcolm's family.[183] But in his marriage to Margaret, all of the known children (Edward, Edmund, Ethelred, Edgar, Alexander, David, Edith [Mathilda], and Mary) had names that originated from Margaret and her line rather than from Malcolm and his.

Margaret was a uniquely powerful queen, but one has to wonder if this was a throwback to the early medieval policy of naming children after the more dominant heritage. Margaret was descended from the Anglo-Saxon ruling house of England that had been deposed approximately four years before her marriage to Malcolm, and also from the Riurikid line that ruled Rus'. It is possible that this ancestral combination would have been more prestigious than a local Scottish royal genealogy, though this may be a difficult suggestion to accept. Buttressing it is the idea, advanced by some, that Malcolm was an anglophile who may have spent time at the court of Edward the Confessor.[184] As part of a larger perspective on the influence of Rusian, or half-Rusian, women, the simplest explanation is that the names for these children were found at home, from his wife Margaret, who was a demonstrable influence in his life and in the course of late eleventh-century Scottish history.[185] Even A. D. M. Barrell, who plays down the idea of Margaret's influence, acknowledges that these names were "novel in the Scottish ruling house."[186]

Onomastics of Female Children

So far this discussion of onomastics has been focused largely on the male children of these marriages, but Rusian women had an influence on the names of their female children as well. This is, perhaps, a more common area of influence for royal women in medieval onomastics, but it is still important to examine the names given by Rusian women to their daughters.

The most common choice of name for a Rusian woman's daughter outside of Rus' (women's names inside of Rus' are rarely recorded) is the name of the Rusian woman's mother. Because of the practice of dynastic marriage, this woman, and consequently the name, was generally not Rusian. The earliest example that we have of this is in Elisabeth Iaroslavna's marriage to Harald Hardrada. Elisabeth bore Harald two daughters. Her first daughter was named Maria, perhaps a continuation of the Christian influence of Rusian women that has been discussed above,[187] while the second was named Ingigerd.[188] Ingigerd was also the name of Elisabeth's mother, the wife of Iaroslav Vladimirich, a Swedish princess.[189] So the name was a Scandinavian one, but also of importance to Elisabeth.

In the next century, two daughters of Mstislav Vladimirich, who also married into Scandinavian royal houses, were able to name a daughter each after their mother, Kristín, daughter of Inge Steinkelsson the king of Sweden.[190] Ingeborg Mstislavna, herself the product of female onomastic influence, was married to Knud Lavard, a Danish duke and king of the Abodrite Slavs, as discussed above. In addition to bearing a son, Waldemar, she had three daughters, one of whom was named Kristín.[191] Ingeborg's sister Malfrid married King Sigurd the Crusader of Norway and had one child, a daughter named Kristín.[192] So, these two half-Rusian women in Scandinavia were able to exercise some of their own onomastic influence to continue their own heritage in their children with their mother's name.[193]

Foreign Onomastics in Rus'?

To emphasize the importance of the contribution of Rusian women to the onomastic heritage of the houses they married into, a brief excursus must be made into foreign onomastic input in the Riurikid family. To do that, I will examine the two principal examples of such influence on male Rusian names prior to 1146, as well as one potential example that might indicate the further research that needs to be undertaken, and also look at several female names that may have been influenced by foreign sources.

The first generation to be raised entirely Christian was that of the grandchildren of Vladimir Sviatoslavich. Christianization has always had an effect on naming patterns throughout the world and the same was true in Rus'. The princes had Christian and also Slavic names, and in the chronicle records that still exist they were more often referred to by their Slavic names. Because the Christian names were not in wide use at the time, as far as we can tell, historians do not often use them now. However, for the women who married out of Rus', sometimes all that is available is a Christian name. For instance, three of Iaroslav's daughters are known only as Elisabeth, Anastasia, and Anna—three Christian names for three Christian princesses who married outside of Rus'. This is not to say that women were given only Christian names, Dobronega/Maria being a prime example to the contrary. Christianity made an impact on Rusian naming patterns—all of the baptized princes had to have a Christian name, whether they used it or not. The names by which chroniclers recorded our historical actors are the names that we must spend the most time examining. In Rus', this was the Slavic, not the Christian name, but there are aberrations that must then be considered even more carefully in this light.

There are three naming aberrations for men in the line of Vsevolod Iaroslavich. The first is Vsevolod's firstborn son, Vladimir. Vladimir acquired the surname Monomakh[194] as a reference to his mother's family, the Byzantine Monomachos clan. This was a powerful family in Byzantium, a son of which became emperor as Constantine IX.[195] The name Monomakh was an indicator of Vladimir's foreign ties and a definite link to his maternal kin and their prestige. The extent of the Monomakhina's influence on the naming of her firstborn son is unknown. It can be safely assumed that he was called Monomakh in a reference to his maternal family, perhaps to emphasize his connection with Byzantium. Whether this was in reference to the early medieval practice of naming a child after the most prestigious ancestry, whether paternal *or* maternal, is unknown. The Monomachos family never again rose to the heights of the empire after the death of Constantine IX in 1055, though the Byzantine name itself may have been appeal enough for those who used it, for Vladimir's mother, or for Vladimir himself.

The second example of an aberration came with Vladimir Monomakh's own firstborn son, Mstislav/Harold. Vladimir was married to

Gyða, daughter of the last Anglo-Saxon king of England, Harold God-winsson. Gyða very definitely had an impact on the naming of her child—she was able to give him her own father's name in addition to his Slavic name. As with the case of Monomakh himself, this was an odd occurrence because the majority of Rusian princes have only one name: Iziaslav, Rostislav, Sviatoslav, and so on. But as Monomakh himself had two names, perhaps he intended his son to as well, while also show-casing the significant foreign origins of his mother, an exiled princess. However, the only sources for the name Harold in reference to Mstislav are non-Rusian sources, indicating that he may not have used the name himself, but it may have been given to him by foreign chroniclers, espe-cially Scandinavians aware of his lineage.[196] The influence of Gyða on her husband is confirmed though by the *Pouchenie* (Instruction) of Vladimir Monomakh. This *Instruction* is an oddity in Rusian history, but was a common feature in the Anglo-Saxon tradition, its goal being to pass on a parting word and legacy to your children on how to rule and be a good Christian.[197] The only one that exists in Rusian history is from the pen of the husband of an Anglo-Saxon woman.

The third potential example is one advanced by A. F. Litvina and F. B. Uspenskii and deals with one of the younger sons of Iaroslav and Ingig-erd.[198] The authors suggest that the name Igor', while being considered a Riurikid name, had not been used since the semilegendary son of Ri-urik. Iaroslav and Ingigerd chose to name their son Igor' as much after his mother and maternal line (due to its Scandinavian equivalent In-gvarr), as because it was an existing Rusian/Riurikid name.[199] The name had special influence because Ingigerd's family line produced no male heirs to inherit, and there was always the potential that a son of hers might inherit the throne.[200] Though this example is not as clear as the first two, it raises the possibility that there might be other hidden exam-ples of foreign onomastic influence yet to be studied.

These three examples establish that foreign princesses did have the potential to influence the naming traditions of their Rusian families, and yet Rusian princes were still largely known by their Slavic names. If they had other names indicative of the western origin of their mothers, they are not extant. When examining the source base we can see that the Latin sources for most of European history are quite rich and provide sub-stantial documentation on royal and noble families. The Rusian sources, however, are rather limited in that regard. For most of the period under discussion the only available source is the *PVL,* which, as discussed elsewhere, is not particularly forthcoming either about the rest of Europe or about the role of women.[201] As such, it is plausible that the monastic authors of the *PVL* played down the role of foreign princesses in Rus' and attempted to minimize their influence.

One of the places that we have female Rusian names is when they married out of the kingdom of Rus'. In those cases in the eleventh century, the names were mostly Christian names, such as Anna, Elisabeth, and Anastasia. However, in the twelfth century we find such names as Ingeborg and Malfrid for the daughters of Mstislav Vladimirich and Kristín, daughter of Inge Steinkelsson.[202] These names are clearly Scandinavian, and though they are primarily found in Scandinavian, such as the *Heimskringla,* we use them as if they were their Rusian names.[203] It is difficult to know if this is true, because no names are recorded in Rusian chronicles for these daughters of Mstislav. Thus we are left with the doubt as to whether these are Rusian names inspired by their mothers, Scandinavian versions of their Rusian names, or Scandinavian names they took upon marriage. Because of the dearth of records it is difficult to determine the birth or baptismal names of Rusian women.

This source weakness may leave the historian in the awkward position of comparing a plethora of foreign examples to only a few domestic ones. However, this dilemma can be addressed by discussing the influence of both Rusian and non-Rusian princesses in their adoptive homes, as has been done in this section. Based on the number of cases on each side, it may seem that the Rusian women played a seemingly unique role in the choice of new names in the dynasties they married into, and that that role was not shared by foreign women in Rus'. It seems more likely that this apparent disparity is actually the result of biased chroniclers and differing onomastic traditions, rather than a difference in the effectiveness of foreign influence. This is a matter that still needs to be pursued, but I would argue that many foreign brides were able to exercise onomastic influence in their new families, and that such influence can help illustrate the power of medieval noble and royal women in their marriages.

The Question of Influence

Karl Schmid wrote, "If new names come into a family through a marriage connexion, this indicates that the family has either wholly or in part associated itself with a different sib."[204] Following this reasoning, the families Rusian princesses married into then associated themselves more closely with the Riurikids. While this may at first appear startling on the basis of a modern perspective of medieval Europe—a picture in which everyone faces west and Rus' is not just on the periphery of Europe, but completely out of the picture—when one looks at the actual political situation of the time (as illustrated in this book), it comes as little surprise. These Rusian princesses were married for a purpose, not, as far as we know, for love, but for politics. Both sides of a dynastic marriage must have desired a political alliance for it to be of utility—both sides must have gained from the agreement. The very existence of these marriages makes clear that these kingdoms were associating themselves with the Riurikids for a mutual advantage. This is simply the other side of the coin from Schmid's analysis of the introduction of new names. The purpose of the marriage was to act as a physical bond of an association between two kingdoms.

The addition of new names through a marriage tie may also be indicative of a continuing or strengthened alliance between the two parties. This is illustrated in two of the examples above. In Hungary, Andrew was the son of one Rusian princess and married to another, thus there were two generations in which a marriage was considered advisable and then made, which would make the transfer of influence more likely. In twelfth-century Denmark Ingeborg married Knud Lavard, and their son Waldemar also married a Rusian princess, showing a continuing desire for a Rusian tie over two generations. This was strengthened more by the fact that Malfrid, Ingeborg's sister, married one of Knud's half brothers. The ties between the Danish royal house and the Riurikids were particularly strong in this time period and so the potential for influence can be easily explained.

One question that remains is what effect these "foreign" names had on their bearers. This is generally unknown, as no medieval memoirs exist that recount Waldemar's shame or pride in his Rusian name. In Hungary, the name Andrew, through Andrew's own actions or those of his family, or because of his name itself, became unpopular for 150 years, while his more traditionally Hungarian-named relatives (such as Béla and Géza) became more common. For the Rusian Mstislav/Harold, the name Harold seems to have given Mstislav more credibility in the Scandinavian world, and he was able to successfully arrange two Scandinavian marriages for his daughters. Unfortunately, the answer to the question of onomastic influence on the bearer is an unknown. It is clear in these situations that the bearer had a nontraditional name for his surroundings, and it is probable that as such it had an effect on his, or her, perception, or more probably others' perception, of them, but this cannot be proved by the extant sources.

The world of medieval Europe as pictured by modern historians has changed a great deal in the past generation. The emergence of good social history, women's history, and a continuing reevaluation of the political and intellectual history that has defined medieval Europe for a hundred years of scholarship have made a fresh look at the medieval world possible. This chapter has aimed to further develop and expand our understanding of the world of medieval Europe, to show that it included the kingdom of Rus' on Europe's eastern end, and to illustrate the importance that dynastic marriage played in drawing Rus' into the web of European politics that bound the whole continent together.

The importance of dynastic marriage has been highlighted in this chapter by the presentation of case studies of Rusian marriages with the other royal houses of Europe. The sheer number of marriages with polities to their west, forty out of fifty-two, shows how closely Rus' was tied in to the world of European politics, but it is in the details of each marriage that the picture of Rusian involvement is truly fleshed out. These details demonstrate that marriages with the Rusians were not, as Bouchard suggested, the last resort for consanguinity-bound European nobles.[205] Instead, they were political agreements designed to advance the needs of both kingdoms. The marriage bound the two kingdoms together in the furtherance of a particular goal, whether that was returning an exiled prince to power, conquering a certain tribe, or buttressing a weak flank. These marriages were all by their very nature in the best interests of the participating families and, except in the case of internecine warfare, in the best interests of the participating kingdoms. The examples provided here serve to show the depth of Rusian commitment to the world of European politics and also their orientation toward the political world to their west.

Another intention of this chapter has been to rehabilitate the image of the Rusian woman in historical scholarship. Political history that ignores women misses half the picture, literally. Women played a role in medieval political history that cannot and should not be ignored by modern historians. This is especially true in Rusian history as Rusian women were the ones who forged the most direct ties with the rest of Europe and because it was through them that Rus' became integrated into Europe. This chapter has attempted to point out the importance of medieval women, particularly Rusian queens. The example provided by Pauline Stafford serves for Rusian women, as well as for those of other medieval kingdoms. "The position of queen was whatever these women could make of it, determined by the framework of rules, contemporary practice, and theory allowed them. In the early Middle Ages that framework was wide, and many great women were able to use it to the full."[206] Many Rusian women fit this description and were able to use their skills to increase their own as well as Rusian influence in their new kingdoms. Examples of these women abound in the descriptions of the Rusian dynastic marriages. These women were able to leave a concrete example of their power for the ages. By influencing the onomastic traditions of their host kingdoms, these Rusian women were able to affect an aspect of royal power and introduce an element of their own heritage into foreign courts.

Rusian men and women participated in the European system of dynastic marriages. Riurikid rulers, like their contemporaries in France, England, or the German and Byzantine Empires, used their sons, daughters, sisters, and brothers as physical tokens to seal agreements and alliances to advance the political interests of their realm, either for or against the will of the participants. These rulers trusted that the individual they gave away in marriage would be true to their home kingdom, attempt to use their influence to hold their host kingdom to the letter of the agreement that the marriage sealed, and also advance the interests of their home kingdom in any way possible. This chapter illustrates not the uniqueness of the Rusian dynastic marriage pro-gram, but its similarity to those of the rest of Europe. Rus' as a political entity functioned in the same manner as the other kingdoms of Europe and participated in European politics by means of dynastic marriages to their own advancement and their enemies' detriment.

— 4 —

Kiev as a Center of European Trade

The study of trade in Rus' has a long and distinguished history.[1] The abundance of scholarship in this area gives us an enormous advantage, but it also presents a problem: so much work has been done over the last two centuries that it is difficult to summarize those results in any systematic fashion (which is one reason there has been no large-scale summary of the vast trading connections and products).[2] Numerous studies have analyzed the archaeology of particular regions, the trading connections implicit in a given type of trade (such as fur), the transfer of coins throughout Rus' and western Eurasia, or even the commercial activities of one group or another.[3] However, there are few venues that allow for this information to be put into a larger survey, other than a national history in which the details are often glossed in the interest of moving rapidly through hundreds of years of history.[4] The importance of trade and the resulting interconnectivity of Rus' with the larger world is self-evident for a work such as this, and therefore this chapter will deal with the position of Russian trade as part of the web of relationships connecting Rus' into Europe. It must be stated quite clearly, though, that this chapter does not introduce new evidence into the historiographical record, nor does it synthesize all of the vast and ever-growing scholarship on Russian commerce. Instead it presents a representative sampling of information from a variety of fields. This will introduce some of the historiography to a wider audience and will use the extensive information already discovered and published about Russian trade specifically, and medieval trade more generally, to bolster the argument that Rus' was in fact part and parcel of Europe and of wider European systems in this period of the Middle Ages.

One additional caveat: the time constraints of this book (988–1146) are awkward for a discussion of Rusian economic relations. The traditional perspective on Rusian trade is that over the course of the tenth century Rus' developed ties with Byzantium, and only in the eleventh century was there a connection with the wider world.[5] In this perspective, the connection to the wider world was brought to an end by a variety of political changes that reshaped European trade in the twelfth century and returned Rus' to a marginal trading position.[6] This traditional model has been challenged by a variety of authors, especially in regard to the supposed decline in trade in the twelfth century.[7] In examining this newer perspective, we will expand our time frame slightly to examine the ninth- and early tenth-century connections that lay the foundation for the very existence of Rus' as a kingdom, as well as for its interconnectivity with the rest of Europe.

Unlike some other interactions that may have clearly delineated boundaries, trade is expansive and crosses territorial, religious, ethnic, and any other boundaries it encounters.[8] Because of this, it is difficult to discuss Rus' separately from a larger Eurasian trading system. Commerce throughout Eurasia has been documented since ancient times, including trade along the famous Silk Roads, parts of which passed through, or very near to, Rusian territory. These routes connected Rus', or the territory that would become Rus', into a hemispheric trading zone in which goods from East Asia, South Asia, the Middle East, and Europe were all exchanged among a variety of traders and merchants. While this represents a potential problem for the larger argument here about Rusian inclusion in Europe, there are ways of narrowing down this vast trading web. In fact, though one can discuss the vastness of trading connections throughout the Eastern Hemisphere, the majority of trade was conducted in smaller regional trading zones. In his expansive work on the early medieval economy, Michael McCormick refers to these as "interlocking exchange zones."[9] Similar to the "interlinked subsystems" used by Janet Abu-Lughod,[10] these are convenient ways to break up a large interconnected world into digestible segments that are created purposefully, though their boundaries are debatable.[11] Each of the interlocking exchange zones is a smaller trading region that contains regular trade routes and exchanges of goods, often oriented around a central trading city or trade route. That exchange zone is connected into a broader network of exchange zones via long-distance merchants (the Radanites as a famous, though rare, example are discussed more below), or connect at their edges, creating the ties that develop into a world trading system.[12] Though it is possible to differentiate multiple exchange zones within the larger European world, these exchange zones are still separate from those that connected Rus' with Central Asia.

"One cannot properly appreciate the economic relationships within this larger region [western Eurasia] unless Kiev's role in the foreign and domestic trade of Rus' is taken into account."[13] This basic argument by Thomas Noonan is at the heart of this chapter, and is part of the larger theme of this book. Kiev, and Rus' in general, are important to understanding broader relationships in Europe during the Middle Ages. Kiev is most commonly discussed in medieval economic history as a center point of the trade between the "Varangians and the Greeks"—a north–south route between Scandinavia and Byzantium—but Kiev was also central to an east–west trade route that extended from Mainz and Regensburg in the German Empire through Bohemia and Poland into Rus', and eventually (passing into another exchange zone) into Central Asia. Rus', though not the city of Kiev itself, was tied into a third exchange zone in Europe as well, one centered on the Baltic Sea that became particularly active in the late eleventh and early twelfth centuries, and saw Rusian merchants as far afield as England. All of this information reinforces Noonan's point that understanding trade in western Eurasia must incorporate Rus'. This chapter utilizes a variety of sources, including archaeology, numismatics, and written sources, to discuss these three exchange zones and demonstrate Rusian interconnectivity with the rest of Europe in the Middle Ages.

Route from the Varangians to the Greeks

The trading path that consumes the most attention amongst historians of Rus' is the one famously referred to in the *PVL* as the "route from the Varangians to the Greeks."[14] In popular imagination, this route stretched from the Baltic Sea, also known as the Varangian Sea,[15] down the waterways of eastern Europe (chiefly down the Dnieper to the Black Sea), and thence to Constantinople.[16] However, even before beginning with the larger discussion of the Russian trade networks it must be pointed out that the route from the Varangians to the Greeks, often quoted, is not illustrated by the *PVL* in the way it is expressed above.[17] The author of the *PVL,* perhaps articulating a Byzantine focus, begins in Constantinople and traces the route from Byzantium up the Dnieper and other rivers to the Baltic Sea.[18] It is true that this is a subtle difference, but one that is important to mention, both for its own sake and as a starting point for the unraveling of the larger story of Rusian trade. The description and orientation of the route is typically changed to reflect the (accurate) historical understanding that the Varangians were descending the eastern European river systems to the Black Sea and Constantinople, and that the Varangians were instrumental in the founding of Rus'. But the chronicler was clear in his depiction of the route as beginning with Constantinople. Regardless of a larger issue of Byzantine influence on the chronicle, this reflects a vision of Constantinople as the center point of the route, especially when considering the rest of the route. The chronicler continues the route past the Baltic, and though this portion is often cut by modern historians, it is of importance to this examination— once you have reached the Varangian Sea, "on to Rome, and from Rome arrive back in that sea to Tsargrad [Constantinople]."[19] It turns out that the route from the Varangians to the Greeks is, in fact, a circle that runs from Constantinople through Rus' around the breadth of the European continent, though these details are elided by the chronicler, to Rome, and finally returning to Constantinople. There is even further description included in the *PVL* that details other routes that one might follow in eastern Europe, all of which were important and relevant to the development of Rusian trade, yet are often omitted in modern histories in favor of a simplification of the trade routes, simply called *the* route from the Varangians to the Greeks.[20] This simplification is representative of a larger trimming of Rusian history in favor of Byzantine connections, consciously or unconsciously. Mark Whittow, a historian of Byzantium, concludes that "the widespread belief in the Dnieper route to Constantinople as one of the great commercial arteries of the early medieval world is no more than an unsubstantiated article of faith."[21]

Further, the chronicler recorded these manifold routes as part of his entry regarding the Apostle Andrew's journey through Rus' in biblical or at least semimythical times. No historians are willing to claim that Andrew truly visited Rus' and that his route was recorded and passed down, and most accept that this, as with many other elements of the *PVL*, is a religious interpolation. I would suggest that the chronicler is detailing contemporaneous travel routes that were used by Rusians, among others, routes that were not solely confined to a path from Scandinavia to Byzantium but in fact encompassed all of Europe. This section discusses the trade routes that existed in eastern Europe and involved Rus', including but not exclusively the route from the Varangians to the Greeks. This is the best-known segment of Rusian trade, and though other trade routes will be discussed later, it is important to begin with this exchange zone and its importance in the development of Rus' and Rusian history.

Long-distance trade routes through the eastern European river systems began before the creation of a Rusian state, with Scandinavians' quest for silver, furs, and other trade goods. The existence of a Middle Eastern exchange zone[22] in the southern part of this region, which extended through Khazar territory into the Dnieper and Volga river basins, was a draw for the Scandinavians. The good that was most in demand was silver, something lacking in Scandinavia and Rus', but held in plenty in the Middle East.[23] The lack of indigenous silver deposits in Scandinavia drew traders deeper and deeper into the eastern European river systems, where they expanded their trade in amber and furs in the mid to late eighth century. The numerous silver dirhams in eastern Europe were gained via trade with Arabs or Khazars, most likely for furs, and were in turn hoarded, used to pay taxes to the Khazars, or passed on to other traders, such as the Scandinavians.[24] Over one-third of the dirhams imported into the Rusian territory in the late eighth to early ninth centuries were exported to Scandinavia.[25] This percentage increased dramatically over time, as did the total number of dirhams coming into this area. Over the next two centuries, especially with the establishment of Scandinavian settlements in this region, Rus' became the middleman, supplying dirhams not only to Scandinavia, but to the Baltic in general, as well as increasing their ties with the various Balts and West Slavs along the rim of the Baltic Sea.[26] Building on Thomas Noonan's data, his student Roman Kovalev concluded that "from the late eighth to the last quarter of the tenth century, millions of Islamic silver coins or dirhams were exported from the Islamic world to northern Europe via European Russia."[27] Rus' also began to use dirhams, in the tenth century especially, as internal currency, both for their full value and cut for use in smaller-value exchanges.[28] The use of dirhams became so prominent that it seems enterprising Kievans began to mint their own imitation dirhams by the tenth century.[29] Whether these were used as a way of fooling merchants (or attempting to), or whether they were a deliberate appropriation of a stable, and useful, currency, we are incapable of saying from the limited archaeological evidence. But the dirham mold itself, along with the numerous hoards of dirhams found throughout Rusian territory, testifies to their enormous importance in and for Rus'.

"By the first half of the ninth century, well before a state of Kievan Rus' formed, northwestern Rus' had become part of a vast commercial network linking the Islamic world and the Baltic region."[30] It is clear from this early period that the Rusian territory was very much a link between European and Central Asian or Middle Eastern exchange zones, with the Volga as the main artery of trade, and with very little mention of the Byzantines. However, over the course of the tenth century the supply of silver from the Middle Eastern exchange zone in the south began to dry up, and the Rusian economy that had been built on that silver was forced to refocus in order to survive.[31] The cities in Rus' that were created or that came to prominence due to the Islamic trade, such as Riurikovo Gorodishche, Gnezdovo, and Staraia Ladoga, could not support themselves any longer.[32] However, the skill sets required for long-distance trade, as well as the existing complement of trade goods, could be applied to another region.[33] During this time we begin to see the rise of Kiev and a Rusian refocusing on both Byzantine and western European exchange zones.[34]

The evidence for the reorientation of trade in Rus' is plentiful—in lieu of trade with the Islamic world, Constantinople was substituted and the main river in this exchange zone changed from the Volga to the Dnieper. Interestingly, the numismatic evidence that was so important in trade with the Middle Eastern exchange zone is largely absent from the discussion of Rusian trade with Byzantium. There have been very few Byzantine coin finds in Rus' from the medieval period, especially compared with the plethora of dirhams or finds of the western European denarius.[35] Constantinople, though, was not simply a market for Rusians, but in the eleventh century was the center of the commercial world for western Eurasia.[36] By reorienting their trade from the failing eastern ties to Constantinople, Rus' reoriented the north–south ex-change zone and continued to play a role in trade in other areas.

Rusian trade ties with Byzantium are first delineated in the written sources by two tenth-century treaties recorded in the *PVL*.[37] The con-tents of the treaties deal with the actual interactions between Byzantium and Rus', providing not just economic, but also legal and political, infor-mation. The language of those treaties, and their specificity, suggests that they were copied into the chronicle from extant versions of the treaty,[38] though there are other ways that such specificity could have been added, as late medieval or early modern chroniclers attempted to "improve" their work and increase the Byzantine connections of Rus', or borrowed from other extant chronicles.[39] T. V. Rozhdestvenskaia points out that the treaties were most likely added to the *PVL* at the end of the fourteenth century, and that thus the information they contain, and its relevance to the tenth century, is suspect,[40] although they do reference contemporary issues in trade and in legal affairs, such as the inclusion of the Rhodian sea law in the treaty of 911.[41] The importance of the treaties has also been called into question. Are they codifications of an existing relationship between the two sides? The delineation of a new relationship? Can they tell us anything about the broader relation-ship between the two sides in the tenth century? This is not to mention the extrapolations of those relationships to the eleventh century and beyond that have occasionally occurred.[42] The treaties themselves do contain a wealth of information about the commercial relationship be-tween Byzantium and Rus', specifying the number of Rusians allowed in Constantinople, the requirements for merchant accreditation, the accommodations for merchants (and others) in Constantinople, the supply of Rusian visitors, and their tax status, among other items. These are important documents in their own right, creating a larger political, legal, diplomatic, and economic relationship between the two states, even while leaving out the specific goods traded.[43]

As noted by the treaties, Rusian and Byzantine merchants frequented each other's cities and carried on a lively trade that has left other traces in both written and material culture. Soon after the second treaty, in the 950s, the regent Ol'ga herself made a visit to Constantinople. The purpose of the trip is most often recorded as Christianization, but refer-ences in both the *PVL* and *De Cerimoniis* seem to suggest that trade may have been at least as important.[44] Additionally, the early date for extant copies of *De Cerimoniis* gives us a greater degree of reliability about the provenance of this particular interaction between Rus' and Byzantium. On her trip, Ol'ga was accompanied to Constantinople by a variety of associates, including over forty merchants, all of whom received gifts from the emperor.[45] These merchants were from "the rulers of Rus',"[46] which most likely refers to the various kniazia from the Rusian cities, and were members of Ol'ga's entourage. When Ol'ga returned to Kiev, she was asked by the Byzantine emperor to provide goods ("slaves, wax, furs, and soldiers") that seem to have been negotiated in Byzantium.[47] Though Christianization may have been a purpose of the trip to Constantinople (see Chapter 5 for more discussion), trade was at least equally as important and receives prominent mentions in each of the primary sources that record information about the event. This is one of the best-recorded trading trips of a Rusian to Constantinople, but it is certainly not the last.[48] There is documentation supporting the presence of Rusian merchants in Constantinople in the tenth, eleventh, and twelfth centuries, and there are reports of a Greek presence in Kiev, and even farther north, reinforcing the important Dnieper connection between Rus' and Byzantium.[49] While Rusian furs, honey, slaves, and wax went south, "Byzantine silks, glass beads and bracelets, and amphorae containing wine, oil, and naphtha" came north along the river.[50] These luxury goods were important to the developing Kievan state, and particularly to the ornament of the Riurikid ruling elite. As discussed in Chapter 1, Byzantine ornamentation was a key way individuals identified themselves with the premier culture in Christian Europe, and Rus' was certainly no different from the German Empire or Scandinavia in wanting to do so.[51] Similar to those other areas, Rus' brought in Byzantine architects and mosaicists, who worked on a variety of buildings, most famously the St. Sophia churches in both Kiev and Novgorod erected in the eleventh century.[52] However, Byzantine goods were found not just in the major cities but throughout Rus', indicating the important internal trading connections within Rus', as well as the external ones.[53]

Though brief, the evidence presented here shows that the route from the Varangians to the Greeks was an important artery of trade for Rus', providing it with merchants, artisans, and luxury goods, as well as trade with the mercantile capital of western Eurasia. The eastern European river systems were important for the creation of Rus' as well. Specifically, the Volga connections drew the Vikings into eastern Europe and allowed Rus' to act as middleman between the Islamic and Baltic worlds. But there were also (trade) routes not taken. For instance, in the tenth century, Sviatoslav attempted to move the capital of Rus' to the Danube, explicitly to better his trading position.[54] Along with Ol'ga's participation in an economic mission to Constantinople, this helps illustrate that as Rus' formed, its rulers were aware of the importance of its position in European trade, and worked to improve that position as best they could.

East–West Trade

In comparison with the "route from the Varangians to the Greeks," the east–west trade route that ran from the German Empire through Bohemia, Poland, and into Rus' is less discussed, though certainly not absent in the general historiography,[55] and there is ample archaeological and textual evidence testifying to its importance. Trade is one of the areas where connections to the rest of Europe have been investigated, in part due to the methodology of archaeology, the main method for discovering such connections—if western European goods are found in Rus' in greater quantities than Byzantine goods, this is difficult to explain away based on a preconceived theory.[56] However, that discussion, while present in certain venues, rarely makes it into the larger discussion of Rusian history. A notable exception is Jonathan Shepard and Simon Franklin's *The Emergence of Rus'*, which acknowledges the enormous importance of the east–west route in early Rusian history, though east–west connections are not generally emphasized in their book.[57] The east–west route not only was important as a source of trade, but also provided the main path for western Europeans to enter and interact with Rus'.[58] The examination here will highlight some of the evidence of people and goods traveling along this route, which provided another avenue of trade and participation in a European exchange zone.

Some of the earliest mentions of Rus' in written sources are in trade documents from the East Frankish Empire dating to the early tenth century, documents that grant trading privileges along the Danube River to Rusians.[59] The Raffelstettin Regulations, as they are known, highlight a trade route that extends from Regensburg down the Danube past Raffelstettin and Passau before turning for Prague and continuing through Cracow, Przemysl, and onto Kiev.[60] The main trade goods listed for the Rusians are furs, slaves, and horses, with attendant prices for each of them, thus overlapping with the goods that we have seen being traded by Rusians on the Dnieper. This establishes an early date for Rusian trade with the rest of Europe, but an even earlier date than the stated 903 and 904 can be surmised from internal textual evidence, as the documents refer to the same laws being in effect back to the reign of Louis the German in the mid-ninth century. Whether Rusians were involved in the mid-ninth century is impossible to say, but if they were, that would put Rusian traders on the Danube shortly after they had visited Louis's court on their way home from Byzantium,[61] about the same time as they raided Constantinople for the first time[62] and while the major river route in eastern Europe was still the Volga trade route to the Muslim world.

Whether or not the Rusian presence can be read back into the ninth century, there is very solid evidence for Rusian trade with central Europe at the beginning of the tenth century, evidence that only grows stronger throughout the century. The Raffelstettin Regulations highlight the beginning of the tenth-century Rusian trade with Europe, while sources from Jewish traders and travelers showcase the growing presence of Rusians and their goods on this east–west trade route. The initial discussion of Jewish traders in Europe always starts with the eighth- to ninth-century Radanite merchants who traveled a variety of routes throughout Eurasia, including the central European route highlighted here.[63] Though these Jewish merchants engaged in trade with the Slavs, and of the Slavs (as slaves), there is no direct connection, other than the route they traveled, with Rus'. Evidence of Rusian involvement in this trade route begins in Jewish sources with the Iberian writer Ibrahim ibn Yakub, who visited Prague in 965.[64] Ibn Yakub recorded the variety of traders present in Prague, including Jews, Rusians, Turks, and Muslims, and explicitly states that the Rusian traders came via Cracow when bringing their wares to Prague.[65] Written half a century after the Raffelstettin Regulations, Ibn Yakub's record provides another crucial data point connecting Rus' into broader patterns of central European trade, as well as highlighting one portion of that route (Rus'–Cracow–Prague; see map on p. 126). The route can be extended into German territory with the addition of other sources on Jewish trade that record the expansion of Jewish settlements in Mainz in the early tenth century and in Regensburg in the mid-tenth century (a result of a decrease in Jewish trade in the Mediterranean due to anti-Jewish laws, primarily in Italian city-states).[66] Mainz and Regensburg then became the base of operations for many of the Jewish traders visiting eastern Europe, indicated by the presence of dirhams in those locations but not in many other German towns, for example, which also indicates trade through Rus'. Further, Russian visitors are known to have visited the German imperial court on multiple occasions, including in 960 and 973. The court was often at Mainz, perhaps lending further weight to the importance of that city as one end of the east–west trade route.[67]

At the other side of the trade route, there is evidence for the existence of multiple Jewish communities in Rusian territory. A Hebrew source, *Or Zaruah,* written in the thirteenth century but citing an eleventh-century work, mentions that the Jewish settlement in the town of Przemysl was carried off into Rus'.[68] This corresponds with the 1031 entry in the *PVL* of Iaroslav and Mstislav's joint sack of the Cherven towns, which would likely include Przemysl, and Iaroslav's subsequent relocation of the people living there deeper into Rusian territory.[69] Additionally, there is a well-attested Jewish community in Kiev from the twelfth century and theoretically present there much earlier.[70] Norman Golb and Omeljan Pritsak's work suggests a Khazarian Jewish presence in Kiev from the mid-tenth century,[71] which coincides with the information provided by Ibn Yakub and others about Jewish traders on this east–west route. The presence of these Jewish communities on this trade route from the tenth and early eleventh centuries attests to its importance to Jewish traders, and also signifies its importance as a main trade route. Kiev also had both Polish and Hungarian gates, indicating two other important trading partners who were part of this east–west exchange zone.[72]

The evidence of traders and travelers only increases over the course of the eleventh and twelfth centuries, as a variety of different trade missions left records.[73] The famous Rabbi Petachia of Regensburg traveled this route in the twelfth century on his way to the Middle East.[74] Brutzkus, who is responsible for the majority of English-language scholarship

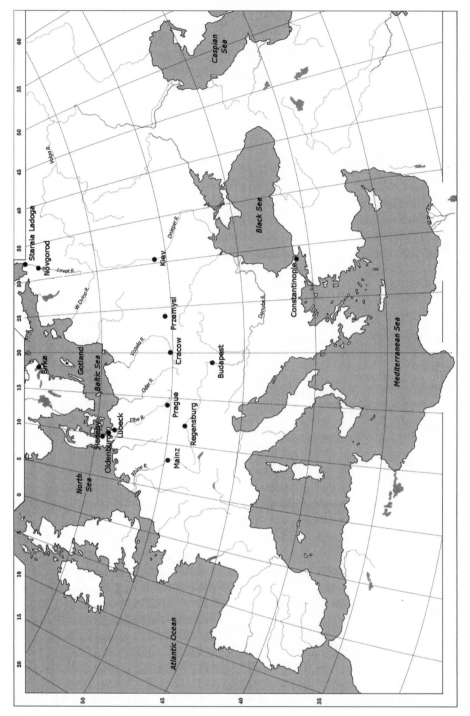

Major European trading cities

on Jewish traders, notes, "In the eleventh and twelfth centuries more was known by the Jews of Germany about Russia than about Poland, and Russian Jews are mentioned more often than Polish Jews."[75] Additionally, there were multiple embassies from Rus' to the German Empire during the eleventh century, including the travels of Iziaslav Iaroslavich and his family after being usurped by his brother Sviatoslav.[76] Nonroyal Rusians are mentioned as present at the eleventh-century translation of the relics of St. Godegard of Hildesheim, while a German stranded in Kiev was assisted home with a gift from the ruler of Kiev and the company of a band of merchants returning to Regensburg.[77] These are just a sampling of the Latin-language sources that record the Rusian people and goods traveling throughout Europe. Rusian sources also provide a glimpse into this trade route in this period. In 1129, Poles captured a group of Rusian merchants coming back from Moravia, eliciting a negotiation between Mstislav of Rus' and Bolesław of Poland.[78] Further, in 1144, Ivan Rostislavich took the city of Berlad and put forth a gramota about trade with Hungary and Bohemia, also testifying to the expansion of Rusian trade routes.[79] This evidence from Latin, Hebrew, and Old East Slavic sources showcases the breadth of connections maintained through this exchange zone and the presence of Rusians in it.

There are further extant sources about traders and travelers, but the commodities traded in this exchange zone must be examined as well. The most common Rusian trade goods were slaves, honey, and furs, though a few others are mentioned as well. Slaves were ubiquitous as part of the early east–west trade route and are mentioned as part of the early trade under the Radanites and in the Raffelstettin Regulations, though they largely disappear after the tenth century.[80] The trade in honey did not leave much of a mark on the historical record, though there are a few mentions of it, such as in Sviatoslav's attempted relocation to the Danube and in the Raffelstettin Regulations.[81] The Rusian fur trade has been extensively studied by Janet Martin, who documented the connections the fur trade created within Rus' and with the rest of Eurasia.[82] There are multiple mentions of Rusian furs as part of the western trade. Rusian furs receive casual mention in saints' lives in the German Empire as objects of luxury,[83] and Benjamin of Tudela's mention of furs is one of the few items about Rus' in his work, in addition to the presence of Rusian traders at Constantinople and elsewhere.[84] All of these Rusian goods were part of this east–west exchange zone, though furs were recorded more than others, perhaps because they were more memorable to elite writers and their sponsors.

Other goods further illustrate the Rusian trading position vis-à-vis the rest of Europe. Weapons were essential pieces of equipment for the warring classes throughout Europe, and many of the knives and swords found in Rus' from this period are similar to those from throughout Europe.[85] The most famous production center for medieval swords was on the middle Rhine River, providing a connection with the Rusian trade route to Mainz, and the swords made there were distributed and copied throughout Europe.[86] Some of the swords bear the names of their makers, almost always in Latin, but that did not deter either Rusian wielders or copiers of the weapons.[87] Rusian-manufactured swords of this type also often contained maker's marks that are copies of the famous names of the Germanic smiths, perhaps in order to increase the value of the weapons.[88] There is even a sword blade that bears a Cyrillic maker's mark, a sword that combines a variety of features, including the Germanic technique for imprinting the blade, Scandinavian ornamentation, and Cyrillic writing, which represents the blending of styles, techniques, and cultures that was Rus'.[89]

In the premodern world, one of the most important commodities (so important that it was often used as currency)[90] was salt, which is mentioned frequently in medieval records.[91] One of the earliest trade embargoes in Rus' came in the late eleventh century, when Sviatopolk Iziaslavich embargoed the salt coming from Galicia, specifically from Przemysl. Though this is recorded in an ecclesiastical source, the *Paterik of the Kievan Caves Monastery,*[92] where it is used to preface the miraculous creation of salt from ashes, the production of salt in Przemysl is mentioned in other sources as well.[93] This salt trade was essential to Rus', and Sviatopolk's attempt to force his rival, David Igorich, into submission through an embargo of the salt trade demonstrates that importance. The salt from Galicia was important more broadly to the central European trade as well, and records from the twelfth and thirteenth centuries show other medieval rulers making use of Galician salt.[94] The presence of salt in this area, and its importance, adds another layer of understanding to the contentious relationship between Rus' and Poland over the Cherven territories.[95] These cities were part of the larger east–west trade route between Rus' and the rest of Europe, and thus their control was important to controlling trade generally, but the salt and saltworks in the region made the cities especially worth fighting for.[96]

The presence of Rusian traders and trade goods along this east–west route, as well as the presence of European merchants and goods in Rus', highlights a second exchange zone that Rus' was part of in the medieval European world, increasing their connections with the rest of Europe.

Baltic Trade

Rusians were also part of another crucial exchange zone, centered on the Baltic Sea. The early relationship between Rus' and the Baltic Sea has been discussed in relation to the creation of Rus' and the Scandinavian expansion into the eastern European river systems. This exchange zone only grew with time, and prospered well beyond the end of the Islamic silver trade.[97] In fact, the sea itself is referenced in primary sources as the Varangian, Scythian, or Rusian Sea, demonstrating the hold that the Rusians had on the imagination of those trading on and writing about the Baltic world.[98] Along the coast of the Baltic there have been numerous finds of Rusian goods, including grivny, spindles, ceramic eggs, and bracelets, all of which are physical manifestations of the depth of Rusian involvement in the Baltic exchange zone.[99] This is not to mention the pan-Baltic goods that show up throughout the region (including Rus'), such as ceramic disks, Frisian combs, and glass beads.[100] Though Scandinavia has its own difficulty being counted as part of the medieval world,[101] Rusian interaction on the Baltic encompassed not only (though primarily) Scandinavia, but also the Balts, the German Empire, and even Flanders and England. This extensive trade demonstrates more of the interconnectivity between Rus' and the rest of Europe.

The mercantile connections between the territory that would become Rus' and the Baltic world began early, but even from the earliest Rusian occupation of important trading cities, such as Ladoga and Novgorod, Rusians participated in the Baltic exchange zone.[102] In an incidental fashion, *Heimskringla* records multiple merchants traveling to Rus' or coming from Rus', indicating the commonplace nature of such travel. The classic example is that of Guthleik, a Scandinavian merchant, who traveled to Novgorod so often that "Gerzki" (of Gartharíki) became his epithet.[103] In one instance Guthleik was commissioned by King St. Olaf of Norway to purchase "valuable things" for him in Novgorod when next he journeyed there. This explicit mention of a merchant traveling to Novgorod in the early eleventh century is only part of the story. The earlier King Olaf, Tryggvason, was captured as a boy on his way to Rus' with his mother and "some merchants,"[104] their purpose being to visit Olaf's uncle Sigurð, who had been in residence in Novgorod for quite some time. Mentions like these occur throughout the eleventh century, with casual notation of Scandinavian merchants and others going to and coming from Rus'.[105]

These commonplace mentions are supplemented by the presence of Rusian merchants and artifacts throughout the major Scandinavian trading centers. Sigtuna had a Rusian trading center with its own church, and Rusian seals have been found there dating to the eleventh century.[106] The lead seals survived, whereas the documents or goods they were attached to did not, but one can hypothesize that the purpose of the seals was to verify provenance and/or represent the authority of the Rusian ruler. The 944 treaty with Byzantium states that all merchants and delegates had previously been known by silver and gold seals issued by the ruler of Kiev.[107] It would not be difficult to imagine that seals would be required or advantageous in the Baltic trade as well, especially considering this precedent. Birka, Hedeby, and Oldenburg also held prominent Rusian trading presences.[108] These towns were all in contact with Rusian towns, such as Staraia Ladoga, and excavations have revealed many of the same trade goods at each place: Frisian bronze combs, found in northern Rus', Scandinavia, Poland, and elsewhere in the Baltic from the eighth through eleventh centuries;[109] glass beads, which were manufactured at both Ladoga and Birka with similar designs;[110] clay disks, which were designed and made in Rus' for export to Scandinavia;[111] glazed ceramic eggs, manufactured in Kiev and found throughout the Baltic.[112] These goods and the similar systems of weights and measures present in these towns[113] all connect them into a Baltic system of trade. Adam of Bremen specifically mentions Hedeby as a port of call for trade with Rus', and notes the travel times for journeys from Birka to Rus';[114] Helmold calls Birka one of the most desirable ports for all the people of "Scythia."[115]

One of the most prominent trading centers in the Baltic was the island of Gotland, with which Rus' had a long association. The creation of Novgorod curtailed Swedish expansion eastward, and, in part, led to the increase in trade with Gotland.[116] This is at least partially due to the fact that the ports at Novgorod and Gotland were quite similar, and the same shallow-draft crafts could be used in both places, as well as from one to the other, without requiring portaging.[117] Trade with Gotland is even referenced in the Novgorod Primary Chronicle (NPL), which is usually quiet in this period regarding foreign interactions. In 1130, however, it records that a group of merchants coming from Gotland ("Got'") were shipwrecked and lost their goods in the process.[118] The long acquaintance between the two led to deeper contacts, and the island was home to a group of Rusian artisans who designed multiple pieces of art for the churches on the island.[119] It is likely that these artisans were designing for a Rusian, or Rusian-influenced, audience who had spent time in Rus' or Rusian churches, as discussed in Chapter 1. It has also been surmised that merchants from Gotland built one of the first foreign churches in Novgorod, around the middle of the twelfth century, providing a clear example of the deep connections that existed.[120]

Finally, Denmark, the earliest centralized kingdom in Scandinavia and one of the most powerful, was a major factor in Rusian foreign relations, not just trade, particularly in the twelfth century. Around 1100 the Danish rulers began to shift their focus from west of Jutland to east of Jutland.[121] The western focus had primarily been because of interaction with England, Normandy, and the German Empire, the last relationship beginning even before the Viking age. However, with power to their west being consolidated in the hands of William the Conqueror and his line, the east began to look more appealing. Diplomatically this can be seen in multiple Rusian marriages in the twelfth century, such as the marriage of Ingeborg Mstislavna to Knud Lavard, as well as political involvement to place a Rusian descendant, Waldemar, on the Danish throne.[122] These political arrangements may even have had economic consequences, as the NPL records not only the presence of Danish merchants in 1130 but also that in 1134 (around the time of struggle for succession in Denmark between a Rusian-backed and a non-Rusian-backed candidate) men of Novgorod (potentially merchants) were killed in Denmark.[123] This small sampling of connections with Scandinavia, including the goods, artisans, and merchants, shows the depth and commonplace nature of the trading relations along the Baltic exchange zone, including Rus'.

The Baltic exchange zone, though primarily involving the Rusians, Scandinavians, and Balts in this period, began to involve others as the twelfth century progressed—particularly the Germans and, eventually, the English. We have already discussed trade with the German Empire in relation to the east–west trade route, but the Baltic exchange zone is a separate (though to some extent overlapping) area. In fact, over the course of the twelfth century it appears that Germans replaced or rivaled Scandinavians as the main Rusian trading partners in the Baltic,[124] a development that set the stage for the creation of the Hanseatic League in the next century.[125] These German traders were largely Saxons, although there were also direct connections with Frisia, which developed its own trading route to Novgorod and back at this time.[126] The Saxons displayed a great appreciation for Rusian goods. Theophilus, the pseudonym of a twelfth-century German monk named Roger, who wrote a treatise on handicrafts, implies that the Rusian enamelwork and niello rivaled anything else in Europe.[127]

The best-known German trading port on the Baltic was Lübeck, which was refounded under Henry the Lion in 1158–1159. Henry was Duke of Saxony, and had been the patron of Knud Lavard, husband of Ingeborg Mstislavna mentioned earlier. After a devastating fire, Henry rebuilt Lübeck with the particular mission of creating a German trading center on the Baltic to compete with Gotland for the Rusian trade.[128] According to Helmold, Henry "sent messengers to the cities and kingdoms of the north—Denmark, Sweden, Norway, Russia—offering them peace so that they should have free access to his city of Lübeck."[129] This open invitation dramatically increased Rusian trade with the German Empire. By the end of the twelfth century there was a trading treaty between the Germans and Novgorodians, and connections only increased in the thirteenth century.[130] This can best be illustrated by the high percentage of German versus other foreign goods found in Rus' during this time. V. P. Darkevich, who examined foreign, specifically western, goods in Rus', found that the majority of objects identifiable as western in Rus' can be traced to the German Empire.[131] Many of these goods are bronze, from the bronze-casting centers in Lotharingia and Lower Saxony. Most famous is the bronze bell, one of two German bells from pre-Mongol Rus' that was found in the *podol* in Kiev.[132] There are also German-manufactured (either imported or produced on German models in Rus') bells in other cities, including one that bears a Latin inscription.[133] Silver found in Rus' after the decline of dirham production, which consisted of coins in the eleventh and early twelfth centuries and bars beginning in the twelfth into the thirteenth centuries, was mostly from the German Empire.[134] Copper was also absent in Rus', and had to be imported from the Baltic, either from Sweden or the German Empire, in the form of ingots or wire to be used as raw material for crafting.[135] These numerous German connections, though beginning at the end of the period under discussion here, represent another element of the Baltic exchange zone in which Rus' participated.[136] In addition to the Scandinavian and German connections, Rus' had other trading partners on the Baltic, a large and profitable exchange zone. Cloth from Ypres began to appear in Novgorod in the early twelfth century and became a medium of exchange throughout the Baltic, setting up a period of Flemish trading strength.[137] Similarly, merchants from England began to trade with Rus', and vice versa. Trade between the two had been going since the middle of our period, with English silver supplementing the German silver in Rus', and English tin even being used to manufacture Rusian goods.[138] The presence of actual merchants from England in Rus', or vice versa, mostly appear only after our time period in the beginning of the thirteenth century; however, it is possible that Rusian traders were in England in the eleventh century.[139] This possibility, when considered alongside the Rusians who married Anglo-Saxon and French royalty, becomes a probability, especially considering that such western goods did not just reach merchants and princes in the cities but extended into the countryside.[140]

This Baltic Sea, or northern European, exchange zone was one in which Rus' was particularly at home and functioned for quite some time, beginning even before a Rusian state was created. Through these northern connections, Rusians were tied into a larger trading sphere that gave them access to goods and merchants and gave them an outlet for their own goods. Most important for our purposes, it provided another avenue of access and communication between Rus' and the rest of Europe.

The picture created here is one of a Rus' that participated in multiple zones of economic exchange, including the route from the Varangians to the Greeks, the east–west route from the German Empire through Poland and Bohemia, or Hungary, and also the Baltic Sea community.

This participation included the presence of Rusian goods, merchants, and artisans in all of those areas, as well as German, Byzantine, Scandinavian, and many other foreign merchants, artisans, and goods in Rus'. From this perspective it is clear that Rus' was part and parcel of a larger European trading world, and that the idea of the Dnieper route to Byzantium as "an economic lifeline" is incorrect.[141] This seems to lend weight to Whittow's supposition, quoted at the beginning of this chapter, that the vital nature of the Dnieper route is "an unsubstantiated article of faith" and has more to do with the later Byzantine importance to the ideology of Rus' than with the actual economic evidence from this period.[142]

All of Rus' participated in these economic connections. However, by way of concluding this chapter we will examine the example of Kiev as a European trading center. Thietmar of Merseburg records in his chronicle that Kiev, "that great city," had eight markets and four hundred churches.[143] Though some have found the number of churches to be an exaggeration, there is little reason to suspect that a city the size of Kiev would not have eight marketplaces.[144] A. P. Novoseltsev and V. T. Pashuto, who have done extensive work on Russian medieval trade, found the number to be quite acceptable, adding that Kiev "was one of the biggest cities in the medieval world."[145] Noonan amplified the latter portion of that statement, adding, "There is no doubt that Kiev was one of the major commercial centers of medieval western Eurasia between ca. 900 and 1240."[146] These comments by scholars who work on medieval Russian trade highlight the position of Kiev in the European world and particularly its economic role. Those eight marketplaces were designed not simply to further intra-Rusian commerce, though that was important, but also to serve the long-distance trade routes and the merchants who traveled them.[147] Many of those marketplaces were likely located in the podol, right on the Dnieper River.[148] The podol was home to a variety of Rusian craft centers that created finished products for shipment throughout all three exchange zones.[149] Johan Callmer has even suggested that the layout of Kiev, specifically the fortress and podol, bears a not coincidental resemblance to the cities of Prague and Cracow, which were also key stops on the east–west land route.[150]

As has been shown throughout this work, it is often hard to find references to Europeans from outside of Rus' and Byzantium in the Rusian sources, and thus subtle references have to be interpreted when found. Though mentions of foreign merchants are few, the Rusian chronicles do mention various "gates" of the city, specifically the Polish, Hungarian, and Jewish gates (mentioned above), all three of which delineated trade routes going west from Kiev.[151] It is not much of a stretch to then expand the mentions of a Polish gate to Poles in Rus', especially when we have foreign evidence about Rusian merchants abroad and Hebrew sources about Jewish merchants traveling the same east–west route to and from the German Empire. Similarly, we find offhand references to foreign merchants in the law codes. The Russkaia Pravda mentions foreign merchants in Rus' and the legal and credit provisions that are attached to them, reassuring us that there were indeed foreign merchants in Rus', though we know little about them from Rusian sources.[152] Finally, the *Paterik* of the Kievan Caves Monastery does mention actual merchants, Byzantine and Abkhazian merchants, who had traveled the north–south route from the Crimea and the Black Sea.[153] This largely subtle evidence goes hand in hand with the increasing archaeological finds of foreign goods in Rus', as well as evidence of the growing Rusian merchant class and merchant sector of Kiev.[154] Though I have not summarized the wealth of material on Rusian trade (or truly scratched the surface), the picture created in this chapter showcases the importance of Kiev, not only as a centerpoint of Rus', but as a major European trading city, as well as making the larger point that Rus' was part of multiple exchange routes that tied it, its people, and its goods into the larger European world.

— 5 —

The Micro-Christendom of Rus'

Through the years many scholars have defined the medieval Christian world as Western Europe.[1] Left out of this framework, or, more often, intentionally set in opposition to this idea of Christendom, was the Byzantine Empire and the Orthodox world.[2] However, for most of the Middle Ages this idea of a single Christendom did not actually exist. There were differences between Byzantine and Roman Christianity, but there was not an opposition between East and West—this later polarization was read back into the historical record. In reality, medieval Europe was a hodgepodge of what Peter Brown calls "micro-Christendoms."[3] Brown's theory will be discussed in more depth below, but, in short, it posits that prior to the papal reform that began in the late eleventh century under Pope Gregory VII and continued through the twelfth century, there were multiple regional micro-Christendoms, each of which thought itself to be a reflection of a perfect Christianity.[4]

The importance of such a theory for the study of the medieval world should be obvious. Much of the subtext of medieval political history is religious history and the history of religious conflict, domination, and repression. Adam of Bremen's *History of the Archbishops of Hamburg-Bremen* tells the story of the archbishops as a means to reinforce the power of their See, but also explicitly as a way to reinforce their claim to control over the entire northern world.[5] Embedded within this wonderful text are multiple stories of conflict between micro-Christendoms as political and religious ends and means were merged to work for control of, or independence from, another kingdom. As is often the case, the histories of Scandinavia and Rus' are similar to each other in this regard. The Rusian princes existed in a world where the main ties were with the Scandinavian kingdoms, with their mix of paganism and semi-independent Latin Christianity; central Europe, largely dominated by the Latin Christianity of the German Empire; and the Orthodox Byzantine Empire, in that order. Traditional histories have focused on the conversion of Rus' to Orthodoxy, relying heavily on the fanciful tale of Vladimir's examination of the various faiths, and have incorporated early modern and modern history back into the eleventh and twelfth centuries, creating Rusian dependence on Constantinople and full conversion to Byzantine Orthodoxy.[6] If, instead, we view this situation through the lens of Brown's theory of micro-Christendoms, our understanding becomes clearer and we can see a more accurate picture of medieval Rus'. That picture shows us a kingdom bordered by multiple micro-Christendoms, each with its own type of Christianity, each trying to influence the other—in other words, a multipolar religious world.[7]

This chapter primarily deals with the micro-Christendom of Rus', but in order to achieve this goal there are several other points that must be addressed. The first section of this chapter deals with Peter Brown's theory of micro-Christendoms and some of his examples. This creates a common ground for later discussion of specific examples of micro-Christendoms and also illustrates some commonalities between Brown's examples and my own. Next, the chapter briefly addresses Scandinavia and Bulgaria as two other examples of European micro-Christendoms that impact heavily on Rus'. Scandinavia was Christianized later than most of Europe, at approximately the same time as Rus' (Norway and Denmark before Rus', Sweden and Iceland after Rus'), and thus its example bears chronologically on the Rusian situation. More so, the Rusians at this time were still strongly influenced by their Scandinavian roots in their manner of thinking and governance, and the Scandinavians faced a similar situation of having multiple micro-Christendoms to draw upon in their process of conversion. The conversion of Bulgaria is widely known because of its inclusion in a variety of primary sources, including the famous letter of Pope Nicholas to Khan Boris detailing what it meant to convert, but its importance to our cause here is just as great.[8] To accomplish his goal of converting his people and bringing them into the Christian world not as subjects, but on their own terms, Khan Boris actively played two micro-Christendoms, Rome and Constantinople, off one another, while also dealing with a third, the East

Frankish Empire.[9] The situation Boris found himself in—between powers, with a goal of maintaining independence—was the same role that Rusian rulers found themselves in later. These two examples both are better documented than the Rusian example, and thus, because of their multiple similarities, illustrate aspects of the Rusian micro-Christendom that can be assumed but not verified.

The second section of this chapter deals with the micro-Christendom of Rus'. In the period discussed in this book, Rus' maintained relations with various micro-Christendoms. Even while converting to Christianity through Byzantine intermediaries Vladimir was exchanging envoys with the pope in Rome, Iziaslav Iaroslavich paid fealty to the pope, and later in the eleventh century Vsevolod Iaroslavich, ruler of Kiev, was involved in the complex pan-European situation involving the pope, the anti-pope, and the patriarch of Constantinople. These are just some of the major political highlights of such interaction. On a smaller scale, the Sázava monastery in Bohemia, which was a Latin monastery of the Slavonic rite, had close ties with Rus', and there were liturgies and saints' lives exchanged between them.[10] The kingdom of Rus' occupied a position between multiple kingdoms, two empires, and at least three micro-Christendoms. The Rusians' goal was to create a powerful independent state of their own, and thus subjugation, whether political, military, or religious, was never an option. To maintain their independence and to create their own micro-Christendom, the Rusian rulers used input from the various micro-Christendoms around them. This chapter is intended to examine the Christianization of Rus' and Rusian Christianity in the light of the idea of these micro-Christendoms and in regard to the place of Rus' in medieval Europe.

Micro-Christendoms

In the later Middle Ages, Christendom was an entity that could be defined as all of the kingdoms that were under the religious aegis of the Latin pope. This world stretched from the far north of Iceland, England, and Scandinavia down through western and central Europe to the tip of Italy. However, this unity did not exist throughout the whole Middle Ages. As Peter Brown writes, in the seventh century "Christianity was a patchwork of adjacent, but separate, 'micro-Christendoms.'

Each region needed to feel that it possessed, if in diminished form, the essence of an entire Christian culture."[11] These micro-Christendoms combined their own local traditions of Christianity with pagan hold-overs and what they knew of Roman practices to create a Christianity that they believed was the most correct. Despite this, these micro-Christendoms still believed they were part of the universal Christian Church. They did not have a sense of themselves as other (whether that is heretic or schismatic), thus the concept of micro-Christendom is a modern one that is being used to help explain phenomena that occurred in the past.[12] This view of the medieval religious world is often not accepted, despite an acknowledgment of the plurality of "Christianities" because of "anachronistic assumptions about what constitutes normative Christianity."[13] These "anachronistic assumptions" will be challenged here especially in regard to Rusian Christianity.

Added to the religious dilemma that these kingdoms faced were the political consequences of whatever their decision might be in regard to which kingdom could Christianize them. Before delving into this in more detail, it must be noted that the conversions discussed in this chapter are what are referred to as ecclesiastical conversions, which are "often the consequence of socio-political strategies, power, economics, intellectual or psychological issues, and other motives or expediencies that have, in fact, very little to do with religious feelings."[14] And though conversion due to true religious feeling and religious motives (what can be referred to as inner conversion) can be found throughout medieval history, including at the royal level, it is the more geopolitical reasoning behind conversion that will be examined here. Because of these social, political, and economic reasons behind medieval royal conversion, historians for years have practically assumed that whoever Christianized a kingdom gained tacit control over that kingdom.[15] That control was enforced by the appointment of bishops by the Christianizing power, bishops who were loyal to those who appointed them rather than to those they ministered to. This created a strong foreign power center in a kingdom that could potentially have strong political consequences for the orientation of the kingdom's foreign policy interests.[16] Brown obliquely acknowledges these concerns in his discussion of micro-Christendoms when he addresses the lengths to which micro-Christendoms went in order to find their own way. These Christian kingdoms all "faced the same problem of creating an ordered and self-sufficient Christian culture,"[17] "self-sufficient" being the key term. The intention of these rulers who opted to convert their kingdoms to Christianity was that their kingdom would become fully Christian, but not under the auspices of any foreign power that might challenge their authority. The ways they came up with to meet those ends are fascinating, and recurred throughout the Middle Ages.

The primary weapon in this fight for control was the creation of native religious centers that rivaled the established Christian cities of Jerusalem, Constantinople, and Rome. Brown discusses two seventh-century examples of this practice, and more occur later in the Middle Ages.[18] Brown's first example is from Britain, where Archbishop Wilfrid of York tried to create a Rome in Britain.[19] Wilfrid, who had personally visited Rome, convinced the king of Northumbria, Oswy, to create his own religious center at Hexham.[20] There they built a basilica, the first of its kind in the northern world, dedicated to St. Peter—saints' relics and depictions of the keys of St. Peter featured prominently. Brown states that "the great church at Hexham was to be a 'Rome' of its own, placed within reach of the Christian populations of northern Britain."[21] This emphasizes the importance of such a symbol. Rome was far away, and thus its relevance to northern Britain was not clear. This was a problem throughout the Christian world as cities attempted to write themselves into ecclesiastical history. Such cities and regions "proclaimed their antiquity through a variety of found and imported objects and rituals that could connect them to the history they wanted."[22] For Northumbria to have its own religious center allowed it to have a place in the larger Christian world and be tied into the map of sacred history, and showed its level of ecclesiastical development and devotion. This was an essential requirement for a micro-Christendom: they wanted to have, or create, their own holy centers (a local locus of worship) that would allow them to have religious legitimacy of their own. Attempts to establish political or ecclesiastical/political independence flowed from this in many cases.

Brown's second example is from the Visigothic kingdoms in Iberia. Bishop Isidore of Seville was an enthusiastic supporter of the creation of a micro-Christendom, working to create a Christian "Holy Commonwealth" that he hoped would rival the one centered in Constantinople.[23]

Brown believes that this imitation was quite conscious. To achieve their desired religious and political ends, the Visigoths had to be independent of foreign spheres of interest, but this required the creation of a central political hierarchy, which was relatively easy, and the creation of a central religious hierarchy, which was not so easy. The best way to do the latter was, as in Hexham, to create a religious center as rival to or equal of a foreign religious center.[24] This allowed the people to view a local religious phenomenon, rather than envying or idealizing/idolizing one both far away and in another kingdom. Spain eventually took this step, and "Toledo [the new royal capital] was spoken of as a 'new Jerusalem.' Its hilltop crowned with palaces and shrines, it was a solemn urban theater where bishops and kings together acted out the great hope of a self-sufficient 'micro-Christendom.'"[25] This "great hope," was shared by many kingdoms of Europe that were working to ensure their own religious and political independence from foreign rulers.

The creation of the Carolingian Empire merged multiple micro-Christendoms that had existed in western Europe. This merger created what, for many people, was the only Christendom that mattered, but regional micro-Christendoms did still continue to exist.[26] The other primary religious empire was somewhat larger than a regional micro-Christendom, and at this time, in Brown's reckoning, transitioned from being the Eastern Roman Empire into the Byzantine Empire.[27] Byzantine Christianity had always run a slightly different course than Roman Christianity, which could be said of most micro-Christendoms. At this time there was a great deal of ferment in Byzantium—the iconoclastic controversy was playing out, and the various heresies, such as monophysitism and monotheletism, were still present at places in the empire. Brown is correct when he says that Byzantium emerged from these struggles with its own unique religious identity. Also standing in opposition to Carolingian Christendom was the Christendom of Anglo-Saxon England. The English had many religious traditions to draw from and had worked at creating a synthesis that suited their needs. They were not interested in being drawn into a continental union.[28] This independent spirit was not only religious, but political as well, more evidence of the interdependence of the two. Offa of Mercia, a contemporary of Charlemagne, called himself "emperor of Britain."[29] Both religious and political independence would continue until at least the eleventh century, at which point England began to send missionaries and missionary bishops throughout the Baltic world. These missionaries opposed the Christendom represented by the Ottonian and Salian empires, and represented a choice for Scandinavia that will be discussed more below.

In the early Middle Ages, there were "many 'micro-Christendoms' which stretched, like so many beads on a string, from Iona across Europe and the Middle East to Iran and Central Asia."[30] These micro-Christendoms shared "a common pool of images and attitudes inherited from ancient Christianity," but they interpreted them in their own ways.[31] This resulted in micro-Christendoms that incorporated unique traditions into a common base of ancient Christian practice. Local saints were incorporated into the menologies,[32] and their histories were written and read throughout specific regions but did not spread to the other micro-Christendoms. Varieties of liturgical practice were formulated, each based on different readings of the Bible and the church fathers, such that the service as practiced in one place was not always identical to that practiced in another.[33] There was also a variety of opinions on language and ecclesiastical marriage peppered throughout the micro-Christendoms. From one to another, the church, its practices, and its officers were mutually recognizable, but differences did exist. When politics entered the picture, those differences were magnified, and these variations in practice and liturgy went from local quirks to micro-Christendoms.

Micro-Christendom and Scandinavia

As Scandinavia began to be Christianized, the question arose as to where their archbishopric should be housed. The answer was delivered by the papacy, in conjunction with the German emperors, who placed them under the archbishop in Hamburg-Bremen. This archbishop had responsibilities to the pope in Rome, his ecclesiastical superior, and to the German emperor, who was quite often his personal patron and sometimes a relative. This was best symbolized by the confirmation process for a new archbishop, in which he received his pallium from the pope and his pastoral staff from the emperor.[34] The placement of the archbishopric for Scandinavia in territory controlled by the German emperor was a clear statement that Scandinavian Christianization was to be undertaken by German missionaries and that the eventual bishops in Scandinavia would be subject to a German archbishop. This would give the German emperor a certain amount of political control in the newly Christianized Scandinavia. Preventing the growth of that political control became a passion for Scandinavian rulers and home-grown ecclesiastics almost from the beginning of Christianization, especially as the archbishop was specifically given powers to appoint bishops, contrary to the wishes of the local rulers.[35] Some of the ways in which Scandinavian rulers struggled to define themselves as separate will be discussed in this section as a means of portraying the creation of a micro-Christendom that occurred in the same time frame as that of Rus'.

There are multiple steps in the process of Christianization of a kingdom. In the medieval world the first step was for the king to convert to Christianity.[36] This was followed by a gradual conversion of the people, beginning with the cities and only later moving to the countryside. Within this framework the important question is, Who is converting the people? In Scandinavia there were a few choices for priests. Those sent out by the archbishop of Hamburg-Bremen were the primary option, and they usually bore gifts to encourage local rulers to pay homage to the archbishop.[37] Priests from Anglo-Saxon England, who spoke a similar language and whose conversion carried no political ties, were the second and more popular choice, and in fact, based on "religious vocabulary," England played a large role in the Christianization of Norway (as will be discussed below).[38] The importance of cultural and linguistic ties was emphasized by Sven Estridsson, king of Denmark and informant of Adam of Bremen, in a conversation with Archbishop Adalbert where he said that people "could more easily be converted by men like them in language and customs rather than by persons unacquainted with their ways and strange to their kind."[39] This was an added incentive for Scandinavian rulers to bring in Anglo-Saxon priests and bishops, who had much more in common with them than the German priests did, and shows an understanding that though conversion to Christianity requires wholesale cultural change, there are differing levels of severity of change (culture shock, if you will) available to converters.[40] Also in the mix were priests from Rus' and potentially Byzantium, who rarely appear in the secondary sources on Scandinavian conversion but whose existence can be inferred from brief mentions in a few primary sources.[41] What the linguistic and cultural similarity of those Rusian and/or Byzantine priests may have been can only be surmised based upon their origins. If they originated in Rus', there would have been a great deal of cultural similarity, though no linguistic similarity if the missionaries were using Old East Slavic. If the priests originated in Byzantium, there would have been neither linguistic nor cultural similarity with any Scandinavian kingdom.

The problem of priests and missionaries was a large one for Scandinavian kings. Knud the Great, after his conquest of England in the early eleventh century, brought English bishops with him back to Denmark. Knud was creating a northern empire by controlling Denmark, Norway, England, and parts of Sweden, and probably had little interest in being controlled ecclesiastically by his southern neighbor. This was a common problem as religion and politics intermingled and clashed—religious control often became caught up with political control. Roger II of Sicily, for example, commissioned the writing of "the Orders and Ranks of the Patriarchal Thrones" as a way to signal to the pope the possibility that the Sicilian Church could move away from Rome to Constantinople if it (or Roger) so chose.[42] Though they did not do so, the threat of a change in allegiance of micro-Christendoms was always there. For Knud, the process was stopped before it got truly started, as agents of Archbishop Unwan of Hamburg-Bremen apprehended one of Knud's English bishops, Gerbrand, and made him, through what means is unknown, pay homage to Unwan and forsake the archbishop of Canterbury, who had consecrated him, in favor of the archbishop of Hamburg-Bremen. Upon Gerbrand's release, Unwan scolded Knud for bringing outside bishops into territory claimed by his see.[43] The life of a missionary bishop was a dangerous one, which is why they normally traveled as part of the king's retinue.[44] This had the added advantage of allowing them higher visibility and taking them around the kingdom on a regular basis. Bishops who did not stay with their kings were made to pay the price, usually by pagans,[45] but occasionally by rival churchmen as illustrated here. Knud's attempt to bring in bishops who were outside of Hamburg-Bremen's control was the first of many attempts by Scandinavian kings to free themselves from German dominion.

The most famous example of a Scandinavian king attempting to establish his independence is that of Harald Hardrada, king of Norway.

Harald as a youth served in Rus' and campaigned in Byzantium and throughout the Mediterranean.[46] This adventuresome existence introduced him to a variety of cultural inputs and allowed him to travel through multiple micro-Christendoms.[47] When king of Norway, he brought in numerous priests and bishops from outside the purview of the archbishop of Hamburg-Bremen. This was not a new phenomenon in Scandinavia, as was noted above, though especially in Norway, as Harald's brother, St. Olaf, had also brought English churchmen back with him to Norway to assist in the Christianization process. In fact, it was one of those English bishops, Grimkell, who was instrumental in commemorating Olaf as a saint after his death at Stiklastaðir.[48] In addition to bringing in foreign priests, though, Harald also sent local priests to England and Normandy to be consecrated and sent back to Norway, an act that particularly outraged Archbishop Adalbert of Hamburg-Bremen, who had one of these bishops kidnapped on his way home from Rome and held in Hamburg until he chose to forsake his previous allegiances and pay homage to Adalbert and the see of Hamburg-Bremen.[49] At this point Adalbert had him released and sent on his way with many fine gifts. This pattern of events seems to show that Harald was attempting to create for himself a clergy that was independent of foreign, particularly German, political influence. This interpretation is buttressed by Adam of Bremen's quotation of Harald, in which Harald states "that he did not know of any archbishop or authority in Norway save only Harold [Harald] himself."[50] Harald may have only been expanding on the common eleventh-century idea that a king who founded a cathedral would be allowed to appoint the bishop who served there and that said bishop would be loyal to the king.[51] This attitude began to change in Europe under the reforming pope Gregory VII and was most visible in the Investiture Controversy between him and German emperor Henry IV. However, even a decade or so before that, Harald received a stern letter from Pope Alexander II telling him to submit to the will and authority of the archbishop of Hamburg-Bremen.[52] The letter from Alexander II is dated either 1061 or 1065, and if the latter, Harald would not have had much chance to comply as he died soon after in an abortive attempt to gain the English throne. Even if time had allowed for a response, an affirmative one would have been unlikely. Harald had made considerable effort to maintain or create an ecclesiastical community in Norway that was not bound to a foreign power. Perhaps such an idea was home-grown or had evolved from a common royal view of filling open bishop-rics, or perhaps it came from years in Byzantine service. Certainly no power in Byzantium was above the emperor at this time, not even the pa-triarch of Constantinople. In fact, some interpret the statement in Cecau-menus's *Strategikon* that Harald "is said to have remained loyal to the Greeks once he returned to his native country" to mean that Harald had converted to Byzantine Christianity and chose to remain that way after his return home from Byzantium and Rus'.[53] Harald may very well have followed different Christian rites while in Rus', Constantinople, Jeru-salem, and throughout his travels, and this may be where he grew so attached to the idea of a church that was independent from foreign in-fluence, but this did not set him apart from or in opposition to Latin Christians (or other micro-Christendoms) in any way.

Sweden has always existed in a borderland; it is the border between the Finns and the Scandinavians, between the micro-Christendoms of Rus' and Scandinavia, and later between the West and the East. The conversion of Sweden happened after the conversion of the rest of Scan-dinavia and of Rus', and there are indications that Rusian and/or Byz-antine priests had some effect on it.[54] Olof Skötkonnung, the first docu-mentable Christian king of Sweden (or part of Sweden)[55] may have had "Orthodox" influences.[56] One of the most interesting examples of this borderland existence of Sweden comes in the person of Bishop Os-mund. Osmund was of Scandinavian heritage (perhaps from England) and trained at Bremen but chose to leave and attempt to be consecrated in Rome.[57] Possibly due to the interference of the archbishop of Hamburg-Bremen, this was refused, and Osmund was later consecrated by an archbishop of "*Polonia.*"[58] The translator of the English-language version of Adam of Bremen translates this as Poland and adds the footnote that he was consecrated by Stephen I, archbishop of Gniezno (1038–1052).[59] Peter Sawyer, following an earlier tradition, believes that Polonia was more likely the land of the Polianians, which was the territory of Kiev.[60] Though Sawyer's conjecture is possible, the Polianian etymology is not ideal in this situation; there were already extensive political ties between Rus' and Sweden at this time, with the Swedish princess Ingigerd mar-ried to the ruler of Kiev, Iaroslav, as well as the extensive retinue that she brought with her.[61] There were also religious ties during this same period, as shown by the Church of St. Olof erected in Kiev in the eleventh century. Further, a priest at Ingigerd's son Vladimir's court in Novgorod left Rus' (after the deaths of both Ingigerd and Vladimir in the mid-eleventh century), and went to Sweden to perform the same role, indicating a continuing ecclesiastical connection between the two.[62] The debate over where Osmund was consecrated continues, but is largely peripheral to our purposes here. What is important to note is that Osmund was not consecrated in the hierarchy of the church at Rome or at Bremen, and Adam refers to him as *"acephalum,"*[63] independent of any Church.

After consecration Osmund traveled to Sweden, where he was installed as bishop (or possibly archbishop, as he had a cross carried before him in archiepiscopal style) in Sigtuna by King Emund "Gamular,"[64] the son of Olof Skötkonnung. Archbishop Adalbert found out about this when his legates arrived in Sigtuna with the Bremen-consecrated candidate for the bishopric, Adalward.[65] These legates and their bishop were thrown out by King Emund and Osmund.[66] The legates reported that Osmund had "by his unsound teaching of our faith corrupted the barbarians."[67] The meaning of "unsound teaching" is precisely unknown, but a case can be made that Osmund's teachings were not in accord with those taught at Bremen, and thus not those practiced in that particular micro-Christendom, but still acknowledged as teachings of "our faith."[68] If this is the case, it only makes more sense why King Emund defended Osmund. By having Osmund he gained an archbishop for his newly Christianized kingdom, which made him ecclesiastically independent from the German Empire, while allowing him to retain Christianity and removing the need, or impetus, for conversion from the south. A fellow Scandinavian as bishop, moreover, was not just of foreign political use, but internally he might be more inclined to support the king and not upset the local beliefs. It has even been advanced that Osmund was part of a system that utilized the runic script as a vernacular alternative to Latin, a practice discontinued once the Swedish Church came under Roman control.[69] It seems then that, as Peter Sawyer put it, "the Swedish king, like Jaroslav [Iaroslav] of Kiev, was attempting to create a 'national' church,"[70] an idea clearly in line with the creation of a Scandinavian micro-Christendom. Sweden was out of communion with Hamburg-Bremen until sometime in 1060, when following a massive famine that devastated northern Europe, a new bishop was invited in, perhaps in an attempt to cure the famine.[71] This was under the auspices of the new king, Stenkil, who had been the only Swede to favorably respond to Adalbert's legates when they came to visit King Emund, according to Adam of Bremen.[72] However, Stenkil's reign was short-lived (and the bishop rarely present), and after Stenkil's death in 1066 there was civil war, and his eventual successor, a son named Inge who had been living in Rus', removed the Swedish Church once again from the aegis of Hamburg-Bremen, but may have brought in priests from elsewhere, as Harald Hardraada had.[73] The church in Sweden would remain outside of the control of Hamburg-Bremen, negotiating directly with the Papacy in the 1080s, who considered it newly converted[74] and eventually subordinated it to the first Scandinavian archbishopric at Lund in the early twelfth century.[75]

As portrayed here, the defender of the Roman Church in both the case of Norway and that of Sweden is Archbishop Adalbert of Hamburg-Bremen. However, his own orthodoxy is in question in multiple ways. Adalbert's ambition was to create a patriarchate of the north, with himself as patriarch.[76] He even turned down the papacy in 1046 to pursue an independent patriarchate for himself.[77] Adam chronicles the changes that Adalbert made, "warranted by what usage of the Romans or of the Greeks I do not know" with some skepticism, including his love of incense, candles, and chant, all outside of the norm of practice in the eleventh-century Roman Church.[78] Though also critical of Adalbert's ambition in this regard, Adam does twice compare Hamburg-Bremen to Rome as he attempts to highlight its importance as *the* center of Christianity for the northern world.[79] It might be that Adalbert was attempting to create his own micro-Christendom and heartily resented the attempts of the Norwegians and Swedes to thwart his plans by doing the same thing.

Apart from large-scale royal interference in ecclesiastical matters, there are also small indications that local priests and bishops were open to creating their own micro-Christendoms through the inclusion of foreign texts that may not have been included in the canon used in Hamburg-Bremen. Many of these traces can only be dated back to the late eleventh and twelfth century, when large-scale (in medieval terms) literacy came to Scandinavia. One of the most interesting and earliest examples is a translation of the *Vita* of the Forty Armenian Martyrs of

Sebaste into Old Norse.[80] This is only one of a handful of Armenian mentions that appear in Scandinavia, and there is always the possibility that this text came via the Old Church Slavonic version, which may have existed in Rus'.[81] In the Grágás, the Icelandic laws, Icelanders were allowed to attend services by both "Armenian" and "Russian" priests.[82] Where these priests came from is a question open to discussion. Returning to the subject of saints' lives, images from Byzantine saints' lives were incorporated into iconography in churches in Gotland, Sweden, and Denmark.[83] These images, as well as those of the Last Judgment (a popular scene), were done in a Byzantine style, reflecting both a foreign influence in their commission as well as the possible presence of foreign artists.[84] Devotional artwork was as important to the lay public as texts, perhaps more so, as the majority of the congregation could not read or understand the liturgy but could understand the images decorating the churches. Those images were also used as teaching tools for the illiterate, so the inclusion of Byzantine saints and Byzantine images reflects an inclusion of those ideas in the church teachings.

As the reforming papacy grew in strength in the twelfth century, its reach eventually encompassed Scandinavia, which became a part of a united Christendom under the Roman pope for at least a few hundred years until the Reformation. Before that time, however, Scandinavian Christianity, through the efforts of local kings as well as through a confluence of events, maintained an independent path. The creation of a Scandinavian micro-Christendom, or multiple micro-Christendoms, allowed the kings and people to resist southern domination and to follow their own path for quite some time. This was a model that was open for Rus' to observe as it went through the same experience at the same time. It was vitally important to Rus' as well, because their micro-Christendom abutted and overlapped with this one, creating a borderland in the eastern Baltic.

Bulgaria's Bid for Ecclesiastical Independence

In the early Middle Ages, Bulgaria was located between two major powers—the East Frankish Empire and the Byzantine Empire. Bulgaria used this situation to its advantage, initially arranging political and military alliances with both sides as need dictated. In the ninth century, conversion entered into the picture, and balancing relations with the two neighboring empires became more complicated. The events of Bulgaria's conversion to Christianity are essential to an understanding of Rusian conversion, for a number of reasons. The first is the most obvious—both Rus' and Bulgaria ended up converting to a Byzantine form of Christianity. The second is that, like Bulgaria, Rus' also maintained politico-ecclesiastical contacts with Rome, the German successors to the East Frankish Empire, and Constantinople, something not every medieval kingdom did.[85] The third reason has to do with the importance, or perceived importance, of Bulgarian Christianity's later effect on Rusian Christianity. Francis Thomsen and others have argued that Rusian Christianity was not Byzantine, but rather Bulgarian.[86] Which is to say that the Bulgarians implemented a Slavonic form of Byzantine Christianity that was then transferred to Rus' on their conversion, thereby simplifying the process. Thus it seems necessary to take a close look at the influences and motives behind Bulgaria's struggle for conversion and ecclesiastical independence, to help understand the less well-documented Rusian case.

In the mid-ninth century Khan Boris ruled a pagan Bulgaria that was composed of both Turkic Bulgars and Slavs. Boris reasoned that through the process of conversion he could solidify his control over both groups within his country, and so in the 860s he decided to convert to Christianity.[87] As all such decisions were, this decision was at least partly political; when he made a move toward the Franks, it was interpreted by the Byzantines as a move away from them. This would only be logical, as the Byzantines and the Bulgarians had been at war off and on for numerous years. In 862 at Tuln, Boris signed an alliance with Louis the German against Rastislav of Moravia.[88] Included in the agreement was a stipulation that Boris and his people would convert to Christianity. Not included but implied was that Christianity would be brought in by Frankish priests and bishops and that this would gain Bulgaria an ally against Byzantium. This alliance was soon countered by Byzantium, who allied with Rastislav of Moravia and agreed to send him priests, namely the now-famous Cyril and Methodius.[89] More momentously, after fending off a Muslim attack, Byzantine emperor Michael III invaded Bulgaria in 864 without much resistance.[90] Under threat, Khan Boris accepted baptism from Byzantine priests and took the emperor's name, Michael, as his baptismal name.[91] This was a victory for Byzantium but an unhappy end for Boris on multiple levels. Many of his boyars revolted against him, both because of their forced conversion and the kingdom's alliance with Byzantium, with whom they were more accustomed to having an adversarial relationship.[92]

The boyars may have had some justification in their anger about conversion to Byzantine Christianity. As soon as Boris converted, Patriarch Photius and Emperor Michael began to treat Boris and Bulgaria as if they were their personal possessions.[93] Byzantine priests flooded the country and began to institute a policy of immediate change in religious practice and life, including widespread use of Greek language and importation of Byzantine customs.[94] While conversion was certainly a process of immense cultural change as one religion and way of life was replaced with another, there were (as discussed in the last section in regard to Scandinavia) multiple ways to go about that. As will be seen below, the Roman Church was much more amenable to a slow and steady progression of conversion, including the cooptation of pagan holy places and holy days. This decreased the rate of rebellion and apostasy and allowed for a more gradual, but full, conversion to the new religion and its practices.[95]

Though Boris could not countenance any revolt against him, he agreed that the situation was untenable. He was facing the same situation as all converting rulers in the Middle Ages—he wanted Christianity, in this case to unify his kingdom, but did not want to subject himself to a foreign power. His attempts at seeking religious independence from Byzantium, including creating his own patriarchate, were met with refusal and metaphors comparing Boris and Bulgaria to children who needed guidance.[96] Boris acted on his displeasure and sent out two separate envoys, one to the pope in Rome, the other to Louis the German in Regensburg.[97] The purpose of these envoys was to request an independent ecclesiastical establishment staffed by priests and bishops from those micro-Christendoms. That Boris sent out two embassies rather than just one to Rome illustrates clearly the nature of his view of Christianity in that time period. His baptism and that of his people was valid and entered them into the Christian world, but the question remained which micro-Christendom offered Boris the best choice, one that would allow him the degree of ecclesiastical independence he required, treat him as he believed he deserved to be treated, and work best for his people. Both of Boris's embassies returned successful, further illustrating the point that converting a kingdom or creating the ecclesiastical framework in a newly converted kingdom was a prize worth having. The papal delegation arrived in November 866, headed by Formosus of Porto. Boris welcomed their arrival and at their insistence began expelling the Byzantine clergy from throughout Bulgaria.[98] Placing second was the Frankish embassy led by Bishop Hermanrich of Passau, which arrived in early 867. Though they wished to stay, the papal envoys asked Boris to expel them as well, which he did. Boris felt safe in his assumption that should he need a check on papal power, he had one (if not two) readily available.[99] This knowledge allowed him to negotiate from a position of strength with all of the kingdoms interested in being his purveyor of Christianity.

The Roman delegation made progress in Christianizing Bulgaria, and late in 867 Boris sent an envoy to Rome to ask that Formosus be named Archbishop of Bulgaria.[100] An independent archbishopric was something Boris had required in his negotiations with his various ecclesiastical vendors. Pope Nicholas I was concerned that Boris and Formosus would turn against him and truly gain ecclesiastical independence, so he denied Boris's request, leaving the post of archbishop vacant. Nicholas died before his envoys reached Boris, and Boris had to reopen negotiations with his successor, Hadrian. At this time other political considerations intruded, specifically Muslim armies that were attacking southern Italy. The papacy, powerless to protect itself, was reliant on Byzantine armies for assistance, and so Hadrian's relations with Boris were much cooler than Nicholas's had been.[101] The interrelationship between religion, foreign policy, and domestic policy in this situation is remarkable and illustrates the complexity required in studying medieval conversion, which historically has not been well recognized.[102] In February 868, Hadrian recalled his bishops from Bulgaria, including Formosus, and sent in their place a subdeacon named Sylvester to become archbishop of Bulgaria, thereby demonstrating his disregard for Boris's preferences.[103] Boris, understandably angry, began negotiations with Byzantium as a means of showing that he had other options available to him, and sent Sylvester back to Rome with the demand that Formosus or Marinus, another bishop of his acquaintance, be named archbishop.[104] The clear breakdown in relations between

Rome and Bulgaria can be traced to the death of Pope Nicholas and, perhaps more importantly, Boris's realization that he was not going to get everything he desired. In the early days of Christianization Boris had received a letter from Patriarch Photius of Constantinople filled with high-sounding language that did not seem relevant to the needs of either Boris or his people. This letter was filled with detailed references to scripture and the church fathers and was rather condescending.[105] In contrast to this, when Boris wrote to Pope Nicholas I with questions regarding details on his conversion and that of his people, Nicholas responded in detailed form, answering even Boris's difficult doctrinal questions with moderation.[106] In addition to ecclesiastical independence, it was good treatment that Boris was looking for, and Nicholas provided this, at least in the wooing stage. Had Nicholas lived, he would most likely have continued his course of denying Boris his choice of candidates for the archbishopric and made the same choice as his successor Hadrian to rely on the Byzantines for military protection, as there was no other option.

Boris's turn away from the papacy was motivated by the clear resolve of the papacy to not give him his choice of candidates and their cooling interest in Bulgaria. This does not immediately explain the turn toward Byzantium, though, as the Franks could have been chosen just as easily. One of the possible motivations for Boris was the creation of the Slavonic Liturgy by Cyril and Methodius for the Moravians. This liturgy would clearly appeal to the majority of Boris's people and grant him linguistic independence, solving one of the problems raised by his boyars earlier. However, the Frankish Church was opposed to the Slavonic Liturgy, more on the political grounds that it removed people from Frankish control than on any ecclesiastical grounds.[107] Both the Byzantine and Roman churches approved the use of the Slavonic Liturgy, and so they were the two viable options if Boris wanted to make use of this new creation.[108] At the Eighth Ecumenical Council held at Constantinople in 869–870, the council, led by the patriarchs of the eastern churches, decided, against the wishes of the Roman representatives, that control of the Bulgarian Church should be passed to the diocese of Constantinople, as per the request of Bulgarian representatives.[109] Thus the Bulgarian Church recognized the supremacy of the patriarch of Constantinople, but they had also attained some of what Boris had wanted. They were able to have their own archbishop, who along with his bishops had a measure of independence from Byzantine control because of the rank they were granted in the ecclesiastical hierarchy.[110]

The story of the creation of the Bulgarian Church does not end there, however. Ten years after the first synod, Rome and Constantinople met again and passed control of the Bulgarian Church back to Rome without consulting with the Bulgarians.[111] Boris was unhappy about the decision and would not agree to expel the Byzantine clergy in the country or to force them to pay homage to Rome instead of Constantinople.[112] Instead matters remained as they were, perhaps as the patriarch of Constantinople had guessed they would when he allowed Rome dominion over the Bulgarian Church. Boris received a gift when in 885 Methodius's disciples, Clement and Naum, appeared with many others on his border asking for asylum.[113] They swiftly set about Slavonicising the clergy and putting the Slavonic Liturgy in place throughout Bulgaria allowing Boris to ease the Byzantine (Greek-speaking) clergy out of Bulgaria or into a secondary position as a new Bulgarian (Slavonic-speaking) clergy came to the fore.[114] At long last, Boris had gained what he wanted. Over the course of twenty years he had taken his kingdom through various struggles and negotiations with the German Empire, the Roman papacy, and the Byzantine Empire so that he and his kingdom could reach a point at which they had a certain measure of ecclesiastical independence from their surrounding kingdoms. Boris's legacy was strong, and within the next fifty years Bulgaria would have an independent patriarchate and an independent micro-Christendom.[115]

Like the Scandinavian kings, Khan Boris was committed to accepting Christianity, but he understood that there were serious political ramifications involved in the selection of the source of his Christianity and more importantly the bishops and priests who delivered it on a daily basis. To ensure that he and his kingdom would receive the best possible arrangement, he negotiated with the three micro-Christendoms nearest him for leverage that would allow him to maintain a measure of ecclesiastical independence. His success at playing one off against another shows the extreme political nature of the process and illustrates the point that though religious conversion could indenture the converted to the converter, it did not have to. Kings and khans could take steps to ensure that they maintained their independence through

him, for comparison's sake Vladimir needed one as well. His well-known grandmother was chosen for the task and posthumously made into a mighty Helen to complete the Constantine-Helen/Vladimir-Ol'ga dyad.[126] This does not, however, invalidate all of the information that was included in the *PVL* entry. Ol'ga did indeed go to Constantinople—that information is also recorded in foreign sources, including a more reliable and contemporary Byzantine source, which will be discussed in more depth shortly.[127]

We must also consider an interesting rebuttal of the emperor and of Byzantium that is placed at the end of the *PVL* entry. When Ol'ga returned home from Constantinople, the emperor sent her an envoy asking her to provide what was agreed upon, mainly trade goods.[128] (My belief, which is shared by others, is that this mission was in fact primarily a trading mission in which religion played a role.)[129] Ol'ga instead refused with a witty rejoinder.[130] Though just having returned from Constantinople after completing some type of negotiations there, upon returning to Kiev Ol'ga distanced herself and Rus' from Byzantium, first by refusing the emperor his trade goods and then by turning to German emperor Otto I.

Although some of the story of her trip may be invented tradition, Ol'ga did, in fact, go to Constantinople, and some of the details of the trip were recorded in *De cerimoniis aulae Byzantinae* (henceforth, *De cerimoniis*), a collection of rituals and appearances of the emperor, ostensibly created as a guide to ceremonial practices but extremely useful as a historical source.[131] Ol'ga's trip is recorded in one other Byzantine source, the account of John Scylitzes, and is mentioned in western sources.[132] Of singular interest in the *De cerimoniis* description is the list of Ol'ga's guests in Constantinople. The majority of her retinue were merchants, which confirms the theory that her trip there was primarily trade oriented, not religious.[133] However, the most interesting member of her entourage was her priest, Gregory.[134] That Ol'ga brought a priest with her indicates that if she was not already Christian, then she was already considering Christianity. Examining the text, it also seems that this priest was not one sent by the emperor to accompany her, as has been advanced.[135] Gregory was excluded from most ceremonies that Ol'ga participated in while in Constantinople—he may have been subtly, or not so, ostracized while there, suggesting that he was a priest from elsewhere, perhaps Rome or the German Empire.[136] The presence of a non-Byzantine priest in Ol'ga's entourage may have been a subtle message to the Byzantine emperor that she realized she had other options and she was examining all of them. There was already evidence in Rus' of Christianity that did not originate from Byzantium, such as the Church of St. Elias in Kiev,[137] and the ongoing effects of such connections can be seen in the Germanic word for church *(tsr'ky/ts'rky)*, which becomes the norm in Old East Slavic.[138]

Ol'ga's awareness of being between two major micro-Christendoms was evident on her return from her trip to Constantinople. After snubbing the Byzantine emperor, in 959 she sent a messenger to German emperor Otto I, asking him to send her a bishop and priests to instruct her and her people.[139] Understandably, Otto was quite receptive to such a request and dispatched Adalbert of Trier, later archbishop of Magdeburg, to Rus', presumably with an entourage of priests.[140] No Rusian records exist detailing the stay of Adalbert and his entourage in Rus', nor the effect that they may have had on the people. The German records resume in 962 when Adalbert returned from Rus' to report that his mission had failed due to pagan opposition.[141] This failure may have occurred through no fault of Ol'ga's—the likely reason for failure comes from her son Sviatoslav, who may have begun to rule or at least exercise his influence at this time. Sviatoslav was a confirmed pagan and would not accept even the trappings of Christianity near him, lest he be thought weak.[142] Regardless of the failure of the Christianizing mission, the fact that Ol'ga requested it remains most important. After negotiating with the Byzantine emperor, she returned to Kiev and requested priests and a bishop from the German emperor. This indicates that she understood her political position, and knew that her conversion and that of her people were the most important pieces of cultural currency she had, in addition to being the most dangerous. The conversion of an entire pagan kingdom was the goal of dominant micro-Christendoms like the German Empire, the Byzantine Empire, and the papacy, all of which were always on the lookout for kings to convert. Through conversion those dominant micro-Christendoms believed they could gain power over that kingdom. Deflecting that power-hungry expansion, yet attaining the goal of Christian conversion, became a high-stakes game that many medieval pagan rulers played, some winning, but most losing.

Vladimir's Religious World

When Ol'ga's grandson Vladimir Sviatoslavich came to the throne of Kiev in approximately 980, he initiated a new era in Rus'. Vladimir understood that the religious traditions of Rus' had to change so that the kingdom could more equally participate in the larger world. His first attempt at changing religious tradition shows his and his advisors' understanding of the complex world in which the Rusians lived and the rival necessities of religion. Christianization of Rus' was not Vladimir's first thought; instead he believed that a reformation and consolidation of the various pagan gods and practices would allow him the control of a centralized religion.[143] Rus' was composed of several different groups of people: Scandinavian conquerors, from whom Vladimir descended; native Slavs who had historically occupied the land west of the Dnieper River; native Iranians who had occupied some of the land east of the Dnieper River; and in Novgorod and its surrounding territory, a healthy leavening of both Balts and Finns. This was quite the multiethnic pastiche, and Vladimir needed something to unite these people behind him and to centralize control of Rus'. To that end, he created a unified pantheon of gods. This eight-god pantheon was designed to appeal to the various peoples under his rule, chiefly those who occupied the heartland of Rus'.[144] Due to the lack of primary sources, the success of this endeavor can be judged only by the fact that less than a decade after creating the pantheon it was abandoned and its statues were pulled down during the conversion to Christianity. The reasons for this can be guessed at, with the main supposition being that though the pagan pantheon may have ideally united the people of the land of Rus', it lacked a necessary controlling and uniting mechanism—a recurring theme in Rus' was the conquest and reconquest of subordinate and wayward tribes. One of the appealing aspects of a common religion was the power it offered a centralizing ruler. Vladimir's goal of unifying Rus' with religion was not working, but he saw another way to make it work: Christianity. The control apparatus inherent in Christianity's hierarchical structure and adherence to one god may have appealed to his desire to solidify administrative control in Kiev. Because his pagan pantheon did not come equipped with a system of priests, bishops, and archbishops, and subgroups of Rusians could maintain a belief in their particular portion of the pantheon, it was doomed to fail in its primary purpose—the centralizing of control and power in Kiev.

This prehistory of Rusian Christianization is meant to illustrate two points. First, Christianity was not the first option for a state religion in Rus'.[145] At a time when the majority of Europe was converted or converting to Christianity and Vladimir's own grandmother had been a convert and urged conversion, he chose to go in another direction. One possible interpretation of this is his understanding of the political baggage inherent in conversion, and that he wanted to avoid it by creating a state paganism. The second point is the historical individuality of Rus'. This consolidation of gods was an original approach in the Middle Ages, and perhaps foreshadowed the creation of a Rusian micro-Christendom over the next decades.

The story of Vladimir's conversion is generally well known, but will be described briefly here because of its importance in the perception of Rus' for history and historians. In 986, representatives of four faiths (including representatives from the micro-Christendoms of Byzantium and the German Empire) came to Kiev to proselytize to Vladimir on their faiths and to gain his conversion and that of Rus'.[146] Not coincidentally, the representatives, in addition to representing different religions, also represented Vladimir's neighbors: the Volga Bulgars (Islam),[147] Khazars (Judaism), Germans (Latin Christianity), and Byzantines (Byzantine Christianity). This is not surprising when we take into account the fact that the process of religious conversion was also meant to entail political alliance or subjugation to the converting party. Thus the people most interested in converting a pagan people to their religion would be those best in a position to exercise some authority over it, as shown in the story of the conversion of Bulgaria above. The main counterexamples to this proposition in medieval history are the conversions that took place due to the Anglo-Saxon missionaries, as discussed in the section above on Scandinavia. Anglo-Saxon England was in no position to exercise control over its neighbors, but it was still interested in fostering their conversion, perhaps out of truly altruistic motives.

In the selection of faiths, the PVL says that Judaism was eliminated from the competition almost out of hand[148] and that Vladimir sent wise elders to the Bulgars, Germans, and Byzantines to examine their faiths more closely.[149] The envoys returned to Kiev and told Vladimir that the

Byzantine church they visited, presumably Hagia Sophia, and its service were so beautiful that it seemed to resemble heaven, and that Byzantine Christianity was the true religion for Rus'.[150] The physical beauty of Hagia Sophia and the beauty of the sights and sounds of the service there seem to have been the contributing factor in the elders' decision to choose Byzantine Christianity.[151] Whatever the reason the Rusian elders chose the beauty of Hagia Sophia and Byzantine Orthodoxy, the *PVL* tells us that after digesting this information Vladimir did nothing.[152] At the end of this entry, there is no conversion, and the next entry begins with the attack on Cherson. This is only one of the three stories of conversion told by the *PVL*, but when this story is told by historians, the later fact of conversion to Byzantine Christianity is added to provide a conclusion. The tale is made to look like a purposeful examination of faiths when, instead, the story is a topos, one used in many conversion stories, such as the conversion of the Khazars to Judaism.[153] It is commonly agreed in Rusian history that this is a much later interpolation, probably by Greek monks who were attempting to make a polemical attack on Latin Christianity, as they did with Vladimir's actual conversion.[154] It can also be seen as an attempt by a redactor of the chronicle to reconcile multiple conversion stories that existed in his time period. Regardless, this tall tale is the first conversion story that was recorded for Rus'. This creates the mistaken impression that the examination of faiths is what actually happened, though it also acts as a metaphor for the search for religious conversion that many pagan kingdoms underwent, minimizing the complexity of the actual decisions.

The second and third stories of Vladimir's conversion recorded by the *PVL* are equally interesting. As reconstructed by Donald Ostrowski, the account of Vladimir's conversion listed under the year 988 in the *PVL*—the account provided by Sil'vestr, the compiler of the *PVL* in the twelfth century—the second story of Vladimir's conversion proceeds from the first.[155] After considering the information his envoys returned to him about the Byzantine faith, Vladimir vowed to be baptized if he was successful in capturing the Byzantine city of Cherson.[156] After capturing the city, now into the third story, he demanded the sister of the Byzantine emperors, Basil and Constantine, be sent to him in marriage.[157] The emperors countered with a demand for Vladimir's conversion before Anna could be sent to marry him, to which Vladimir responded that he would be baptized by her priests when she arrived.[158] The emperors agreed and dispatched Anna to Cherson with gifts and an entourage of priests.[159] According to the *PVL,* when she arrived in Cherson Vladimir was blind. This had been a mystery of the conversion story until Ostrowski looked at the conversion stories as a whole and saw the blindness as divine punishment for Vladimir's theoretical broken vow to convert if he took Cherson.[160] The blindness was healed only by Vladimir's actual conversion upon Anna's arrival.[161] This story of Vladimir's personal conversion ends on this miraculous note, but the *PVL* entry continues to include Vladimir and his entourage of Anna and the Chersonite priests returning to Kiev, herding the populace in to the Dnieper, and baptizing them en masse.[162]

All three of the conversion stories as recorded in the *PVL* seem to leave out the political/military/diplomatic/religious wrangling that seems to be essential to the conversion of a high political figure in the Middle Ages.[163] I believe that the conversion of Rus' seems to have grown out of a political decision to create a more united kingdom[164] buttressed by a goal of gaining international renown through marriage, rather than an actual religious devotion to Orthodoxy experienced by Vladimir, which certainly was not felt by the Rusian people.[165] The lack of interest in religious education or in proselytizing the faith beyond the Riurikid elites demonstrated by the church hierarchy in Rus' seems to confirm that position.

My reconstructed version of the Rusian conversion story, the fourth in this telling, begins with a political agreement.[166] Emperor Basil II of Byzantium was faced with a political crisis in the late 980s when he had two simultaneous rebellions, one by a well-known general, Bardas Phokas.[167] To fight these uprisings he needed soldiers, and for this he turned to Vladimir. Vladimir agreed to send him 6,000 soldiers to help put down the rebellions,[168] but in return he wanted to marry Basil's sister, the porphyrogenite princess Anna. This request was a momentous one, as a porphyrogenite princess was the most sought-after bride in the world of dynastic marriage. This same Anna had also been sought as a bride by Otto II[169] and Robert Capet,[170] without success.[171] However, as Basil was in dire straits, he agreed to the request with the stipulation that Vladimir convert to Christianity. To this, Vladimir agreed. After the rebellion had been put down, Basil did not deliver Anna, and Vladimir besieged the city of Cherson on the Black Sea in retaliation. His capture of the city was dependent on one of the inhabitants, a priest named Anastasius, betraying the city to him.[172] After Vladimir's capture of Cherson and some further negotiations, Basil turned over Anna and sent along with her an entourage of priests and dignitaries.[173] The *PVL* then records the baptism of Vladimir at Cherson by the bishop of Cherson with Anna's priests assisting, but it also acknowledges that some people believe he was baptized in Kiev.[174] After his baptism, Vladimir collected his wife, the priests of Cherson, the relics of St. Clement, and Anastasius, the betrayer of Cherson,[175] for the return journey to Kiev, where Vladimir was to baptize the whole population.[176] This is most probably the story of the conversion of Rus'—a political agreement that resulted in the Christianization of Vladimir and his people. The Byzantines did not send a bishop to minister to Rus', for accompanying Anna were merely priests *(prozvutery)*,[177] although the actual baptism of Vladimir as recorded in the *PVL* was presided over by the bishop of Cherson. The lack of a missionary bishop for Rus' indicates that Byzantium did not plan on the conversion of Rus', but only on the conversion of Vladimir.[178] The conversion of Rus' to Christianity was thus accomplished by Vladimir, with both the Chersonite priests he brought back with him and Anna's priests taking part.[179] Further enhancing this perception is Vladimir's installation of Anastasius, the betrayer of Cherson, as the head of the first postconversion church, with the priests from Cherson serving under Anastasius.[180] Had there been a strong Byzantine ecclesiastical presence in Rus' at the time, this would not have occurred. Anastasius, a person heretofore known only for betraying Cherson, a Byzantine city, was appointed to head the first church Vladimir built in Kiev after conversion. In addition, assisting Anastasius were priests Vladimir brought with him from Cherson, not priests sent from Constantinople. These facts strongly indicate that Vladimir had not given up his intention of remaining ecclesiastically independent, which he had demonstrated with the attempt at a pagan pantheon. Instead he accepted personal conversion from Byzantium and then acted on his own terms as the initiator of the conversion of the kingdom of Rus'. When considered in this light, the conversion of Rus' is not the Byzantine-driven action it is often perceived to be. Instead it seems clear that Vladimir was attempting to create his own Christian kingdom independent of outside influence, a micro-Christendom of Rus'.

Contacts with Latin Micro-Christendoms

Let us return briefly to the relics of St. Clement that the *PVL* says Vladimir took with him from Cherson to Kiev. On his way through Cherson in 860, Constantine (St. Cyril) discovered the relics of Pope St. Clement I, the third successor to St. Peter, who hagiographical tradition says was banished to the Crimea, where he died a martyr.[181] These relics Constantine carried with him on his mission to the Khazars, and in 867 he eventually brought the relics to Rome and gave them to Pope Hadrian II.[182] There are two hypotheses as to how Vladimir came in possession of relics of St. Clement over a century later. The first is that not all of the relics were taken by Constantine, which seems unlikely, because any he found he would have taken for the glory of the church. The second is that the relics were sent back. The second option has historical evidence to support it, as one Rusian chronicle records an embassy from the papacy to Vladimir at Cherson in 988.[183] This embassy is recorded as having come to bring holy relics to Vladimir, perhaps to celebrate his conversion or to influence him toward the micro-Christendom of Rome. This action had occurred before as Rome sent out relics to attempt to reinforce and strengthen their ecclesiastical position. The recipients of the relics were then connected to Rome, and the new churches or chapels built to house the relics became instant centers of Christian devotion.[184] These relics were important to Vladimir and he erected a chapel for them in his first Kievan church, and it is in that chapel that both Vladimir and his Byzantine wife Anna were laid to rest on their deaths.[185] Vladimir's possession of such important relics signaled the divine sanction of his, and his people's, conversion. Moreover, the placement of the relics in Vladimir's palace chapel was a constant reminder of the sanctity and power of his rule.[186] The relics of St. Clement continued to play a role in the Rusian Church for years to come. In the mid-twelfth century, the second native metropolitan was consecrated metropolitan of Kiev "by the head of St. Clement, as the Greeks consecrate by the head of St. John."[187] Thus, the relics played a large role in the creation of the Rusian Church.

The pope's overtures to Vladimir were not entirely one-sided. The Nikon chronicle records that in 994, just a few years after Vladimir received the embassy in Cherson, he himself sent an embassy to the pope in Rome.[188] This embassy would have met with Pope John XV, and the topics of discussion are anyone's guess. The Nikon chronicle does not record the purpose of such a visit, but its existence does not seem unlikely in light of the other religious contacts that Vladimir and his fellow Rusian rulers were known to have. Nor does it seem unlikely in the larger Christian world; Byzantine clerics traveled to Rome to speak with their religious colleagues there, and Romanos I Lekapenos used papal emissaries to crown his son as patriarch of Constantinople earlier in the decade.[189]

The papacy had actually gotten involved in Rus' a few years prior to Vladimir's conversion when, in 979, Pope Benedict VII sent an embassy to Kiev.[190] The purpose of this embassy is not stated, but the general overture was most likely one of introduction and an attempt by the papacy to involve itself in the bidding for Rusian conversion. The Rusian situation had been brought to the papacy's attention a few years earlier when in 973 Iaropolk Sviatoslavich of Kiev sent an embassy to Quedlinburg to consult with Otto I and some of the rulers of the other central and eastern European kingdoms.[191] The primary topic of discussion was probably the creation of the see of Prague, but other topics were no doubt discussed, and as Iaropolk's was one of the only two pagan kingdoms there, the Christianization of his realm must have been very interesting to the others. A likely conjecture would be that the pope heard of this unconverted pagan realm that had been approached by both Byzantium and the German Empire and attempted to get involved. The embassy arrived at a bad time in Rus'—Iaropolk was at war with his brother Vladimir and steadily losing.[192] This was a potential opportunity missed by the Rusians. Had a capable ruler been in full control, an embassy from the papacy might have been welcome. Just as the Khazars had converted to Judaism to avoid the choice between their two powerful neighbors, who represented Christianity and Islam, Rus' might have escaped its perceived bind by choosing to convert with the papacy, a distant master who could exercise little local control. This would have been a preferable option to choosing one of two powerful neighbors and allying fully with either's particular micro-Christendom.

Vladimir's conversion entered his kingdom into the wider family of Christian kingdoms of Europe. This was illustrated in the early eleventh century by the arrival of Bruno of Querfurt in Kiev. Bruno was a German missionary inspired by the missionary spirit of Otto III to convert pagan peoples. He came to Rus' to speak with Vladimir about the possibility of converting the nomadic Pechenegs, the southern neighbors of the Rusians.[193] Vladimir was described by Bruno as a "good Christian," and Bruno seemed uninterested in converting the Rusians.[194] In fact, he worked with Vladimir's cooperation and the use of one of Vladimir's sons as hostage to secure the conversion of the Pecheneg leaders.[195] Bruno does not share much information about Rus', or Rusian Christianity, but what he does say is enough. He makes it clear, through a lack of words on the subject, that Rus' was Christian, that Vladimir was Christian, and that he had no problems with their Christianity. As he was designated missionary archbishop of Magdeburg, the see responsible for the Slavs, he would have been interested in the Christianity of the Rusians.[196] His lack of detail about them tells us he accepted them and was more interested in the pagan Pechenegs.

Bruno's passive portrayal of Rus' as a part of Christendom is confirmed only a few years later when Sviatopolk Iaropolchich married a daughter of Bolesław Chrobry of Poland. This Boleslavna brought with her Reinbern, bishop of Kolobrzeg, as her personal confessor.[197] As was described in Chapter 2, it was a common practice for brides to take a personal confessor with them when they married, and the rank of that confessor was an indicator of their own rank. What is interesting is the role that Thietmar describes Reinbern as playing in Rus'. Thietmar says of Reinbern that he is a good Christian bishop who did much to evangelize Sviatopolk's people, who were mainly still pagans.[198] By this time Christianity had been in Rus' for more than twenty years, and at the court of the eldest Riurikid prince there would most likely have been other Christian figures from the Rusian Church. It is then interesting to have a well-informed contemporary discuss the proselytizing activities of a Polish/Latin priest in Rus' at this time. This evidence corroborates Bruno's work to show that the image of Rusian Christianity in the period shortly after the conversion was broadly Christian (not polemicized), and that this ecumenical Christianity was recognized as such by Latin churchmen.[199]

Papal Fealty

One of the most interesting ties with a foreign micro-Christendom developed by the Rusian rulers was an oath of fealty taken by Iziaslav

Iaroslavich to Pope Gregory VII. Iziaslav had been ruler of Kiev, but was ousted by his brothers Sviatoslav and Vsevolod in the 1070s. Iziaslav fled with his wife and son first to Poland and then to the German Empire. While asking Henry IV for assistance to regain his kingdom, Iziaslav also dispatched his son, Iaropolk, to Rome to meet with the pope to request the same.[200] This was an ambitious and interesting move, for a number of reasons. The first is simply that, using the traditional model of a Europe divided post-1054 into Orthodox and Latin, the prospect of an Orthodox ruler, even in exile, appealing to the Roman pope for assistance would be well-nigh impossible. However, when viewed through the lens of multiple micro-Christendoms, this becomes a much more plausible negotiation. The second reason is that Iziaslav was appealing to both Henry IV and Pope Gregory VII while Henry IV and Gregory VII were at odds with one another. A ruler from the eastern edge of Europe was suddenly playing two of the largest actors in European politics off each other in order to help him regain his throne.

The decisions reached by Iaropolk and the pope are recorded in a papal letter from April 17, 1075.[201] In that letter it is stated that Iaropolk, who throughout is stated to be acting on behalf of his father, Iziaslav, professed *fidelitas* to Gregory VII and in return requested to receive the kingdom *(regnum)* of Rus' as a gift from St. Peter. Gregory VII for his part promised Iziaslav all of these things and sent with Iaropolk two papal legates who were to act as the pope's hands in directing assistance for Iziaslav's return.[202] A further action of the conference is recorded in another papal letter, in which Gregory VII instructs Bolesław of Poland to return the money he had stolen from Iziaslav, obviously in response to such a request from Iaropolk.[203] This instruction seems to have been followed, and by winter of the next year Iziaslav and his family were in Poland, probably accompanied by the papal envoys. It was at Christmas of that year, 1076, that Bolesław II was crowned rex at Gniezno.[204] It is possible that Bolesław was crowned by the same papal envoys who accompanied Iziaslav and his family,[205] but all that is recorded is that there were fifteen bishops, of which the legates could have been part.[206] The coronation of Bolesław seems to be in exchange for his agreement to help Iziaslav regain the throne in Kiev. Though only supposition, this proposition is logical and fits with facts known about Gregory VII's pontificate. Gregory VII was very interested in expanding the influence of the papacy, and he used royal crowns as his main method of diplomacy with Rus', Dalmatia, and elsewhere.[207] Further, it cost him nothing to give such a crown to Bolesław, but increased Bolesław's position vis-à-vis his, and Gregory VII's, main rival, the German Empire, and ultimately created a papal ally.

As for the position of Rus' in this whole affair, it is more than interesting that an exiled Rusian ruler would turn to the papacy for support in regaining his kingdom. The idea that there was a gross political divide between the east and west after 1054 is a fallacy, although ecclesiastically there was indeed a falling out between the Orthodox and papal sides.[208] This action makes it clear that the negativity was not felt on the political side in Rus'. When pressed, Iziaslav had no compunction about turning to the papacy, who had consistently been sending embassies to Rus' for one hundred years, for assistance and even going so far as to pledge his fidelitas to the pope and accept Rus' as a gift from St. Peter. This is a testament not only to the lack of animosity between Rusian rulers and the Latin Church, but also to the lack of monopoly control by the Byzantine churchmen in Rus'. Iziaslav's exile was condemned by the abbot of the Kievan Caves Monastery, the holiest monastery in Rus', and Abbot Feodosii would not eat with the usurpers Sviatoslav and Vsevolod.[209] The *PVL* condemns the usurpation in very similar words,[210] and although we do not know the position of the metropolitan, it can be safely assumed that the Rusian Church was against the usurpation. Their opposition did not lend strength to Iziaslav's cause or place him back on the throne. Instead, Iziaslav was forced to turn to the Latin Church for assistance. This is a telling incident in the history of the Rusian Church and its relations with both Constantinople and Rome. Despite receiving their initial Christianizers from Byzantium, the political elite very rarely chose to seek Byzantine political or ecclesiastical assistance. Instead the rulers almost always choose to look to the Latin world for assistance—they did not feel their initial conversion had created a barrier between them and the rest of medieval Europe, but instead believed that it united them with a larger Christian world.

Iziaslav was restored to the throne of Kiev in 1077 only to die the next year in battle. At his death he was honored by the Kievan Caves Monastery and the *PVL* with a glowing eulogy.[211] The *PVL* describes all of Kiev turning out to see his body return and be laid to rest in the Church of the Holy Virgin.[212] Further, the *Paterik* of the Kievan Caves

Monastery, written by monks of the monastery, describes him as a "Christ-loving prince."[213] Most interestingly, the *Paterik* compares Iziaslav favorably to St. Peter, one of only two mentions of that particular saint contained there.[214] All of this adds up to a very favorable posthumous impression of Iziaslav portrayed by the Rusian Church. Posthumous recollections in chronicles and other medieval documents are often used to determine the estimation of the person before his death. For a Rusian "Orthodox" ruler who was twice ousted, twice turned to Poland for assistance, received halfhearted assistance from the German emperor, and paid homage to the pope in Rome, this is a remarkably positive picture, which seems to indicate that the Rusian micro-Christendom, through its monastic chroniclers of both the *Paterik* and the *PVL,* did not find fault with these things. One would assume that the Byzantine Church would have felt more strongly about it, as they did in their struggle in Hungary when contenders for the throne would go as supplicants to the pope, but in the Rusian instance this does not seem to be the case.[215] The typically anti-Latin monks (at least in their polemics) did not look negatively on Iziaslav, despite his strong connections to and support from Rome and the Latin world. The relatively unique reference to St. Peter is also important to consider. The pope was the heir to St. Peter and thus this saint was particularly affiliated with the Latin Church. To compare a Rusian ruler to him, especially one who paid homage to the pope and was granted the title rex, indicates a relationship between the two. This is further buttressed by the erection of the first Church of the Holy Apostle Peter in Kiev by Iaropolk Iziaslavich, who had made the journey to Rome and had pledged on his father's behalf.[216] The particular association of St. Peter with Rome and with Iziaslav and his son who had pledged to Rome, indicates a connection between the two that would have been unthinkable in the traditional picture of Rus'.

Negotiating with Two Papacies

In 1084 Henry IV's conflict with Pope Gregory VII escalated with the confirmation of Wibert of Ravenna as Pope Clement III.[217] However, unlike his father, who had successfully placed multiple popes in Rome,[218] Henry IV had to fight an uphill battle for the confirmation and continuing support of his pope against Gregory VII (d. 1085), and more strongly against Pope Urban II (elected and confirmed 1088). It is this struggle that brings Rus' into the picture. Clement III was attempting to enlist the support of various micro-Christendoms in his campaign to be accepted as pope. At the time of Gregory VII's death, Clement III was recognized as pope "not only in the imperial territories but in Hungary and Croatia and perhaps also in England and Southern Italy."[219] So, Clement III already had broad support outside of the territory of Henry IV, and he was attempting to extend that support to Rus'. The evidence we have for this attempt is a letter from Metropolitan Ioann II of Kiev from the late 1080s.[220] This letter is obviously a reply to an original letter from Clement III, the content of which can be surmised through Ioann II's reply. Clement III, perhaps soon after his confirmation in Rome in 1084, was feeling out the Rusian metropolitan[221] in regard to church unification. This would have served both religious and political goals for Clement III, as well as his patron Henry IV, allowing them not only to build a larger coalition, but to show their power by garnering the support of the micro-Christendom of Rus', the largest kingdom in Europe.[222] Henry IV also attempted to bring Rus' into his party at this time with the dynastic marriage of one of his noblemen, Henry of Stade, with the daughter of the ruler of Kiev, Evpraksia Vsevolodovna.[223] Though the dating for this marriage may predate the original letter from Clement III, the two overtures were most likely attempts to bring Rus' closer to the party of Henry IV.

Unfortunately for Clement III, unlike the political hierarchy in Rus' the religious hierarchy was often dominated by Byzantine-oriented metropolitans such as Ioann II.[224] Ioann II's reply to Clement III was cordial in tone, yet mainly consisted of a considered attack on various Latin practices that precluded ecclesiastical unification, and went so far as to refer any further inquiries on the subject to the patriarch of Constantinople.[225] From prior German relations with Rus' it would have been impossible to know the nature of Ioann II. Where the Rusian rulers were more than happy to be guided by politics and ally themselves with rulers of Latin micro-Christendoms,[226] Ioann II was a Byzantine religious conservative who opposed relations with the Latins.[227] This doomed Clement III's attempt to failure, as Ioann II would not agree even to discuss ecclesiastical unification, much less (it seems) to take sides in a struggle for the papacy. The death-knell for Clement III's chances with Rus' was sounded in 1089 when Byzantium and newly confirmed pope Urban II began to grow closer.[228]

There is, however, a Rusian denouement to the story. As related in the next section, in 1091 an embassy arrived from the "pope from Rome" bearing relics of St. Nicholas and the service for the Feast of the Translation of the Relics of St. Nicholas of Myre to Bari.[229] As it was Urban II who consecrated the relics of St. Nicholas in their new home in Bari,[230] it seems likely that it was also he who sent the text of the Latin feast day to Rus', as well as the relics. The arrival of this embassy may then be read as an offering from Urban II to join his camp, as the Rusians had already rejected Clement III. It is possible that this overture was accepted, and that this was the reason for Evpraksia Vsevolodovna to turn on her husband Henry IV and join the camp of Urban II in 1094.[231] Unfortunately this cannot be proven. It does seem, however, that the claimants for the papacy in Rome were trying to attract Rus' to their respective camps, and each attempted this in their own way.

The Role of the Metropolitan

The foundation of Christianity in a newly converted kingdom is a difficult process that requires the establishment of churches as well as a hierarchy to manage those churches and their accompanying priests and bishops. At the top of that hierarchy is, eventually, an archbishop or metropolitan. The first metropolitan recorded in the *PVL* in Rus' was Theopemptos in 1039,[232] though whether he was the first metropolitan in Rus' is a matter of debate. Later chronicles mention metropolitans prior to him, and the *Skazanie of Boris and Gleb* of Nestor composed in the late eleventh century mentions a Metropolitan (or archbishop) John as preceding Theopemptos.[233] There is also the notation in the *Chronicon* of Thietmar of Merseburg that an archbishop received Bolesław Chrobry when he took Kiev in 1018.[234] The editor of the English-language translation of Thietmar identifies that archbishop as Metropolitan John, presumably the same as Nestor's, with dates as metropolitan from 1008 to 1033,[235] although he is never named as such in Thietmar's work. This lack of a clear record for a metropolitan presence in early Christian Rus' has led to a variety of theories in regard to the origins of the Rusian ecclesiastical hierarchy.[236] The position advanced here has similarities to the arguments advanced by many scholars, but because of the language of micro-Christendoms, I do not feel the need to enter explicitly into this academic quagmire.[237] My position, as discussed above in "Vladimir's Religious World," is that the Rusian Church was founded by Vladimir because of his political and marital goals and that the first priests were from Cherson, including the head of Vladimir's first church in Kiev, Anastasius. It seems clear from the chronicles that Vladimir and his son Iaroslav exercised control over the church at least prior to the arrival of Metropolitan Theopemptos, as they appointed priests and bishops themselves, occasionally against the wishes of other churchmen.[238] This follows the model of kingdoms throughout Europe prior to the papal reform begun under Gregory VII—the ruler who founded a church had the power to place priests, including at larger churches, bishops.[239] This does not then make the church necessarily autocephalous, but it does demonstrate a measure of autonomy, as do the other acts of the rulers discussed in this chapter. However, all metropolitans in this period, with the exception of Ilarion,[240] were appointed from Constantinople and were, to a greater or lesser degree, agents of Constantinople. The remainder of this part will be devoted to the question of their influence as agents of Constantinople and their position in Rus' as can be determined from the sources.

The metropolitan of Kiev was Rusian in position only; for the vast majority of the history of Rus', he was Byzantine.[241] This creates multiple immediate problems, the first of which is that he was primarily a Greek speaker; in fact, very few of the Byzantine metropolitans in Rus' were able to speak Old East Slavic or write in it or Church Slavonic.[242] This is especially odd when considered in the light of the German priests and rulers on the border of Slavic territories who knew Slavic languages,[243] and leads to the creation of an environment in which the Byzantine metropolitans lived isolated from their Rusian parishioners.[244] This was quite in contrast to the advice Sven Estridsson gave to Archbishop Adalbert about missionaries, and priests generally, being more effective if they shared language and customs.[245] The second problem that arises is the issue of loyalty. While a priest's loyalty is assumed to be to his Church and ecclesiastical superiors first, this may be in contrast with his mission in a foreign land. As was seen in the discussions of Scandinavia and Bulgaria, rulers were often interested in acquiring independent religious hierarchies for the express purpose of having ecclesiastics loyal to them, and distant masters, such as the pope, feared such things. This is one of the reasons put forward for the creation of the first native Rusian metropolitan, Ilarion. The question that follows from these two main problems is, what kind of influence did the metropolitan have on the political elite in Rus', or similarly, how much power did he have in Rus'? These are difficult questions to answer because of the paucity of sources and the nature of the sources that we do have, but using a few of the main examples, I will attempt an answer.

We must begin with the idea that though there was a metropolitan see in Kiev from at least 1039 through the end of our period, there was not always a metropolitan resident in Kiev or in Rus'. The tenure of metropolitans in Kiev was often short,[246] and the time required to send to Constantinople for a replacement, for Constantinople to make a decision, and for the replacement to return could be long.[247] This left intervals without a metropolitan presence in Kiev, and the Rusian Church without a functional head. Into that vacuum it is easy to imagine that the most powerful person in the kingdom, the ruler of Kiev, would have a voice in church affairs, as Iaroslav did during his appointment of Luka Zhidyata in Novgorod and Ilarion as metropolitan.

When there was a metropolitan in Kiev, what did he do? The metropolitan founded and consecrated churches, installed bishops, and was occasionally present at meetings of the rulers. In the majority of these cases he was fulfilling typical ecclesiastical functions. In the story of the blinding of Vasil'ko, however, he had a diplomatic function as Vsevolod's widow and Metropolitan Nicholas were sent as emissaries to make peace between the rival factions.[248] It is clearly stated that Vladimir Monomakh honored the metropolitan and loved him as he loved all churchmen.[249] The metropolitan's role as emissary is clearly political, and though he played a secondary role to Vladimir's stepmother, he was still one of the ones chosen as an ambassador for peace. Alternatively, he could have been chosen because of a sense of ecclesiastical immunity so that he could have crossed the warring principalities without harm, and his rank would have supplied him clout to have easy access to all the parties. This political role is similar to one mentioned above from Thietmar of Merseburg's work, where an unnamed archbishop acted as a representative of Kiev in surrendering the city to Bolesław Chrobry.[250] Whether these leaders of the Kievan Church acted through translators or on their own behalf, it is clear that at times they did play more than a ceremonial religious role.

In the story of the blinding of Vasil'ko, the metropolitan is "honored" and is able to fulfill his task of bringing about peace. However, the metropolitans' wishes were not always so easy for the princes to agree to. The prime example of this is found in the *Canonical Responses of Metropolitan Ioann II* (henceforth, *Canonical Responses*), a listing of answers to doctrinal and practical questions by Metropolitan Ioann II.[251] Ioann II is noted in the *PVL* as being a well-educated and respected bookman, and he is known in secondary sources for his anti-Latin polemics.[252] Part of that reputation for anti-Latin writings is from these *Canonical Responses,* where he implores the Riurikids to stop marrying their daughters out of the faith, the implicit subtext of which is that they were marrying them to Latins.[253] This is a normal post-1054 Schism understanding of the Orthodox-Latin world, but it is one limited to churchmen. The rulers of Rus' continued intermarrying their families with Latin Christians well after Ioann II's time. Though the material does not exist to provide a complete analysis of Rusian political-ecclesiastical interaction, this was probably how it generally worked. The metropolitan's advice was followed only if it did not conflict with the political realities of the current situation. In the case of Vladimir Monomakh and Metropolitan Nicholas's peace mission, it was in Vladimir's interest to listen to the metropolitan and make peace.[254] In the case of Metropolitan Ioann II's admonition, it was in the best interests of the princes to continue marrying their daughters "outside of the faith." This reflects the metropolitan's actual position in Rus', an outsider by his ethnicity and language, who may or may not have influence on the rulers, depending on the situation. This is a different picture than what we find when we read the majority of the scholarship, which portrays the metropolitan as the controlling agent of Byzantium in Rus'.[255] The metropolitan was an agent of Byzantium in that he was a Byzantine appointee with more in common with the Constantinopolitan court than with the Kievan, but he was not as influential as some have argued.[256]

Part of the reason for his lack of influence is that during our time period the metropolitan of Kiev was not the only metropolitan in Rus'.

There is an interesting period in the second half of the eleventh century when there may have been as many as three metropolitans resident in Rus'.[257] The reason given for the division is often that the new metropolitanates mirrored the post-Iaroslav triumvirate.[258] There was the original see of Kiev and then also sees in Pereiaslavl' and Chernigov.[259] However, other authors have their own opinions about when these additional metropolitanates were added and why.[260] The interesting point for the purposes of this discussion is that they did exist. The policy of the Byzantine Church was not to split the see of Rhosia, as they called it, despite the fact that it was the single largest ecclesiastical see in Europe and extremely unwieldy.[261] Nevertheless, in the 1070s and 1080s there were three metropolitanates in Rus'. The best-known of the other metropolitans is Metropolitan Ephraim of Pereiaslavl', who founded churches, attended ecclesiastical conferences, and is known as the sole metropolitan in Rus' after Ioann III's death in 1089.[262] It has been theorized that Ephraim did not have as close a relationship with Byzantium as the metropolitans of Kiev did, which allowed for the acceptance of the Feast of the Translation of the Relics of St. Nicholas under his care in the early 1090s.[263] Though there is no good evidence for Ephraim's political orientation, it is possible that he had a different relationship with Byzantium than the metropolitans of Kiev. The presence of additional metropolitans in Rus' can easily be read as an attempt at increasing Rusian control over the Church, a common denominator in the creation of medieval micro-Christendoms.

The Creation of a National Church

When discussing the Christianization of any kingdom in the Middle Ages, it is important to remember that Christian doctrine prohibited the existence of any kind of national church.[264] This was set forth by the early church fathers. Augustine and Jerome wrote that all Christians "belonged to a single *populus* called *Christianus*, to which belonged equally all the baptized, be they male or female, slave or free, poor or privileged."[265] This also gave rise later in the Middle Ages to the idea of a single Christendom to which all nations belonged and was part of the basis for the pope's claim to ascendancy over kings. When Rus' and Muscovy are brought into the discussion of national churches, there is even more discussion of the issue. In the late fourteenth century the patriarch of Constantinople sent a missive to Grand Prince Vasillii I saying, "It is not possible for Christians to have the church and not to have the emperor."[266] This was in response to Vasillii I removing the emperor's name from the liturgy in the Muscovite Church. By that time, Byzantium was much less powerful than Muscovy, but the patriarch needed to raise money to rebuild and defend Constantinople and as such reached back to the early fathers for a precedent.[267] As with so many other pieces of evidence from Muscovite Russia, this one too was read back into Kievan Rus'.[268] However, Simon Franklin, a scholar of Rus' and the Rusian Church in particular, can find no evidence that the Byzantine emperor was ever included in the Rusian Liturgy in the Kievan period.[269] It seems that the patriarch was incorrect, and for at least some time Rus' was able to have the church without the emperor.

This debate has extended into modern historiography, with various well-known figures taking opposing positions throughout the twentieth century. Early in the century, Georges Florovsky defended his position on the Byzantine view: "From the strict canonical point of view, which was held in Byzantium, all claims for independence on the side of 'national Churches' were illegitimate, if only because, from that point of view, there was but *one nation,* the 'Christian Nation'."[270] Florovsky clearly drew on the ideas of the early church fathers in his explication of Byzantine ideas.[271] However, Florovsky's position is that of Byzantium, not that of Rus'. It makes sense that the Byzantine emperor as well as the church would want to defend the ideals of the church fathers as part of their larger practice of viewing the Christian world as their domain to rule. Later, Roman Jakobson defended the idea of a Rusian Church and wrote that there existed a "conscious patriotism" in Rus' during the Kievan period and that the idea of a "national church" did exist.[272] Jakobson's idea is founded on the Romantic era identification of language and culture.[273] A national church was possible then because there was a relatively unified language group in Kievan Rus', and as that produced its own culture, it could also have its own religion. While Jakobson's ideas are not my own, I do agree and think that I have illustrated that Rus' was able to create a national church, and that the creation of such a church was a conscious desire of the Rusian rulers,[274] despite whatever the Byzantine Church and emperor thought about the matter.

The remainder of this chapter is devoted to an exploration of the ways this national church was differentiated from the Byzantine.

Slavonic Liturgy in Rus'

As we saw in Bulgaria, Khan Boris was eager to spread the Slavonic Liturgy throughout his kingdom to create a measure of independence from Byzantium, as well as to aid in the proselytization of his people.[275] In Rus', the use of the Slavonic Liturgy seems to have been a foregone conclusion. The majority of the religious materials were brought in from Bulgaria, for which they had originally been translated.[276] Rus' was then connected to the ecclesiastical world of the Bulgarians, but linguistically to no one else. The Byzantines and the various Latin churches used different, but uniform, languages for their ecclesiastical services, and even the metropolitans sent to Rus' by Byzantium probably did not know much, if any, Slavonic.[277] Thus the use of Slavonic in Rus' led to a situation in which it was separated from both the church that was its titular head, the patriarchate of Constantinople, and the churches to whom it related in the west. However, as Ilarion seemed to imply in his "Sermon on Law and Grace," the new must succeed the old, perhaps in language as well.[278] So the Slavonic Liturgy in Rus' differentiated Rus' and its church from its neighbors but put it in sync with its new religion.

Linguistic unity was vital, however, in creating lasting ties both politically and religiously. The Rusian rulers formed complex political relationships with the Hungarians, Poles, and others, but as politics shifted over the course of the twelfth and thirteenth centuries, religious and linguistic ties proved stronger than familial and political ones. The fact that Rus' was not part of the homogenizing Latin-language community was a major factor in their exclusion from the Western Christian world in that period of change. Therefore, though the use of the Slavonic liturgy assisted in the creation of a micro-Christendom of Rus' in the period under discussion, it also laid the groundwork for the status of Rus' as an outsider to the Latin-speaking Roman Church in later centuries.

Saints in Rus'

When a king and kingdom convert to Christianity, they absorb the religion through their converters. In the medieval world, an essential part of that religion was a collection of saints to venerate. For Rus', the basic package of saints came via Byzantium, but that group did not exist long without modification. These modifications are particularly interesting to discuss in the context of the development of the micro-Christendom of Rus'.

Essential to this package, though not necessarily venerated throughout the micro-Christendoms, were the creators of the Slavonic Liturgy, Saints Constantine/Cyril and Methodius.[279] Their exploits, but not their canonizations, are recorded in the prehistory in the *PVL*.[280] Following this is a defense of the Slavonic Liturgy delivered by the pope, condemning those who did not believe that there should be a fourth liturgical language beyond Hebrew, Greek, and Latin.[281] Given that both the papacy and the patriarch of Constantinople endorsed the Slavonic Liturgy, it is interesting to find a papal endorsement of it here but not one from the patriarch. The unstated main opponents of the Slavonic Liturgy were the Frankish priests and their backer, the East Frankish Empire, which had opposed the Slavonic Liturgy in an attempt to increase its own power in Moravia.[282] This was an early sign that there were more than just two players in the game. The German Empire (successor to the East Franks) was a third major party, Latin in confession, that was interested in converting pagan peoples to its own micro-Christendom. The *PVL* intimates that it was the pope who then dispatched Constantine/Cyril to Bulgaria and Methodius back to Moravia to continue their teachings.[283] The involvement of the papacy in this section of the *PVL* is interesting because, as discussed elsewhere, the *PVL* was composed by Byzantine monks or Rusian monks trained and supervised by Byzantines, and it contains a variety of anti-Latin polemics. However, the composer or compiler of the *PVL* chose to portray the papacy (as opposed to the patriarchate) as the propagator and defender of the Slavonic Liturgy, even though the composition (and certainly compilation) occurred after the papacy changed its position and repudiated Slavonic as a liturgical language.[284] The anti-Slavonic stand of the papacy post-1080 should have uncomplicated the situation in the

PVL, and the patriarchate should have stood as the sole defender of the Slavonic liturgy. The fact that this does not happen suggests a more complicated story than simply the foundation of Byzantine Christianity in Rus' in 988 and thereafter a Byzantine focus to worship.

The history of the Rusian menology indicates that there was actually very little updating of Rusian religious texts in this time period. The vast majority of saints in Rusian menologies were early Christian saints. During the ninth, tenth, and early eleventh centuries nearly every patriarch of Constantinople was placed into the Byzantine menologies upon his death and honored with his own feast day.[285] However, after Nikifor (d. 828), none of these patriarchs appear in the Rusian menologies of the eleventh and twelfth centuries.[286] Why is this, when we know that during this time period there was interaction between Rus' and Constantinople? In the opinion of O. V. Loseva, who has made an extensive study of Rusian menologies, the menologies were translated into Slavonic in the early to mid-ninth century, presumably for/by the Bulgarians, and were not updated by the Rusians with regard to Byzantine menologies until the fourteenth century.[287] The lack of updating in this period is corroborated by the fact that the "flowering of Byzantine scholarship of the eleventh and twelfth centuries" is completely absent from any Rusian sources.[288] So it appears that, despite the contacts that existed because of the importation of metropolitans and the monastic traffic between Rus' and Byzantium, very little new Byzantine liturgical or other material reached Rus' in this period.

The inclusion of certain saints or their saints' days also tells a story about the Rusian Church. Certain saints, especially ones from the first centuries of Christianity, are celebrated in almost all micro-Christendoms. But not all micro-Christendoms celebrated the saint on the same day. Determining which day was used by various menologies helps to indicate the provenance of that menology and/or the influences upon its construction. Rusian menologies in fact contain quite a few Latin saints that are not listed in Byzantine menologies, but more importantly, for the moment, the dates they use for many early Christian saints are the ones used in Rome.[289] For instance, Pope Sylvester (d. 335) is listed in the Rusian menology on December 31, though in Byzantine menologies he has a place on January 2.[290] Though the difference is only one of a few days, it marks the border between a Roman and a Byzantine dating.

Many other saints from the Rusian menologies also follow Latin dates, including the apostles Matthew and Paul, the martyrs Cosmas and Damian, and all of the zealots *(podvizhniki)*.[291] The only possible source for these dates would have been menologies or monks from a western micro-Christendom that used the Roman dates.[292] Their presence in Rusian menologies of the eleventh and twelfth centuries shows the extent of religious interaction between Rus' and western micro-Christendoms at that time. The use of Roman dates for saints and the lack of new Byzantine saints from the early ninth century onward shows once again the path Rus' was treading as an independent micro-Christendom.

One of the best ways to increase the strength and centralization of a particular micro-Christendom was to create indigenous saints, as they acted as rallying points for religious independence and directed devotion inward, rather than outward to a foreign source. Rus', however, created two native saints quite early in its Christian history, with the martyrdom of two sons of St. Vladimir, Boris and Gleb, in the first quarter of the early eleventh century. These two saints have an interesting place in Rusian history, both political and ecclesiastical—not only are they the first Rusian saints, but they are also sainted members of the ruling Riurikid family. Where the model for their sanctification comes from has become something of a question.[293] The *Lesson on the Life and Murder of the Blessed Passion-Sufferers Boris and Gleb*, written by Nestor in the last quarter of the eleventh century, contains reference to a Metropolitan Ioann who helped create the cult of Boris and Gleb.[294] But this is the only reference to such a metropolitan's existence in Rus', and its presence in a hagiographical text has created some skepticism. It is much more certain that the Byzantine metropolitans in Kiev subscribed to the later cult, as the chronicles agree that the metropolitan was present at the translation of the relics of Boris and Gleb in both 1072 and 1115.[295] Nestor's inclusion of Metropolitan Ioann may have been an attempt to read that involvement back into the crucial development of the cult, and the use of the name Ioann may have been a mistake for the later Metropolitan Ioann II.[296]

Despite this support, or simple acquiescence, of the Byzantine-appointed metropolitan, it appears that the actual model for Boris and Gleb's sanctification comes from the idea of the martyred ruler, much more common in central and western Europe. The prototypical Slavic example of this is King Wenceslas of Bohemia, who was martyred in the ninth century and became one of the first national saints of Bohemia along with his mother, also a martyr, Ludmila.[297] The martyred prince was an important national saint in Britain and in Scandinavia, where prior to the creation of Sts. Boris and Gleb there existed multiple national saints who were all from the royal family and all died in a Christian manner.[298] Wenceslas does appear in numerous eleventh- and twelfth-century Rusian menologies, and a full liturgical office was created for him.[299] Also present in at least one Rusian litany of saints are numerous other martyred princes, including St. Olaf of Norway,[300] St. Knud of Denmark, and St. Magnus of Orkney.[301] The veneration of these western martyred rulers, as well as the importation of the model itself, is indicative of the religious contacts that Rus' maintained with its fellow European micro-Christendoms.[302]

Wenceslas's story most likely passed to Rus' through ties with the Sázava monastery in Bohemia, one of the few Slavonic monasteries under the Roman Church. Through the same return path, the tale of Boris and Gleb spread to Bohemia and central Europe. The Sázava chronicle even mentions that relics of Boris and Gleb were brought to Bohemia to be venerated.[303] This tie is bolstered by additional Bohemian saints who made their way into Rus', including St. Vitus, the patron saint of Prague, who appears in the Molitva of Sv. Troicě,[304] and St. Adalbert of Prague.[305] There is open discussion about the place of composition of many Slavonic texts, including the liturgical office for St. Wenceslas and the Molitva mentioned above. The debates center around whether they moved east or west and were composed in Rus' or in Bohemia.[306] The conclusion of the debates may be that the texts were written in the more established ecclesiastical center of Sázava, but this in no way detracts from their importance in Rusian history.[307] The presence of Sázava-composed texts in Rus' shows the willingness of Rusian ecclesiastics and noble lay individuals to import texts from multiple micro-Christendoms, building on the base that was appropriated from Byzantium and thus enhancing their own, Rusian, micro-Christendom.

An easy explanation for these ties, as well as for the veneration of Constantine/Cyril and Methodius, has always been that Rus' recognized its Slavic connection with both the West and South Slavs. Although they recognized ethnic similarities,[308] Rus' actually had less contact with

Slavic Europe than with the rest of Europe. This translated into few Rusian-Slavic marriages and fewer foreign Slavic saints in Rus' than there were saints from the rest of Europe.[309] Rus' seemed to be far less interested in ethnic ties with the Slavs in the tenth through twelfth centuries than they would be later.[310] For instance, in the thirteenth century the Rusians had a monastery on Mt. Athos where they maintained close connections to other Slavic monasteries, including trading monasteries with the Serbs and sheltering other Slavic Orthodox monks and priests.[311] But during the tenth through twelfth centuries, instead of focusing on ethnic ties, Rus' evinced an ecclesiastical interest in only some of its neighbors—Scandinavia, Bohemia (and by extension the German Empire), Poland, Hungary, and Byzantium. This is logical because Rus', though with a largely Slavic population, was still at this time a multiethnic kingdom composed of a ruling elite that had little Slavic blood.

The Rusian Church also went its own way regarding the saints that they appropriated from Byzantium. An excellent example of this is St. Nicholas. In the late 1080s the relics of St. Nicholas were stolen from Myra by Italian merchants and resettled in Bari.[312] To commemorate this theft, Pope Urban II in September 1089 instituted the Feast of St. Nicholas on May 9. This was a celebration that naturally antagonized the Byzantines, and they repudiated it.[313] However, this feast was on the Rusian calendar[314] and was most likely brought to Rus' in 1091 when a papal delegation came to Kiev bearing relics.[315] To celebrate properly the feast of the translation of the relics of St. Nicholas, the Rusian Church needed an office. The one created was clearly borrowed from the Latin version, which might also have been introduced by the 1091 expedition.[316]

The year in which this celebration reached Rus' was one that may help account for the acceptance of such a feast—1091 was one of the many gaps in the occupancy of the metropolitanate of Kiev. Metropolitan Ioann III "the Castrate" had died in 1090/1091[317] after being in place only a year, and his successor, Nicholas, did not arrive until approximately 1096. Thus, during that time period there was no Byzantine-appointed metropolitan in Rus', and thus less of a Byzantine connection for the Rusian Church.[318] This is emphasized by the translation of the relics of Theodosius, the founder of the Kievan Caves Monastery, to the Cathedral of the Transfiguration.[319] The monks had reason to believe that the glorification of another national saint would be opposed by the Byzantine Church.[320] As discussed above, the glorification of a national saint gave the people of Rus' somewhere local to direct their prayers and attention, potentially distracting them from the veneration of Constantinople. This was also, obviously, a necessary step in the establishment of an independent micro-Christendom, as a micro-Christendom requires a local locus of holiness so that it is not dependent on an outside holy place.

Locus of Worship

The establishment of a locus of worship inside Rus' can be seen to have been a goal of the Rusian rulers. They recognized the power that places and objects hold and were eager to focus their growing kingdom on Kiev, rather than on Constantinople or elsewhere. A locus of worship, however, is more than just a church; it is a religious center and a focal point for a kingdom. Recall Brown's example of Toledo, where the city was self-consciously hailed as a new Jerusalem in an effort to direct the attention of the people inward, rather than outward.[321] The way in which Rus' accomplished this was to mirror Constantinople in Kiev: the icons of Constantinopolitan architecture, such as the Golden Gate and most importantly Hagia Sophia, were re-created in Kiev.[322] These icons were deliberately appropriated with the express purpose of lending Kiev some of the majesty of Constantinople. Historiography has long viewed this as an outgrowth of Byzantine influence in Rus' and interpreted it as a clear sign that Rus' was in the power of Byzantium. In addition to the interpretation offered in Chapter 1 regarding the Byzantine Ideal, I would suggest that this deliberate appropriation of symbols had the politico-ecclesiastical purpose of furthering the establishment of a micro-Christendom, and that in fact this was one of the crucial steps in that process.[323] It is likely that such a step worked for this period, as Adam of Bremen writing in the 1070s described Kiev as "rival of the Scepter of Constantinople, the brightest ornament of Greece."[324] Adam's description of Kiev and his comparison of it to Constantinople are wonderfully evocative. Constantinople is set as the center and brightest ornament of the entire Byzantine Empire, with Kiev as the center and brightest ornament of Rus'. The comparison between the two evokes the point discussed here, which is that just as Constantinople was the ecclesiastical center of Byzantium, Kiev became the ecclesiastical center of Rus'. This deliberate attempt to create a locus of worship inside Rus', largely engineered under the long and prosperous rule of Iaroslav the Wise, culminates in one final action—the appointment of a Russian metropolitan of Kiev. In 1051 Iaroslav appointed the monk Ilarion to the post of metropolitan of Kiev. He was the first native Russian to fill that post and the only to do so in the eleventh century.[325] This appointment was against the wishes of the patriarch of Constantinople,[326] and represents another approach in Iaroslav's campaign toward the creation of an ecclesiastically independent Rus'.

Peter Brown's theory of the creation of multiple micro-Christendoms before the age of papal consolidation of power beginning in the twelfth century has been used and expanded in this chapter to discuss the creation of a Rusian micro-Christendom. The rulers of Rus' realized that they had to convert to Christianity to fulfill their goals of participation in the European world, but they wanted to maintain their independence, both political and ecclesiastical. Their initial steps toward conversion, by Ol'ga as well as by Vladimir, illustrate this point. Conversion was an inherently political process in the medieval world, where the targets of missionaries were kings and kingdoms. As has been shown in this chapter, it seems that the Rusian leaders understood these complex ties between politics and religion and worked to balance their interests by maintaining ties with a variety of micro-Christendoms, including accepting relics from Rome and metropolitans from Constantinople. They also strove to create a Rusian locus of worship in Kiev by replicating some of the famous locations of Constantinople in an attempt to turn the Rusian people's devotion inward, rather than directing it at an outside source. The Rusian Church accepted Latin dates for saints' days and holidays that were at variance with the Byzantine micro-Christendom, or even flouted Byzantium itself. The goal of the rulers of Rus' was the maintenance of their own independence from foreign domination. Ecclesiastically the result was the creation of a Rusian Church that was unique. It was easily identifiable as a Christian church, it was ruled at the top by a Byzantine metropolitan, and had many Byzantine practices and structures, but it also incorporated elements from western micro-Christendoms. This is a new picture of the Christian Church in Rus', different from the traditionally articulated picture, and it showcases the creation of a new micro-Christendom—of Rus'.

Conclusion

Rus' in a Wider World

After the middle of the twelfth century Rus' began to change, and many of its connections with Europe began to attenuate. The disintegration of centralized political control in the mid-twelfth century in Rus', and the subsequent creation of multiple warring polities, made contact with outside powers of any sort, except as military or political assets, more difficult. The increase in the crusading mentality in Western Europe led to the increasing separation of the Latin and Orthodox Churches and the spread beyond the monasteries of the idea of Orthodox Christians as heretics, and eventually as objects of crusade. This is exemplified by the Fourth Crusade's sack of Constantinople in 1204, and the multiple crusades against Rusian city-states in the late twelfth and thirteenth centuries by Swedish crusaders and the Teutonic Knights. These actions increased the Rusians's appreciation of their own religion and increased their identification with Byzantium as part of a larger "us versus them" mentality shift. Finally, the invasion of the Mongols in the mid-thirteenth century cemented the separation of Slavic eastern Europe from the rest of the continent. The subjugation of the Rusian city-states to Mongol rule increased their otherness in the eyes of the rest of Europe. It also led to internal changes in Rus', including a shifting of power to the northeast, farther from their former European connections, increasing the power of the Orthodox Church, and finally leading to the creation of those most permanent ties to Byzantium—imperial ideology and the use of the title *tsar'*. These changes, which took place over the course of one hundred years after the end of the period covered in this book, radically changed the place and perception of Rus' in Europe. In fact, by the mid-thirteenth century there was no entity known as Rus'. The fact that these Slavic states passed back out of contact with the rest of Europe should not stop us from acknowledging that they *were* part of medieval Europe for a time. Despite the historically brief time of approximately two hundred years, from Vladimir Sviatoslavich's conversion to Christianity in 988 to the dissolution of central control in Rus' in 1146, Rus' was part of medieval Europe during that period, and deserves to be fully acknowledged and studied as such.

The goal inherent in this book's title is to reimagine Europe, specifically the place of Rus' in the medieval European world. The ideas laid out here present a picture of Rus' that differs from the traditional one subscribed to by medievalists, Byzantinists, and Slavists, while the importance of the goal has also been made clear through the evidence and arguments presented. The investigation of Rus' as separate from Europe, as part and parcel of Byzantium, or the study of medieval Europe excepting Rus', all decrease our understanding of events in the medieval world, because interaction existed between the various parts of medieval Europe. Despite what I believe to be the success of this study in presenting Rus' as an integral part of medieval Europe in the tenth through mid-twelfth centuries, it is also only a beginning. The study of a larger medieval Europe, inclusive of Rus', has to be increased through a variety of monographic studies that will cement this relationship in the historiography. The groundwork for many such ideas, including studies of comparative Rusian and Germanic rulership, female onomastic influence, women's entourages and courts, central European politico-military alliances, and the influence of dominant micro-Christendoms on emerging Christian kingdoms have been laid in this book. It is only with the completion of these studies and many others that the place of Kievan Rus' in Europe will truly be established.

On a broader level, we must examine the findings of this book in regard to the growing trend toward studies of world history. World history has steadily replaced studies based solely on Western history at the undergraduate level, and world history programs are proliferating at the graduate level. This is a new phenomenon in academia, but an old one among practitioners of the historical craft. Two thousand years ago Cicero noted that the effects of prosperity in China, or lack thereof, were related to the trends of currency of Rome.[1] The same is true in regard to the study of Rus'. Rus' was a part of Europe, but it was also on the easternmost border of Europe, the last Christian kingdom before the pagan steppe tribes and Muslims on the Volga and in central Asia. Rus' was the preferred route for many travelers to those lands. The account of Rabbi Petachia of his journey from Regensburg to Baghdad covers Regensburg through Kiev in the first paragraph because the journey was so commonplace, and only after Rus' does the travel description begin.[2] Rus', then, was familiar to European travelers, and it was beyond it that things became exotic. This opens up a wide variety of studies, almost nonexistent in English,[3] of Rus' and its relationship with Asia or with central Europe, of Christianity (including Rus') and Islam or paganism on the eastern frontiers of Europe, and of steppe influences on the eastern kingdoms of Europe, including Rus' and Hungary. Acknowledging the place of Rus' in Europe helps to open up not only European but also world history topics for further study.

Nationalist studies of one country read back into history largely went out of favor in the second half of the last century. It is only places that have been separated from modern Western Europe for political reasons for which such studies have continued. Scholars in Hungary,[4] Russia,[5] and Ukraine[6] often read their modern territorial boundaries back into history for the purposes of creating, defining, or defending their modern national identity. American and Western European scholars have largely been content to let them do this, as they have also passively absorbed modern political phenomenon and read them back into history. This trend is breaking down in the twenty-first century, and Western academia is beginning to explore the history of medieval eastern Europe.[7] The next step for these studies is the one outlined in this book—the integration of those medieval eastern European kingdoms into medieval European history as a whole.

Life, and thus history, does not occur in isolation, and yet it is often studied that way, as if events on the European continent do not affect England, for instance. Cicero's quotation above is merely one data point of a larger phenomenon. Clearly it is impossible to study in the depth required every country, kingdom, or empire on every continent in every time period. But it is important to realize that interactions were occurring between polities, however separate. Such interactions might dramatically affect even the smallest of microhistories in such a way as to create local folklore, economic impetus, religious practice, medical conditions, or any of a variety of other possibilities. Examining the connections between medieval kingdoms outside of modern political or even geographical conceptions (European studies versus Asian studies) allows us to see the plethora of connections that existed for medieval people about which we have been unaware. Though this book does not explore every Rusian connection with non-Rusian peoples, it does attempt to thoroughly explore a subsection of those interactions in order to achieve a clearer understanding of history as a whole.

The medieval kingdom of Rus' was involved in a variety of ways with the other kingdoms and empires of medieval Europe, including via dynastic marriages, religious exchange, military enterprises, artistic exchange, and many other ways not covered. Those ties illustrate the connection of Rus' to the rest of Europe in this period and show that the place of Rus' is firmly in Europe.

Appendix: Rulers of Rus'

The following are all technically rulers of Kiev, but it is generally agreed (with some exceptions) that the ruler of Kiev is the ruler of Rus'. The rulers are listed in chronological order, with their dates of rule in parentheses.

Igor' (913–945)
Ol'ga (regent, 945–ca. 964)
Sviatoslav Igorevich (945–972)
Iaropolk Sviatoslavich (973–980)
Vladimir Sviatoslavich (ca. 980–1015)
Sviatopolk Iaropolchich (1015–1016, 1018)
Iaroslav "the Wise" Vladimirich (1016–1018, 1018–1054)
Iziaslav Iaroslavich (1054–1068, 1069–1073, 1077–1078)
Vseslav Briacheslavich (1068–1069)
Sviatoslav Iaroslavich (1073–1076)
Vsevolod Iaroslavich (1076–1077)
Vsevolod Iaroslavich (1078–1093)
Sviatopolk II Iziaslavich (1093–1113)
Vladimir "Monomakh" Vsevolodich (1113–1125)
Mstislav "Harald" Vladimirich (1125–1132)
Iaropolk Vladimirich (1132–1138)
Viacheslav Vladimirich (1138)
Vsevolod Olgovich (1138–1146)

Notes

Introduction

1. *The Hagiography of Kievan Rus'*, trans. Paul Hollingsworth, in *Harvard Library of Early Ukrainian Literature: English Translations*, vol. 2 (Cambridge, Mass.: Harvard University Press, 1992).

2. Gerd Althoff, *Otto III,* trans. Phyllis G. Jestice (University Park: Pennsylvania State University Press, 2003), 57.

3. The eminent German historian Karl Leyser advocated this principle as well, though failed to follow it in the same book, and excluded Rus' from his picture of Germany's horizons. "The inner working of early medieval societies cannot be understood without also studying their links, religious, cultural, economic, and political, with their neighbours." K. J. Leyser, *Medieval Germany and Its Neighbours, 900–1250* (London: Hambledon Press, 1982), ix.

4. The influence of Benedict Anderson on these ideas must be noted here, as, although he works on the modern world, he cogently states the situation in the medieval world as a preface to his larger discussion. Anderson, *Imagined Communities: Reflections on the Origin and Spread of Nationalism* (London: Verso, 2006).

5. The period dealt with in this book is largely late tenth, eleventh, and first half of the twelfth centuries. Marc Bloch, *Feudal Society,* vol. 1, *The Growth of Ties of Dependence,* trans. L. A. Manyon (Chicago: University of Chicago Press, 1961), 81.

6. This should be differentiated from the "Schism" of 1054, which, while historically relevant, did not see an immediate impact on political relations between medieval states of different Christian orientations.

7. Timothy C. Champion, "Medieval Archeology and the Tyranny of the Historical Record," in *From the Baltic to the Black Sea: Studies in Medieval Archeology,* ed. David Austin and Leslie Alcock (London: Unwin Hyman, 1990), 79.

8. There are numerous examples, but a sampling includes Clifford R. Backman, *The Worlds of Medieval Europe* (Oxford: Oxford University Press, 2003); and R. W. Southern, *The Making of the Middle Ages* (New Haven, Conn.: Yale University Press, 1974). Robert Bartlett deals much more with the Slavs than most medieval historians, but he deals with the Slavs not as actors, but as those acted upon, and includes them in the story for the purpose of telling the German story more than for telling their own. Bartlett, *The Making of Europe: Conquest, Colonization and Cultural Change, 950–1350* (Princeton N.J.: Princeton University Press, 1993).

9. For an interesting bibliographic review of Soviet scholarship to the mid-1970s that shows some of these trends, see M. B. Sverdlov, "Rus' i evropeiskie gosudarstva," in *Sovetskaia istoriografiia Kievskoi Rusi,* ed. V. V. Mavrodin (Leningrad: Nauka, 1978). Two of the most famous names from this period are B. D. Grekov and V. V. Mavrodin. B. D. Grekov, *Kievskaia Rus'* (Moscow: Uchebno-pedagogicheskii izdatel'stvo, 1949); V. V. Mavrodin, *Obrazovanie drevnerusskogo gosudarstva* (Leningrad: Leningradskogo universiteta, 1945). Though there is also some excellent later, especially post-Soviet, scholarship that attempts to deal with larger visions of Rus'. For example, A. V. Nazarenko, *Drevniaia Rus' na mezhdunarodnykh putiakh: Mezhdistsiplinarnye ocherki kulturnykh, torgovykh, politicheskikh sviazei IX–XII vekov* (Moscow: Iazyki russkoi kul'tury, 2001). However, this work is not without its problems as well. See Charles Halperin's review of Nazarenko's book, in which he discusses the lack of a complete framework for the book. Halperin, *Slavic Review* 61, no. 2 (2002). In English-language scholarship the same problem exists, even in such excellent works as Janet Martin, *Medieval Russia, 980–1584* (Cambridge: Cambridge University Press, 1995); and Simon Franklin and Jonathan Shepard, *The Emergence of Rus', 750–1200* (New York: Longman, 1996).

10. The Normanist controversy seems largely concluded, with the anti-Normanist position having lost its major backer with the fall of the Soviet Union. The origin of the original Rusians in Scandinavia and their domination of local Slavic, Finnic, and other tribes along the eastern European river systems created the foundations for the Rusian state that is discussed here.

11. Dimitri Obolensky, *The Byzantine Commonwealth: Eastern Europe, 500–1453* (London: Weidenfeld and Nicolson, 1971).

12. For more information on the history of the idea of Sweden and the problems with discussing "Sweden" in a medieval context, see Thomas Lindkvist, "The Emergence of Sweden," in *The Viking World,* ed. Stefan Brink in collaboration with Neil Price (London: Routledge, 2008), 668–674.

13. German historians typically refer to this political entity simply as the "Reich," a tradition occasionally followed in English-language works as well, such as Lisa Wolverton, *Hastening toward Prague: Power and Society in the Medieval Czech Lands* (Philadelphia: University of Pennsylvania Press, 2001), 228, where it is simply referred to as "the 'Empire'" and its ruler as "the German emperor."

14. A fascinating introduction to the topic, as related to medieval Europe, is Josiah Russell, *Medieval Regions and Their Cities* (Bloomington: Indiana University Press, 1972). For a brief discussion of this in another context, see Anderson, *Imagined Communities,* 19–22.

15. Which is not to say that current studies do not exist; they just do not address the problem as definitely as it could be addressed. For two examples, see Iaroslav Isaievych, "On the Titulature of Rulers in Eastern Europe," *Journal of Ukrainian Studies* 29, nos. 1–2 (2004): 219–244; Aleksander Filiushkin, *Tituly Russkikh gosudarei* (Moscow: Al'ians-Arkheo, 2006).

16. See my papers "What Was a Kniaz'?" (paper delivered at the Medieval Slavic and Early Modern Culture Workshop, UCLA, February 25, 2005); "Kniaz'=Rex=King" (paper presented at the Eighth Midwest Medieval Slavic Workshop, University of Chicago, April 29, 2005); "Why Titles Matter: Titulature in Eleventh- and Twelfth-Century Rus'" (paper delivered at the 41st International Congress on Medieval Studies, University of Western Michigan, May 6, 2006); "The Forgotten Kingdom of Rus'" (paper presented at the Midwest Medieval History Conference, University of Notre Dame, September 25–26, 2009); "What's in a Name? The Case of the Kingdom of Rus'" (public lecture presented at Wittenberg University, December 3, 2009).

17. For the title "grand prince," see, most recently, Martin Dimnik, "The Title 'Grand Prince' in Kievan Rus'," *Mediaeval Studies* 66 (2004): 253–312.

18. Omeljan Pritsak, *The Old Rus' Kievan and Galician-Volhynian Chronicles: The Ostroz'kyj (Xlebnikov) and Četvertyns'kyj (Pogodin) Codices* (Cambridge, Mass.: Harvard University Press, 1990), xv. Donald Ostrowski notes that the *Povest' vremennykh let (PVL)* began to be compiled roughly in 1116, using earlier sources, perhaps including an unfinished chronicle. Ostrowski, *The Povest' vremennykh let: An Interlinear Collation and Paradosis,* ed. Donald Ostrowski, with David Birnbaum and Horace G. Lunt (Cambridge, Mass.: Harvard University Press, 2004), xvii–xviii.

19. Samuel Hazzard Cross and Olgerd P. Sherbowitz-Wetzor, eds., transls., *The Russian Primary Chronicle* (Cambridge, Mass.: Mediaeval Academy of America, 1953), 4. This is also, currently, the only English-language translation of the *PVL,* and while it has its faults, it is generally fine and has excellent notes.

20. See Ostrowski's stemma in the introduction. There is further discussion of the process by which this information is arrived at there as well in the section entitled "Use of the Stemma." *The Povest' vremennykh let*, xxxix.

21. A. A. Shakhmatov, *Razyskaniia o russkikh letopisiakh* (Moscow: Akademicheskii Proekt, 2001); Pritsak, *The Old Rus' Kievan and Galician-Volhynian Chronicles;* Ostrowski, *The Povest' vremennykh let;* Ostrowski, "The Načalnyj Svod Theory and the Povest' vremennyx let," *Russian Linguistics* 31 (2007): 269–308; Ostrowski, "Striving for Perfection: Transcription of the Laurentian Copy of the Povest' vremennykh let," *Russian Linguistics* 30 (2006): 437–451.

22. *The Povest' vremennykh let.*

23. *The Paterik of the Kievan Caves Monastery,* trans. Muriel Heppell (Cambridge, Mass.: Harvard University Press, 1989); *Sermons and Rhetoric of Kievan Rus',* trans. Simon Franklin (Cambridge, Mass.: Harvard University Press, 1991); O. V. Loseva, *Russkie Mesiateslovy XI–XIV vekov* (Moscow: Pamiatniki istoricheskoi mysli, 2001); "Kanonicheskie otvety mitropolita Ioanna II," *Russkaia istoricheskaia biblioteka* 6 (1908).

24. A small sampling includes the following: "Nicolai I. Papae Epistolae," in *Monumenta Germanica historiae epistolarum,* ed. Ernestus Perels (Berolini: Apud Weidmannos, 1925); Adomnán of Iona, *Life of St. Columba,* trans. Richard Sharpe (New York: Penguin, 1995); Adamus Bremensis, *Adami gesta Hammaburgensis ecclesiae pontificum,* ed. J. M. Lappenberg, Scriptores rerum germanicarum in usum scholarum ex Monumentis Germaniae historicis recusi (Hannover: Impensis Biblipolii Hahniani, 1876); I. I. Reiske, ed., *De cerimoniis aulae Byzantinae,* vol. 9 of Corpus Scriptorum Historiae Byzantinae (Bonn: Impensis Ed. Weberi, 1829); John Scylitzes, *Ioannis Scylitzae synopsis historiarum,* ed. Ioannes Thurn, Corpus fontium historiae Byzantinae (Berolini: De Gruyter, 1973); Albert Bauer and Reinhold Rau, eds., *Fontes ad historiam aevi Saxonici illustrandam: Widukindi res gestae Saxonicae; Adalberti continuato Reginonis; Liudprandi opera* (Darmstadt: Wissenschaftliche Buchgesellschaft, 1971); *Ottonian Germany: The "Chronicon" of Thietmar of Merseburg,* trans. David A. Warner (Manchester: Manchester University Press, 2001); V. Cl. Lud. Frid. Hasse, ed., *Lamberti Hersfeldensis Annales,* in Monumenta Germaniae Historica Scriptores, vol. 5, ed. G. Pertz (Hannover: Impensis Bibliopolii Avlici Hahniani, 1844).

25. Something that may be seen as very similar to Charles Halperin's ideology of silence regarding the Mongols. Halperin, "Ideology of Silence: Prejudice and Pragmatism on the Medieval Religious Frontier," *Comparative Studies in Society and History* 26, no. 3 (1984): 442–466.

26. Multiple examples of this will be seen throughout this book. Iziaslav Iaroslavich, for example, travels widely in Poland and the German Empire and no mention (positive or negative) is made of this in the Rusian sources, apart from a brief note that he went to the Poles. Evpraksia Vsevolodovna marries two Germans, including the emperor, leaves the emperor to side with the pope during the Investiture Controversy, and receives a prestigious burial in Rus' upon her death—the burial and her admittance to a nunnery being her only mentions in Rusian sources at all. These are the two most prominent examples, highlighting the problems inherent in the Rusian sources when dealing with the rest of Europe.

1. The Byzantine Ideal

1. Dimitri Obolensky, *The Byzantine Commonwealth: Eastern Europe, 500–1453* (London: Weidenfeld and Nicolson, 1971), 1.
2. Francis Thomson has gone so far as to say that "the reception of Byzantine culture forms the foundation of East Slav civilization." Francis J. Thomson, "The Intellectual Silence of Early Russia," in *The Reception of Byzantine Culture in Mediaeval Russia* (Brookfield, Vt.: Ashgate, 1999), ix.
3. Obolensky consciously limited his work based upon geography, as well as levels of influence. Obolensky, *The Byzantine Commonwealth*, 1–2. Among other sources that deal with the Byzantine influence on a broader Europe, see Michael McCormick, "Byzantium's Role in the Formation of Early Medieval Civilization: Approaches and Problems," *Illinois Classical Studies* 12, no. 2 (1987): 208. In the past decade or so there has been an increase in scholarship on such connections. In addition to McCormick's article-length study, Anthea Harris and Krijnie Ciggaar have offered book-length studies of the topic in various time periods, and Julia M. H. Smith has dealt with the issue as well, though through a slightly different lens.

   In addition to Europe, parts of the Middle East and North Africa were influenced by Byzantium as well, but they are generally not discussed here. However, as a brief example, the Fatimids borrowed some aspects of Byzantine court ceremonial. Jonathan Shepard, "Byzantine Diplomacy, A.D. 800–1204: Means and Ends," in *Byzantine Diplomacy: Papers from the Twenty-Fourth Spring Symposium of Byzantine Studies, Cambridge, March 1990*, ed. Jonathon Shepard and Simon Franklin (Brookfield, Vt.: Variorum, 1990), 58.
4. Donald M. Nicol, "The Byzantine View of Western Europe," in *Byzantium: Its Ecclesiastical History and Relations with the Western World* (London: Variorum Reprints, 1972), 316. The internal quotation is from Franz Dölger.

5. Ibid., 319. Fredegar recording that Childeric was sent from the emperor to rule Gaul is one example of this. See Anthea Harris, *Byzantium, Britain and the West: The Archeology of Cultural Identity, AD 400–650* (Charleston, S.C.: Tempus, 2003), 31.

6. This lack might also be illustrated in pagan Scandinavian and Germanic kingdoms by the recourse to heavenly genealogies for the ruling families. Genealogies that traced the descent of the ruler back to Odin/Wodan/Wotan provided increased legitimation for that person or family to rule. Additionally, some medieval families concocted Trojan ancestries for themselves as a way to increase their own legitimacy by drawing on the larger Greco-Roman heritage.

7. For a fascinating critique of Obolensky's formulation that mentions some of these same points, in more pointed language, see Anthony Kaldellis, *Hellenism in Byzantium: The Transformations of Greek Identity and the Reception of the Classical Tradition* (Cambridge: Cambridge University Press, 2007), 109–110.

8. Obolensky, *The Byzantine Commonwealth,* 3, for his description and definition of commonwealth.

9. Ruth Macrides, "Dynastic Marriages and Political Kinship," in *Byzantine Diplomacy: Papers from the Twenty-Fourth Spring Symposium of Byzantine Studies, Cambridge, March 1990,* ed. Jonathan Shepard and Simon Franklin (Brookfield, Vt.: Variorum, 1990). Though the amount of "honor" fluctuated widely based upon time and place. The crusaders of the late-eleventh and twelfth centuries were certainly less interested in the Roman heritage than were, perhaps, the Ottonian emperors. Similarly, the Rusians appropriated many things from Byzantium, but an understanding of the culture of antiquity was not necessarily one of them. For more on these ideas in regard to Rus', see Francis J. Thomson, *The Reception of Byzantine Culture in Medaeval Russia* (Brookfield, Vt.: Ashgate, 1999); Simon Franklin, "The Empire of the Rhomaioi as Viewed from Kievan Russia: Aspects of Byzantino-Russian Cultural Relations," in *Byzantium—Rus'—Russia: Studies in the Translation of Christian Culture* (Burlington, Vt.: Ashgate/Variorum, 2002).

10. I believe this is in keeping with some of Obolensky's core ideas about the idea of Byzantium's "cultural" supremacy. Obolensky, *The Byzantine Commonwealth,* 2–3. This process also continued for much of the Middle Ages as dynasties established themselves throughout Europe. As will be discussed, in western Europe, the Franks, Germans, and Anglo-Saxons appropriated from Byzantium in the early and high Middle Ages, but the Serbs and others were still appropriating from Byzantium in the late Mid-

dle Ages. This does not mean, however, that the appropriation meant the same thing to all of those people throughout that time, rather that Byzantium (the Roman Empire) held a lasting prestige for kingdoms and royal families seeking their own legitimacy.

11. For the early medieval period, see Harris, *Byzantium, Britain and the West*; and Julia M. H. Smith, *Europe after Rome: A New Cultural History, 500–1000* (Oxford: Oxford University Press, 2005).

12. *Adam of Bremen: History of the Archbishops of Hamburg-Bremen,* trans. Francis J. Tschan (New York: Columbia University Press, 1959), bk. 3, xxxii. Henry III "was the grand-grand-grand nephew of Otto II and Empress Theophano," n111.

13. Kaldellis, *Hellenism in Byzantium,* 43.

14. See the introduction to Paolo Squatriti's excellent recent translation of Liudprand for an estimation of his linguistic abilities and their appreciation by his contemporaries. Liudprand of Cremona, *The Complete Works of Liudprand of Cremona,* trans. Paolo Squatriti (Washington, D.C.: Catholic University of America Press, 2007), 16–17.

15. As is well known, Liudprand's views of the Byzantines changed over time. The positive portrayal can be found in the *Antapadosis* (bk. 3, ch. 26, for example), while the negative can be seen most clearly in *De Legatione.* He also refers to the Byzantine emperor briefly as emperor of the Romans as well, though appends "or Greeks" (*De Legatione,* ch. 40). Liudprand of Cremona, *Relatio de Legatione Constantinopolitana* (online at Patrologia Latin, http://www.documentacatholicaomnia.eu/30_10_0922-0972-_Liutprandus _Cremonensis_Episcopus.html); *Historia Gestorum Regum et Imperatorum Sive Antapadosis* (online at Patrologia Latina, http://www.documentacath olicaomnia.eu/30_10_0922-0972-_Liutprandus_Cremonensis_Episcopus .html).

16. Kaldellis, *Hellenism in Byzantium,* 43. Kaldellis notes: "For many western historians Rome also belongs to antiquity and so anything later than it can at best constitute a 'reception,' despite the fact that in the case of Byzantium *alone* are we dealing with direct political, social, and cultural continuity from Julius Caesar to Konstantinos XI Palaiologos."

17. Smith, *Europe after Rome,* 255–277. This is seen quite quotably on p. 277— "the rhetoric of Romanness added a patina of ancient respectability to the new forms of hegemonic kingship that emerged in northern Europe from the end of the eighth century onwards."

18. Paul Magdalino, "The Empire of the Komnenoi (1118–1204)," in *The Cambridge History of the Byzantine Empire, c. 500–1492,* ed. Jonathan Shepard (Cambridge: Cambridge University Press, 2009), 647, 654.

19. Harris, *Byzantium, Britain and the West,* 98–99.

20. Byzantine coinage maintained Roman prestige and weight as well (for obvious reasons) and thus was still the main currency to be appropriated in style, weight, and fineness throughout Europe. Pamela Nightingale, "The Evolution of Weight-Standards and the Creation of New Monetary and Commercial Links in Northern Europe from the Tenth Century to the Twelfth Century," *Economic History Review* 38, no. 2 (1985): 194–199.

21. Krijnie N. Ciggaar, *Western Travellers to Constantinople: The West and Byzantium, 962–1204; Cultural and Political Relations* (Leiden: Brill, 1996), 354.

22. Obolensky, *The Byzantine Commonwealth,* 1, 203, 208. More recently one can see the same phenomenon in James Howard-Johnston, "Byzantium and Its Neighbors," in *The Oxford Handbook of Byzantine Studies,* ed. Elizabeth Jeffreys with John Haldon and Robin Cormack (Oxford: Oxford University Press, 2009), 954.

23. Ciggaar, *Western Travellers to Constantinople,* 7. Michael McCormick has also commented on the problem of the word *influence:* "It implies that the society which 'receives' the foreign 'influence' plays a passive role, inertly absorbing the output of another society. In reality, the process is usually quite the opposite: the borrower takes the initiative in appropriating from the 'donor' society an element which it deems useful." McCormick, "Byzantium's Role," 216.

24. Peter Brown, "Eastern and Western Christendom in Late Antiquity: A Parting of the Ways," in *The Orthodox Churches and the West,* ed. Derek Baker (Oxford: Basil Blackwell, 1976), 5.

25. Obolensky, *The Byzantine Commonwealth.* For a more concise explanation of what Obolensky terms "cultural imbalance," see Dimitri Obolensky, "Byzantine Frontier Zones and Cultural Exchanges," in *Actes du XIVe congrès international des études Byzantines* (Bucharest: Editura Academiei Republicii Socialiste România, 1974); and Robert Bartlett, *The Making of Europe: Conquest, Colonization and Cultural Change, 950–1350* (Princeton, N.J.: Princeton University Press, 1993). This idea has been adopted by a wide variety of scholars, so much so that Jan Piskorski was able to state that "historians are generally in agreement that medieval German colonization and colonization of so-called German law were the second great step after Christianity in the development of East Central Europe at the turn of the first and second millennia." Piskorski, "Medieval Colonization in East Central Europe," in *The Germans and the East,* ed. Charles Ingrao and Franz A. J. Szabo (West Lafayette, Ind.: Purdue University Press, 2008), 31.

26. Kathleen Ashley and Véronique Plesch, "The Cultural Processes of 'Appropriation,'" *Journal of Medieval and Early Modern Studies* 31, no. 1 (2002): 8.

27. Ibid., 2–3.

28. Ibid., 3. Piskorski adds a relevant quote here that speaks to the essence of the idea of appropriation: "cultures which are open and independent are not afraid of borrowings and foreign inspiration, and they are well able to take advantage of these." Piskorski, "Medieval Colonization in East Central Europe," 33.

29. John Lowden, "The Luxury Book as Diplomatic Gift," in *Byzantine Diplomacy: Papers from the Twenty-Fourth Spring Symposium of Byzantine Studies, Cambridge, March 1990,* ed. Jonathan Shepard and Simon Franklin (Brookfield, Vt.: Variorum, 1990), 260.

30. Wilhelm Koehler, "Byzantine Art in the West," *Dumbarton Oaks Papers* 1 (1941).

31. McCormick, "Byzantium's Role."

32. See Chapter 2 for more discussion of the importance of Byzantine brides and their desirability to multiple European royal houses. Also, Otto III himself chose to pursue a dynastic marriage with Byzantium as one of his first sole decisions after coming of age as a ruler. Gerd Althoff, *Otto III,* trans. Phyllis G. Jestice (University Park: Pennsylvania State University Press, 2003), 56.

33. Altoff, *Otto III,* 81.

34. Though Constantine I also used the term *renovatio* on his coinage, which was perhaps indicative of his founding of the empire in Constantinople.

35. Ibid., 83.

36. Though addressed in a variety of Schramm's works, it is most fully dealt with in the expansive *Kaiser Könige und Päpste* (Stuttgart: Anton Hieresmann, 1969), esp. 3:200–296.

37. Julia Smith talks in some detail about Carolingian appropriations, later Roman/Byzantine appropriations in Europe she then attributes to Charlemagne. Smith, *Europe after Rome,* 275. Otto of Freising provides the medieval context for Charlemagne's *translatio imperii.* Bishop of Freising Otto, *The Two Cities: A Chronicle of Universal History to the Year 1146* a.d., trans. Charles Christopher Mierow (New York: Octagon Books, 1966), bk. 7, sec. 35.

38. Althoff, *Otto III.*

39. Gerbert of Aurillac, *The Letters of Gerbert with His Papal Privileges as Sylvester II,* trans. Harriet Pratt Lattin (New York: Columbia University Press, 1961), 297. Otto was not the only ruler who received a Byzantine, or even Byzantine-style, education. Roger II of Sicily, as well, was educated

by "exponents of Graeco-Byzantine culture," and that became clear in his use of the language and symbols of Byzantium. Hubert Houben, *Roger II of Sicily: A Ruler between East and West,* trans. Graham A. Loud and Diane Milburn (Cambridge: Cambridge University Press, 2002), 100.

40. For more discussion of this influence, see Smith, *Europe after Rome,* 275–277.

41. Jonathan Shepard, "Western Approaches (900–1025)," in *The Cambridge History of the Byzantine Empire, c. 500–1492,* ed. Jonathan Shepard, 537–559 (Cambridge: Cambridge University Press, 2009), 550.

42. Ibid., 545, 549, 552.

43. Althoff, *Otto III,* 81.

44. *Ottonian Germany: The "Chronicon" of Thietmar of Merseburg,* trans. David A. Warner (Manchester: Manchester University Press, 2001), bk. 4, ch. 47.

45. Ibid., ch. 45.

46. Gallus Anonymous, *Gesta principum Polonorum: The Deeds of the Princes of the Poles,* trans. Paul W. Knoll and Frank Schaer (New York: Central European University Press, 2003), 37.

47. Thietmar of Merseburg, "Die Chronik des Bischofs Thietmar von Merseburg," in Monumenta Germaniae Historica Scriptores rerum Germanicarum, Nova series, vol. 9, ed. Robert Holtzmann (Berlin: Weidmannsche Buchandlung, 1935), bk. 5, ch. 10.

48. For an in-depth analysis of the event, see Jonathan Shepard, "Otto III Boleslaw Chrobry and the 'Happening' at Gniezno, A.D. 1000: Some Possible Implications of Professor Poppe's Thesis concerning the Offspring of Anna Porphyrogenita," in *Byzantium and East Central Europe,* ed. Günter Prinzing and Maciej Salamon, with the assistance of Paul Stephenson (Cracow: Byzantina et Slavica Cracoviensia III, 2001), 27–48.

49. There is a fascinating discussion of the role of the Ottonian emperors in the *Reichskirche,* as Leyser calls it, in Karl Leyser, *Rule and Conflict in Early Medieval Society: Ottonian Saxony* (London: Arnold, 1979). It must be mentioned, as well, that Otto III may have been acting with the permission of Pope Sylvester II, as he ordained Gaudentius, Adalbert's brother, as archbishop; though multiple ecclesiastics were unhappy about the whole affair because land had been taken away from them in the reorganization. See *Ottonian Germany,* bk. 4, ch. 45, and n130.

50. *Ottonian Germany,* bk. 4, ch. 46. Elaborated upon by Gallus Anonymous, *Gesta principum Polonorum,* 37–39.

51. *Ottonian Germany,* bk. 4, ch. 59.

52. Karl Leyser, "The Tenth Century in Byzantine-Western Relationships," in *Relations between East and West in the Middle Ages,* ed. Derek Baker (Edinburgh: Edinburgh University Press, 1973), 31.

53. Althoff, *Otto III,* 84–85. There is an excellent reproduction of the miniature on p. 85.

54. Ibid., 86.

55. Ibid., 86–87.

56. Ibid., 19. Shepard, "Western Approaches," 553–554. See also Shepard,
"Byzantine Diplomacy," 58, on the Fatimid rulers' view of Constantinople
as the model of a capital city.

57. Bernhardt's book is a fascinating look at itinerant kingship in Germany.
John W. Bernhardt, *Itinerant Kingship and Royal Monasteries in Early Medieval Germany, c. 936–1075* (Cambridge: Cambridge University Press, 1993).

58. The Visigothic kings of Spain also worked to create a powerful capital from
which they could rule, with the intent of copying Rome, both old and new.
Peter Robert Lamont Brown, *The Rise of Western Christendom: Triumph
and Diversity, AD 200–1000,* 2nd ed. (Malden, Mass.: Blackwell, 2003), 366.

59. Leyser, "The Tenth Century," 44.

60. And those two are separated by approximately eighty years. Robert L. Benson, "Political *Renovatio:* Two Models from Roman Antiquity," in *Renaissance and Renewal in the Twelfth Century,* ed. Robert L. Benson and Giles
Constable (Cambridge, Mass.: Harvard University Press, 1982), 374n181.

61. Ibid., 373. This was also the title that Pope Leo had controversially awarded
to Charlemagne in 800, though he more often chose to use the title *rex fran-
korum et longobardum,* perhaps out of political expediency, or because of a
compromise with the Byzantines, who maintained the view that their ruler
was truly *rex,* or *basileus, Romanorum.*

62. Ibid., 373n177.

63. See the analysis of Paolo Squatriti in Liudprand of Cremona, *Complete
Works,* 18.

64. Though typically referred to as "rex," Roger II was called "basileus" by his
court preacher Philagathos Keramides, indicating his perception of Roger's status. Houben, *Roger II of Sicily,* 101–102.

65. Brown, *Rise of Western Christendom,* 477. Shepard mentions this title
briefly, as well, and notes that there were direct contacts with Byzantium
in the tenth century that involved gift exchange. Shepard, "Western Approaches," 542.

66. Walter de Gray Birch, "Index of the Styles and Titles of English Sovereigns," *Report of the First Annual Meeting of the Index Society* (London,
1879), 52–53. Birch's article contains a listing of all of the titles used by the
rulers of both Anglo-Saxon and Norman England.

67. Ibid., 55.

68. Ciggaar, *Western Travellers to Constantinople,* 132.

69. Ibid., 141.

70. Bernard S. Bachrach, "On the Origins of William the Conqueror's Horse Transports," *Technology and Culture* 26, no. 3 (1985): 505.

71. Ibid., 45.

72. Ciggaar, *Western Travellers to Constantinople,* 139–141; Krijnie Ciggaar, "Byzantine Marginalia to the Norman Conquest," *Anglo-Norman Studies* 9 (1986): 57–59.

73. Ciggaar, "Byzantine Marginalia, 60–61.

74. Simon Franklin, *Writing, Society and Culture in Early Rus, c. 950–1300* (Cambridge: Cambridge University Press, 2002), 13; Thomson, "Intellectual Silence," xxi–xxii.

75. Franklin, "Empire of the Rhomaioi." For an example of such a use of *tsar'* for a deceased ruler, see the inscription in Kiev's St. Sofia church, recorded in S. A. Vysotskii, *Drevnei-russkie nadpisi sofii Kievskoi, XI–XIV vv.* vyp. 1 (Kiev: Naukova Dumka, 1966), 39–41, tables IX and X.

76. This represents one of the key things to note in this chapter, and more generally in this book—that there was considerable absorption of Byzantine ideas, religion, and so forth after the period under discussion, but not until after the dissolution of a united Rus' in the mid-twelfth century. John Meyendorff, *Byzantium and the Rise of Russia: A Study of Byzantino-Russian Relations in the Fourteenth Century* (Cambridge: Cambridge University Press, 1981), 274. See also the article on the Russo-Byzantine connections of Muscovy in the handling of autocracy by Robert Lee Wolff, "The Three Romes: The Migration of an Ideology and the Making of an Autocrat," *Daedalus* 88, no. 2 (1959).

77. V. L. Ianin, "Pechati Feofano Muzalon," *Numizmatika i sfragistika* 2 (1965): 82.

78. I. I. Reiske, ed., *De ceremoniis aulae Byzantinae,* vol. 9 of Corpus Scriptorum Historiae Byzantinae (Bonn: Impensis Ed. Weberi, 1829), 594–598.

79. Jeffrey Featherstone, "Ol'ga's Visit to Constantinople," *Harvard Ukrainian Studies* 14, nos. 3–4 (1990): 309n27. Featherstone makes the observation that *archontissa* was a common title for a noble woman in Byzantine Greek and separate from the titulature of rulers.

80. Cecily Hilsdale, "Diplomacy by Design: Rhetorical Strategies of the Byzantine Gift" (PhD diss., University of Chicago, 2003), 66, citing Reiske, *De ceremoniis,* 694. This titulature changed in the eleventh century, however, when the Byzantines begin to call the Hungarian ruler "kral." Cecily J. Hilsdale, "The Social Life of the Byzantine Gift: The Royal Crown of Hungary Re-Invented," *Art History* 31:5 (2008), 618, 620.

81. Jonathan Shepard, "Byzantium and Russia in the Eleventh Century: A Study in Political and Ecclesiastical Relations" (PhD diss., University of Oxford, 1973), 74.

82. Shepard theorizes that the Byzantines gave the title to the Rusians because they lacked *autokratia* in their land. The Rusian rulers completely abandoned the title in the twelfth century when they switched entirely to Slavonic seals and coins. Ibid., 353–356.

83. Gray Birch, "Index of the Styles and Titles of English Sovereigns," 69. This understanding of archon as rex, if true, further points out the problems in attempting to understand medieval titulature as no modern reader of Greek or Latin would ever assign an equivalency to those titles. Historians and linguists must not only understand the language, but the perception of language of a thousand years ago, often by only half-trained speakers, to truly get at the heart of this issue.

84. Following Thomson and others, the appropriation must be looked at as selective, though not necessarily self-selected, a point that may be debated. Thomson, "Intellectual Silence of Early Russia." The Muscovites, of course, created a rhetoric in which they were the "Third Rome" and a direct descendant of the Byzantine Empire.

85. Those who shared frontiers with Byzantium were more greatly influenced than those farther away, in Obolensky's analysis. Obolensky, "Byzantine Frontier Zones."

86. Robert Browning, *Byzantium and Bulgaria: A Comparative Study across the Early Medieval Frontier* (Berkeley: University of California Press, 1975), 58–67.

87. For a nice rendering of *basileus Romaion,* see Veselin Beševliev, *Die Protobulgarischen Inschriften* (Berlin: Akademie Verlag, 1963), 330–331.

88. Browning, *Byzantium and Bulgaria,* 62. Though the Byzantines soon repented this and claimed that it meant nothing, coincidentally once Symeon and his armies were removed from the area around Constantinople.

89. Ibid., 67.

90. Ibid., 69. For a better picture of Peter's reign, see John V. A. Fine Jr., "A Fresh Look at Bulgaria under Tsar Peter I (927–969)," *Byzantine Studies/ Etudes Byzantines* 5, nos. 1–2 (1978).

91. Jonathan Shepard, "A Marriage Too Far? Maria Lekapena and Peter of Bulgaria," in *The Empress Theophano: Byzantium and the West at the Turn of the Millennium,* ed. Adalbert Davids (Cambridge: Cambridge University Press, 1995), 140–148.

92. Paul Stephenson, "Balkan Borderlands (1018–1204)," in *The Cambridge History of the Byzantine Empire, c. 500–1492,* ed. Jonathan Shepard (Cambridge: Cambridge University Press, 2009), 669.

93. John V. A. Fine Jr., *The Late Medieval Balkans: A Critical Survey from the Late Twelfth Century to the Ottoman Conquest* (Ann Arbor: University of Michigan Press, 1987), 309. The differences in usage between the Serbian

and Greek ("Greek" v. "Roman") most likely result from the lack of a "Roman" image of Byzantium in some of the Slavic states. This has been discussed already, briefly, in regard to the Rusians and their perception of Byzantium as a "Christian" rather than a Roman empire. Nonetheless, the Rusians and Serbs both placed a certain weight on the image of Byzantium and appropriated from it accordingly to buttress their own legitimacy.

94. Nicol, "Byzantine View of Western Europe," 319.

95. Brown, *Rise of Western Christendom,* 378.

96. Krijnie Ciggaar, "England and Byzantium on the Eve of the Norman Conquest (The Reign of Edward the Confessor)," *Anglo-Norman Studies* 5 (1982): 84.

97. Ibid., 90.

98. *Ottonian Germany,* bk. 8, ch. 33.

99. Not to mention the simpler possibility that, as he had also informed the German emperor of his actions (though the emperor had lent troops to this campaign as well), he also felt the need to inform the other major power center in Europe.

100. Werner Ohnsorge, "Otto I. und Byzanz," in *Konstantinopel und der Okzident* (Darmstadt: Wissenschaftliche Buchgesellschaft, 1966), 214

101. Aurillac, *The Letters of Gerbert,* letter 119.

102. A. A. Vasiliev, "Hugh Capet of France and Byzantium," *Dumbarton Oaks Papers* 6 (1951): 229, 232.

103. Wladislaw Duczko, "Viking Sweden and Byzantium—An Archeologist's Version," in *Byzantium: Identity, Image, Influence—XIX International Congress of Byzantine Studies, University of Copenhagen, 18–24 August, 1996,* ed. Karsten Fledelius (Copenhagen: Eventus, 1996), 194, 199.

104. Snorri Sturluson, *Heimskringla: History of the Kings of Norway,* trans. Lee M. Hollander (Austin: University of Texas Press, 1964), 697–698. Though the story there is outwardly not one of easily impressed Norsemen. Instead the tale has been embroidered with saga motifs to illustrate that the Norse king was superior to the emperor, a traditional tactic used when faced with awe of a foreign ruler. There is an even more embellished story in *Morkinskinna: The Earliest Icelandic Chronicle of the Norwegian Kings (1030–1157),* trans. Theodore M. Andersson and Kari Ellen Gade (Ithaca, N.Y.: Cornell University Press, 2000), 323–324.

105. Karsten Fledelius, "Royal Scandinavian Travellers to Byzantium: The Vision of Byzantium in Danish and Norwegian Historiography of the Early 13th Century—and in the Danish Historical Drama of the Early 19th Century," in *Byzantium: Identity, Image, Influence—XIX International Con-*

gress of Byzantine Studies, University of Copenhagen, 18–24 August, 1996, ed. Karsten Fledelius (Copenhagen: Eventus, 1996), 215.

106. Liudprand of Cremona, *Liudprandi Opera,* ed. Joseph Becker, Scriptores rerum Germanicarum (Hannover: Impensis Bibliopolii Hahniani, 1915), bk. VI, ch. 5.

107. George Ostrogorsky, *History of the Byzantine State,* trans. Joan Hussey, rev. ed. (New Brunswick, N.J.: Rutgers University Press, 1969), 240, 477. The second citation specifically refers to Serbian legal practice.

108. Daniel Kaiser, *The Growth of the Law in Medieval Russia* (Princeton, N.J.: Princeton University Press, 1980), 172. As noted elsewhere, after the period covered in this book the Rusian ties with Byzantium become much stronger, and the pan-European political connections, including the Scandinavian roots of the Riurikids, fade away in favor of Byzantinization.

109. Benson, "Political *Renovatio,*" 362.

110. This could have stemmed, in part, from Constantine IX's creation of a legal school for the clarification and codification of Byzantine legal statutes and the regularization of the practice of law. Angold, "Belle Époque or Crisis (1025–1118)," in *The Cambridge History of the Byzantine Empire, c. 500–1492,* ed. Jonathan Shepard (Cambridge: Cambridge University Press, 2009), 599.

111. Houben, *Roger II of Sicily,* 141–142.

112. Ibid., 143.

113. For a fascinating article on Byzantine blinding, including multiple specific examples, moral reasoning behind the examples, as well as the physical consequences, see John Lascaratos and S. Marketos, "The Penalty of Blinding during Byzantine Times: Medical Remarks," *Documenta opthalmologica* 81, no. 1 (1992).

114. Althoff, *Otto III,* 60.

115. Thietmar of Merseburg notes two additional blindings in the German Empire, neither for the purpose of making someone ineligible for a throne, and both disapproved of by Thietmar as voice of the ecclesiastical establishment. *Ottonian Germany,* bk. 2, ch. 42, and bk. 4, ch. 21.

116. Timothy Reuter, *Germany in the Early Middle Ages, c. 800–1056* (London: Longman, 1991), 260.

117. Lisa Wolverton, *Hastening toward Prague: Power and Society in the Medieval Czech Lands* (Philadelphia: University of Pennsylvania Press, 2001), 189–190. Wolverton notes that this may have been a creation of Cosmas of Prague for his chronicle.

118. Ciggaar, *Western Travellers to Constantinople,* 142.

119. *The Povest' vremennykh let,* 256:24–273:6.

120. For more on the idea that the tale is a later addition, if not an interpolation, see M. Kh. Aleshkovskii, *Povest' vremennykh let: Sud'ba literaturnogo proizvedeniia v drevnei Rusi* (Moscow: Nauka, 1971), 34–35. Aleshkovskii and most, though, do accept the tale is true, even if added by a different author.

121. Vladimir Monomakh states that such a thing had not occurred before in Rus'. *The Povest' vremennykh let,* 262:8–10.

122. Donald Ostrowski, *Muscovy and the Mongols: Cross-Cultural Influences on the Steppe Frontier, 1304–1589* (Cambridge: Cambridge University Press, 1998), 24.

123. Wolverton, *Hastening toward Prague,* 86.

124. John Kinnamos, *Deeds of John and Manuel Comnenus,* trans. Charles M. Brand (New York: Columbia University Press, 1976), 17.

125. Ostrogorsky, *History of the Byzantine State,* 331.

126. Nightingale, "Evolution of Weight-Standards," 194–199.

127. For examples, see the excellent collection of Cécile Morrisson, *Catalogue des monnaies byzantines de la bibliothèque nationale* (Paris: Bibliothèque nationale, 1970).

128. Robert Sabatino Lopez, "The Dollar of the Middle Ages," *Journal of Economic History* 11, no. 3 (1951).

129. Philip Grierson notes explicitly that "the pennies of the feudal age are of an almost infinite variety of types." Grierson, *Numismatics* (Oxford: Oxford University Press, 1975), 25.

130. Wolverton, *Hastening toward Prague,* 166.

131. Philip Grierson, "Harold Hardrada and Byzantine Coin Types in Denmark," *Byzantinische Forschungen* 1 (1966): 129. Brita Malmer discusses moneyers, though not necessarily their influence on Byzantine-inspired Scandinavian coinage. Malmer, "Some Observations on the Importation of Byzantine Coins to Scandinavia in the Tenth and Eleventh Centuries and the Scandinavian Response," *Russian History/Histoire Russe* 28, nos. 1–4 (2001): 295–302.

132. David Warner has an excellent introduction to this subject in his "Ritual and Memory in the Ottonian Reich: The Ceremony of Adventus," *Speculum* 76, no. 2 (2001): 255–283.

133. The main source for information about Byzantine seals is the extensive list of publications by Nikolas Oikonomidès, such as Nicolas Oikonomidès, *A Collection of Dated Byzantine Lead Seals* (Washington, D.C.: Dumbarton Oaks Research Library and Collection, 1986); and especially John Nesbitt and Nicolas Oikonomidès, eds., *Catalogue of Byzantine Seals at Dumbarton Oaks and in the Fogg Museum of Art* (Washington, D.C.: Dumbarton Oaks Research Library and Collection, 1991–2005).

134. McCormick, "Byzantium's Role," 216.

135. Ibid.

136. Althoff, *Otto III*, 83.

137. Ibid. Otto also issued other seals with a clear Byzantine influence, including one showing him "standing frontally with orb and tall scepter, very much in the manner of Byzantine emperors." Otto Demus, *Byzantine Art and the West* (New York: New York University Press, 1970), 85.

138. Anthony Cutler, "Misapprehension and Misgivings: Byzantine Art and the West in the Twelfth and Thirteenth Centuries," in *Byzantium, Italy and the North: Papers on Cultural Relations* (London: Pindar Press, 2000), 487.

139. Ibid.

140. Ibid.

141. Ciggaar, *Western Travellers to Constantinople*, 283.

142. John Nesbitt, "Sigillography," in *The Oxford Handbook of Byzantine Studies,* ed. Elizabeth Jeffreys with John Haldon and Robin Cormack (Oxford: Oxford University Press, 2009), 150.

143. Houben, *Roger II of Sicily,* 119–120.

144. Houben spends significant time discussing the various depictions of Roger II, including pictures, the vast majority of which continue the theme of Byzantine appropriation. Ibid., 113–122. Vera von Falkenhausen has done significant work on the language and style of the Normans of Sicily as well. For her discussion of their use of Greek, see Vera von Falkenhausen, "I Diplomi Rei Re Normanni in Lingua Greca," in *Documenti Medievali Greci e Latini: Studi Comparativi,* ed. Giuseppe De Gregorio e Otto Kresten (Spoleto: Centro Italiano di Studi Sull'alto Medioevo, 1998), 253–308.

145. Anne Kromann and Jørgen Steen Jensen, "Byzantine Inspired Nordic Coinage from the 11th Century," in *Byzantium: Identity, Image, Influence—XIX International Congress of Byzantine Studies, University of Copenhagen, 18–24 August, 1996,* ed. Karsten Fledelius (Copenhagen: Eventus, 1996), 183; Malmer, "Some Observations."

146. Philip Grierson, *Byzantine Coins* (Berkeley: University of California Press, 1982), pl. 54, nos. 951, 952, 954.

147. Brita Malmer, "The Byzantine Empire and the Monetary History of Scandinavia during the 10th and 11th Century A.D.," in *Les pays du nord et Byzance (Scandinavie et Byzance): Actes du colloque Nordique et international de Byzantinologie,* ed. Rudolf Zeitler (Uppsala: Almqvist and Wiksell, 1981), 126.

148. Kromann and Jensen, "Byzantine Inspired Nordic Coinage," 183.

149. Sven and Magnus the Good (r. 1042–1047) engaged in a civil war to succeed Harthacnut.

150. Malmer, "Some Observations," 298; Grierson, "Harold Hardrada," 131.

151. By political stability I mean continuity of empire, rather than continuity of a particular dynasty, though prior to the death of Theodora in 1056 the Macedonian dynasty had been ruling for nearly 200 years.

152. Malmer also points out that it is important to consider the fact that Byzantine coins were "simply more beautiful, larger, and better made than most coins from other parts of Europe." This also would have had an important role to play in appropriation and use. Malmer, "Some Observations," 302.

153. Malmer, "The Byzantine Empire," 126. The article also contains photographs of the relevant coins, and drawings that illustrate the appropriate terms, such as *cross crosslet*.

154. Kromann and Jensen, "Byzantine Inspired Nordic Coinage," 183.

155. M. F. Hendy, "Michael IV and Harold Hardrada," *Numismatic Chronicle* 10 (1970): 187. Hendy is able to narrow the Michael of the coin down to Michael IV, due to a special issue of coinage relating to the suppression of Peter Deljan's revolt in Bulgaria.

156. Ibid., 197. This was a problem in the early Germanic kingdoms of western Europe as well, which appropriated Roman coin types and copied them "with declining fidelity" through the generations. Grierson, *Numismatics*, 25.

157. Grierson, "Harold Hardrada," 125.

158. Ibid.

159. Liudprand of Cremona would often intersperse Greek words and phrases into his Latin texts as a way to impress the largely non-Greek reading group of Latin readers. Though they could not read the Greek, it was viewed as a "prestigious, scriptural language." Liudprand of Cremona, *Complete Works*, 16.

160. This difficulty is not limited to Greek text, but also occurs for other languages. The Latin inscriptions on Bohemian coins were "badly garbled," which was due, most likely, to the illiterate moneyers or their assistants. Wolverton, *Hastening toward Prague*, 167.

161. Kromann and Jensen, "Byzantine Inspired Nordic Coinage," 126.

162. Grierson, "Harold Hardrada," 136. The only decipherable letters are an X, an N, and a W.

163. For a full version of the story, see *Morkinskinna*, chs. 9–50.

164. For instance, I use it to discuss Harald's religious policy in Chapter 5.

165. Malmer, "The Byzantine Empire," 127.

166. Hendy, "Michael IV and Harold Hardrada."

167. Grierson, "Harold Hardrada," 127.

168. Michael IV is traditionally named as the emperor who debased the coinage; recently, however, Constantine IX has been blamed as the culprit, in

which case Harald might not have been around long enough to see many effects of the debasement. Michael Angold, "Belle Époque or Crisis," 590.

169. Malmer, "The Byzantine Empire," 128.

170. Ibid.

171. Grierson, "Harold Hardrada," 128.

172. Ciggaar, "Byzantine Marginalia," 60–61.

173. A. P. Kazhdan and Ann Wharton Epstein, *Change in Byzantine Culture in the Eleventh and Twelfth Centuries* (Berkeley: University of California Press, 1985), 115–116; Antony Eastmond, "An Intentional Error? Imperial Art and 'Mis'-Interpretation under Andronikos I Komnenos," *Art Bulletin* 76, no. 3 (1994): 507; For the classic view reaffirming Skylitzes, see Angold, "Belle Époque or Crisis," 603.

174. Grierson, "Harold Hardrada," 137.

175. Kromann and Jensen, "Byzantine Inspired Nordic Coinage," 183.

176. Franklin, *Writing, Society and Culture,* 51.

177. M. P. Sotnikova and I. G. Spasskii, *Tysiacheletie drevneishie monet Rossii: Svodnyi catalog russkikh monet X–XI vekov* (Leningrad: Iskusstvo, 1983), 60–61. The book also contains images of all of the extant Rusian coins from this period, as well as the authors' analysis of them.

178. Ibid., 69–81.

179. Sotnikova and Spasskii provide a table showing the evolution of the symbol through four generations of rulers and their coins. Ibid., 84.

180. Ibid., 82.

181. Ibid.; Shepard, "Byzantium and Russia," 30.

182. Shepard, "Byzantium and Russia," 31–32.

183. Martin Dimnik, *The Dynasty of Chernigov, 1054–1146* (Toronto: Pontifical Institute of Mediaeval Studies, 1994), 171.

184. Ibid., 172. See the coins of Michael VII in Cécile Morrisson, *Catalogue des monnaies Byzantines de la bibliothèque nationale,* vol. 2 (Paris: Bibliothèque nationale, 1970), 654–658.

185. For more information about which, see the note on Oleg Sviatoslavich at Rusian Genealogy (http:// genealogy.obdurodon.org/).

186. Sotnikova and Spasski, *Tysiacheletie drevneishie monet Rossii,* 96–98.

187. Ibid., 96.

188. Franklin, *Writing, Society and Culture,* 49.

189. V. L. Ianin, "Nakhodka drevnerusskikh vislykh pechatei v Sigtune (Shvetsiia)," in *Vostochnaia evropa v drevnosti i srednevekov'e: X Cheteniia k 80-letiiu chlena-korrespondenta AN SSSR Vladimira Terent'evicha Pashuto,* ed. E. A. Mel'nikova (Moscow: RAN, 1998), 140. Vsevolod's Christian name was Andrei.

190. Franklin, *Writing, Society and Culture,* 103–104. There also have been assumptions about the use of Slavonic versus Greek as part of a campaign either for or against Byzantine influence.

191. V. L. Ianin, *Aktovye pechati Drevnei Rusi X–XV vv,* vol. 1 (Moscow: Nauka, 1970), 170, 251. A record of all extant seals available to Ianin are collected here and displayed in multiple views.

192. Ianin, "Pechati Feofano Muzalon," 82.

193. Ianin, *Aktovye pechati Drevnei Rusi X–XV vv,* vol. 1.

194. Shepard, "Byzantium and Russia," 142. A. V. Solov'ev, in "O pechati i titule Vladimira Sviatogo," *Byzantinoslavica* 9 (1947–1948): 31, 43–44, advanced the idea that it may have been "autocrator" in Latin letters. Ianin disagrees with the attribution to Vladimir; see Ianin, "Nakhodka drevnerusskikh vislykh pechatei v Sigtune (Shvetsiia)," 41–42.

195. Shepard, "Byzantium and Russia," 142.

196. Omeljan Pritsak, *The Origins of the Old Rus' Weights and Monetary Systems: Two Studies in Western Eurasian Metrology and Numismatics in the Seventh to Eleventh Centuries* (Cambridge, Mass.: Harvard Ukrainian Research Institute, 1998), 97–99.

197. M. P. Sotnikova, ed., *Drevneishie russkie monety X–XI vekov: Katalog i issledovanie* (Moscow: Banki i birzhi, 1995).

198. Franklin, *Writing, Society and Culture,* 50. For Scandinavian and English coins, see A. V. Nazarenko, *Drevniaia Rus' na mezhdunarodnykh putiakh: Mezhdistsiplinarnye ocherki kulturnykh, torgovykh, politicheskikh sviazei IX–XII vekov* (Moscow: Iazyki russkoi kul'tury, 2001), 499.

199. Shepard, "Byzantium and Russia," 181.

200. Cutler, "Misapprehension and Misgivings," 488.

201. Koehler, "Byzantine Art."

202. Demus, *Byzantine Art,* vii–viii.

203. Ibid., 25.

204. Herbert Bloch, "Monte Cassino, Byzantium, and the West in the Earlier Middle Ages," *Dumbarton Oaks Papers* 3 (1946): 194.

205. *Chronica monasterii Casinensis,* ed. Hartmut Hoffmann, vol. 34 of Monumenta Germaniae Historica (Hannover: Impensis Bibliopolii Hahniani, 1980), III.27.

206. Ibid.

207. Margaret English Frazer, "Church Doors and the Gates of Paradise: Byzantine Bronze Doors in Italy," *Dumbarton Oaks Papers* 27 (1973), 147.

208. Ernst Kitzinger, "The Byzantine Contribution to Western Art of the Twelfth and Thirteenth Centuries," in *The Art of Byzantium and the Me-*

dieval West: Selected Studies, ed. W. Eugene Kleinbauer (Bloomington: Indiana University Press, 1976), 367. Demus, *Byzantine Art,* 26.

209. Herbert Bloch, "The New Fascination with Ancient Rome," in *Renaissance and Renewal in the Twelfth Century,* ed. Robert L. Benson and Giles Constable (Cambridge, Mass.: Harvard University Press, 1982), 618.

210. Bloch, "Monte Cassino," 165.

211. This influence reached as far as Iceland, where traces of Monte Cassino's influence can be seen on a Last Judgment carving. Selma Jónsdóttir, *An 11th Century Byzantine Last Judgement in Iceland* (Reykjavík: Almenna Bókafélagið, 1959), 85.

212. Koehler, "Byzantine Art," 76.

213. Demus, *Byzantine Art,* 18–19.

214. Otto Demus, "Vorbildqualität und Lehrfunktion der byzantinischen Kunst," in *Stil und Überlieferung in der Kunst des Abendlandes* (Berlin: Verlag Gebr Mann, 1967), 93.

215. Demus, *Byzantine Art,* 19. The wall mosaic had been a forgotten art in the West until it was revived by Byzantine and Byzantine-trained artists in the second half of the eleventh century. Kitzinger, "The Byzantine Contribution," 364

216. Frazer, "Church Doors," 147.

217. Ernst Kitzinger, "The Arts as Aspects of a Renaissance," in *Renaissance and Renewal in the Twelfth Century,* ed. Robert L. Benson and Giles Constable (Cambridge, Mass.: Harvard University Press, 1982), 647.

218. Kitzinger, "The Byzantine Contribution," 364.

219. Kitzinger, "The Arts as Aspects," 652.

220. Ibid.

221. Ibid.

222. Demus, *Byzantine Art,* 122.

223. Kitzinger, "The Arts as Aspects," 665.

224. Ciggaar, *Western Travellers to Constantinople,* 291. For more on the discussion of this tomb and its significance, see Houben, *Roger II of Sicily,* 133.

225. Kitzinger, "The Arts as Aspects," 665.

226. Demus, *Byzantine Art,* 85.

227. K. N. Ciggaar and Jos. M. M. Hermans, "Byzantium and the West in the Tenth Century: Some Introductory Notes," in *Byzantium and the Low Countries in the Tenth Century: Aspects of Art and History in the Ottonian Era,* ed. V. D. van Aalst and K. N. Ciggaar (Hernen: A. A. Brediusstichting, 1985), 9. This continued all the way through Henry III at least. Krijnie Ciggaar, "The Empress Theophano (972–991): Political and Cultural Implications of Her Presence in Western Europe for the Low Countries, in Particular for the

County of Holland," in *Byzantium and the Low Countries in the Tenth Century: Aspects of Art and History in the Ottonian Era,* ed. V. D. van Aalst and K. N. Ciggaar (Hernen: A. A. Brediusstichting, 1985), 54.

228. Demus, *Byzantine Art,* 79.

229. Ciggaar, *Western Travellers to Constantinople,* 208.

230. Ibid., 133.

231. Demus, *Byzantine Art,* 79.

232. Ibid. This would be vehemently disagreed with by Althoff and others, who believe that the Ottonians, specifically Otto III, were interested in resurrecting Rome and not in imitating Byzantium. Althoff, *Otto III.*

233. Obolensky, "Byzantine Frontier Zones."

234. Ibid., 305.

235. Arthur Voyce, *The Art and Architecture of Medieval Russia* (Norman: University of Oklahoma Press, 1977), 87–140.

236. Elena Boeck, "Simulating the Hippodrome: The Performance of Power in Kiev's St. Sophia," *Art Bulletin* 41, no. 3 (2009): 293.

237. Demus, *Byzantine Art,* 121.

238. Ibid.

239. Meyendorff, *Byzantium and the Rise of Russia,* 19. More recently, Elena Boeck has said the same thing, arguing that "St. Sophia is the most ambitious Orthodox church built in the eleventh century." Boeck, "Simulating the Hippodrome," 283.

240. Demus, *Byzantine Art,* 121.

241. *The Povest' vremennykh let,* 110:19–21.

242. A good illustration of the traditional hypothesis is in map 26 of the *Cambridge History of the Byzantine Empire,* where Novgorod, Chernigov, and Kiev are marked as having "buildings and other works probably (when not certainly) commissioned or supplied by the Byzantine emperor." Angold, "Belle Époque or Crisis," map 26.

243. Ibid., 240.

244. Ciggaar, *Western Travellers to Constantinople,* 169. For further Byzantine–French connections, see the catalog from the 1958 exposition, *Byzance et la France médiévale: Manuscrits à peintures du IIe au XVIe siècle* (Paris: Bibliothèque nationale, 1958).

245. Ciggaar, *Western Travellers to Constantinople,* 169.

246. Ibid., 177–179.

247. Anthony Cutler, "Garda, Kallunge, and the Byzantine Tradition on Gotland," *Art Bulletin* 51, no. 3 (1969): 429.

248. The Scandinavian flow of mercenaries to Constantinople trickled out over the course of the early eleventh century, and they were replaced after 1066 by Anglo-Saxons, among others.

249. Ulla Haastrup, "Byzantine Elements in Frescoes in Zealand from the Middle of the 12th Century," in *Les Pays du Nord et Byzance (Scandinavie et Byzance): Actes due colloque Nordique et international de Byzantinologie*, ed. Rudolf Zeitler (Uppsala: Almqvist and Wiksell, 1981), 331.

250. Ibid., 329.

251. Signe Horn Fuglesang, "A Critical Survey of Theories on Byzantine Influence in Scandinavia," in *Byzantium: Identity, Image, Influence—XIX International Congress of Byzantine Studies, University of Copenhagen, 18–24 August, 1996,* ed. Karsten Fledelius (Copenhagen: Eventus, 1996).

252. Haastrup, "Byzantine Elements."

253. Christofer Klasson, "The Byzantine Heritage in Sweden," *Byzantium and the North: Acta Byzantina Fennica* 1 (1985).

254. Jonathan Shepard and Simon Franklin, *The Emergence of Rus, 750–1200: Longman History of Russia* (New York: Longman, 1996), 330.

255. Cutler, "Garda, Kallunge," 392–393. For the many other connections between Gotland and Ladoga, as well as the larger Baltic world, see Chapter 4.

256. Cutler, "Garda, Kallunge," 399, 422.

257. Anthony Cutler, "Byzantine Art and the North: Meditations on the Notion of Influence," in *Byzantium: Identity, Image, Influence—XIX International Congress of Byzantine Studies, University of Copenhagen, 18–24 August, 1996,* ed. Karsten Fledelius (Copenhagen: Eventus, 1996), 176.

258. Ibid., 171–172.

259. Anthony Cutler, "The Sculpture and Sources of 'Byzantios,'" in *Byzantium, Italy and the North: Papers on Cultural Relations* (London: Pindar Press, 2000), 431.

260. Ibid., 454.

261. Fuglesang, "A Critical Survey," 144.

262. Though it is possible that the icon type was brought from Rus' during the multiple marriages with Danish rulers in the twelfth century.

263. Krijnie Ciggaar, "Denmark and Byzantium from 1184 to 1212," *Mediaeval Scandinavia* 13 (2000): 130.

264. Ibid., 142.

265. Ibid., 129–130.

266. Jónsdóttir, *Byzantine Last Judgement.*

267. Ibid., 25.

2. The Ties That Bind

1. Counted in this number are the known marriages in which both the male and the female parties are identifiable. Countries to the west of Rus' are

identified here as Hungary, Poland, the German Empire, France, Sweden, Norway, Denmark, and England.

2. T. Rymer, *Foedera, conventiones, literae . . .* , 4 vols. (1816–1869), i, 209, cited in John Carmi Parsons, "Mothers, Daughters, Marriage, Power: Some Plantagenet Evidence, 1150–1500," in *Medieval Queenship,* ed. John Carmi Parsons (Gloucestershire: Sutton, 1994), 63.

3. Georges Duby, "Towards a History of Women in France and Spain," in *Love and Marriage in the Middle Ages,* ed. Georges Duby (Cambridge: Polity Press, 1994), 96. Of course, the history of medieval women is incredibly rich, with many publications in recent years. Two excellent recent works on the influence of noble women in France are Amy Livingstone, *Out of Love for My Kin: Aristocratic Family Life in the Lands of the Loire, 1000–1200* (Ithaca, N.Y.: Cornell University Press, 2010); and Valerie L. Garver, *Women and Aristocratic Culture in the Carolingian World* (Ithaca, N.Y.: Cornell University Press, 2009).

4. Parsons, "Mothers, Daughters, Marriage, Power," 69.

5. Such as Jane Tibbetts Schulenburg who writes that "daughters were definitely valued by their families, particularly as players of major roles in the formation of marriage alliances and extended connections, as childbearers, and as abbesses of family monasteries, interceders for their families' souls, etc." Schulenburg, *Forgetful of Their Sex: Female Sanctity and Society, ca. 500–1100* (Chicago: University of Chicago Press, 1998), 240.

6. For a particular example of how two Rusian princesses changed Scandinavian politics as part of their dynastic marriages, see Christian Raffensperger, "Dynastic Marriage in Action: How Two Rusian Princesses Changed Scandinavia," in *Imenoslov: Istoricheskaia semantika imeni* Ed. F. B. Uspenskii (Moscow: Indrik, 2009), 187–199.

7. Saxo Grammaticus, *Danorum regum heroumque historia Books X–XVI: The Text of the First Edition with Translation and Commentary in Three Volumes,* trans. Eric Christiansen, vol. 1: bks. X, XI, XII and XIII (Oxford: B.A.R., 1980), 58, bk. XI, 6. Though Saxo does occasionally attribute motives, such as for Queen Margaret of Denmark's marriage of her nephew Knud to Ingeborg Mstislavna, explicitly to increase Knud's familial ties and backing. Bk. XIII, 110.

8. The term "state" is, of course, misused here in the modern sense, but with the enormous variety of empires, kingdoms, duchies, etc., throughout western Eurasia, there is no equally usable term.

9. Though referring to the Ottonian quest for a porphyrogenite bride, Jonathan Shepard is particularly eloquent on the enormous amount to be gained. "A Greek marriage alliance would not merely demonstrate that

Otto's predominance in the west was acknowledged by the other outstanding Christian ruler; it would also transfuse purple-born blood into his own descendants' line, enhancing their imperial status." Shepard, "Western Approaches," 546.

10. Especially considering that at the same time the Bulgarians received an autocephalous church, and Peter received the title *basileus*. *De administrando imperio / Constantine Porphyrogenitus*, trans. R. J. H. Jenkins (Washington D.C.: Dumbarton Oaks Center for Byzantine Studies, 1967); and Jonathan Shepard, "A Marriage Too Far? Maria Lekapena and Peter of Bulgaria," in *The Empress Theophano: Byzantium and the West at the Turn of the Millennium*, ed. Adalbert Davids (Cambridge: Cambridge University Press, 1995).

11. Many sources discuss this attempt. Albert Bauer and Reinhold Rau, eds., *Fontes ad historiam aevi Saxonici illustrandam: Widukindi res gestae Saxonicae; Adalberti continuato Reginonis; Liudprandi opera* (Darmstadt: Wissenschaftliche Buchgesellschaft, 1971). Anna specifically is mentioned in *Ottonian Germany: The "Chronicon" of Thietmar of Merseburg*, trans. David A. Warner (Manchester: Manchester University Press, 2001), bk. 7. ch. 72. For analysis, see Karl Leyser, " 'Theophanu divina gratia imperatrix augusta': Western and Eastern Emperorship in the Later Tenth Century," in *The Empress Theophano: Byzantium and the West at the Turn of the First Millennium*, ed. Adalbert Davids (Cambridge: Cambridge University Press, 1995), 16; and Werner Ohnsorge, "Otto I. und Byzanz," in *Konstantinopel und der Okzident* (Darmstadt: Wissenschaftliche Buchgesellschaft, 1966), 222.

12. Gerbert of Aurillac, *The Letters of Gerbert, with His Papal Privileges as Sylvester II*, trans. Harriet Pratt Lattin (New York: Columbia University Pres, 1961), 151–152.

13. *The Povest' vremennykh let: An Interlinear Collation and Paradosis*, ed. Donald Ostrowski, with David Birnbaum and Horace G. Lunt (Cambridge, Mass.: Harvard University Press, 2004), 109:26–110:12.

14. Harald Fairhair did something similar when he finally united Norway: he married a daughter of the king of Denmark, the political prize of the north in the ninth century, giving up all of his pagan wives. Snorri Sturluson, *Heimskringla: History of the Kings of Norway*, trans. Lee M. Hollander (Austin: University of Texas Press, 1964), 76–77. The similarities between Harald and Vladimir may be more than coincidental, however. See Christian Raffensperger, "Shared (Hi)Stories: Vladimir of Rus' and Harald Fairhair of Norway," *Russian Review* 68, no. 4 (2009): 569–582.

15. The marriage of Vsevolod Iaroslavich and a member of the Byzantine family of Constantine Monomachos.

16. Georges Duby, "Marriage in Early Medieval Society," in *Love and Marriage in the Middle Ages,* ed. Georges Duby (Cambridge: Polity Press, 1994), 8. This is similar to an idea advanced to me in personal conversation by Edward Keenan that the Riurikids may have been eager to marry other families of Viking descent. Keenan, personal communication, August 10, 2004.

17. Sisters and daughters of Bolesław Chrobry married Scandinavian kings. For details, see Sturluson, *Heimskringla;* and *Ottonian Germany.*

18. Saxo as interpreted by Inge Skovgaard-Petersen, "Queenship in Medieval Denmark," in *Medieval Queenship,* ed. John Carmi Parsons (Gloucestershire: Sutton, 1994), 27.

19. Almost any history of Byzantium will corroborate this picture. George Ostrogorsky, *History of the Byzantine State,* trans. Joan Hussey, rev. ed. (New Brunswick, N.J.: Rutgers University Press, 1969); Michael Angold, *The Byzantine Empire, 1025–1204* (New York: Longman, 1997).

20. Or as Pauline Stafford put it, "The household was not only the center of government but a model for it." Stafford, *Queens, Concubines, and Dowagers: The King's Wife in the Early Middle Ages* (Athens, Ga.: University of Georgia Press, 1983), 28.

21. N. F. Kotliar discusses this in relation to the rulers of Galich. Kotliar, "Stranstvuiushchie dvory galitskikh kniazei," in *Vostochnaia evropa v drevnosti i srednevekov'e* (Moscow: Institut vseobshchei istorii RAN, 2008), 110–115. The German example is discussed by John W. Bernhardt in *Itinerant Kingship and Royal Monasteries in Early Medieval Germany, c. 936–1075* (Cambridge: Cambridge University Press, 1993).

22. Alexander Kazhdan, "Rus'-Byzantine Princely Marriages in the Eleventh and Twelfth Centuries," *Harvard Ukrainian Studies* 12–13 (1988–1989): 428.

23. Ruth Macrides, "Dynastic Marriages and Political Kinship," in *Byzantine Diplomacy: Papers from the Twenty-Fourth Spring Symposium of Byzantine Studies, Cambridge, March 1990,* ed. Jonathan Shepard and Simon Franklin (Brookfield, Vt.: Variorum, 1990), 270.

24. *De administrando imperio / Constantine Porphyrogenitus.*

25. There are references to "Scythians," a term that Byzantine sources occasionally use for Rusians, among others, but outside sources show that in this case they are clearly references to steppe peoples. *The Alexiad of Anna Comnena,* trans. E. R. A. Sewter (New York: Penguin Books, 1969).

26. Kazhdan, "Rus'-Byzantine Princely Marriages," 425.

27. The number of Latin sources mentioning Rus' are too many to list here, but they can be found in the complete bibliography. For just a brief English sample, there are two major sources that are in good edited translations: *Adam of Bremen: History of the Archbishops of Hamburg-Bremen,* trans. Francis J. Tschan (New York: Columbia University Press, 1959); and *Ottonian Germany.*

28. N. de Baumgarten, "Généalogies et mariages Occidentaux des Rurikides Russes du X-e au XIII-e siècle," *Orientalia Christiana* 9, no. 25 (1927).

29. Kazhdan, "Rus'-Byzantine Princely Marriages." I have no intention of duplicating Kazhdan's work. This section serves only to illustrate that there have been other marriages by Rusians listed in other places that are not included here, and why they have not been included. I have included in the count of total known marriages marriages that Kazhdan cannot disprove but cannot find overwhelming evidence for either.

30. *The Povest' vremennykh let,* 160:30–31.

31. Ibid., though there are other examples in the text.

32. Kazhdan, "Rus'-Byzantine Princely Marriages"; N. M. Karamzin, *Istoriia gosudarstva Rossiiskogo,* vol. 2 (repr., Moscow: Kniga, 1988).

33. Paul White discusses, in some detail, the reasons for chroniclers "improving" their chronicles. Paul A. White, *Non-Native Sources for the Scandinavian Kings' Sagas* (New York: Routledge, 2005), 11.

34. Vernadsky discusses Evpraksia and Anna, but not the broad patterns of Rusian dynastic marriage ties. George Vernadsky, *Kievan Russia* (New Haven, Conn: Yale University Press, 1948), 340–343.

35. Macrides, "Dynastic Marriages," 265.

36. More on this marriage and its purpose can be found in Chapter 3.

37. *The Povest' vremennykh let,* 154:28–155:3, 155:19–21. Though, of course, the *PVL* did not mention the dynastic marriages or the politics and alliances involved. In general the *PVL* is silent in regard to western ties with Rus'—the Poles are the only ones who get treatment, and even that is less than one would imagine.

38. As mentioned, there are multiple examples of this effect in Rusian history. For details, see the marriages of Sviatopolk Iaropolchich, Iziaslav Iaroslavich, and Sbyslava Sviatopolkovna.

39. Macrides, "Dynastic Marriages," 275.

40. Ibid.

41. The best example of which is probably Sviatopolk's campaigns against the Rostislavichi at the end of the eleventh century, to which the Sviatoslavichi were openly opposed. *The Povest' vremennykh let,* 272:6–273:1.

42. Though consent was increasingly stressed by the medieval church, in practice it was acknowledged that parents were the ones that made the decisions, and children often had no choice but to consent. See Michael M. Sheehan, "Choice of Marriage Partner in the Middle Ages: Development and Mode of Application of a Theory of Marriage," in *Marriage, Family, and Law in Medieval Europe: Collected Studies*, ed. James K. Farge (Toronto: University of Toronto Press, 1997). Saxo Grammaticus provides an interesting example of a churchman trying to show that consent was required that also indicates the realities of the time. Saxo Grammaticus, *Gesta Danorum: The History of the Danes*, ed. Hilda Ellis Davidson, trans. Peter Fisher (Totowa, N.J.: Rowman and Littlefield, 1979).

43. The two main sources for the embassy are the Psalter of Odalric (the relevant sections are quoted in full in "'Paris' Roger II, XLIVe eveque de Chalons, sa vieet sa mission en Russie," in *La Chronique de Champagne* 2 [1837] : 95–96); and the Chronicle of Clarius ("Chronicon Sancti-Petri-Vivi Senonensis: Auctore Clario," in *Bibliothèque Historique de'Lyonne*, vol. 2 [Auxerre: Perriquet et Rouillé, Imprimeurs de la Société, 1863], 506). There is also discussion that Gosselin of Chauny may have been mistaken for Roger of Chalons in the sources. "Roger II, XLIVe eveque de Chalons," 93.

44. The marriage, though not the date, is also recorded by Adam of Bremen. *Adam of Bremen*, xiii.12, schol. 62 (63).

45. Duby, "Marriage in Early Medieval Society," 8.

46. Unless we accept the later evidence of Tatishchev as to the agreement between Sviatopolk Iziaslavich and Władysław Herman of Poland. Tatishchev, *Istoriia Rossiiskaia* (Moscow: Akademii Nauk SSSR, 1963), 2:117. The validity of Tatishchev as a source, at all, has been challenged by many, most recently by Aleksei Tolochko, *"Istoriia Rossiiskaia" Vasiliia Tatishcheva: Istochniki i izvestiia* (Moscow: Novoe literaturnoe obozrenie, 2005).

47. Timothy Reuter, *Germany in the Early Middle Ages, c. 800–1056* (London: Longman, 1991), 277.

48. There are multiple articles on this marriage. A good introduction is Shepard, "A Marriage Too Far?"

49. "One way to determine how the ties created by foreign marriages functioned and what benefits were gained from them is to examine the contexts in which they were proposed and how they were described." Macrides, "Dynastic Marriages," 273.

50. Ibid., 276.

51. For a table depicting these degrees of kinship, see Constance B. Bouchard, "Consanguinity and Noble Marriages in the Tenth and Eleventh Centuries," *Speculum* 56, no. 2 (1981).

52. My understanding of consanguinity in the Middle Ages is to a great part informed by the excellent work of Constance Bouchard and her work on medieval consanguinity. Ibid.

53. The dispensation from Pope Paschal II is noted by the chronicler Gallus Anonymous. Anonymous, *Gesta principum Polonorum: The Deeds of the Princes of the Poles,* trans. Paul W. Knoll and Frank Schaer (New York: Central European University Press, 2003), 158–161.

54. This became easier by the early twelfth century, when the Riurikid families had separated to a larger degree.

55. John Carmi Parsons, "Family, Sex, and Power: The Rhythms of Medieval Queenship," in *Medieval Queenship,* ed. John Carmi Parsons (Gloucestershire: Sutton, 1994). Parsons discusses this briefly in his introductory remarks to this edited volume. There have been several relevant dissertations written on Rusian medieval women in the past few decades, but little follow-up work has been done. For an example of the relevant dissertations, see Eve Levin, "The Role and Status of Women in Medieval Novgorod" (PhD diss., Indiana University, 1983). And for the follow-up work, see N. L. Pushkareva, *Zhenshchiny Drevnei Rusi* (Moscow: Mysl', 1989), which is weak on Rusian material, though much better in Muscovite history.

56. Lois Hunneycutt, "Female Succession and the Language of Power in the Writings of Twelfth-Century Churchmen," in *Medieval Queenship,* ed. John Carmi Parsons (Gloucestershire: Sutton, 1994), 191. Hunneycutt asserts that medieval writers could only acknowledge a woman holding power for someone else, not completely on her own.

57. André Poulet, "Capetian Women and the Regency: The Genesis of a Vocation," in *Medieval Queenship,* ed. John Carmi Parsons (Gloucestershire: Sutton, 1994), 101.

58. Parsons, "Mothers, Daughters, Marriage, Power," 63–65.

59. Ibid., 65. See also Carla Freccero, "Marguerite de Navarre and the Politics of Maternal Sovereignty," in *Women and Sovereignty,* ed. Louise Olga Fradenburg (Edinburgh: Edinburgh University Press, 1992), 133.

60. Parsons, "Family, Sex, and Power," 10.

61. Hunneycutt, "Female Succession," 190.

62. Suzanne Fonay Wemple, *Women in Frankish Society: Marriage and the Cloister, 500–900* (Philadelphia: University of Pennsylvania Press, 1981), 122.

63. Armin Wolf, "Reigning Queens in Medieval Europe: When, Where, and Why," in *Medieval Queenship,* ed. John Carmi Parsons (Gloucestershire: Sutton, 1994).

64. Parsons, "Mothers, Daughters, Marriage, Power," 65.

65. Poulet, "Capetian Women," 104–105.

66. Parsons, "Mothers, Daughters, Marriage, Power" 68–69.

67. This is not correct in Rus' or Scandinavia, where daughters could and did inherit land. However, in Rus', at least, they were not the primary beneficiaries and did not receive their own principalities. For details on Rusian female inheritance, see *Medieval Russian Laws,* trans. George Vernadsky (New York: Oxford University Press, 1947), 51, 53. The rest of Parsons's argument, and even the gist of this portion, is still very relevant to Rus'.

68. An example of this genre of behavior, though not necessarily peacemaking, is seen in Rus'—Predslava Vladimirovna acted as informant to her brothers about their father's intentions, according to the *PVL,* though the full extent of her actions remains hidden. *The Povest' vremennykh let,* 140:26–141:1.

69. Parsons, "Mothers, Daughters, Marriage, Power," 68–69.

70. Ibid.

71. Parsons, "Family, Sex, and Power," 4.

72. *The Povest' vremennykh let,* 110:17–19.

73. *Ottonian Germany,* bk. 7, ch. 72.

74. Ibid.

75. This subject will be discussed more in Chapter 5 with the creation of the idea of a micro-Christendom of Rus'.

76. J. Vogt, ed., *Chronica ecclesiae Rosenfeldensis seu Hassefeldensis: Monumenta inedita rerum Germanicarum* (Bremen: Precipue Bremensium, 1740), 125, cited in S. P. Rozanov, "Evpraksiia-Adel'geida Vsevolodovna (1071–1109)," *Izvestiia Akademii Nauk SSSR VII,* ser. 8 (1929).

77. *Ottonian Germany,* bk. 2, ch. 15.

78. Sturluson, *Heimskringla,* 342–343.

79. Theophano's exact identity and her relation to the Byzantine emperor have been a matter for scholarly debate for some time. The classic article on the subject is Franz Dölger, "Wer war Theophano?" *Historisches Jahrbuch* 69 (1949).

80. Davids, *The Empress Theophano.* The negative reception of her by some in medieval Germany is echoed by the title given to her by the modern German historian, Werner Ohnsorge, of "Nichtporphyrogenita Theophano." Ohnsorge, "Otto I. und Byzanz," 224.

81. Judith Herrin, "Theophano: Considerations on the Education of a Byzantine Princess," in *The Empress Theophano: Byzantium and the West at the Turn of the First Millennium,* ed. Adalbert Davids (Cambridge: Cambridge University Press, 1995), 64.

82. Francis J. Tschan, ed., *Saint Bernward of Hildesheim*, vol. 2, *His Works of Art* (South Bend, Ind.: University of Notre Dame, 1951), 8–9; K. Ciggaar, "Theophano: An Empress Reconsidered," in *The Empress Theophano: Byzantium and the West at the Turn of the First Millennium*, ed. Adalbert Davids (Cambridge: Cambridge University Press, 1995), 54, 59, 61.

83. See, for example, Ingigerd's shaming of Iaroslav into fostering Magnus Olafsson, recorded in *Morkinskinna*. While exaggerated, it does correspond to the picture of Ingigerd present in all of the Scandinavian sources as a wise woman and advisor to Iaroslav. *Morkinskinna: The Earliest Icelandic Chronicle of the Norwegian Kings (1030–1157)*, trans. Theodore M. Andersson and Kari Ellen Gade (Ithaca, N.Y.: Cornell University Press, 2000), ch. 1.

84. Saška Georgieva, "The Byzantine Princesses in Bulgaria," in *Byzantino-Bulgarica IX*, ed. N. Evtimova (Sofia: Editions de L'Academie Bulgare des Sciences, 1995), 167–168.

85. Hunneycutt, "Female Succession," 189.

86. Ibid. Pauline Stafford also provides multiple examples of queens being asked to defend their homes or homelands while kings were away on campaign. Stafford, *Queens, Concubines, and Dowagers*, 117–119.

87. Hunneycutt, "Female Succession," 190. This, of course, did change beginning in the twelfth century, when bureaucracies began to evolve to manage kingdoms. The twelfth century was a turning point for the power of royal women in general, as this was a time when their right to hold land was restricted and female monastic movements began to decline. Stafford, *Queens, Concubines, and Dowagers*, 194–196.

88. Thomson, "The Intellectual Silence of Early Russia," in *The Reception of Byzantine Culture in Medaeval Russia* (Brookfield, Vt.: Ashgate, 1999), xxiin89.

89. Evpraksia's situation will be discussed in more detail in Chapter 5. See also Christian Raffensperger, "Evpraksia Vsevolodovna: Between East and West," *Russian History/Histoire Russe* 30, nos. 1–2 (2003): 23–34.

90. Parsons, "Family, Sex, and Power," 8.

91. Ibid.

92. Ibid., 9.

93. Stafford, *Queens, Concubines, and Dowagers*, 25.

94. Parsons, "Family, Sex, and Power," 9–10.

95. Stafford makes the argument that in this age of personal kingship the king was supposed to be an impartial decision maker, while the queen had no such restrictions and was expected to be an emotional balance to his impartiality. Stafford, *Queens, Concubines, and Dowagers*, 25.

96. Parsons, "Mothers, Daughters, Marriage, Power," 71.

97. Sedulius Scottus, *On Christian Rulers and the Poems*, trans. Edward Gerard Doyle (Binghamton: Medieval and Renaissance Texts and Studies, 1983), 59–61.

98. Stafford, *Queens, Concubines, and Dowagers*, 28–29.

99. Parsons, "Mothers, Daughters, Marriage, Power," 74. Stafford would, most likely, not disagree with this view, as she holds that "queens were expected to have an education to match their status" and that those who did not were chided for it. Stafford, *Queens, Concubines, and Dowagers*, 55.

100. Parsons, "Mothers, Daughters, Marriage, Power," 75.

101. Leo the Deacon, *The History of Leo the Deacon: Byzantine Military Expansion in the Tenth Century*, trans. Alice-Mary Talbot and Denis F. Sullivan (Washington, D.C.: Dumbarton Oaks Research Library and Collection, 2005), bk. 5, ch. 6; for the Bulgarian princesses, see also ch. 3. Cecily Hilsdale discusses the education of princesses in "Constructing a Byzantine 'Augusta:' A Greek Book for a French Bride." *The Art Bulletin* 87:3 (2005).

102. S. P. Rozanova, "Evpraksiia-Adel'geida Vsevolodovna (1071–1109)," *Izvestiia Akademii Nauk SSSR* 8, ser. 7 (1929): 168.

103. Andrew W. Lewis, *Royal Succession in Capetian France: Studies on Familial Order and the State* (Cambridge, Mass.: Harvard University Press, 1981), 46.

104. Maurice Prou, ed., *Recueil des actes de Philippe I-er, roi de France (1059–1108)* (Paris: Imprimerie Nationale, 1908). An example of this is from a royal proclamation of January 26, 1065, that is signed "Philippus gratia Dei Francorum rex. Anna regina." Ibid., 53.

105. Wladimir V. Bogomoletz, "Anna of Kiev: An Enigmatic Capetian Queen of the Eleventh Century: A Reassessment of Biographical Sources," *French History* 19 (2005), 317, citing Prou, *Recueil des actes de Philippe I-er*, nos. XIX, XXXVI.

106. George Pertz, ed., *Lamberti Hersfeldensis Annales* (Hannover: Impensis Bibliopolii Hahniani, 1843), 166, where there is, unfortunately, no mention of Anastasia. She does appear a few years later in 1071, rewarding Otto, the Duke of Bavaria, for his work in restoring her son Salomon to the throne. See ibid., p. 185. More on this marriage is discussed in Chapter 3.

107. These women have been treated in multiple individual studies, and they are often addressed in histories of Germany. See Carolyn Edwards, "Dynastic Sanctity in Two Early Medieval Women's *Lives*," in *Medieval Family Roles: A Book of Essays*, ed. Cathy Jorgensen Itnyre (New York: Garland, 1996); Stafford, *Queens, Concubines, and Dowagers*; Davids, *The Empress Theoph-*

ano; Reuter, *Germany in the Early Middle Ages;* and I. S. Robinson, *Henry IV of Germany, 1056–1106* (Cambridge: Cambridge University Press, 1999).

108. For more details, see the excellent collection of articles on Theophano in Davids, *The Empress Theophano.*

109. For more details, see Robinson, *Henry IV of Germany.*

110. Macrides, "Dynastic Marriages," 280.

111. Macrides states that "exporting a bride was more desirable because in this way a Byzantine ruler could establish a presence in the centers of power, and beside the potentates he was trying to bring into his sphere of influence." Ibid., 272.

112. Cecily Hilsdale, "Diplomacy by Design: Rhetorical Strategies of the Byzantine Gift" (PhD diss., University of Chicago, 2003), 77–79.

113. Sturluson, *Heimskringla,* 538.

114. *Annalista Saxo,* in Monumenta Germaniae Historica Scriptores, vol. 6, ed. George Pertz (Hannover: Impensis Bibliopolii Avlici Hahniani, 1844), s.a. 1062, 1103. There is an additional Rusian-related example as well, little more than a decade before this one, when Oda of Stade, wife of Sviatoslav Iaroslavich, returned home following her husband's death. Martin Dimnik, *The Dynasty of Chernigov, 1054–1146* (Toronto: Pontifical Institute of Mediaeval Studies, 1994), 129.

115. Though, not insignificantly, Anna Iaroslavna dedicates a church foundation in memory of her father's soul. Bogomoletz, "Anna of Kiev," 318, citing Prou, *Recueil des actes de Philippe I-er,* no. XLIII.

116. Raffensperger, "Evpraksia Vsevolodovna."

117. *The Povest' vremennykh let,* 281:16–17, 283:23–27.

118. There is one example, but the situation is aberrant. Euphemia Vladimirovna married Koloman of Hungary in 1112 but was repudiated by him in 1113, ostensibly for having an affair, and she returned to Rus' pregnant. S. P. Rozanova, "Evfimiia Vladimirovna i Boris Kolomanovich: Iz evropeiskoi politiki XII v," *Izvestiia akademii nauk SSSR* 8 (1930).

119. Ibid.

3. Rusian Dynastic Marriage

1. There are another fourteen relationships that can be assumed, if not proven. For instance, there are recorded in the Rusian chronicles Riurikid men and their sons, with no mother listed for the children. Some of the mothers must surely have been wives (as opposed to concubines or mistresses), but unfortunately there is no information on them.

2. For a complete listing and discussion of Rusian dynastic marriages during this period, see Christian Raffensperger, "Reexamining Rus': The Place of Kievan Rus' in Europe, ca. 800–1146" (PhD diss., University of Chicago, 2006), appendix. Some of this discussion can also be found online at http//genealogy. obdurodon.org.

3. For example, see Christian Raffensperger, "Evpraksia Vsevolodovna: Between East and West," *Russian History/Histoire Russe* 30, nos. 1–2 (2003): 23–34.

4. Marrige as a tool of conversion, specifically that of Vladimir Sviatoslavich and Anna *Porphyrogenita,* is discussed in detail in Chapter 5.

5. *The Povest' vremennykh let: An Interlinear Collation and Paradosis,* ed. Donald Ostrowski, with David Birnbaum and Horace G. Lunt (Cambridge, Mass.: Harvard University Press, 2004), 149:28–150:2.

6. Samuel Hazzard Cross and Olgerd P. Sherbowitz-Wetzor, eds., transls., *The Russian Primary Chronicle* (Cambridge, Mass.: Mediaeval Academy of America, 1953), n158. Though it may have begun earlier than 1034, because Mieszko initially had to abdicate in 1031 to his brother Otto, but he regained the throne at Otto's death in 1032, only to die insane in 1034.

7. Gallus Anonymous, *Gesta principum Polonorum: The Deeds of the Princes of the Poles,* trans. Paul W. Knoll and Frank Schaer (New York: Central European University Press, 2003), 81. Casimir joined the Benedictine order and enrolled at the monastery of Cluny in France. He returned to Saxony after receiving a papal dispensation to marry. N. I. Shchaveleva, ed., *"Velikaia khronika" o Pol'she, Rusi i ikh sosediakh XI–XIII vv* (Moscow: Izdatel'stvo Moskovskogo universiteta, 1987), 69.

8. Anonymous, *Gesta principum Polonorum,* 81.

9. *The Povest' vremennykh let,* 153:24–25.

10. Anonymous, *Gesta principum Polonorum,* 83–85.

11. Ibid., 80–81. Mazovia and Pomerania were still in revolt and were dealt with in separate expeditions sometime after the initial conquering and after Casimir's marriage.

12. *The Povest' vremennykh let,* 154:28–155:3.

13. Emphasis mine. Shchaveleva, *Velikaia khronika,* 70. The description of Dobronega as "daughter" of the Rusian prince is an interesting feature of this text. Some modern historians have wondered if she was indeed a daughter of Iaroslav, rather than his sister. This view gains endorsement here, but is generally considered incorrect, and could simply be another case of a chronicler confusing father and son (Vladimir and Iaroslav, in this case). See the discussion in E. V. Pchelov, *Genealogiia drevnerusskikh*

kniazei, IX–nachala XI v (Moscow: Rossiiskii gosudarstvennyi gumani-tarnyi universitet, 2001), 206–209.

14. Shchaveleva, *Velikaia khronika,* 70.

15. *The Povest' vremennykh let,* 154:28–155:3.

16. Ibid., 153:24–25.

17. George Pertz, ed., *Annalista Saxo,* in Monumenta Germaniae Historica Scriptores, vol. 6 (Hannover: Impensis Bibliopolii Avlici Hahniani, 1844), s.a. 1039.

18. V. Cl. Lud. Frid. Hasse, ed., *Lamberti Hersfeldensis Annales,* in Monumenta Germaniae Historica Scriptores, vol. 5 (Hannover: Impensis Bibliopolii Avlici Hahniani, 1844), s.a. 1039.

19. For instance, Baumgarten complicates the issue and adds a hypothetical 1038 marriage date based on the 1039 birth of their son, Bolesław. N. de Baumgarten, "Généalogies et mariages Occidentaux des Rurikides Russes du X-e au XIII-e siècle," *Orientalia Christiana* 9, no. 25 (1927): table 1. And the editors of the *Gesta* went so far as to include, in a footnote to the marriage date of 1041, the birth dates of 1039 for Bolesław and 1040 for Władysław. Anonymous, *Gesta principum Polonorum,* 82n1.

20. *The Povest' vremennykh let,* 153:24–25.

21. Anonymous, *Gesta principum Polonorum,* 83.

22. The *Great Chronicle* is equally unhelpful here, as it devotes only a small part of a passage to the campaign against the Mazovians. It also says that the Mazovians were aided by many groups, including Rusians, though the editor rightly contradicts the statement. Shchaveleva, *Velikaia khronika,* 70n13.

23. *The Povest' vremennykh let,* 153:24–25, 155:19–21, which contains only the 1041 and 1047 raids; *Letopisnyi sbornik, imenuemyi: Patriarshei ili Nikonovskoi letopis'iu,* vol. 9 of *Polnoe sobranie russkikh letopisei* (Moscow: Iazyki russkoi kul'tury, 2000) (hereafter cited as *PSRL 9*), 82–83, which contains all three raids; and *Rogozhskii letopisets / Tverskoi sbornik,* vol. 15 of *Polnoe sobranie russkikh letopisei* (Moscow: Iazyki slavianskoi kul'tury, 2000) (hereafter cited as *PSRL 15*), 148–150, which also contains all three.

24. *PSRL 9,* 82; and *PSRL 15,* 149.

25. *PSRL 9,* 83; *PSRL 15,* 149. This marriage is interesting as well for its consanguinity problems. Casimir and Dobronega were not related by blood, nor were Iziaslav and Gertrude. However, Latin consanguinity laws viewed a marriage as a new blood relationship, and thus siblings-in-law were treated as siblings for consanguinity purposes. Thus, in this view, the marriage of Iziaslav and Gertrude was consanguineous, as Gertrude

would have been treated as Iziaslav's aunt and related in the second degree.

26. *The Povest' vremennykh let*, 155:19–21. *Ziat'*, confusingly for Dobronega's paternity, can be translated as either "brother-in-law" or "son-in-law," but it does provide a familial connection between the two men. *PSRL 15*, 150.

27. *The Povest' vremennykh let*, 154:28–155:3.

28. Children are specifically mentioned in other Rusian chronicles. *PSRL 15*, 149.

29. Anonymous, *Gesta principum Polonorum*, 81. Pchelov also reads this as recognition of a large dowry brought into the marriage. E. V. Pchelov, "Pol'skaia kniagina—Mariia Dobronega Vladimirovna," in *Vostochnaia Evropa v drevnosti i srednevekov'e*, ed. V. T. Pashuto (Moscow: RAN, 1994), 32.

30. The Polovtsy are part of a complicated history of nomadic people of the Eurasian steppe and are also referred to as Cumans and Qipchaks, depending on the origin of the source. For more information on them specifically, see S. A. Pletneva, *Polovtsy* (Moscow: Nauka, 1990).

31. We see this most clearly in the names given to some of these women, which are Christian saints' names and betray no Turkic influence whatsoever; Iaropolk Vladimirich's Turkic wife was named Elena, for instance. *Ipat'evskaia letopis'*, vol. 2 of *Polnoe sobranie russkikh letopisei* (Moscow: Iazyki slavianskoi kul'tury, 2001) (hereafter cited as *PSRL 2*), 319.

32. Charles Halperin, "The Ideology of Silence: Prejudice and Pragmatism on the Religious Frontier," *Comparative Studies in Society and History* 26, no. 3 (1984): 442–466. Márta Font contrasts these perspectives as well in regard to the Rusian rulers and their steppe neighbors. Font, "Old-Russian Principalities and Their Nomadic Neighbours: Stereotypes of Chronicles and Diplomatic Practices of the Princes," *Acta Orientalia Academiae Scientiarum Hungaricae* 58, no. 3 (2005): 267–276.

33. *The Povest' vremennykh let*, 226:3–5.

34. Ibid., 226:5–6.

35. For a fascinating look at the Xiongnu, nomadic pastoralists, and their interaction with sedentary populations, see Thomas Barfield, *The Perilous Frontier: Nomadic Empires and China* (New York: Blackwell, 1989).

36. *The Povest' vremennykh let*, 226:3–5.

37. Długosz, *Annales*, 157.

38. *The Povest' vremennykh let*, 231:9–232:8.

39. Ibid., 231:10.

40. Ibid., 232:3–8.

41. Pertz, *Annalista Saxo*, a. 1082, 721.

42. For a further discussion of such issues, see the chapter on marriage in Eve Levin, *Sex and Society in the World of the Orthodox Slavs, 900–1700* (Ithaca, N.Y.: Cornell University Press, 1989). Levin states that the approved marriage age for women in the Orthodox world was twelve, though many marriages (or betrothals) occurred earlier. In the Latin world, women often married later, around the age of fifteen, most likely because consummation was required for marriage in the Latin world and menarche did not begin until an average age of fourteen. Carol Jean Diers and Darrell W. Amundsen, "The Age of Menarche in Medieval Europe," *Human Biology* 45 (1973).

43. A. V. Nazarenko, *Drevniaia Rus' na mezhdunarodnykh putiakh: Mezhdistsiplinarnye ocherki kulturnykh, torgovykh, politicheskikh sviazei IX–XII vekov* (Moscow: Iazyki russkoi kul'tury, 2001), 540, citing J. Vogt, ed., *Chronica ecclesiae Rosenfeldensis seu Hassefeldensis: Monumenta inedita rerum Germanicarum* (Bremen: Precipue Bremensium, 1740), 125.

44. Bishop of Naumburg Walram, *Liber De Unitate Ecclesiae Conservanda, Scriptores Rerum Germanicarum* (Hannover: Impensis Bibliopolii Hahniani, 1883), lib. II.35, 114.

45. Oda may have been quite influential in Rus'. A. F. Litvina and F. B. Uspenskii have suggested that she may have been responsible for the dedication of a monastery to St. Simeon (of Trier) in Kiev. Litvina and Uspenskii, "'Monastyr' Sv. Simeona v Kieve: K istorii russko-nemetskikh sviazei XI v," *Slaviane i ikh sosediakh* 12 (2008): 276–284.

46. S. P. Rozanov, "Evpraksiia-Adel'geida Vsevolodovna (1071–1109)," *Izvestiia Akademii Nauk SSSR* 8, ser. 7 (1929): 622–623.

47. One of the most interesting reasons he suggests for the second marriage is, quite simply, love. Rozanov, "Evpraksiia-Adel'geida Vsevolodovna," 626. The Annals of St. Disibodi mentions Evpraksia's attractiveness, specifically. George Pertz, ed., *Annales Sancti Disibodi*, in Monumenta Germaniae Historica Scriptores, vol. 17 (Hannover: Impensis Bibliopolii Avlici Hahniani, 1861), a. 1093.

48. I. S. Robinson, *Henry IV of Germany, 1056–1106* (Cambridge: Cambridge University Press, 1999), 269. Henry IV had notorious Saxon problems, and Margrave Udo II, Henry III's father, had been one of the leaders of the Saxon uprisings of the 1070s.

49. See also A. B. Golovko, *Drevniaia Rus' i Pol'sha v politicheskikh vzaimootnosheniiakh X-pervoi treti XIII vv* (Kiev: Naukova Dumka, 1988), 58.

50. Nazarenko, *Drevniaia Rus',* 540–546, 553.

51. In addition to Iziaslav's marriage to Gertrude, daughter of the king of Poland, Sviatopolk II married his sister Evdoksia (both were Gertrude's

children and thus half-Polish) to Mieszko, the son of Władysław Hermann, Duke of Poland (1079–1102). Sviatopolk II also married his son Iaroslav to one of Władysław Hermann's daughters, and his daughter Sbyslava, to Władysław Hermann's son, Bolesław III, a marriage that received a papal dispensation, though all of them required it according to both Latin and Orthodox Church consanguinity laws. See the discussion on consanguinity in Chapter 2.

52. Even non-Iziaslavichi occupants of the western principalities were more closely tied to the Poles than were other Rusians, as shown by David Igorevich, who, after he inherited Volhynia upon the death of Iaropolk Iziaslavich, made an alliance with Władysław Hermann. Golovko, *Drevniaia Rus'*, 59.

53. "Canonical Responses of Metropolitan Ioann II," in *Russkaia istoricheskaia biblioteka* (Saint Petersburg: RIB, 1908), art. 13.

54. Many historians make this claim, beginning with N. M. Karamzin, *Istoriia gosudarstva rossiiskogo*, vol. 2 (Moscow: Kniga, 1988), 60. Nazrenko fleshes this out further with other examples from the writings of Ioann II. A. V. Nazarenko, " 'Zelo nepodobno pravovernym': Mezhkonfessional'nye braki na rusi v XI–XII vekakh," in *Drevniaia Rus' i Slaviane* (Moscow: RAN, 2009), 272, 272n9. The only other explanation would be marriages to Jews or Muslims, both of which would have been extraordinary enough to preserve mention of it elsewhere.

55. N. V. Ponyrko and D. S. Likhachev, eds., *Epistoliarnoe nasledie Drevnei Rusi XI–XIII: Issledovaniia, teksty, perevody* (Saint Petersburg: Nauka, 1992), 30–35.

56. The chronicler makes the common mistake of confusing son and father.

57. George Pertz, ed., *Ekkehardi Chronicon,* in Monumenta Germaniae Historica Scriptores, vol. 6 (Hannover: Impensis Bibliopolii Avlici Hahniani, 1844), a. 1089, p. 207. Also listed in Pertz, *Annalista Saxo,* a. 1089, p. 726.; Frutolf of Michelsburg, *Chronica,* ed. F.-J. Schmale and I. Schmale-Ott (Darmstadt: Ausgewahlte Quellen zur deutschen Geschiste des Mittelalters, 1972), a. 1089, p. 104.

58. Walram, *Liber De Unitate Ecclesiae Conservanda,* lib. II.26, 100. Her enthronement is also recorded in one of Henry's diplomata from 1089. F. Hausmann, ed., *Monumenta Germaniae Historica: Diplomatum Regum Et Imperatorum Germaniae,* vol. 6, *Heinrici IV: Diplomata* (Weimar: Hermann Bohlaus Nachfolger, 1953), 407.

59. Anna Iaroslavna, Dobronega Vladimirovna, Anastasia Iaroslavna, and Elisabeth Iaroslavna, respectively.

60. These stories describe Henry IV, with references to the book of Revelation, as a Nicoletian, a member of a sect that practiced sexually "deviant" acts and held orgies. This was not the first time such charges had been brought against Henry IV—in the 1070s he briefly separated from his first wife, Bertha, and she, also in the company of pro-papacy forces, brought such charges against him. In Evpraksia's version, she at first participated in such rites out of naiveté and love for her husband. However, once she found herself pregnant, she was unable to determine who was the father of the baby, and she was filled with disgust and a resolve to do something. This something translated into leaving her husband and joining the pro-papacy side of Mathilda of Tuscany. For more information on Evpraksia, see Raffensperger, "Evpraksia Vsevolodovna."

61. The consequences of this marriage and the separation are discussed more in Chapter 5.

62. George Pertz, ed., *Bernoldi Chronicon,* in Monumenta Germaniae Historica Scriptores, vol. 5 (Hannover: Impensis Bibliopolii Avlici Hahniani, 1844), a. 1095, p. 462.

63. I. M. Lappenberg, ed., *Annales Stadenses Auctore M. Alberto,* in Monumenta Germaniae Historica Scriptores, vol. 16, ed. G. Pertz (Hannover: Impensis Bibliopolii Avlici Hahniani, 1859), 316–317.

64. *Povest' vremennykh let,* 218:16–17a, 283:23–27.

65. *Adam of Bremen: History of the Archbishops of Hamburg-Bremen,* trans. Francis J. Tschan (New York: Columbia University Press, 1959), xiii, 12, 124; Snorri Sturluson, *Heimskringla: History of the Kings of Norway,* trans. Lee M. Hollander (Austin: University of Texas Press, 1964), 577.

66. Both Iaroslav and Olaf married daughters of Olof Skötkonnung, king of Sweden. In fact, Olaf was arranged to marry Ingigerd before Iaroslav married her. Sturluson, *Heimskringla,* 340–341.

67. Ibid., 578; *Morkinskinna: The Earliest Icelandic Chronicle of the Norwegian Kings (1030–1157),* trans. Theodore M. Andersson and Kari Ellen Gade (Ithaca, N.Y.: Cornell University Press, 2000), ch. 9. The information in *Heimskringla* and *Morkinskinna* is substantially similar, but as *Morkinskinna* is slightly earlier, it provides a nice check on *Heimskringla.*

68. Sturluson, *Heimskringla,* 486. With a slightly different version of the story, one less favorable to Iaroslav, in *Morkinskinna,* ch. 1.

69. *Morkinskinna,* ch. 9; Sturluson, *Heimskringla,* 578.

70. Sturluson, *Heimskringla,* 581, 590; *Morkinskinna,* ch. 10.

71. Though *Morkinskinna* specifically refers to "confidential messengers" as the bearers of this immense wealth. This description does not invalidate

the idea of Varangian and/or Rusian merchants being used, but does add a layer of secrecy that must be acknowledged. *Morkinskinna,* ch. 10.

72. Other reasons have been suggested, such as claiming his betrothed Elisabeth, or fleeing the wrath of the Empress Zoe in Constantinople. *Morkinskinna,* ch. 13; Sturluson, *Heimskringla,* 587–589.

73. *Morkinskinna,* ch. 13; Sturluson, *Heimskringla,* 589–591; *Adam of Bremen,* xiii, 12, 124, schol. 62 (63).

74. Sturluson, *Heimskringla,* 589.

75. Ibid., 587–589; *Morkinskinna,* ch. 13.

76. *Morkinskinna,* ch. 13.; C. R. Unger, ed., *Flateyjarbók,* vol. 3 (Christiania: P. T. Mallings, 1868), 290.

77. Sturluson, *Heimskringla,* 473–486; *Morkinskinna,* ch. 1.

78. Sturluson, *Heimskringla,* 590.

79. Ibid., 590–591; *Morkinskinna,* ch. 13.

80. Lambert of Hersefeld, "Lamberti Hersfeldensis Annales." Ed. V. Cl. Lud. Frid. Hasse, *Monumenta Germaniae Historica. Scriptores V.* ed. Pertz, (Hannover: Impensis Bibliopolii Avlici Hahniani, 1844), s.a. 1043.

81. Andrew W. Lewis, *Royal Succession in Capetian France: Studies on Familial Order and the State* (Cambridge, Mass.: Harvard University Press, 1981), 45.

82. Ibid.

83. The two main sources for the embassy are the Psalter of Odalric (the relevant sections are quoted in full in Louis Paris, "Roger II, XLIVe eveque de Chalons, sa vieet sa mission en Russie," in *La Chronique de Champagne* [1837], 2:95–96) and the Chronicle of Clarius ("Chronicon Sancti-Petri-Vivi Senonensis: Auctore Clario," in *Bibliothèque Historique de'Lyonne* [Auxerre: Perriquet et Rouillé, Imprimeurs de la Société, 1863], 2:506). There is also discussion that Gosselin of Chauny may have been mistaken for Roger of Chalons in the sources. "Roger II, XLIVe eveque de Chalons," 93.

84. Which was nonchalantly covered in Clarius by the phrase *cum aliis.* "Chronicon Sancti-Petri-Vivi Senonensis: Auctore Clario." In *Bibliothèque Historique de'Lyonne.* Vol. 2. (Auxerre: Perriquet et Rouillé, Imprimeurs de la Société, 1863), 506.

85. "Roger II, XLIVe eveque de Chalons," 95.

86. Clarius records that "Quos ille cum pluribus donis et cum filia remisit in Francia." "Chronicon Sancti Petri-Vivi Senonensis," 506.

87. Prou's synthesis and explanation of the dates is excellent. Maurice Prou, ed., *Recueil des actes de Philippe I-er, roi de France (1059–1108)* (Paris: Imprimerie Nationale, 1908), xix–xxiii. The marriage, though not the

date, is also recorded by Adam of Bremen. *Adam of Bremen*, xiii.12, schol. 62 (63).

88. George Pertz, ed., *Bertholdi Annales*, in Monumenta Germaniae Historica Scriptores, vol. 5 (Hannover: Impensis Bibliopolii Avlici Hahniani, 1844), s.a. 1060. Berthold records that Anna was regent for Philip, but not this specific decree. The specific decree can be found in André Poulet, "Capetian Women and the Regency: The Genesis of a Vocation," in *Medieval Queenship*, ed. John Carmi Parsons (Gloucestershire: Sutton, 1994), 107. As well as Prou, *Recueil des actes de Philippe I-er*, 19–20.

89. Constance B. Bouchard, "Consanguinity and Noble Marriages in the Tenth and Eleventh Centuries," *Speculum* 56, no. 2 (1981): 277.

90. Ibid.

91. Robert-Henri Bautier, "Anne de Kiev, reine de France, et la politique royale au XI-e siècle, étude critique de la documentation," *Revue des études Slaves* 57, no. 4 (1985), 545; and Poulet, "Capetian Women and the Regency," 100.

92. These marriages are discussed earlier in this chapter.

93. Jean Dunbabin, "What's in a Name? Phillip, King of France," *Speculum* 68, no. 4 (1993): 956.

94. I. S. Robinson, *Henry IV of Germany, 1056–1106* (Cambridge: Cambridge University Press, 1999), 21–25.

95. Dunbabin, "What's in a Name?" 956.

96. *PSRL 2*, 273.

97. For a breakdown of those sources, as well as an interesting perspective on the marriage, see S. P. Rozanov, "Evfimiia Vladimirovna i Boris Kolomanovich: Iz evropeiskoi politiki XII v," *Izvestiia Akademii Nauk SSSR* 8 (1930).

98. Mór Wertner, *Az Árpádok családi története* (Nagy: 1892), 216–217.

99. For more on the marriage of Predslava Sviatopolkovna, see her entry at http://genealogy.obdurodon.org.

100. Rozanov, "Evfimiia Vladimirovna i Boris Kolomanovich," 591.

101. "Boguphali II episcopi Posnaniensis Chronicon Poloniae, cum continuatione Basconis custodis Posnaniensis," in *Monumenta Poloniae Historica*, ed. August Bielowski (Warsaw: Mouton, 1961), 508.

102. "Cosmae chronicon Boemorum cum continuatoribus," in *Fontes rerum Bohemicarum*, ed. Jos. Emler (Prague: Nákladem Musea Království Ceského, 1874), 215–216; and Otto, Bishop of Freising, *The Two Cities: A Chronicle of Universal History to the Year 1146 A.D.*, trans. Charles Christopher Mierow (New York: Octagon Books, 1966), bk. 7, sec. 21.

103. There are multiple examples of Hungarian support for Iaroslav in the various chronicles. *PSRL 2*, 285, 287.

104. John Kinnamos, *Deeds of John and Manuel Comnenus*, trans. Charles M. Brand (New York: Columbia University Press, 1976), 93; Shchaveleva, *Velikaia khronika*, 103–106.

105. Tatishchev, for instance, records her original name as Sofiia and her monastic name as Evfimiia. V. N. Tatishchev, *Istoriia Rossiiskaia* (Moscow: Akademii Nauk SSSR, 1963), 128, 149.

106. *Lavrent'evskaia letopis'*, vol. 1 of *Polnoe sobranie russkikh letopisei* (Moscow: Iazyki slavianskoi kul'tury, 2001), 305.

107. One classic example is the one recorded by Othlo of St. Emmerman in his *Liber visionum,* in which a nun dreams of the Empress Theophano being punished after death for her introduction of luxury and jewelry to the West. The traditional interpretation of this is simply as a posthumous denunciation of the powerful Empress Theophano. Othlo, "Ex Libro Visionum," in *Monumenta Germanica Historiae Scriptores*, vol. 11, ed. George Pertz (Hannover: Impensis Bibliopolii Hahniani, 1854), 385.

108. F. B. Uspenskii, *Imia i vlast': Vybor imeni kak instrument dinasticheskoi bor'by v srednevekovoi Skandinavii* (Moscow: Iazyki russkoi kul'tury, 2001). 13.

109. Constance B. Bouchard, "Patterns of Women's Names in Royal Lineages, Ninth–Eleventh Centuries," *Medieval Prosopography* 9, no. 1 (1988): 1–2.

110. M. Chaume, *Les origines du duché de Bourgogne* (Dijon: Librarie E. Rebourseau, 1925), 1:519–520.

111. Bouchard, "Patterns of Women's Names," 4.

112. Ibid.

113. Constance B. Bouchard, "The Migration of Women's Names in the Upper Nobility, Ninth–Twelfth Centuries," *Medieval Prosopography* 9, no. 2 (1988): 11.

114. Karl Schmid, "The Structure of the Nobility in the Earlier Middle Ages," in *The Medieval Nobility: Studies on the Ruling Classes of France and Germany from the Sixth to the Twelfth Century,* ed. Timothy Reuter (Amsterdam: North-Holland, 1979), 47. "The names of ancestors, used again and again in families and sibs, were the distinguishing mark of a group of persons with a group consciousness."

115. Dunbabin, "What's in a Name?," 949–950.

116. Bouchard, "Patterns of Women's Names," 14. Though it is clear that this was not the norm, eleven out of twelve of the known daughters born to the Ottonians from the late ninth through the tenth centuries had names from their paternal families. Bouchard, "Patterns of Women's Names," 15.

117. Constance B. Bouchard, "Family Structure and Family Consciousness among the Aristocracy in the Ninth to Eleventh Centuries," *Francia* 14 (1986): 645.

118. Bouchard, "Patterns of Women's Names," 4.

119. Ibid. 12.

120. The image of the queen, including her rights and responsibilities, seems to have solidified in the thirteenth century into the queen-as-intercessor image, modeled on that of the medieval Virgin Mary. Therese Martin, "The Art of a Reigning Queen as Dynastic Propaganda in Twelfth-Century Spain," *Speculum* 80, no. 4 (2005): 1135.

121. The definitive study of Matilda is Marjorie Chibnall, *The Empress Matilda: Queen Consort, Queen Mother and Lady of the English* (Cambridge, Mass.: Blackwell, 1992).

122. Dunbabin, "What's in a Name?," 949.

123. Henry's own name was, indirectly, the product of female influence on Capetian onomastics. Hugh the Great married Hadvise, sister of Otto I of Germany. Hugh then named his second and third sons Otto and Henry, respectively, after Hadvise's brothers. Dunbabin, "What's in a Name?," 949–950.

124. See Figure 1.

125. Hugh and Henry's younger brother was named Robert in a continuation of the pattern.

126. Dunbabin, "What's in a Name?," 952.

127. F. G. Holweck, *A Biographical Dictionary of the Saints* (St. Louis: B. Herder, 1924), 810–811.

128. O. V. Loseva, *Russkie mesiatseslovy* (Moscow: Pamiatniki istoricheskoi mysli, 2001), 174, 202.

129. Prou, ed., *Recueil des actes de Philippe I-er,* xxiii.

130. Juan Mateos, *Le typicon de la grande église,* in Orientalia Christiana Analecta, vol. 165 (Rome: Pont. Institutum Orientalium Studiorum, 1962), 233.

131. Jean Dunbabin, *France in the Making, 843–1180* (Oxford: Oxford University Press, 1985), 215.

132. Dunbabin, "What's in a Name?," 954.

133. Dunbabin, *France in the Making,* 136, for example. Lewis, *Royal Succession in Capetian France,* 46, also suggests as much.

134. Dunbabin, "What's in a Name?," 960. For an interesting account of Philip's Christianity and perhaps the reason he was not well remembered as a Christian ruler, see Irfan Shahîd, *Rome and the Arabs: A Prolegomenon to the Study of Byzantium and the Arabs* (Washington, D.C.: Dumbarton Oaks Research Library and Collection, 1984), 78–79.

135. Dunbabin, "What's in a Name?," 961–962. See the discussion on titulature in Chapter 1, as well.

136. Her name as recorded by the Liubech Sinodik is "Kelikia"; however, a simple scribal error could have changed the Greek and Slavonic *Kekilia* into *Kelikia*. R. V. Zotov, *O Chernigovskikh kniaz'iakh po Liubetskomu sinodiku v Tatarskoe vremia* (Saint Petersburg: Tipografiia brat'ev Panteleevykh, 1892), 24, 33. The name Cecilia (Kekilia) was certainly known in Rus' and occupied a saints' day on November 22. Loseva, *Russkie mesiatseslovy*, 207.

137. By this I mean that each of the descendants of Árpád had multiple children, whereas the line from Riurik to Vladimir is a series of mostly only children. Of course, these genealogies are semilegendary at best until, in the Rusian case, Igor' and Ol'ga.

138. In secondary sources her name is given as Premislava, but this is a creation of modern historiography. For secondary source attribution of the name, see Baumgarten, "Généalogies," table 1; Wertner, *Az Árpádok családi története*, 112.

139. There is no dated reference to the marriage, but it is recorded without a name for the "wife from Ruthenia" in Dezso Dercesnyi, ed., *The Hungarian Illuminated Chronicle: Chronica de gestis Hungarorum* (Budapest: Corvina Press, 1969), 113.

140. A. F. Litvina and F. B. Uspenskii, *Vybor imeni u russkikh kniazei v X–XVI vv* (Moscow: Indrik, 2006), 507–508. The first recorded Andrew (Andrei) in the Rusian chronicles is Andrei Vladimirich, son of Vladimir Monomakh, who was born in 1102. *The Povest' vremennykh let*, 276:30, variant reading from the Hypatian chronicle. Beginning in the twelfth and thirteenth centuries the name began to become more familiar in Rus'. Baumgarten, "Généalogies," tables 4–6, 10–12.

141. *The Povest' vremennykh let*, 7:25–9:4.

142. Loseva, *Russkie mesiatseslovy*, 214–215.

143. Ibid.

144. Dercesnyi, *Hungarian Illuminated Chronicle*, 111.

145. Ibid., 113. Wertner, *Az Árpádok Családi Története*, 114–115. See Figure 3 for dates. This marriage is clearly in violation of consanguinity laws, as the two participants were first cousins. There is no mention of a dispensation for the marriage, nor any discussion of the consanguinity in the primary sources, which has led some to suspect that the marriage of the unknown Vladimirovna to Ladislaus is a later confusion.

146. David was the saint's name given to Gleb Vladimirich, Anastasia's uncle, and thus was already well known in Rus' at this time.

147. The image of David was especially powerful for a medieval ruler. The late Roman and Byzantine emperors took the name "New David" as an indicator of their inheritance of the mantle of King David. Charlemagne, as well as Merovingian kings, copied this imagery and used the name and/or image of David to legitimate their sovereignty. Ildar Garipzanov, "*David Imperator Augustus, Gratia Dei Rex*: Communication and Propaganda in Carolingian Royal Iconography," in *Monotheistic Kingship: The Medieval Variants*, ed. Aziz Al-Azmeh and János M. Bak (Budapest: Central European University, 2004), 92.

148. Ilarion, *Slovo o zakone i blagodati Ilariona*, ed. A. M. Moldovan (Kiev: Naukova Dumka, 1984), 97.

149. David's birth date is unknown, but the second half of the 1050s is a rough approximation. Baumgarten places it in 1058 conjecturally. Baumgarten, "Généalogies," table 1.

150. Dercesnyi, *Hungarian Illuminated Chronicle*, 115.

151. Ibid., 113.

152. Z. J. Kosztolynik, *Hungary under the Early Árpáds, 890s to 1063* (Boulder, Colo.: East European Monographs, 2002), 400.

153. For more information on the monastery and excellent background citations, see Walter K. Hanak, "Saint Procopius, the Sázava Monastery, and the Byzantine-Slavonic Legacy: Some Reconsiderations," in *Byzantina et Slavica Cracoviensie III: Byzantium and East Central Europe*, ed. Günter Prinzing and Maciej Salamon, with the assistance of Paul Stephenson (Cracow: Jagiellonian University, 2001), 71–80. In fact, testifying not only to Anastasia's probable influence but also to the concerted proselytizing of the Byzantines, Orthodox monasteries existed in Hungary into the twelfth century. Márta Font, "Missions, Conversions, and Power Legitimization in East Central Europe at the Turn of the First Millennium," in *East Central and Eastern Europe in the Early Middle Ages*, ed. Florin Curta (Ann Arbor: University of Michigan Press, 2008), 288.

154. Dercesnyi, *Hungarian Illuminated Chronicle*, 116.

155. Ibid., 115.

156. Kosztolynik, *Hungary under the Early Árpáds*, 376. See Dercesnyi, *Hungarian Illuminated Chronicle*, 125, for one late example.

157. Wilhelm, "Wilhelmi Abbatis Genealogia Regum Danorum," in *Scriptores Minores Historiae Danicae Medii Aevi*, ed. M. C. L. Getz (Copenhagen, 1917), 180. No date for the wedding exists, but it can be inferred to have occurred in the 1120s because of Knud's death in 1131 and the need for the wedding to have occurred before the birth of their last child, and obviously before Knud's death. For more on this marriage, see Christian

Raffensperger, "Dynastic Marriage in Action: How Two Rusian Princesses Changed Scandinavia," in *Imenoslov*, ed. F. B. Uspenskii (Moscow: Indrik, 2009), 187–199.

158. Wilhelm, "Wilhelmi abbatis genealogia regum Danorum," 180. *The Chronicle of the Slavs by Helmold, Priest of Bosau*, trans. Francis J. Tschan (New York: Columbia University Press, 1935), 152. Knud later became king of the Abodrite Slavs, a position he also received from Lothar, probably in approximately 1128. *Chronicle of the Slavs*, 153.

159. Saxo Grammaticus, *Danorum Regum Heroumque Historia Books X–XVI: The Text of the First Edition with Translation and Commentary in Three Volumes*, trans. Eric Christiansen (Oxford: B.A.R., 1980), bk. 13, 130.

160. For a Scandinavian example, which might be the most relevant in this case, see Snorri Sturluson, *Heimskringla*, ed. Bjarni Adalbjarnarson (Reykjavík: Hid Íslenzka Fornritagélag, 1951), 3:258.

161. An extensive examination of Riurikid genealogy will show the obvious popularity of the name, especially for firstborn sons. Interestingly, the name often occurs for younger sons when an older relative with the name dies.

162. *Chronicle of the Slavs*, 153.

163. Wilhelm, "Wilhelmi abbatis genealogia regum Danorum," 180, where the fact that he had conquered the Slavs rather than inherited their rule is pointed out as well; "rex Sclauorum, quos non hereditario iure sed armis potenter obtinuit."

164. Baumgarten, "Généalogies," 22–23, table 5.

165. *Knytlinga Saga: The History of the Kings of Denmark*, trans. Hermann Pálsson and Paul Edwards (Odense: Odense University Press, 1986), 135–136. For a secondary source reference that accepts the vaiildity of *Knytlinga saga*, see Uspenskii, *Imia i vlast'*, 18, n10

166. Beyond the use as a name in the royal dynasty of Denmark, the name Waldemar also became used for many noble families in the Baltic area. See examples in the works of William Urban on the Baltic Crusades, including Urban, *The Baltic Crusade* (Chicago: Lithuanian Research and Studies Center, 1994); and Urban, *The Samogitian Crusade* (Chicago: Lithuanian Research and Studies Center, 1989).

167. Alastair H. Thomas and Stewart P. Oakley, *Historical Dictionary of Denmark* (Lanham, Md.: Scarecrow Press, 1998), 418.

168. Waldemar married Sophia Vladimirovna, who was the grandniece of Ingeborg and daughter of Prince Vladimir Vsevolodovich of Novgorod. Wilhelm, "Wilhelmi abbatis genealogia regum Danorum," 182. Baumgarten, "Généalogies," 22–23, table 5.

169. This is another consanguineous marriage without any mention of a dispensation. Sophia and Waldemar are first cousins once removed.

170. Birgit Sawyer and Peter Sawyer, *Medieval Scandinavia: From Conversion to Reformation, circa 800–1500* (Minneapolis: University of Minnesota Press, 1993), 62, 89.

171. To continue the Hungarian parallel, Waldemar had also lived through a time of dynastic turmoil. During his youth there were multiple claimants to the Danish throne, and his mother Ingeborg had to fight for Waldemar's right to rule.

172. Sawyer and Sawyer, *Medieval Scandinavia*, 90, 117. For more on St. Knud and this ceremony, see Thomas A. Dubois and Niels Ingwersen, "St. Knud Lavard: A Saint for Denmark," in *Sanctity in the North: Saints, Lives, and Cults in Medieval Scandinavia*, ed. Thomas A. Dubois (Toronto: University of Toronto Press, 2008).

173. Nordstrom, ed., *Dictionary of Scandinavian History*, 333–334.

174. Norman W. Ingham, "Has a Missing Daughter of Iaroslav Mudry Been Found?" *Russian History* 25, no. 3 (1998); Norman W. Ingham, "A Slavist's View of Agatha, Wife of Edward the Exile, as a Possible Daughter of Yaroslav the Wise," *New England Historical and Genealogical Register* 152, no. 606 (1998); and René Jetté, "Is the Mystery of the Origin of Agatha, Wife of Edward the Exile, Finally Solved?," *New England Historical and Genealogical Register* 150, no. 600 (1996). The *Leges Edwarde confessoris* records the marriage of Agatha—daughter of Iaroslav, who was king of the Rusians—to Edward. Ingham, "Missing Daughter," 252–254.

175. Or for that matter in the Hungarian or German traditions, common alternative beliefs for the origin of Agatha. Jetté, "Origin of Agatha," 424–425.

176. Christine did appear later in the century in the Swedish royal house, of which Agafia's mother, Ingigerd, was a member. Wilhelm, "Wilhelmi abbatis genealogia regum Danorum," 180–182.

177. "Margaret" may also have been the name of a sister of Malcolm III of Scotland. The name does not appear in the Scottish line, as far as I have been able to find, and the precise identity of the mother of Malcolm and his siblings is unknown, though the best guesses point to a Scandinavian connection.

178. Loseva, *Russkie mesiatseslovy*, 391, 385–386. Loseva lists Margaret as Marina, the Orthodox version of the saint's name. Also Ingham, "Slavist's View of Agatha," 223.

179. Wilhelm, "Wilhelmi abbatis genealogia regum Danorum," 180–182. Kristin, daughter of Inge Steinkelsson, who later married Mstislav Vladimirich.

180. See, for example, Derek Baker, "'A Nursery of Saints': St. Margaret of Scotland Reconsidered," in *Medieval Women,* ed. Derek Baker (Oxford: Basil Blackwell for the Ecclesiastical History Society, 1978); Lois Hunneycutt, "The Idea of the Perfect Princess: The Life of Saint Margaret in the Reign of Matilda II, 1100–1118," *Anglo-Norman Studies* 12 (1989); Valerie Wall, "Queen Margaret of Scotland (1070–1093): Burying the Past, Enshrining the Future," in *Queens and Queenship in Medieval Europe: Proceedings of a Conference Held at King's College London, April 1995,* ed. Anne J. Duggan (Woodbridge: Boydell Press, 1997); and Alan Wilson, *St. Margaret, Queen of Scotland* (Edinburgh: John Donald, 1993).

181. The first instance of the name David in Rus' was as the Christian name of Gleb Vladimirich. M. D. Prisëlkov suggests that this name came from Bulgaria, via a brother of Tsar' Samuel. Prisëlkov, *Ocherki po tserkovno-politicheskoi istorii Kievskoi Rusi X–XII vv* (Saint Petersburg: M. M. Stasiuloevicha, 1913), 37–38. This fits in nicely with his theory of the Bulgarian origin of Rusian Christianity but cannot be proven conclusively. For some minor differences with Prisëlkov's portrayal of Samuel and David, see John V. A. Fine Jr., *The Early Medieval Balkans: A Critical Survey from the Sixth to the Late Twelfth Century* (Ann Arbor: University of Michigan Press, 1983), 188–190.

182. The East Slavic calendar had seven separate saints' days for Alexanders, three of whom appear in a large number of menologies. Loseva, *Russkie mesiatseslovy,* 338–339, 358, 418. Also Ingham, "Slavist's View of Agatha," 223.

183. Eileen Dunlop, *Queen Margaret of Scotland* (Edinburgh: National Museums of Scotland, 2005), 42.

184. Peter Somerset Fry and Fiona Somerset Fry, *The History of Scotland* (New York: Barnes and Noble, 1982), 54–55. A. D. M. Barrell notes that the Norman rulers of England supported Malcolm's children, against Malcolm's brother, multiple times. Barrell, *Medieval Scotland* (Cambridge: Cambridge University Press, 2000), 14, 27; Malcolm himself may have opposed the Norman invasion and assisted the Anglo-Saxons, 70.

185. Among other things, Margaret "assumed a prominent, truly collaborative position as partner and indispensable counselor of the king. She was involved in improving the image and honor of the royal court. She encouraged the business of foreign merchants. She played a significant role as a supporter of Gregorian reform policies in Scotland and occupied a prominent position in the reform councils of the period." Jane Tibbetts Schulenburg, *Forgetful of Their Sex: Female Sanctity and Society, ca. 500–1100* (Chicago: University of Chicago Press, 1998), 20. See also Pauline Staf-

ford, "The Portrayal of Royal Women in England, Mid-Tenth to Mid-Twelfth Centuries," in *Medieval Queenship,* ed. John Carmi Parsons (Gloucestershire: Sutton, 1994), 153–154.

186. Barrell, *Medieval Scotland,* 14.

187. Or perhaps a sly reference to Harald's love interest in Byzantium, the Byzantine princess Maria. See *Morkinskinna,* ch. 13.

188. Sturluson, *Heimskringla,* 602.

189. Ibid., 340; *Morkinskinna,* ch. 9.

190. Sturluson, *Heimskringla,* 702; *Morkinskinna,* ch. 66.

191. Sturluson, *Heimskringla,* 702.

192. Ibid., 751; *Morkinskinna,* ch. 66.

193. For more on the marriages of these two women and the influential role they played in Scandinavian politics of the early twelfth century, see Raffensperger, "Dynastic Marriage in Action," 187–199.

194. *PSRL 2,* col. 276, for one example of the name in use in a primary source.

195. George Ostrogorsky, *History of the Byzantine State,* trans. Joan Hussey, rev. ed. (New Brunswick, N.J.: Rutgers University Press, 1969), 333–337.

196. I. M. Ivakin, *Kniaz' Vladimir Monomakh i ego pouchenie* (Moscow: Universitetskaia tipografia, 1901), 208. A. V. Nazarenko also devotes a whole chapter of *Drevniaia Rus'* to Mstislav/Harald. There is substantial discussion of his genealogy and the sources in Litvina and Uspenskii, *Vybor imeni u russkikh kniazei.*

197. M. P. Alekseev, "Anglo-saxonskaia parallel' k Poucheniu Vladimira Monomakha," *Trudy otdela drevno-russkoi literatury* 2 (1935).

198. Litvina and Uspenskii, *Vybor imeni u russkikh kniazei,* 38–39.

199. Ibid.

200. For commentary on Scandinavian-Slavic legal practices in regard to inheritance through the female line, see Francis Butler, "The House of Rogvolod," in *Imenoslov: Istoricheskaia semantika imeni* (Moscow: Indrik, 2007).

201. Of the numerous foreign contacts in Rusian history, only a small number, chiefly those with Byzantium, have been listed in the *Povest' vremennykh let (PVL).* The number of mentions of the Poles, the main contact to the west of Rus', is in the single digits in the period before 1110, and there are only two mentions of the Hungarians. In Latin-language records, contacts with Rus' are mentioned much more frequently. For more on this topic, see the Introduction.

202. Grammaticus, *Danorum regum heroumque historia,* bk. XIII, 110; Sturluson, *Heimskringla,* 702. The name of their sister, Rogned', does appear in the Hypatian chronicle. *PSRL 2,* 529, 531. Hers is also, clearly, a

Scandinavian name, but it has a strong Rusian antecedent. See Butler, "The House of Rogvolod."

203. Sturluson, *Heimskringla*, 702. Litvina and Uspenskii offer the fascinating, and probably correct, argument that Ingeborg was named after Kristín's father, Ingi, and that Rogned' was named after Kristín's brother, Rögnvaldr. Though, of course, the name Rogned' has a place in Rusian onomastic tradition as well; its reappearance after more than a century is too much for coincidence. Litvina and Uspenskii, *Vybor imeni u russkikh kniazei*, 39–40.

204. Schmid, "Structure of the Nobility," 47.

205. Bouchard, "Consanguinity," 277.

206. Pauline Stafford, *Queens, Concubines, and Dowagers: The King's Wife in the Early Middle Ages* (Athens, Ga.: University of Georgia Press, 1983), 197.

4. Kiev as a Center of European Trade

1. The field is truly vast, especially in Russian. A. P. Novoseltsev and V. T. Pashuto summarize a great deal of the classic works in their article "Vneshniaia torgovlia drevnei Rusi do serediny XIII," *Istoriia SSSR* 3 (1967). Additionally, much work has been done since then by a variety of scholars on both sides of the Atlantic. Thomas Noonan and Janet Martin have written extensively in English on trade, as have a large number of scholars in Russian, such as E. A. Rybina, B. A. Rybakov, P. P. Tolochko, V. L. Ianin, and, most recently, V. B. Perkhavko.

2. Thomas S. Noonan, "The Flourishing of Kiev's International and Domestic Trade, ca. 1100–ca. 1240," in *Ukrainian Economic History: Interpretive Essays*, ed. I. S. Koropeckyj (Cambridge, Mass.: Harvard University Press, 2001), 104. Noonan notes explicitly that M. K. Karger's two-volume study of Kiev from the late 1950s has been supplanted, and challenged, by more-recent works, but has not been replaced by a similar large-scale study.

3. As Thomas Noonan eloquently notes, "Historians tend to focus upon written sources and thus do not always fully utilize the vast archeological and numismatic data. Numismatists do not always put the evidence of coin hoards and finds into a historical context. And, archeologists all too often adopt a highly selective and superficial approach to the written sources. Obviously, we cannot expect a single scholar to be a specialist on all aspects of all the various sources. But, we can ask that a study of Kiev's commerce in the pre-Mongol era should try to incorporate in a critical

fashion as much of the extant evidence as possible. The different types of evidence (e.g., written sources, archeology, numismatics, etc.) are not isolated, water-tight compartments; rather, they all reflect, if only imperfectly, a single historical reality. Consequently, we must try to integrate the insights from all the various disciplines into a more perfect vision of the past." Ibid., 104–105.

4. Though to some extent a national history, as it deals with early Russia, Janet Martin's book does deal extensively with Rusian, and Russian, trading connections throughout Eurasia. Martin, *Medieval Russia, 980–1584,* 2nd ed. (Cambridge: Cambridge University Press, 2008).

5. Volodymyr I. Mezentsev, "The Territorial and Demographic Development of Medieval Kiev and Other Major Cities of Rus': A Comparative Analysis Based on Recent Archeological Research," *Russian Review* 48, no. 2 (1989): 145–146.

6. Noonan, "Flourishing," 105–106.

7. Mezentsev, "Territorial and Demographic Development," 146.

8. Witness the dramatic expansion of trade in the fourteenth and fifteenth centuries with the advent of the age of exploration.

9. Michael McCormick, *Origins of the European Economy: Communications and Commerce,* a.d. *300–900* (Cambridge: Cambridge University Press, 2001), 612.

10. Janet L. Abu-Lughod, *Before European Hegemony: The World System,* a.d. *1250–1350* (New York: Oxford University Press, 1989), 33, 34 (map).

11. This method of viewing economic exchange in the medieval world is steadily replacing the narrow view based upon medieval (or modern, then read back in time) polities. Mark Whittow noted recently that the Byzantine economy should be viewed in light of larger Mediterranean economics, rather than falsely segmented off. Whittow, "The Middle Byzantine Economy," in *The Cambridge History of the Byzantine Empire, c. 500–1492,* ed. Jonathan Shepard (Cambridge: Cambridge University Press, 2009), 465.

12. Similarly, one might speak of major trading cities as "nodal points" connecting the various trading networks into a larger web. Søren Michael Sindbæk, "Local and Long-Distance Exchange," in *The Viking World,* ed. Stefan Brink in collaboration with Neil Price (London: Routledge, 2008), 154.

13. Noonan, "Flourishing," 103–104.

14. *The Povest' vremennykh let: An Interlinear Collation and Paradosis,* ed. Donald Ostrowski, with David Birnbaum and Horace G. Lunt (Cambridge, Mass.: Harvard University Press, 2004), 7:2.

15. *The Povest' vremennykh let,* 4:7, 7:7, and elsewhere.

16. The whole route is detailed, with specific rivers and lakes, in *Povest' vremennykh let,* 7:2–7:7.

17. In this context it is worth noting the collection of articles in *Vostochnaia Evropa* about the path from the Varangians to the Greeks, specifically the fascinating article by E. A. Mel'nikova about the path as a mental map. Mel'nikova, "Put' kak strukturnaia osnova mental'noi karti sostavitelia 'povesti vremennykh let'," in *Vostochnaia evropa v drevnosti i srednevekov'e* (Moscow: Institut vseobshchei istorii RAN, 2008), 150–156.

18. *The Povest' vremennykh let,* 7:2–7:7.

19. Ibid., 7:7–7:9.

20. Ibid., 7:9–7:24, in regard to the travels of Apostle Andrew. This is not an entirely original observation. The work of Thomas Noonan, which is drawn on heavily in the early portions of this chapter, demonstrated the interconnectivity between the Scandinavian, Rusian, and Islamic worlds in the eighth to tenth centuries. His work, chiefly, on numismatics, put Rus' into a larger trading world than simply the route from the Varangians to the Greeks.

21. Mark Whittow, *The Making of Byzantium, 600–1025* (Berkeley: University of California Press, 1996), 249.

22. I refer to the exchange zone centered on the Abbasid capital, Baghdad, and extending into the Caucasus and Central Asia as a Middle Eastern exchange zone, though the boundaries of it, stretching to the Caspian, are slightly broader than our current definition of the Middle Eastern world.

23. Thomas S. Noonan, "Why the Vikings First Came to Russia," in *The Islamic World, Russia and the Vikings, 750–900: The Numismatic Evidence* (Brookfield, Vt.: Ashgate, 1998), 340.

24. *The Povest' vremennykh let,* 65:4–5.

25. Noonan, "Why the Vikings," 343–344.

26. Ibid., 344–345.

27. Roman K. Kovalev, "Mint Output in Tenth-Century Bukhārā: A Case Study of Dirham Production and Monetary Circulation in Northern Europe," *Russian History/Histoire Russe* 28, nos. 1–4 (2001): 245. "In fact, dirhams appear to have been struck by the Sāmānid specifically for this great northern trade" (n2).

28. Thomas S. Noonan, "Medieval Islamic Copper Coins from European Russia and Surrounding Regions: The Use of the Fals in Early Islamic Trade with Eastern Europe," *Journal of the American Oriental Society* 94, no. 4 (1974): 452. This was certainly not uncommon and seems to have

been the case also in Scandinavia, the final destination of many of the dirhams transiting Rus'. Svein H. Gullbekk, "Coinage and Monetary Economies," in *The Viking World*, ed. Stefan Brink in collaboration with Neil Price (London: Routledge, 2008), 166.

29. Johan Callmer, "The Archeology of Kiev, ca A.D. 500–1000: A Survey," in *Les Pays du Nord et Byzance (Scandinavie et Byzance): Actes du colloque nordique et international de byzantinologie,* ed. Rudolf Zeitler (Uppsala: Almqvist and Wiksell, 1981), 37.

30. Janet Martin, "Coins, Commerce, and the Conceptualization of Kievan Rus'," in *Pre-Modern Russia and Its World: Essays in Honor of Thomas S. Noonan,* ed. Kathryn L. Reyerson, Theofanis G. Stavrou, and James D. Tracy (Wiesbaden: Harrassowitz, 2006), 165.

31. Various reasons have been put forth for the decrease in the minting of silver dirhams, from the dishonesty of minters, to the overexporting of silver to Rusian territory, to fund conquest of India, among others. E. Ashtor, *A Social and Economic History of the Near East in the Middle Ages* (Berkeley: University of California Press, 1976), 175–177.

32. However, Petr Sorokin notes that "from the middle of the 8th until the 14th century, the settlement of Ladoga . . . was the main port in north-western Russia." Sorokin, "Staraya Ladoga: A Seaport in Medieval Russia," in *Connected by the Sea: Proceedings of the Tenth International Symposium on Boat and Ship Archeology, Roskilde 2003,* ed. Lucy Blue, Fred Hocker, and Anton Englert (Oxford: Oxbow Books, 2006), 157.

33. Martin, "Coins, Commerce," 167, 169; Noonan, "Flourishing," 107–109.

34. Callmer, "Archeology of Kiev," 44.

35. Ibid., 46. There is more discussion of denarius finds in Rus' in regard to the East–West trade ties in Rus', below, but briefly, Georges Duby puts forward the idea that denarius finds increase as dirhams decrease in Slavic areas as a marker of Western influence. Duby, *The Early Growth of the European Economy: Warriors and Peasants from the Seventh to the Twelfth Century* (Ithaca, N.Y.: Cornell University Press, 1973), 126–127. The reasons for the lack of coin finds are many, including the increase in a monetary economy, as well as simply a possible failure to hoard properly. For instance, Ol'ga and her entourage were given large sums of money when she visited Constantinople in the 950s, but where that money ended up is unknown. *De cerimoniis aulae Byzantinae,* ed. I. I. Reiske, vol. 9 of *Corpus Scriptorum Historiae Byzantinae,* ed. B. G. Niebuhrii (Bonn: Impensis Ed. Weberi, 1829), 597–598. Further, unlike the enormous transit of dirhams through Rus', only 635 Byzantine coins have been found in Swedish hoards, 80 percent of which are on Gotland. The timing, however, does

coincide with the rise of the north–south trade route in Rus', as the majority of those coins were minted in the mid-tenth century (945–989). Brita Malmer, "Some Observations on the Importation of Byzantine Coins to Scandinavia in the Tenth and Eleventh Centuries and the Scandinavian Response," *Russian History/Histoire Russe* 28, nos. 1–4 (2001): 295.

36. Steven Runciman, *A History of the Crusades* (Cambridge: Cambridge University Press, 1962), 1:51.

37. There is also the 907 treaty, which is often viewed as a preliminary treaty to the 911 one. *The Povest' vremennykh let,* 30:25–32:7, 32:24–38:15, 46:11–54:15. The treaties are discussed in the most detail in Frank Edward Wozniak Jr., "The Nature of Byzantine Foreign Policy toward Kievan Russia in the First Half of the Tenth Century: A Reassessment" (PhD diss., Stanford University, 1973); Jana Malingoudi, *Die russisch-byzantinischen Verträge des 10. Jahrhunderts aus diplomatischer Sicht* (Thessaloniki: Vanias, 1994).

38. Wozniak, *Byzantine Foreign Policy,* 79–80.

39. V. Ia. Petrukhin, "Pokhod Olega na Tsar'grad: K problem istochnikov letopisnogo rasskaza," in *Slaviane i ikh sosedi: Grecheskii i slavianskii mir v srednie veka i rannee novoe vremia* (Moscow: Institut slavianovedeniia i balkanistiki RAN, 1994), 15–16.

40. T. V. Rozhdestvenskaia, "Dogovory Rusi s Vizantiei X v. v strukture letopisnogo povestvovaniia," in *Vostochnaia evropa v drevnosti i srednevekov'e: X Cheteniia k 80-letiiu chlena-korrespondenta AN SSSR Vladimira Terent'evicha Pashuto,* ed. E. A. Mel'nikova (Moscow: RAN, 1998), 101. Though, of course, it is relevant to point out that the extant copies of the *PVL* date only from this same time and thus all of the information contained therein has some problems as well.

41. *The Rhodian Sea-Law,* ed. and trans. Walter Ashburner (Oxford: Clarendon Press, 1909). Though this law did not appreciably change throughout the Middle Ages, and theoretically could have been known in Rus' at a later date as well.

42. For different perspectives on the treaties, see Whittow, *The Making of Byzantium,* 249; Simon Franklin and Jonathan Shepard, *The Emergence of Rus, 750–1200* (New York: Longman, 1996), 103–104; A. P. Novoseltsev and V. T. Pashuto, "Vneshniaia torgovlia drevnei Rusi do serediny XIII," *Istoriia SSSR* 3 (1967): 82–83.

43. At the end of the second major treaty, listed in the *PVL* under the year 944, Igor' sends the Greeks home with "furs, slaves, and wax." This is the only reference to trade goods in the whole of the latter treaty. *The Povest' vremennykh let,* 54:9–10.

44. Catherine Holmes briefly mentions the multiple purposes involved in the trip as well. Catherine Holmes, *Basil II and the Governance of Empire (976–1025)* (Oxford: Oxford University Press, 2005), 513.

45. *De cerimoniis,* 597, 598.

46. Ibid., 595.

47. *The Povest' vremennykh let,* 62:26–63:1.

48. It is also interesting to note, though not necessarily relevant for our purposes here, that this is the only such visit to Constantinople by a high-ranking Rusian. In fact, as recorded in the extant sources, it is the only visit to a foreign capital made by any Rusian ruler.

49. Janet Martin, *Treasure of the Land of Darkness: The Fur Trade and Its Significance for Medieval Russia* (Cambridge: Cambridge University Press, 1986), 39, 40, 41, 45, and elsewhere; Novoseltsev and Pashuto, "Vneshniaia torgovlia drevnei Rusi," 84.

50. Martin, *Treasure,* 45. The majority of this kind of information comes from archaeological studies such as Iu. L. Shchalova, "Nekotorye materialy k istorii russko-vizantiiskikh otnoshenii v xi–xii vv.," *Vizantiiskii vremennik* 19 (1961): 60–75.

51. For a concise description not by this author, see Per Jonas Nordhagen, "Byzantium and the West," in *Les Pays du Nord et Byzance (Scandinavie et Byzance): Actes du colloque nordique et international de byzantinologie,* ed. Rudolf Zeitler (Uppsala: Almqvist and Wiksell, 1981), 346–347.

52. For an overview of Byzantine influence on Western art, see Otto Demus, *Byzantine Art and the West* (New York: New York University Press, 1970); Oleg M. Ioannisyan, "Archeological Evidence for the Development and Urbanization of Kiev from the 8th to the 14th Centuries," trans. Katharine Judelson, in *From the Baltic to the Black Sea: Studies in Medieval Archeology,* ed. David Austin and Leslie Alcock (London: Unwin Hyman, 1990), 297, 304. Though it must be noted that Ioannisyan has a significantly different interpretation of the quality of the work done by the Byzantine craftsmen than does Demus. Demus, *Byzantine Art and the West,* 121.

53. N. Makarov, "Traders in the Forest: The Northern Periphery of Rus' in the Medieval Trade Network," in *Pre-Modern Russia and Its World: Essays in Honor of Thomas S. Noonan,* ed. Kathryn L. Reyerson, Theofanis G. Stavrou, and James D. Tracy (Wiesbaden: Harrassowitz, 2006), 123; Martin, *Treasure,* 45.

54. Sviatoslav's stated goal was to trade Rusian wax, furs, honey, and slaves for Byzantine, Bohemian, and Hungarian goods such as gold, silks, wine, fruit, horses, and silver. *The Povest' vremennykh let,* 67:20–27.

55. This trade route has been under investigation for some time, The first major work on the subject (still relevant) is from the nineteenth century. V. Vasil'evskii, "Drevniaia torgovlia Kieva s Regensburgom," *Zhurnal' ministerstva narodnago prosveshcheniia* (1888): 121–150.

56. Soviet archaeologists in particular did an enormous amount of work on these connections, which resulted in some fine periodicals, though occasionally Marxist interpretations need to be challenged. In relation to this topic, some of the best sources are the volumes of *Arkheologiia SSSR,* such as V. P. Darkevich, "Proizvedeniia zapadnogo khudozhestvennogo remesla v vostochnoi evrope (X–XIV vv.)," *Arkheologiia SSSR,* E1–57. (1966), or the run of *Arkheologicheskii sbornik,* which is also cited extensively here.

57. Franklin and Shepard, *The Emergence of Rus,* 88, 92.

58. Some examples include the French embassy sent for Anna Iaroslavna, Rabbi Petachia on his travels, as well as a host of other Jewish travelers and traders. Louis Paris, "Roger II, XLIVe eveque de Chalons, sa vieet sa mission en Russie," in *La Chronique de Champagne* 2 (1837): 89–99; Pethahiah of Regensburg, *Travels of Rabbi Petachia of Ratisbon,* trans. A. Benisch (London: Trubner, 1856); J. Brutzkus, "Trade with Eastern Europe, 800–1200," *Economic History Review* 13, nos. 1–2 (1943): 31–41.

59. "Addition Decima: Leges Portorii c.a. 906," in Monumenta Germaniae Historica, Leges, vol. 3 (Hannover: Impensis Bibliopolii Avlici Hahniani, 1863), 480–481; Vasil'evskii, "Drevniaia torgovlia Kieva," 124–127, where the trading regulations are translated into Russian.

60. Martin, *Treasure,* 47–48.

61. *The Annals of St-Bertin,* trans. Janet L. Nelson (New York: Manchester University Press, 1991), 44.

62. *The Povest' vremennykh let,* 21:10–22:3; Cyril Mango, *The Homilies of Photius Patriarch of Constantinople* (Cambridge, Mass.: Harvard University Press, 1958), homilies III and IV. The best source on the attack that analyzes all of the relevant primary source material is A. A. Vasiliev, *The Russian Attack on Constantinople* (Cambridge, Mass.: Harvard University Press, 1946).

63. L. Rabinowitz, *Jewish Merchant Adventurers: A Study of the Radanites* (London: Edward Goldston, 1948), 139–143; see also Ashtor, *A Social and Economic History,* 105–107, where the same trade goods as Rusians sold, slaves and furs, are discussed.

64. Brutzkus, "Trade with Eastern Europe," 33–34.

65. "Prague is the richest city, by reason of its trade. Russians and Slavs come to it from Cracow with their wares, and Moslems, Jews and Turks come

from Turkey [Chazaria and Crimea] with goods and money, and take away slaves, lead and various furs." Ibid., 34.

66. Ibid., 33–34.

67. "Annales Quedlinburgenses," in Monumenta Germaniae Historica Scriptores, vol. 3, ed. George Pertz (Hannover: Impensis Bibliopolii Avlici Hahniani, 1839), s.a. 960; *Lamberti Hersfeldensis Annales,* ed. V. Cl. Lud. Frid. Hasse, in Monumenta Germaniae Historica Scriptores, vol. 5, ed. George Pertz (Hannover: Impensis Bibliopolii Avlici Hahniani, 1844), s.a. 960, 973. Lambert, however, notes that the 973 meeting took place in Quedlinburg.

68. Brutzkus, "Trade with Eastern Europe," 34, where he cites *Or Zaruah* (Zhitomir, 1862), I, ch. 694, p. 196. I am unable to read Hebrew, and have merely used Brutzkus's interpretation of the events.

69. *The Povest' vremennykh let,* 150:3–8.

70. *Ipat'evskaia letopis',* vol. 2 of *Polnoe sobranie russkikh letopisei* (Moscow: Iazyki russkoi kul'tury, 2001) (hereafter cited as *PSRL 2*), 275–276, 326.

71. Norman Golb and Omeljan Pritsak, *Khazarian Hebrew Documents of the Tenth Century* (Ithaca, N.Y.: Cornell University Press, 1982).

72. *PSRL 2,* 427–428.

73. Brutzkus discusses this route in some detail with copious references to Hebrew sources. Brutzkus, "Trade with Eastern Europe."

74. Rabbi Petachia disposes of this portion of his journey in a short paragraph before embarking on telling the tale of his travels in the Middle East. The brevity of his relation of this whole trade route showcases its unremarkableness to his audience, and thus how common it was for people to travel from the German Empire to Rus'. Pethahiah of Regensburg, *Travels of Rabbi Petachia.*

75. Brutzkus, "Trade with Eastern Europe," 36.

76. Two examples of Rusian embassies in the German Empire, in 960 and 973, have already been mentioned, but there are others, including in 1043 and 1075. *Lamberti Hersfeldensis Annales,* s.a. 1043, 1075. The 1075 example is particularly relevant, as it is in regard to Iziaslav Iaroslavich's travels with his family throughout Europe, made possible (along with his knowledge of the area), because of the interconnectivity of Rus' and the rest of Europe.

77. "Vita Mariani," in *Acta Sanctorum,* vol. 4 (February, 1894): 369.

78. Though stemming from Tatishchev, who is often a questionable source, it is reasonable that this took place in this period. V. N. Tatishchev, *Istoriia Rossiiskaia* (Moscow: Akademii Nauk SSSR, 1963), 2:142.

79. Novoseltsev and Pashuto, "Vneshniaia torgovlia drevnei Rusi," 87.

80. Rabinowitz, *Jewish Merchant Adventurers,* 174–175; "Addition Decima: Leges Portorii c.a. 906," 481.

81. "Addition Decima: Leges Portorii c.a. 906," 481; *The Povest' vremennykh let,* 67:24–27.

82. Martin, *Treasure.*

83. Novoseltsev and Pashuto, "Vneshniaia torgovlia drevnei Rusi," 89, 92, citing Vita Meinwerci epispopi Patherbrunnensis. *Scriptores Rerum Germanicarum* Ed. F. Tenckhoff (Hannover: Impensis Bibliopolii Hahniani, 1921), cap. 44, 56, 85, 86, 111, 112, 123.

84. Benjamin of Tudela, *The Itinerary of Benjamin of Tudela,* trans. Masa'ot shel Tabi Benjamin (Cold Spring, N.Y.: NightinGale Resources, 2005), 139.

85. R. S. Minasian, "Chetyre gruppy nozhei Vostochnoi Evropy epokhi rannego srednevekov'ia: K voprosu o poiavlenii slavianskikh form v lesnoi zone," *Arkheologicheskii Sbornik* 21 (1980): 73.

86. A. N. Kirpichnikov, "Drevnerusskoe oruzhie: Vypusk pervyi, mechi i sabli IX–XIII vv.," *Arkheologiia SSSR* E1–36 (1966): 38, 43. According to a more recent analysis, this was the "largest weapons manufacturer in Europe during the Middle Ages, which produced internationally regarded cold weapons of high quality." A. N. Kirpichnikov, Lena Thålin-Bergman, and Ingmar Jansson, "A New Analysis of Viking-Age Swords from the Collection of the Statens Historiska Musser, Stockholm, Sweden," *Russian History/Histoire Russe* 28, nos. 1–4 (2001): 227.

87. For an exhaustive study of the inscriptions, see D. A. Drboglav, *Zagadki latinskikh kleim na mechakh IX–XIV vekov: Klassifikatsiia, datirovka i chtenie nadpisei* (Moscow: Izdatel'stvo Moskovskogo universiteta, 1984).

88. Kirpichnikov, "Drevnerusskoe oruzhie," 38–39, 41, 43–44; B. A. Rybakov, *Remeslo Drevnei Rusi* (Moscow: Akademii Nauk SSSR, 1948), 228–229.

89. Kirpichnikov, "Drevnerusskoe oruzhie," 41. Also, Simon Franklin, *Writing, Society and Culture in Early Rus', c. 950–1300* (Cambridge: Cambridge University Press, 2002), 59.

90. Henryk Samsonowicz, "The City and the Trade Route in the Early Middle Ages," in *Central and Eastern Europe in the Middle Ages: A Cultural History,* ed. Piotr Górecki and Nancy van Deusen (London: Tauris, 2009), 24.

91. For instance, the Raffelstettin regulations mention salt much more often than any other single commodity. "Addition Decima: Leges Portorii c.a. 906," 480–481.

92. *The Paterik of the Kievan Caves Monastery,* trans. Muriel Heppell (Cambridge, Mass.: Harvard University Press, 1989), 172.

93. V. B. Perkhavko, "Kievo-Pecherskii paterik o torgovle sol'iu v drevnei rusi," in *Vostochnaia evropa v drevnosti i srednevekov'e,* ed. V. T. Pashuto (Moscow: Akademii nauk SSSR, 1990), 105–109.

94. Ibid., 106–109.

95. A. V. Nazarenko, *Drevniaia Rus' na mezhdunarodnykh putiakh: Mezhdistsiplinarnye ocherki kulturnykh, torgovykh, politicheskikh sviazei IX–XII vekov* (Moscow: Iazyki russkoi kul'tury, 2001), 76–78.

96. Nazarenko, *Drevniaia Rus',* 76–78.

97. Novoseltsev and Pashuto, "Vneshniaia torgovlia drevnei Rusi," 87. Christian Radke illustrates this continued prosperity by highlighting the immense amount of German silver that quite quickly replaced the Islamic silver flowing into the entire Baltic region. Christian Radke, "Money, Port and Ships from a Schleswig Point of View," in *Connected by the Sea: Proceedings of the Tenth International Symposium on Boat and Ship Archeology, Roskilde 2003,* ed. Lucy Blue, Fred Hocker, and Anton Englert (Oxford: Oxbow Books, 2006), 147.

98. *The Povest' vremennykh let,* 7:2–7; *Adam of Bremen: The History of the Archbishops of Hamburg-Bremen,* trans. Francis J. Tschan (New York: Columbia University Press, 2002), bk. 4, 193.x.10 and schol. 116 (115); *The Chronicle of the Slavs by Helmold, Priest of Bosau,* trans. Francis J. Tschan (New York: Columbia University Press, 1935), 46, ch. 1.

99. Novoseltsev and Pashuto, "Vneshniaia torgovlia drevnei Rusi," 87–88.

100. Iu. I. Shtakel'berg, "Glinianye diski iz Staroi Ladogi," *Arkeologicheskii sbornik* 4 (1962): 109–115; O. I. Davidan, "K voprosu o proiskhozhdenii i datirovke rannikh grebenok staroi ladogi," *Arkheologicheskii Sbornik* 10 (1968): 54–63; Z. A. L'vova, "K voprosu o prichinakh pronikhoveniia stekliannykh bus X–nachala XI veka v severnye raiony vostochnoi evropy," *Arkheologicheskii sbornik* 18 (1977): 106–109.

101. The majority of references to Scandinavia in most medieval survey textbooks, for instance, have to do with the Vikings and/or Christianization, but fail to include them in the broader picture of medieval Europe. Similarly, even in Scandinavian histories, the periodizations for Viking and medieval history are separate.

102. Ladoga itself dates from the eighth century, and the interaction with the larger Baltic world is part of the earliest strata of archeological finds. Sorokin, "Staraya Ladoga"; Sindbæk, "Local and Long-Distance Exchange," 151–152; Evgeny N. Nosov, "The Problem of the Emergence of Early Urban Centres in Northern Russia," in *Cultural Transformations and Interactions in Eastern Europe,* ed. John Chapman and Pavel Dolukhanov (Brookfield, Vt.: Aldershot, 1993), 254.

103. Gartharíki is the Old Norse name for Rus'. Snorri Sturluson, *Heimskringla: History of the Kings of Norway*, trans. Lee M. Hollander (Austin: University of Texas Press, 1964), 297.

104. Ibid., 147.

105. For example, "Sigvat often asked merchants who had dealings with Hólmgarth what they could tell him about Magnús Óláfsson." Ibid., 547.

106. Novoseltsev and Pashuto, "Vneshniaia torgovlia drevnei Rusi," 91; V. L. Ianin, "Nakhodka drevnerusskikh vislykh pechatei v Sigtune (Shvetsiia)," in *Vostochnaia evropa v drevnosti i srednevekov'e: X Cheteniia k 80–letiiu chlena-korrespondenta AN SSSR Vladimira Terent'evicha Pashuto*, ed. E. A. Mel'nikova (Moscow: RAN, 1998), 139.

107. *The Povest' vremennykh let*, 48:7–9.

108. Martin, *Treasure*, 40–41.

109. O. I. Davidan, "K voprosu o proiskhozhdenii i datirovke rannikh grebenok Staroi Ladogi," *Arkheologicheskii Sbornik* 10 (1968): 54–63.

110. Z. A. L'vova, "Stekliannye busy Staroi Ladogi: Chast II. Proiskhozhdenie bus," *Arkheologicheskii sbornik* 12 (1970): 111.

111. Iu. I. Shtakel'berg, "Glinianye diski iz Staroi Ladogi," *Arkehologicheskii sbornik* 4 (1962): 113.

112. Noonan, "Flourishing," 108–110; Per Beskow. "Byzantine Influence in the Conversion of the Baltic Region?," in *The Cross Goes North: Processes of Conversion in Northern Europe, AD 300–1300*, ed. Martin Carver (York: York Medieval Press, 2003), 560; Wladislaw Duczko, "Viking Sweden and Byzantium: An Archaeologists Version," in *Byzantium: Identity, Image, Influence: XIX International Congress of Byzantine Studies, University of Copenhagen, 18–24 August, 1996*, ed. Karsten Fledelius (Copenhagen: Eventus, 1996), 199.

113. O. I. Davidan, "Vesovye gir'ki Staroi Ladogi," *Arkheologicheskii sbornik* 28 (1987): 122.

114. *Adam of Bremen*, bk. 4, 187.i.1; bk. 4, schol. 126 (121).

115. *Chronicle of the Slavs*, 66, ch. 8.

116. Martin, *Treasure*, 40.

117. Birgit Sawyer and Peter Sawyer, *Medieval Scandinavia: From Conversion to Reformation, circa 800–1500*, The Nordic Series vol. 17 (Minneapolis: University of Minnesota Press, 1993), 154–155. Else Roesdahl discusses these boats, including archaeological finds, and a modern reconstruction, in slightly more depth. Roesdahl, *The Vikings* (London: Penguin, 1991), 91.

118. *Novgorodskaia pervaia letopis': Starshego i mladshego izvodov*, vol. 3 of *Polnoe sobranie russkikh letopisei* (Moscow: Iazyki russkoi kul'tury, 2000) (hereafter cited as *PSRL 3*), 22.

119. Anthony Cutler, "Garda, Källunge and the Byzantine Tradition on Gotland," in *Byzantium, Italy and the North: Papers on Cultural Relations* (London: Pindar Press, 2000), 422, 399.

120. Martin, *Treasure*, 50. The connections actually go much deeper, and we see a whole host of merchants and artisans operating on Gotland and in the Rusian north, both. For just one example, see Davidan, "Bronzoliteinoe delo v Ladoge," *Arkheologicheskii Sbornik* 21 (1980), 66–67.

121. Kurt Villads Jensen, "The Blue Baltic Border of Denmark in the High Middle Ages: Danes, Wends, and Saxo Grammaticus," in *Medieval Frontiers: Concepts and Practice,* ed. David Abulafia and Nora Berend (Burlington, Vt.: Ashgate, 2002), 177.

122. Wilhelm, "Wilhelmi abbatis genealogia regum Danorum," in *Scriptores minores historiae danicae medii aevi,* ed. M. C. L. Getz (Copenhagen, 1917), 182; Christian Raffensperger, "Dynastic Marriage in Action: How Two Rusian Princesses Changed Scandinavia," in *Imenoslov: Istoricheskaia semantika imeni* (Moscow: Indrik, 2009), 187–199.

123. *PSRL 3*, 22, 23.

124. Martin, *Treasure*, 49.

125. When the Germans will come to dominate the Baltic trade. Sawyer and Sawyer, *Medieval Scandinavia,* 155–156.

126. Martin, *Treasure*, 49; V. M. Potin, *Drenviaia Rus' i evropeiskie gosudarstva v X–XIII vv.: Istoriko–numismakitcheskii ocherk* (Leningrad: Sovetskii Khudozhnik, 1968), 63.

127. Theophilus, *De Diversis Artibus: The Various Arts,* trans. C. R. Dodwell (London: Thomas Nelson and Sons, 1961), xxxix, 4.

128. Robert-Henri Bautier, *The Economic Development of Medieval Europe,* trans. Heather Karolyi (New York: Harcourt Brace Jovanovich, 1971), 121.

129. *Chronicle of the Slavs,* 229 ch. 86 (85).

130. Samuel H. Cross, "Medieval Russian Contacts with the West," *Speculum* 10, no. 2 (April 1935): 142.

131. Darkevich, "Proizvedeniia zapadnogo," 9–42.

132. Ibid., 52, 10.

133. Edward V. Williams, *The Bells of Russia: History and Technology* (Princeton, N.J.: Princeton University Press, 1985), 36.

134. Martin, *Treasure*, 51–52; Novoseltsev and Pashuto, "Vneshniaia torgovlia drevnei Rusi," 98–99; Radke, "Money, Port and Ships," 147.

135. Irina E. Zaitseva, "Metal Ornaments in the Rural Sites of Northern Russia: Long Distance Trade or Local Metalwork?," in *Centre, Region, Periphery: Medieval Europe—Basel 2002,* vol. 3, ed. Guido Helmig et al. (Hertingen: Folio Verlag Dr. G. Wesselkamp, 2002), 117.

136. And for Robert Bartlett represent the German civilizing process that extended into Rus' through Lübeck. Bartlett, *The Making of Europe: Conquest, Colonization and Cultural Change, 950–1350* (Princeton, N.J.: Princeton University Press, 1993), 293.

137. Bautier, *Economic Development*, 107; Martin, *Treasure*, 51.

138. Novoseltsev and Pashuto, "Vneshniaia torgovlia drevnei Rusi," 98–99; Iu. A. Limonov, "Etnicheskii i geograficheskii 'spravochnik' cheloveka drevnei rusi (IX–XIII vv)," in *Vostochnaia evropa v drevnosti i srednevekov'e,* ed. V. T. Pashuto (Moscow: RAN, 1994), 99.

139. Novoseltsev and Pashuto mention an eleventh-century trading mission recorded in the chronicles, but I have not been able to find their evidence in the Monumenta Germaniae Historica. Novoseltsev and Pashuto, "Vneshniaia torgovlia drevnei Rusi," 98.

140. Makarov, "Traders in the Forest"; Sergey Zakharov, "Beloozero Town: An Urban Centre on the Periphery," in *Centre, Region, Periphery: Medieval Europe—Basel 2002*, vol. 3, ed. Guido Helmig et al. (Hertingen: Folio Verlag Dr. G. Wesselkamp, 2002), 120; Zaitseva, "Metal Ornaments," 114–119.

141. Dimitri Obolensky, *The Byzantine Commonwealth, Eastern Europe, 500–1453* (London: Weidenfeld and Nicolson, 1971), 41.

142. Whittow, *The Making of Byzantium*, 249.

143. *Ottonian Germany: The 'Chronicon' of Thietmar of Merseburg,* trans. David A. Warner (Manchester: Manchester University Press, 2001), bk. 8, ch. 32.

144. In fact, the Laurentian Chronicle records a large number of churches, perhaps also inflated, but similarly so, when referencing the 1124 fire in Kiev. *Lavrent'evskaia letopis',* vol. 1 of *Polnoe sobranie russkikh letopisei* (Moscow: Iazyki russkoi kul'tury, 2000) (hereafter cited as *PSRL 1*), 293. As for the size of the city, the most recent estimate that I am aware of is by V. I. Mezentsev, who suggests an approximate population of 40,000 people in the eleventh to the twelfth century. Mezentsev, "Territorial and Demographic Development," 160.

145. Novoseltsev and Pashuto, "Vneshniaia torgovlia drevnei Rusi," 103.

146. Noonan, "Flourishing," 103.

147. Kiev was also a center of transshipment of goods throughout Rus'. Martin, *Treasure*, 44.

148. The classic work on the podol is K. N. Gupalo, *Podol v drevnem Kieve* (Kiev: Naukova Dumka, 1982). Some of the conclusions, such as regarding the extent of its spread and the height of development, are constantly under revision as new finds are made. See, for example, Mezentsev, "Territorial and Demographic Development," 150, 154.

149. Gupalo discusses these at length; for example, there was a workshop for ornamental metal plates for bridles found in the podol, whose work was widespread. *Podol v drevnem Kieve,* 74.

150. Callmer, "Archeology of Kiev," 45.

151. *PSRL 2,* 326, 427–428, for selected examples.

152. Daniel H. Kaiser, "The Economy of Kievan Rus': Evidence from the *Pravda Rus'kaia,*" in *Ukrainian Economic History: Interpretive Essays,* ed. I. S. Koropeckyj (Cambridge, Mass.: Harvard University Press, 2001), 47–48, discussing and quoting *Pravda russkaia,* ed. B. D. Grekov (Moscow: Izdatel'stvo akademii nauk SSSR, 1947), arts. 48, 55.

153. *Paterik of the Kievan Caves Monastery,* 11.

154. V. B. Perkhavko, "Zarozhdenie kupchestva na Rusi," in *Vostochnaia evropa v drevnosti i srednevekov'e: X Cheteniia k 80–letiiu chlena-korrespondenta AN SSSR Vladimira Terent'evicha Pashuto,* ed. E. A. Mel'nikova (Moscow: RAN, 1998), 89–90. Or his recent book, *Torgovyi mir srednevekovoi Rusi* (Moscow: Academia, 2006).

5. The Micro-Christendom of Rus'

1. The classic example would be R. W. Southern, *The Making of the Middle Ages* (New Haven, Conn.: Yale University Press, 1953).

2. Also relevant here is the work of Ricardo Picchio, who developed the ideas of Slavia Orthodoxa and Slavia Romana in his work. For example, see Rikardo Pikio, *Provoslavnoto slavianstvo i starob'lgarkata kultura traditsiia* (Sofia: Sv. Kliment Okhridski, 1993).

3. Peter Robert Lamont Brown, *The Rise of Western Christendom: Triumph and Diversity, AD 200–1000,* 2nd ed. (Malden, Mass.: Blackwell, 2003).

4. Ibid., 359. This might actually be taken much further, enumerating smaller regions as their own pieces of micro-Christendoms (even unique micro-Christendoms), with their own particular representations of divinity based on their own self-perception.

5. *Adam of Bremen: History of the Archbishops of Hamburg-Bremen,* trans. Francis J. Tschan (New York: Columbia University Press, 1959). For analysis of his aims, see Hans-Werner Goetz, "Constructing the Past: Religious Dimensions and Historical Consciousness in Adam of Bremen's *Gesta Hamburgensis ecclesiae pontificum,*" in *The Making of Christian Myths in the Periphery of Latin Christendom (c. 1000–1300),* ed. Lars Boje Mortensen (Copenhagen: Museum Tusculanum Press, University of Copenhagen, 2006), 32–33.

6. John Meyendorff, *Byzantium and the Rise of Russia: A Study of Byzantino-Russian Relations in the Fourteenth Century* (Cambridge: Cambridge University Press, 1981), 5–6.

7. This chapter is not intended to serve as a definitive history of the Christianization of Rus' or of Christianity in Rus'. Those topics have had many books and articles written on them over the last few hundred years, and this chapter alone could not do justice to such a rich topic. For such history, see Ernest Honigmann, "Studies in Slavic Church History," *Byzantion* 17 (1944–1945); Ia. N. Shchapov, *Gosudarstvo i tserkov': Drevnei Rusi X–XIII vv.* (Moscow: Nauka, 1989); A. V. Poppe, "Russkie mitropolii konstantinopol'skoi patriarkhii v XI stoletii," *Vizantiiskii vremennik* 28 (1968); Poppe, "The Political Background to the Baptism of Rus': Byzantine-Russian Relations between 986–989," in *The Rise of Christian Russia* (London: Variorum, 1982); A. P. Vlasto, *The Entry of the Slavs into Christendom* (Cambridge: Cambridge University Press, 1970); Francis Dvornik, *Byzantine Missions among the Slavs* (New Brunswick, N.J.: Rutgers University Press, 1970).

8. "Nicolai I. Papae Epistolae," in *Monumenta Germanica historiae epistolarum*, ed. Ernestus Perels (Berolini: Apud Weidmannos, 1925).

9. The East Frankish Empire was, by this time, already making the transition to becoming the German Empire, which will be discussed throughout the rest of the chapter.

10. The issue of the relevance of Sázava Monastery to Rus' is under debate. I have chosen to accept its role in fostering Rusian Christianity, but others do not. For a refutation of the view of Sázava's importance, see A. de Vincenz, "West Slavic Elements in the Literary Language of Kievan Rus'," *Harvard Ukrainian Studies* 12–13 (1988–1989). For a brief review of some of the literature surrounding Sázava and the importance of the Slavonic Liturgy, see Walter K. Hanak, "Saint Procopius, the Sázava Monastery, and the Byzantine-Slavonic Legacy: Some Reconsiderations," in *Byzantina et Slavica Cracoviensie III: Byzantium and East Central Europe*, ed. Günter Prinzing and Maciej Salamon, with the assistance of Paul Stephenson (Cracow: 2001), 71–80.

11. Brown, *Rise of Western Christendom*, 364.

12. There are two reasons I have chosen not to simply use the word *Church* to designate these areas. One is my preference for Peter Brown's theory and his eloquent terminology; the second is that I believe *Church* would send the message that they were schismatic.

13. Julia M. H. Smith, *Europe after Rome: A New Cultural History, 500–1000* (Oxford: Oxford University Press, 2005), 224. M. A. Claussen discusses

the progression of historiography on this topic briefly as well. Claussen, *The Reform of the Frankish Church: Chrodegang of Metz and the Regula canonicorum in the Eighth Century* (Cambridge: Cambridge University Press, 2004), 263–276.

14. Jane Tibbetts Schulenburg, *Forgetful of Their Sex: Female Sanctity and Society, ca. 500–1100* (Chicago: University of Chicago Press, 1998), 178.

15. For example, see Premysław Urbańczyk, "The Politics of Conversion in North Central Europe," in *The Cross Goes North: Processes of Conversion in Northern Europe, AD 300–1300,* ed. Martin Carver (York: York Medieval Press, 2003), 20.

16. Which was actually a very similar process to the centers of power created via dynastic marriages, as seen in Chapters 2 and 3.

17. Brown, *Rise of Western Christendom,* 368.

18. Claussen discusses the attempt to model many aspects of Rome in Metz in the eighth century, for instance. Claussen, *Reform of the Frankish Church,* 279.

19. Brown, *Rise of Western Christendom,* 362–363.

20. Henry Mayr-Harting, *The Coming of Christianity to Anglo-Saxon England* (University Park: Pennsylvania State University Press, 1972), 107.

21. Brown, *Rise of Western Christendom,* 363. Mayr-Harting also notes the Roman flavor of the church at Hexham, in regard to architecture as well as decoration. Mayr-Harting, *The Coming of Christianity,* 156–158.

22. Claussen continues with his specific example: "By importing the relics of its saints, Chrodegang linked his city to Rome, and by reorganizing, at least partially, the topography of sacred history, he reconfigured the map of Christendom's holy places." Claussen, *Reform of the Frankish Church,* 281.

23. This is Brown's term used in reference to Obolensky's usage in regards to Byzantium. Brown, *Rise of Western Christendom,* 366.

24. Multiple such "local renditions of Rome" were built throughout Europe at this time. Smith, *Europe after Rome,* 288.

25. Brown, *Rise of Western Christendom,* 366.

26. Ibid., 378. Claussen complexifies this statement and adds to the discussion of what the Carolingians were doing and why. Claussen, *Reform of the Frankish Church,* 263–276.

27. Brown, *Rise of Western Christendom,* 378. I am not sure that I agree with Brown's argument at this point, but it does serve to aptly illustrate the common medievalist point of view that with the creation of the Carolingian Empire there was a Roman Empire in the West again and that the Eastern Roman Empire ceased to be Roman.

28. Ibid., 368.

29. Ibid., 477. The same is true for Oswald of Northumbria, who was called "emperor of all Britain" after his victory over the British king, Cadwallon. Adomnán of Iona, *Life of St. Columba,* trans. Richard Sharpe (New York: Penguin, 1995), 111. This is discussed in Chapter 1, but for a full list of English rulers who used the imperial title, see Walter de Gray Birch, "Index of the Styles and Titles of English Sovereigns," *Report of the First Annual Meeting of the Index Society* (London, 1879).

30. Brown, *Rise of Western Christendom,* 378.

31. Ibid.

32. An ecclesiastical calendar that details saints' days, and often their stories, as they should be celebrated in a monastic setting.

33. For an extreme example of this, see the practices of Archbishop Adalbert as discussed in *Adam of Bremen,* bk. 3, xxvii.

34. Ibid., bk. 2, xxix, among other places. Archbishop Adalbert, the main subject of Adam's *gesta,* is noted to have "prided himself on having only two masters, that is, the pope and the king, to whose dominion all the powers of the world and of the Church of right were subject." Ibid., bk. 3, lxxviii.

35. Ibid.

36. It should also be noted that in most kingdoms there were Christians before the kingdom as a whole converted. In Rus', there was a Church of St. Elias in Kiev prior to Vladimir's conversion of the whole of Rus'. However, this Christian population was never dense enough to convert a kingdom en masse without the impetus of a royal conversion. For the Church of St. Elias, see *The Povest' vremennykh let: An Interlinear Collation and Paradosis,* ed. Donald Ostrowski, with David Birnbaum and Horace G. Lunt (Cambridge, Mass.: Harvard University Press, 2004), 52:26–27.

37. *Adam of Bremen,* bk. 2, xlix.

38. John Lindow, "St. Olaf and the Skalds," in *Sanctity in the North: Saints, Lives, and Cults in Medieval Scandinavia,* ed. Thomas A. DuBois (Toronto: University of Toronto Press, 2008), 108.

39. *Adam of Bremen,* bk. 3, lxxii. Goetz notes that this very easily could have simply been a facile explanation for the abandonment of Adalbert's plan to begin proselytizing himself, though it fits nicely with other evidence regarding conversion. Goetz, "Constructing the Past," 36.

40. For an excellent work that delves much more deeply into conversion and its social consequences in the early medieval world, including lessons that are very applicable here, see James C. Russell, *The Germanization of Early*

Medieval Christianity: A Sociohistorical Approach to Religious Transformation (Oxford: Oxford University Press, 1994).

41. An example of such a mention is Bishop Osmund, who is discussed more below. Adamus Bremensis, *Adami gesta Hammaburgensis ecclesiae pontificum,* ed. J. M. Lappenberg, Scriptores rerum germanicarum in usum scholarum ex Monumentis Germaniae historicis recusi (Hannover: Impensis Biblipolii Hahniani, 1876), xv.14. Carl Hallencreutz has developed a fascinating view of Adam's account by matching it with runic inscriptions in Sweden. Carl F. Hallencreutz, "What Do the Runic Stones and Adam Tell Us about Byzantine Influences?," In *Rom und Byzanz im Norden: Mission und Glaubenswechsel im Ostseeraum während des 8.–14. Jahrhunderts,* vol. 1, ed. Michael Müller-Wille (Stuttgart: Franz Steinar Verlag, 1997), 331–340. Which builds on a foundation established by, among others, Anders Sjöberg, "Pop Upir' Lichoj and the Swedish rune-carver Ofeigr Upir," *Scando-Slavica* 28, no. 1 (1982): 109–124.

For contrasting views on these mentions, see Peter Sawyer, *Kings and Vikings: Scandinavia and Europe, AD 700–1100* (London: Methuen, 1982), 141; and Per Beskow, "Byzantine Influence in the Conversion of the Baltic Region?," in *The Cross Goes North: Processes of Conversion in Northern Europe, AD 300–1300,* ed. Martin Carver (York: York Medieval Press, 2003) 559–563.

42. Hubert Houben, *Roger II of Sicily: A Ruler between East and West,* trans. Graham A. Loud and Diane Milburn (Cambridge: Cambridge University Press, 2002), 102.

43. *Adam of Bremen,* bk. 2, lv.

44. Birgit Sawyer and Peter Sawyer, *Medieval Scandinavia: From Conversion to Reformation, circa 800–1500* (Minneapolis: University of Minnesota Press, 1993), 107.

45. A convenient, and well-known, example is Adalbert of Prague's beheading by the Prussians in the late tenth century. *Ottonian Germany: The "Chronicon" of Thietmar of Merseburg,* trans. David A. Warner (Manchester: Manchester University Press, 2001), bk. 4, ch. 28.

46. Harald's adventures are numerous and can be found in multiple primary and secondary sources. Perhaps most complete is the chapter on him in Snorri Sturluson, *Heimskringla: History of the Kings of Norway,* trans. Lee M. Hollander (Austin.: University of Texas Press, 1964).

47. Those cultural inputs will appear in a variety of venues in Harald's Norway. See Chapter 1.

48. Lindow, "St. Olaf and the Skalds," 106. As an additional side note, for our purposes it is interesting that Grimkell also followed Olaf to Rus' and

back, and may be in part responsible for the creation of an eleventh-century church of St. Olaf in Novgorod. Sjöberg, "Pop Upir' Lichoj," 115–116.

49. *Adam of Bremen,* bk. 3, xvii, and schol 68 (69).

50. Ibid., bk. 3, xvii.

51. Sawyer and Sawyer, *Medieval Scandinavia,* 136.

52. *Adam of Bremen,* schol. 69 (70). Alexander II was also a reforming pope, in the tradition of his predecessor Nicholas II and successor Gregory VII, and was a strong advocate for the rights of the papacy and proper hierarchy. But the contradiction between one pope consecrating a bishop for Norway and another protesting such consecration reflects the constantly changing ecclesiastical circumstances in the eleventh century. For more on this discussion, see Lesley Abrams, "The Anglo-Saxons and the Christianization of Scandinavia," *Anglo-Saxon England* 24 (1995): 213–249.

53. Cecaumenus, *Strategikon,* ed. B. Wassiliewsky and V. Jernstedt (Saint Petersburg: Imperatorksaia Akademiia Nauk, 1896), 97; interpretation from Krijnie N. Ciggaar, *Western Travellers to Constantinople: The West and Byzantium, 962–1204—Cultural and Political Relations* (Leiden: Brill, 1996), 105.

54. Sawyer, *Kings and Vikings,* 141.

55. Sawyer and Sawyer, *Medieval Scandinavia,* 104. The traditional date of conversion is 1008, but Olof had coinage with Christian symbols from the mid-990s. Sweden was actually divided into two separate kingdoms of the Svear and the Götar, which were not united until the late twelfth century. Olof was king of the Svear. Ibid., 60.

56. Ciggaar, *Western Travellers to Constantinople,* 119.

57. *Adam of Bremen,* bk. 3, xv. He was selected and sent to Bremen by the bishop of Norway, Sigefrid.

58. Adamus Bremensis, *Adami gesta Hammaburgensis ecclesiae pontificum,* ed. J. M. Lappenberg, Scriptores rerum germanicarum in usum scholarum ex Monumentis Germaniae historicis recusi (Hannover: Impensis Biblipolii Hahniani, 1876), bk. 3, xv.14.

59. *Adam of Bremen,* bk. 3, xv, and n52. Goetz agrees with this location for the confirmation of Osmund. Goetz, "Constructing the Past," 37.

60. Sawyer, *Kings and Vikings,* 141. Sawyer presents this as part of a larger Byzantine or Rusian ecclesiastical influence on eastern Sweden. In contrast to this, Per Beskow presents an argument against Osmund's Orthodox orientation and, more probably, against Byzantine influence on Scandinavia. Beskow, "Byzantine Influence," 559–563. For the anti-Kievan argument, see also Władysław Duczko, "The Fateful Hundred Years: Swe-

den in the Eleventh Century," in *The Neighbours of Poland in the 11th Century,* ed. P. Urbańczyk (Warsaw: Wydawnistwo DiG, 2002), 22–24. Duczko makes the persuasive argument that for Adam, Rus' was *Ruzzia,* while Poland was *Polania,* while the Poliani of the *PVL* were unknown to Adam, and may have been an invention of the chronicler.

61. That retinue included at least one jarl, her kinsman Ragnvald Úlfsson who ruled Aldeigjuborg [Ladoga] in Rus'. Sturluson, *Heimskringla,* 342–343.

62. Sjöberg, "Pop Upir' Lichoj."

63. *Adami gesta Hammaburgensis,* bk. 3, xv.

64. *Gamular* means "the old" or "the bad" and the name was probably given to him by the royals who succeeded him in reference to this whole episode.

65. *Adam of Bremen,* bk. 3, xv.

66. For more on Osmund and this episode, see Sjöberg, "Pop Upir' Lichoj," 120.

67. *Adam of Bremen,* bk. 3, xv.

68. Ibid.

69. Sjöberg, "Pop Upir' Lichoj," 119–123.

70. Sawyer, *Kings and Vikings,* 141. A thought that has been expressed before, in particular by Anders Sjöberg: "King Emund, like his brother-in-law Great Prince Jaroslav and King Harald of Norway (who was married to Jaroslav's daughter), all attempted to organize independent national churches." Sjöberg, "Pop Upir' Lichoj," 122.

71. *Adam of Bremen,* bk. 3, xvi.

72. Ibid., xv. Though even Stenkil forbade Bishop Adalward (Archbishop Adalbert's appointee) to trespass on the grounds of the pagan temple at Uppsala. Ibid., bk. 4, xxx.

73. *Adam of Bremen,* bk. 3, liii, and schol. 84. Pope Gregory VII in a letter to King Inge notes that priests of the "Gallican church" have been active in Sweden, and asks to send priests from Rome to clarify their teachings. *The Register of Pope Gregory VII, 1073–1085,* ed. and trans. H. E. J. Cowdrey (Oxford: Oxford University Press, 2002), 8.11.

74. *Register of Pope Gregory,* 9.14.

75. *Adam of Bremen,* bk. 3, liii, and schol. 84. See also Sjöberg, "Pop Upir' Lichoj," 120–121.

76. *Adam of Bremen,* bk. 3, xxxiii.

77. Sjöberg, "Pop Upir' Lichoj," 119.

78. *Adam of Bremen,* bk. 3, xxvii.

79. Ibid., xxiv, lxxiii. For further discussion on this topic, see Goetz, "Constructing the Past," 44–45.

80. Ciggaar, *Western Travellers to Constantinople,* 124–125.

81. See F. Miklosich, ed., *Codice Suprasliensi,* Monumenta Linguae Palaeo-slovenicae (Vindobonae: Carl Gerold's Sohn, 1851).

82. *Laws of Early Iceland: Gragas, The Codex Regius of Gragas with Material from Other Manuscripts,* trans. Andrew Dennis, Peter Foote, and Richard Perkins (Winnipeg: University of Manitoba Press, 2006), 38; though, interestingly, priests "not versed in the Latin language" could not consecrate churches or confirm children. "Armenian" could be from Armenia, or alternately from a Slavic region of the Baltic coast (n53). "Russian" is actually *"girzkr"* and most likely denotes priests from Rus' (gardariki), but there is a great deal of discussion available on the term. F. B. Uspenskii, *Skandinavy, variagi, Rus': Istoriko-filologicheskie ocherki* (Moscow: Iazyki slavianskoi kul'tury, 2002), 299–337.

83. André Grabar, "Pénétration Byzantine en islande et en Scandinavie," *Cahiers Archéologiques* 13 (1962); and Anthony Cutler, "Garda, Kallunge, and the Byzantine Tradition on Gotland," *Art Bulletin* 51, no. 3 (1969).

84. All of these issues are discussed in more depth in Chapter 1. Their presence here simply indicates the interpenetration of types of influence in medieval Europe.

85. Hungary is another example of a medieval kingdom that maintained such ties, but the conversion of the Hungarians is less well documented and does not have the other points to recommend it for use in this context.

86. Francis J. Thomsen, "The Bulgarian Contribution of the Reception of Byzantine Culture in Kievan Rus': The Myths and the Enigma," in *The Reception of Byzantine Culture in Mediaeval Russia* (Brookfield, Vt.: Variorum, 1999).

87. Richard E. Sullivan, "Khan Boris and the Conversion of Bulgaria: A Case Study of the Impact of Christianity on a Barbarian Society," *Studies in Medieval and Renaissance History* 3 (1966): 67.

88. Ibid., 69.

89. George Ostrogorsky, *History of the Byzantine State,* trans. Joan Hussey, rev. ed. (New Brunswick, N.J.: Rutgers University Press, 1969), 229; and Dvornik, *Byzantine Missions,* 73, 74, 104. Ostrogorsky's *History of the Byzantine State,* though dated in many ways, is still one of the best secondary sources on the events surrounding the Bulgarian conversion. Newer works such as *The Oxford History of Byzantium* mention the conversion in passing, but do not investigate it in any depth. Because of this, I have chosen to use Ostrogorsky, though carefully, for this section.

90. Ostrogorsky, *History of the Byzantine State,* 230, though Ostrogorsky confuses the order of alliances between Bulgaria and the Franks and Moravia and Byzantium.

91. Ibid.

92. Sullivan, "Khan Boris," 71–73; and Ostrogorsky, *History of the Byzantine State,* 230, who says that Boris had fifty-two of the rebellious boyars beheaded.

93. Paul Magdalino notes that although the conversion of Bulgaria to Byzantine Christianity was a victory for Byzantine diplomacy, it may not have been of importance to Byzantium had it not clearly been an important goal for the Frankish Church and the papacy. Magdalino, "The Medieval Empire (780–1204)," in *The Oxford History of Byzantium,* ed. Cyril Mango (Oxford: Oxford University Press, 2002), 172–173.

94. Sullivan, "Khan Boris," 70–71; and Robert Browning, *Byzantium and Bulgaria: A Comparative Study across the Early Medieval Frontier* (Berkeley: University of California, 1975), 147.

95. These are the two extremes of conversion practiced in medieval Christianity. The cooptation and steady absorption has been illustrated in a variety of places, such as Russell, *Germanization of Early Medieval Christianity.* The alternative—a full and immediate conversion, or nothing, resulting in apostasy and rebellion—has many examples, from Charlemagne's "conversion(s)" of the Saxons to the crusades. Henry of Livonia's descriptions of multiple conversions and rebellions by the same groups and the Baltic crusaders' (and Henry's) fury are the most eloquent and telling of what was expected. Henricus Lettus, *The Chronicle of Henry of Livonia,* trans. James Brundage (New York: Columbia University Press, 1961).

96. Ostrogorsky, *History of the Byzantine State,* 231.

97. Browning, *Byzantium and Bulgaria,* 148.

98. Ibid.

99. Ibid.

100. Ibid., 150.

101. Ibid., 150–151.

102. For instance, in his well-known book on the first Bulgarian empire, Steven Runciman summarized this whole intricate struggle with brevity: Boris "outwitted the Pope and used the Patriarch to secure for his country the Church that he desired." Runciman, *A History of the First Bulgarian Empire* (London: G. Bell and Sons, 1930), 259.

103. Browning, *Byzantium and Bulgaria,* 150.

104. Ibid., 151.

105. For an annotated translation of the letter, see Despina Stratoudaki White and Joseph R. Berrigan Jr., *The Patriarch and the Prince: The Letter of Patriarch Photios of Constantinople to Khan Boris of Bulgaria* (Brookline, Mass.: Holy Cross Orthodox Press, 1982).

106. For instance, Pope Nicholas I allowed as how it would take some time to phase out polygamy among the Bulgarian elite. Sullivan discusses this letter in some detail. Sullivan, "Khan Boris"; and for the letter itself, see "Nicolai I. Papae Epistolae."

107. Dvornik discusses this extensively. For the political ramifications, see Dvornik, *Byzantine Missions,* 154.

108. Byzantine support for this liturgy is clear, as they dispatched Cyril and Methodius. Papal support was confirmed by Pope Hadrian II (dating from 868–869) and lasted at least until the eleventh century. Ibid., 102.

109. For three interesting versions of events, see Ostrogorsky, *History of the Byzantine State,* 234–235; Browning, *Byzantium and Bulgaria,* 151–152; and Sullivan, "Khan Boris," 93.

110. For more information on the rank of the archbishop and his bishops, see Ostrogorsky, *History of the Byzantine State,* 235n1.

111. Sullivan, "Khan Boris," 95.

112. The pope protested Boris's actions, or lack thereof, in 881 and 882, to no avail. Ibid.

113. Browning, *Byzantium and Bulgaria,* 153.

114. Sullivan, "Khan Boris," 98–99.

115. Bulgaria gained ecclesiastical independence in 927 with the granting of a patriarch in conjunction with the marriage of a porphyrogenite princess to the Bulgarian tsar'. Jonathan Shepard, "A Marriage Too Far? Maria Lekapena and Peter of Bulgaria," in *The Empress Theophano: Byzantium and the West at the Turn of the Millennium,* ed. Adalbert Davids (Cambridge: Cambridge University Press, 1995).

116. For examples, see K. Ericsson, "The Earliest Conversion of the Rus' to Christianity," *Slavonic and East European Review* 44, no. 102 (1966); and Immanuel Bekker, ed., *Theophanes continuatus: Chronographia* (Bonn: Weber, 1838), IV.33.

117. To quote Michael Angold, "It had little impact at the time, but it was important for the future, because it underlined the unbridgeable gulf that was developing between Byzantium and the west." Angold, "Belle Époque or Crisis (1025–1118)," in *The Cambridge History of the Byzantine Empire, c. 500–1492,* ed. Jonathan Shepard (Cambridge: Cambridge University Press, 2009), 601.

118. The exact origins of a division between Eastern and Western Europe can be discussed at some length. Medieval dates have been given due to religious or crusading divisions, as well as Mongol invasions. Twentieth-century divisions due to the Cold War are also popularly discussed. However, the perception of Eastern Europe as different, and thus "other," seems to trace back in modern history to the Enlightenment, as discussed in Larry Wolff, *Inventing Eastern Europe: The Map of Civilization on the Mind of the Enlightenment* (Stanford: Stanford University Press, 1996).

119. At the time, Ol'ga was regent for her minor son Sviatoslav, and thus the ruler of Rus'.

120. *The Povest' vremennykh let*, 60:25–63:4.

121. Ibid., 61:15–16.

122. The Empress Helen, wife of Constantine VII.

123. Francis Butler discusses the Ol'ga–Helen comparisons, and their historicity. Francis Butler, *Enlightener of Rus': The Image of Vladimir Sviatoslavich across the Centuries* (Bloomington, Ind.: Slavica, 2002), 21, 29, 74.

124. *The Povest' vremennykh let*, 61:18–22.

125. A. A. Shakhmatov, *Razyskaniia o russkikh letopisiakh* (repr., Moscow: Akademicheskii Proekt, 2001), 11.

126. Ibid., 19–21.

127. I. I. Reiske, ed., *De cerimoniis aulae Byzantinae,* vol. 9 of *Corpus Scriptorum Historiae Byzantinae* (Bonn: Impensis Ed. Weberi, 1829), 594–598. The sections relevant to Ol'ga's visit have been translated by Jeffrey Featherstone, "Ol'ga's Visit to Constantinople," *Harvard Ukrainian Studies* 14, nos. 3–4 (1990).

128. *The Povest' vremennykh let*, 62:29. "Slaves, wax, and furs."

129. George Ostrogorsky also emphasizes the trading over the religious aspects of the trip. G. Ostrogorskii, "Vizantiia: Kievskaia kniaginia Ol'ga," in *To Honor Roman Jakobson: Essays on the Occasion of his Seventieth Birthday* (1967), 2:1464.

130. *The Povest' vremennykh let*, 63:2–4.

131. *De cerimoniis.*

132. John Scylitzes, *Ioannis Scylitzae synopsis historiarum,* ed. Ioannes Thurn, Corpus fontium historiae Byzantinae (Berolini: De Gruyter, 1973), 240. Continuator Reginionis in Albert Bauer and Reinhold Rau, eds., *Fontes ad historiam aevi Saxonici illustrandam: Widukindi res gestae Saxonicae; Adalberti continuato Reginonis; Liudprandi opera* (Darmstadt: Wissenschaftliche Buchgesellschaft, 1971), 214, 216. I have chosen not to discuss in this chapter whether or not Ol'ga was actually baptized in Constantinople. There is a great deal of scholarship on the matter, best summarized

in A. V. Nazarenko, *Drevniaia Rus' na mezhdunarodnykh putiakh: Mezh-distsiplinarnye ocherki kulturnykh, torgovykh, politicheskikh sviazei IX–XII vekov* (Moscow: Iazyki russkoi kul'tury, 2001), ch. 5.

133. *De cerimoniis, 597.*

134. Ibid.

135. Featherstone himself finds no contradiction with the presence of a priest in Ol'ga's entourage upon her arrival. Featherstone, "Ol'ga's Visit to Constantinople," 311.

136. This could be inferred from the comparatively low level of remuneration he receives from the emperor. On the first occasion he receives slightly more than the servants of Ol'ga's merchants and half that of the interpreter. *De cerimoniis, 598.*

137. *The Povest' vremennykh let,* 52:26–27. The history of the first Christian church in Kiev is investigated in S. A. Ivanov, "Kogda v Kieve poiavilsia pervyi khristianskii khram?," *Slaviane i ikh sosedi* 11 (2004): 9–18. For the possible affiliation of the church, see Samuel Hazzard Cross and Olgerd P. Sherbowitz-Wetzor, eds., transls., *The Russian Primary Chronicle* (Cambridge, Mass.: Mediaeval Academy of America, 1953), 77n53.

138. Sjöberg, "Pop Upir' Lichoj," 116.

139. Bauer and Rau, *Fontes ad historiam,* 214.

140. *Ottonian Germany,* 108, bk. 2, ch. 22; and Bauer and Rau, *Fontes ad historiam,* 214, 216. Otto's first choice, Adaldag, died shortly after his consecration, and Adalbert was quickly chosen to replace him.

141. Bauer and Rau, *Fontes ad historiam,* 218. Though in 968 Adalbert was appointed bishop of Magdeburg, which was the center of German missionary activity among the Slavs, so perhaps this was a continuation of his earlier mandate or he was able to use the skills he had learned in Rus'. *Ottonian Germany,* bk. 2, ch. 22.

142. *The Povest' vremennykh let,* 63:23–24.

143. Numerous parallels could be made here to the brief rule of Roman Emperor Julian the Apostate, who attempted to return the Roman Empire to paganism through a highly centralized and codified form of paganism in the mid-fourth century. Further, Przemysław Urbańczyk has argued that "in pre-Christian societies progressive hierarchisation of the social structure was paralleled by the hierarchisation of the pagan pantheons. Attempts at establishing a paramount power centre needed ideological support, which often led to religious henotheism like that imposed c. 986 by Vladimir in Kiev." Urbańczyk, "The Politics of Conversion," 15–27.

144. The eight-god pantheon was made up of Perun, Khors, Dazhbog, Stribog, Simargl, Mokosh, Volos/Veles, and Svarog. Multiple of these gods have

Indo-European backgrounds and would naturally appeal to a wide array of peoples. For more information on these gods, see Marija Gimbutas, "Ancient Slavic Religion: A Synopsis," in *To Honor Roman Jakobson: Essays on the Occasion of His Seventieth Birthday,* vol. 1 (1967).

145. The term *state* is inappropriate in a medieval context, but the reader must bear with me as there is no other term appropriate for a kingdom-encompassing religion in the premodern era.

146. *The Povest' vremennykh let,* 84:17–87:22.

147. Jonathan Shepard advances the idea, based on Marzawi's text, that Khorezm was in fact the Muslim proponent. Shepard, "Some Remarks on the Sources for the Conversion of Rus'," in *Le origini e lo sviluppo della Cristianità Slavo-Bizantina,* ed. S. W. Swierkosz-Lenart (Rome: Nella Sede Dell'istituto Palazzo Borromini, 1992), 77–78.

148. The Khazar reference may in fact be a later interpolation. Shakhmatov, *Razyskaniia o russkikh letopisiakh,* 51–52, 147–148. Vladimir's father, Sviatoslav, had mortally wounded the Khazar Empire with a major attack on its capital in 965. *The Povest' vremennykh let,* 65:6–11.

149. *The Povest' vremennykh let,* 107:9–14.

150. Ibid., 107:26–30.

151. Richard Hellie, additionally, has expressed the idea that there existed a Rusian belief that beauty = good; he bases his argument on his understanding of left- and right-brain development. Hellie, "Late Medieval and Early Modern Russian Civilization and Modern Neuroscience," in *Cultural Identity in a Multicultural State: Muscovy, 1359–1584,* ed. A. M. Kleimola and G. D. Lenhoff (Moscow: ITS-Garant, 1997).

152. *The Povest' vremennykh let,* 109:1.

153. Jonathan Shepard lists the topoi, even though he does not ultimately agree that the "Examination of the Four Faiths" is just a topos. Shepard, "Some Remarks," 64–65, 80. For an alternative view of the conversion of the Khazars and religious oral arguments, see Francis Butler, "The Representation of Oral Culture in the *Vita Constantini,*" *Slavic and East European Journal* 39, no. 3 (1995).

154. Shepard, "Some Remarks," 64–65.

155. Donald Ostrowski, "The Account of Volodimer's Conversion in the *Povest' vremennykh let:* A Chiasmus of Stories," *Harvard Ukrainian Studies* 28, nos. 1–4 (2006 [2009]): 568–569.

156. Capture of the city of Cherson recorded in *The Povest' vremennykh let,* 109:1–24.

157. Ibid., 109:24–110:2.

158. Ibid., 110:2–8.

159. Ibid., 110:12–19.
160. Ostrowski, "Account of Volodimer's Conversion," 569, 569n18, 573–574. Blindness as divine punishment for broken vows is a topos used often in medieval hagiography and conversion stories.
161. *The Povest' vremennykh let*, 111:6–16.
162. Ibid., 117:2–9. This final conversion of the people of Kiev stemming from both Vladimir and Anna (as well as Anna's involvement in healing Vladimir's blindness) is taken by Ostrowski to denote Sil'vestr's understanding of Rusian Christianity as stemming from Byzantium. Important to note here, of course, is that this is Sil'vestr's understanding in the early twelfth century, not necessarily the reality of the situation in the late tenth. Ostrowski, "Account of Volodimer's Conversion," 576, 578.
163. Urbańczyk notes that there are "numerous examples of conscious decisions to change religion taken by political leaders who carefully consider their geopolitical situations." Urbańczyk, "The Politics of Conversion," 20.
164. This idea is, of course, reinforced by the conversion passage in the *PVL*, which contains the notations that upon Christianization, Vladimir sent priests to the various cities of Rus' and assigned his sons to rule over those cities. These measures in unison paint a picture of Vladimir creating a centralized control mechanism for Rus'. *The Povest' vremennykh let*, 118:23–25, 121:5–16.
165. I certainly do not mean to suggest that no one in Rus' ever actually believed. Religious feeling in Rus' was certainly strong, at least among monks, for whom we have sources, by a few decades after the conversion. See *The Paterik of the Kievan Caves Monastery*, trans. Muriel Heppell (Cambridge, Mass.: Harvard University Press, 1989); or *Sermons and Rhetoric of Kievan Rus'*, trans. Simon Franklin, Harvard Library of Early Ukrainian Literature (Cambridge, Mass.: Harvard University Press, 1991).
166. For a fascinating history of theories of the Rusian conversion and a unique approach to the idea, see Poppe, "Political Background."
167. Catherine Holmes, *Basil II and the Governance of Empire (976–1025)* (Oxford: Oxford University Press, 2005), 240ff.
168. Michael Psellus, *Fourteen Byzantine Rulers: The Chronographia of Michael Psellus*, trans. E. R. A. Sewter (New York: Penguin Books, 1966), bk. 1, 14–15.
169. Karl Leyser, "'Theophanu divina gratia imperatrix augusta': Western and Eastern Emperorship in the Later Tenth Century," in *The Empress Theoph-*

ano: Byzantium and the West at the Turn of the First Millennium, ed. Adalbert Davids (Cambridge: Cambridge University Press, 1995), 16; and *Ottonian Germany,* bk. 7, ch. 72.

170. Adalbert Davids, "Marriage Negotiations between Byzantium and the West and the Name of Theophano in Byzantium (Eighth to Tenth Centuries)," 109; and Judith Herrin, "Theophano: Considerations on the Education of a Byzantine Princess," 68; both in *The Empress Theophano: Byzantium and the West at the Turn of the First Millennium,* ed. Adalbert Davids (Cambridge: Cambridge University Press, 1995).

171. For more on Vladimir's marriage to Anna and the importance of porphyrogenite brides, see Chapter 2.

172. *The Povest' vremennykh let,* 109:15–19.

173. Ibid., 110:17–19.

174. Ibid., 111:24–25. This is part of the fusion of conversion stories in the *PVL,* as shown also by the examination-of-faiths story.

175. Ibid., 116:9–20.

176. Ibid., 117:2–12.

177. Which may be odd, as many royal brides traveled to their dynastic marriages with a bishop as personal confessor. See the example of Sviatopolk's bride, a Polish princess who arrives with the Bishop Reinbern of Kolobrzeg, discussed below. *Ottonian Germany,* bk. 7, ch. 72

178. Jonathan Shepard in his discussion of the Rusian conversion also states that conversion was due to Vladimir's initiative, and not to the initiative of the Byzantine Church or emperor. Additionally, though he does not provide a sequence of events, Shepard portrays Vladimir as a rational actor searching for a faith, and using a political opportunity in Byzantium to secure a marriage and a religious embassy. Shepard, "Some Remarks," 81, 94–95. Similarly, Ostrowski notes that in many of the stories of the conversion compiled by Sil'vestr, Vladimir was acting as his own "internal converting agent." Ostrowski, "Account of Volodimer's Conversion," 573. Sergey A. Ivanov also notes the lack of a metropolitan or missionary presence in Anna's entourage in reference to the larger history of conversion. Ivanov, "Religious Missions," in *The Cambridge History of the Byzantine Empire, c. 500–1492,* ed. Jonathan Shepard (Cambridge: Cambridge University Press, 2009), 326.

179. *The Povest' vremennykh let,* 117:20–21.

180. Ibid., 121:24–122:3. Jonathan Shepard also notes the importance of Anastasius's installation in this church as a clear testament to Vladimir's victory over the Byzantines at Cherson. Shepard, "Conversions and Regimes Compared: The Rus' and the Poles, ca. 1000," in *East Central and Eastern*

Europe in the Early Middle Ages, ed. Florin Curta (Ann Arbor: University of Michigan Press, 2008), 261.

181. Francis Dvornik, *Les légendes de Constantin et de Méthode vues de Byzance* (Prague: Orbis, 1933), 359.

182. Ibid., 378.

183. *Letopisnyi sbornik, imenuemyi: Patriarshei ili Nikonovskoi letopis'iu,* vol. 9 of *Polnoe sobranie russkikh letopisei* (Moscow: Iazyki russkoi kul'tury, 2000) (hereafter cited as *PSRL 9*), 57. Though written late, the Nikon chronicle contains the majority of extant references to the papal ties of the Rusian rulers. There are two possible reasons for this: the first is that the later chronicler simply created ties with the papacy to fulfill the political purpose of his sponsor. The second possibility is that the later chronicler had access to different sources than the earlier chroniclers. Serge Zenkovsky believes that various ecclesiastical archives were used in the compilation of the Nikon text. As yet, I have found no papal records corroborating the Nikon chronicle's accounts of papal contacts in this period. Though disappointing, this is not surprising, as papal records for the tenth and early eleventh centuries are almost nonexistent and do not become plentiful until the papacy of Gregory VII. However, none of the papal contacts included in the Nikon chronicle are outrageous or implausible; instead they conform to a regular pattern and seem perfectly normal, and thus I have chosen to accept the second possibility mentioned above and will use this information, though judiciously. For more information, see *The Nikonian Chronicle: From the Beginning to the Year 1132,* ed. Serge A. Zenkovsky, trans. Serge A. Zenkovsky and Betty Jean Zenkovsky (Princeton, N.J.: Kingston Press, 1984), xxxvi; and Andrzej Poppe, "Political Background," 200, n11.

184. Claussen, *Reform of the Frankish Church,* 258–261.

185. *Ottonian Germany,* bk. 7, ch. 74.

186. Shepard, "Conversions and Regimes Compared," 159–160.

187. *Ipat'evskaia letopis',* vol. 2 of *Polnoe sobranie russkikh letopisei* (Moscow: Iazyki slavianskoi kul'tury, 2001) (hereafter cited as *PSRL 2*), 341. *Staviat'* is not precisely "consecrate," but "install" as in a bishop. I have chosen a term with religious implications rather than the more prosaic *install,* for a more understandable, and symmetrical, translation.

188. *PSRL 9,* 68.

189. Jonathan Shepard, "Western Approaches (900–10252)," in *The Cambridge History of the Byzantine Empire, c. 500–1492,* ed. Jonathan Shepard (Cambridge: Cambridge University Press, 2009), 539.

190. Ibid., 39.

191. V. Cl. Lud. Frid. Hasse, ed., *Lamberti Hersfeldensis Annales,* in Monumenta Germaniae Historica Scriptores, vol. 5 (Hannover: Impensis Bibliopolii Avlici Hahniani, 1844), s.a. 973. "Id est Romanorum, Grecorum, Beneventorum, Italorum, Ungariorum, Danorum, Sclavorum, Bulgariorum atque Ruscorum." It is also likely that there were papal representatives present, but they are not mentioned explicitly.

192. *The Povest' vremennykh let,* 74:22–78:19.

193. Bruno of Querfurt, "List Brunona do Henryka II, ok. 1008," in *Monumenta Poloniae Historica* (Lwow: Nakladem Wlasynm, 1864), 224.

194. Ibid., 224–225.

195. Ibid., 225. A. P. Vlasto does not rate the conversion highly but does believe that it kept the peace until 1015. Vlasto, *Entry of the Slavs,* 274.

196. Vlasto, *Entry of the Slavs,* 274. We should also remember that Archbishop Adalbert, who came to proselytize the Rusians under Ol'ga, also became archbishop of Magdeburg, a position that had some interest in Rus' and was a figure of interest to Bruno, as he wrote the saint's *vita.*

197. *Ottonian Germany,* bk. 7, ch. 72.

198. Ibid.

199. This is reinforced by an analysis of liturgical material culture, which shows that Rusian, Scandinavian, and "Westeuropean" liturgical objects were very similar. Alexandr Musin, "Two Churches of Two Traditions: Common Traits and Peculiarities in Northern and Russian Christianity before and after 1054 AD through the Archeological Evidence—A View from the East," in *Rom und Byzanz im Norden: Mission und Glaubenswechsel im Osteraum während des 8.—14. Jahrhunderts,* vol. 2, ed. Michael Müller-Wille (Stuttgart: Franz Steiner Verlag, 1997), 288.

200. H. E. J. Cowdrey, *Pope Gregory VII, 1073–1085* (Oxford: Clarendon Press, 1998), 452.

201. P. Athanasius, ed., *Documenta pontificum Romanorum historiam Ucrainae illustrantia (1075–1953),* vol. 1 (1075–1700) (Rome: P. P. Basiliani, 1953), 5–6.

202. Ibid.

203. Ibid. For the theft of the money, see *The Povest' vremennykh let,* 183:2–5.

204. George Pertz, ed., *Lamberti Hersfeldensis Annales* (Hannover: Impensis Bibliopolii Hahniani, 1843), s.a. 1077.

205. Papal scholars do not believe this, as there is no evidence for it; Slavists, perhaps accustomed to working from more scanty records, accept the possibility. For differing opinions, see Cowdrey, *Pope Gregory VII,* 452; and Jukka Korpela, *Prince, Saint and Apostle: Prince Vladimir Svyatoslavic*

of Kiev, His Posthumous Life, and the Religious Legitimization of the Russian Great Power (Wiesbaden: Harassowitz, 2001), 109.

206. Pertz, *Lamberti Hersfeldensis Annales,* s.a. 1077.

207. Cowdrey, *Pope Gregory VII,* 440–444.

208. There are multiple anti-Latin polemics from eleventh-century Rus' written by Greek churchmen to show that the idea of the schism was known. See "Kanonicheskie otvety mitropolita Ioanna II," *Russkaia istoricheskaia biblioteka* 6 (1908): 1–2; and Vladimir's conversion story, which contains an anti-Latin polemic, *The Povest' vremennykh let.*

209. *Paterik of the Kievan Caves Monastery,* 74–75.

210. *The Povest' vremennykh let,* 182:20–21.

211. Ibid., 202:9–20.

212. Ibid.

213. *Paterik of the Kievan Caves Monastery,* 48–51, for example.

214. Ibid., 49–50.

215. Z. J. Kosztolnyik, *Five Eleventh Century Hungarian Kings: Their Policies and Their Relations with Rome* (New York: Columbia University Press, 1981), 90–91.

216. *The Povest' vremennykh let,* 206:23–25. There is also the possibility that Iaropolk took the baptismal name Peter when he was in the West. N. I. Shchaveleva, "Kniaz' Iaropolk Iziaslavich i khristianskaia tserkov' XI v.," in *Vostochnaia Evropa v drevnosti i srednevekov'e: X cheteniia k 80-letiiu chlena-korrespondenta AN SSSR Vladimira Terent'evicha Pashuto,* ed. E. A. Mel'nikova (Moscow: RAN, 1998), 134.

217. Wibert had first been elected at Brixen in 1080, but this was the first time since then that Henry IV had possessed Rome and thus when he could have Wibert officially confirmed. I. S. Robinson, *Henry IV of Germany, 1056–1106* (Cambridge: Cambridge University Press, 1999), 228.

218. Cowdrey, *Pope Gregory VII,* 228.

219. I. S. Robinson, *The Papacy, 1073–1198: Continuity and Innovation* (Cambridge: Cambridge University Press, 1990), 413.

220. I am here accepting the identification of the writer as Ioann and the identification of the recipient as Clement III. For proofs of these, see N. V. Ponyrko and D. S. Likhachev, eds., *Epistoliarnoe nasledie drevnei rusi XI–XIII: Issledovaniia, teksty, perevody* (Saint Petersburg: Nauka, 1992), 24.

221. Or to be more exact, the main Rusian metropolitan. For more information, see the section titled "The Role of the Metropolitan."

222. Bernard Leib, *Rome, Kiev et Byzance à la fin du XIe siècle* (Paris: Auguste Picard, 1924), 34.

223. For more on this marriage, see Chapter 3. For Nazarenko's theory on the relations of this marriage to Clement III's papacy, see Nazarenko, *Drevniaia Rus'*, 540–546.

224. Leib, *Rome, Kiev et Byzance*, 34, 41.

225. Ponyrko and Likhachev, *Epistoliarnoe nasledie drevnei rusi*, 30–35. Ioann II does say that Clement III could write him again if he so wished. Ibid., 35.

226. For more on this, see Chapters 2 and 3.

227. As illustrated in his *Canonical Responses,* where he chides Rusian princes for marrying their daughters "out of the faith." "Kanonicheskie otvety mitropolita Ioanna II," 7.

228. Ponyrko and Likhachev, *Epistoliarnoe nasledie drevnei rusi,* 28. Prior to this, Henry IV and Byzantium had been allied against Robert Guiscard. Robinson, *Henry IV of Germany,* 214, 222, 227; ironically this was just as Clement III was coming to the height of his power (283).

229. *PSRL 9,* 116; and Leib, *Rome, Kiev et Byzance,* 51–71.

230. Leib, *Rome, Kiev et Byzance,* 69.

231. Nazarenko advances the idea that the cause for Evpraksia's betrayal of the emperor was the realignment of Rusian politics in line with Byzantine loyalty to Urban II, though he does not consider the relics of St. Nicholas to be part of this political realignment. Nazarenko, *Drevniaia Rus',* 557.

232. *The Povest' vremennykh let,* 153:20–22.

233. *The Hagiography of Kievan Rus',* trans. Paul Hollingsworth, vol. 2 of Harvard Library of Early Ukrainian Literature, English Translations (Cambridge, Mass.: Harvard University Press, 1992), 20

234. *Ottonian Germany,* bk. 8, ch. 32.

235. Ibid., bk. 8, ch. 32, n77.

236. M. D. Prisëlkov originally argued that the early Rusian Church was under the jurisdiction not of Constantinople but of the patriarch of Ochrid. Prisëlkov, *Ocherki po tserkovno-politicheskoi istorii Kievskoi Rusi X–XII vv* (Saint Petersburg: M. M. Stasiuloevicha, 1913). Ernest Honigmann has argued against this theory and put Vladimir's church firmly under the patriarch of Constantinople. Honigmann, "Studies in Slavic Church History." Baumgarten advanced his own idea about the western affiliation of the early Rusian church, while Nicholas Zernov originally staked out the position that the church was autocephalous. N. de Baumgarten, *Saint Vladimir et la conversion de la Russie* (Rome: Pontifical Institute of Oriental Studies, 1932); Nicholas Zernov, "Vladimir and the Origin of the Russian Church," *Slavonic and East European Review* 28 (1949–1950).

237. While I have only listed a bare few academic citations on this topic, there are many more. Andrzej Poppe, *The Rise of Christian Russia* (London: Variorum Reprints, 1982), contains numerous articles in which Poppe engages in this debate, and the bibliographies contained therein are excellent.

238. Vladimir, after Christianizing the population of Kiev, placed priests in the cities of Rus'. *The Povest' vremennykh let*, 118:23–24. While his son, Iaroslav, made Luka Zhidyata bishop of Novgorod. *The Povest' vremennykh let*, 150:25–27; In so doing, Iaroslav displaced the prior bishop's choice of successor. Cross and Sherbowitz-Wetzor, *The Russian Primary Chronicle*, n162. There is also the extreme example of Iaroslav's appointment of Ilarion as metropolitan in 1051. *The Povest' vremennykh let*, 155:26–28. In fact, Rusian rulers continued to appoint at least some of their own bishops through this time period. Shchapov, *Gosudarstvo i tserkov'*, 172.

239. This is all of a piece with the *Eigenkirchensystem* that was a Germanic accretion to early medieval Christianity. Russell, *Germanization of Early Medieval Christianity*, 212 and elsewhere.

240. Although there are people who believe that Ilarion was appointed in agreement with Constantinople, rather than in opposition to Constantinople. Dimitri Obolensky, "Byzantium, Kiev and Moscow: A Study in Ecclesiastical Relations," in *Byzantium and the Slavs: Collected Studies*, ed. Dimitri Obolensky (London: Variorum Reprints, 1971), 142.

241. By one count there were twenty-three metropolitans of Kiev between 988 and 1281, and only two were Rusian. Anthony-Emil N. Tachiaos, "The Greek Metropolitans of Kievan Rus': An Evaluation of Their Spiritual and Cultural Activity," *Harvard Ukrainian Studies* 12–13 (1988–1989), 431.

242. Ibid., 436; Ivanov, "Religious Missions," 327 (in reference to Metropolitan Nikephoras).

243. *Ottonian Germany*, bk. 7, ch. 73; and *The Chronicle of the Slavs by Helmold, Priest of Bosau*, trans. Francis J. Tschan (New York: Columbia University Press, 1935), 154, ch. 49.

244. Tachiaos, "Greek Metropolitans," 436.

245. *Adam of Bremen*, bk. 3, lxxii.

246. As in the case of Ioann III "the Castrate," who was metropolitan for less than a full year. *The Povest' vremennykh let*, 208:14–18.

247. And could thus account for the unusual step of Vsevolod Iaroslavich sending his daughter Ianka to Constantinople in 1089, perhaps to expe-

dite the process of returning a metropolitan after the death of Ioann II. Ibid., 208:14–20.

248. Ibid., 263:20–21.

249. Ibid., 264:15–20.

250. *Ottonian Germany,* bk. 8, ch. 32.

251. "Kanonicheskie otvety mitropolita Ioanna II."

252. *The Povest' vremennykh let,* 208:8–14. For discussion of his, and others', polemics, see Leib, *Rome, Kiev et Byzance,* 33–40.

253. "Kanonicheskie otvety mitropolita Ioanna II," art. 13. It is clear from the context, and elsewhere, that Ioann II does not mean Jews, Muslims, or pagans, by this. There are no recorded marriages, postconversion, between Rusian men and non-Christians. The only exceptions to this are the daughters of Polovtsian khans who convert to Christianity upon their marriage to Rusians.

254. As well as in the best interest of his image, which was probably the primary purpose for the inclusion of the story in the chronicle. The general pattern of events may be true, while the details often appear to have been supplemented or fabricated.

255. Dimitri Obolensky, *The Byzantine Commonwealth: Eastern Europe 500–1453* (London: Weidenfeld and Nicolson, 1971), 226.

256. For an excellent discussion of this issue and Byzantine ecclesiastical and textual influence on Rus', see Simon Franklin, "The Empire of the Rhomaioi as Viewed from Kievan Russia: Aspects of Byzantino-Russian Cultural Relations," in *Byzantium—Rus'—Russia: Studies in the Translation of Christian Culture* (Burlington, Vt.: Ashgate, 2002).

257. Shchapov discusses this at length and reviews the scholarship on the matter. Shchapov, *Gosudarstvo i tserkov',* 56–62.

258. The most recent work on this topic was done by A. V. Nazarenko. Nazarenko, "Mitropolii iaroslavichei vo vtoroi polovine XI veka," in *Drevniaia Rus' i Slaviane* (Moscow: RAN, 2009), 207–245.

259. Shchapov, *Gosudarstvo i tserkov',* 59.

260. For examples, see Martin Dimnik, *The Dynasty of Chernigov, 1054–1146* (Toronto: Pontifical Institute of Mediaeval Studies, 1994), 105–107.

261. Territorially speaking, this statement is definitively true and an argument could be made about population, but there are very few accurate population statistics for the eleventh century. Poppe attributes the impetus for the division to Byzantium, but this seems unlikely. Poppe, "Russkie mitropolii," 98–104.

262. *PSRL 9,* 116, where he is anachronistically referred to as the metropolitan of Kiev and all Rus'. This also helps to refute Poppe's claim that the two

additional metropolitanates were titular. If Ephraim was founding churches, they were probably within his see.

263. Leib, *Rome, Kiev et Byzance,* 72–74. For more on Ephraim and his possible "Western" orientation, see D. G. Khrustalev, *Razyskaniia o Efreme Pereiaslavslom* (Saint Petersburg: Evraziia, 2002).

264. The word *national* is used only out of convenience to delineate the church of a particular kingdom, and does not carry its modern political meaning.

265. Edward Reisman, "Determinants of Collective Identity in Rus', 988–1505" (PhD diss., University of Chicago, 1987), 176.

266. Fr. Miklosich and Ios. Müller, eds., *Acta Patriarchatus Constantinopolitani,* vol. 2 (Vindobonae: Carolus Gerold, 1862), 188–192. This is not entirely unheralded earlier in medieval history as well. E.g., Liudprand of Cremona's "*Retribution* betrays few doubts that the new Rome of the east harbored Christendom's supreme authority." Liudprand of Cremona, *The Complete Works of Liudprand of Cremona,* trans. Paolo Squatriti (Washington, D.C.: Catholic University of America Press, 2007), 17.

267. Anthony Kaldellis argues that the statement of Patriarch Antonios IV is against almost all precedent in the Byzantine Empire and is a symptom of the late imperial need for funds, rather than an accurate representation of the political or religious situation of the day. This makes it even harder to apply to Muscovy, not to mention Rus'. Kaldellis, *Hellenism in Byzantium: The Transformations of Greek Identity and the Reception of the Classical Tradition* (Cambridge: Cambridge University Press, 2007), 104–105.

268. Franklin, "Empire of the Rhomaioi," 508.

269. Ibid., 510.

270. Georges Florovsky, introduction to P. L. Sokolov, *Russkii arkhierei iz Vizantii i pravo ego naznacheniia do nachala XV veka* (repr., Kiev: I. I. Chokolov, 1970).

271. Reisman, "Determinants" 176.

272. Roman Jakobson, "The Beginnings of National Self-Determination in Europe," *Review of Politics* 7, no. 1 (1945): 39.

273. Reisman, "Determinants," 36.

274. This opinion is shared by a variety of other scholars, including Peter Sawyer. Sawyer, *Kings and Vikings,* 141; and Anders Sjöberg, "Pop Upir' Lichoj," 122.

275. Or to again quote Jakobson, "the Church-Slavonic ideology helped Bulgaria to preserve its national individuality." Jakobson, "Beginnings of National Self-Determination," 39.

276. Thomsen, "Bulgarian Contribution."
277. Tachiaos, "Greek Metropolitans," 431.
278. *Sermons and Rhetoric of Kievan Rus'.*
279. Norman W. Ingham, "The Litany of Saints in 'Molitva Sv. Troicě,'" in *Studies Presented to Professor Roman Jakobson by His Students* (Cambridge, Mass.: Slavica, 1968), 125; and O. V. Loseva, *Russkie mesiatseslovy* (Moscow: Pamiatniki istoricheskoi mysli, 2001), 270.
280. *The Povest' vremennykh let,* 26:5–29:2.
281. Ibid.
282. Dvornik, *Byzantine Missions,* 152–160, specif. 154.
283. *The Povest' vremennykh let,* 27:12–28:1. Though this itinerary for Constantine-Cyril is incorrect, as he became a monk in Rome, took the name Cyril, and died all after his return from the initial trip to Moravia. Dvornik, *Byzantine Missions,* 143–144.
284. *Register of Pope Gregory VII,* 7.11.
285. Loseva, *Russkie mesiatseslovy,* 60.
286. Ibid.
287. Ibid., 61–62.
288. Franklin, "Empire of the Rhomaioi," 519.
289. Loseva discusses this issue extensively with large lists of saints from the various Rusian menologies of the time period. Loseva, *Russkie mesiatseslovy,* 63–69.
290. Ibid., 63.
291. Ibid., 65–66, 68.
292. If one doubts the importance of saints' days to a micro-Christendom, one has only to look at the *Paterik of the Kievan Caves Monastery,* where there is a story about Agapit. Agapit was a monk of the Kievan Caves Monastery who one day was joined by a visitor. Agapit offered food to the visitor, who replied that he could not eat, as it was one of the four days of the month that he was supposed to fast. Hearing this, Agapit was greatly agitated and angrily asked the monk who he was and what faith he was. The monk responded that he was Armenian, and Agapit told him, "Get away from me, you impious heterodox!" *Paterik of the Kievan Caves Monastery,* 151. In his analysis of this episode, Edward Reisman suggests that the Armenian was honoring St. Sergius, a saint who was not accepted in Rus'. Reisman, "Determinants," 221.
293. Simply on the issue of whether or not it was supported by the Byzantine micro-Christendom one can find multiple views. Jonathan Shepard and Paul Hollingsworth, for instance, believe it certainly was supported by

the local metropolitans, while Shchapov does not. Shepard, "Byzantium and Russia in the Eleventh Century: A Study in Political and Ecclesiastical Relations" (PhD diss., University of Oxford, 1973), ch. 3; Hollingsworth, introduction to *The Hagiography of Kievan Rus'*; Shchapov, *Gosudarstvo i tserkov'*, 177–178.

294. *The Hagiography of Kievan Rus'*, 20.

295. Metropolitan George in 1072, *The Povest' vremennykh let*, 181:18–182:19; and Metropolitan Nikephoras in 1115, *PSRL 2*, 280.

296. Also complicating the picture is the fact that the first office for the saints is ascribed to Metropolitan Ioann, but it is unclear whether this is Nestor's Ioann from the 1020s or Ioann II from the 1070s to the 1080s. *The Hagiography of Kievan Rus'*, 20, n46.

297. Norman W. Ingham, "The Martyred Prince and the Question of Slavic Cultural Continuity in the Early Middle Ages," in *Medieval Russian Culture*, ed. Henrik Birnbaum and Michael S. Flier (Berkeley: University of California Press, 1984), 33.

298. Ibid., 33–34.

299. Francis Butler, "Wenceslas: The Saint and His Name in Kievan Rus," *Slavic and East European Journal* 48, no. 1 (2004): 66.

300. Who plays a role in the history of Rus', as a visitor to Iaroslav's court while in exile, and having left his son, Magnus, to be fostered by Iaroslav and Ingigerd. In addition to these better-known observations is the note by one of Olaf's skalds, Sighvatr, that Olaf cured the blindness of "Valdemar" while in Rus'. Though no other information is available, it is an intriguing note—for the consequences of a possible miraculous healing for Vladimir Iaroslavich (as a possible identity), for the relationship with the tale of the blinding of Vladimir Sviatoslavich prior to his conversion, and for the site of one of Olaf's first miracles to be in Rus'. Lindow, "St. Olaf and the Skalds," 117, 119, 126.

301. Ingham, "Litany of Saints," 132.

302. Tibor Živković has noted similar trends of appropriation of saints from multiple traditions as a way of attempting to understand political influence. Živković, "The Earliest Cult of Saints in Ragusa," in *Forging Unity: The South Slavs between East and West, 550–1150* (Belgrade: Institute of History, 2008), 147–156

303. "Mnich Sázavsky," in *Fontes rerum Bohemicarum*, ed. Jos. Emler (Prague: Nákladem Musea Království Ceského, 1874), 251.

304. Ingham, "Litany of Saints," 131.

305. Vlasto, *Entry of the Slavs*, 291.

306. Butler, "Wenceslas," 66; and Ingham, "Litany of Saints," 130.

307. A number of Latin religious texts reached Rus' in Bohemian form, including the *Life of Saint Benedicts of Nursia,* the *Martyrdom of Pope Stephen,* the *Martyrdom of Saint Apollinarius of Ravenna,* the *Life of Saint Conrad,* the *Life of St. Julian of Le Mans,* and the sermons of Pope Gregory the Great. Vlasto, *Entry of the Slavs,* 292.

308. *The Povest' vremennykh let,* 11:4–13:6.

309. See the litany of saints preserved in the *Molitva Sv. Troicĕ,* Ingham, "Litany of Saints."

310. Edward Reisman deals with this in his dissertation, concluding that there was no sense of Slavic solidarity in Rus', especially in this time period. Reisman, "Determinants."

311. For a discussion of relations between Slavic monks on Athos, see John V. A. Fine Jr., *The Late Medieval Balkans: A Critical Survey from the Late Twelfth Century to the Ottoman Conquest* (Ann Arbor: University of Michigan Press, 1987), 38 and elsewhere.

312. The position of the merchants is that they rescued the relics, which were in an area close to Arab attacks.

313. Vlasto, *Entry of the Slavs,* 291.

314. Loseva, *Russkie mesiatseslovy,* 336.

315. *PSRL 9,* 116.

316. Bernard Leib goes into extensive detail with translations of the various versions of the office that were created at this time, in order to show the provenance of the Rusian version. Leib, *Rome, Kiev et Byzance,* 56–68.

317. *The Povest' vremennykh let,* 208:7–8.

318. Whether the metropolitan acted as a control mechanism on the church or on Rus' in general and whether or not Ephraim was acting as metropolitan of Rus' at this time and had Western sympathies are discussed above in the section "The Role of the Metropolitan."

319. *The Povest' vremennykh let,* 209:10–214:13.

320. Cross and Sherbowitz-Wetzor, *The Russian Primary Chronicle,* 274–275, n273.

321. Brown, *Rise of Western Christendom,* 366.

322. Elena Boeck, "Simulating the Hippodrome: The Performance of Power in Kiev's St. Sophia," *Art Bulletin* 41, no. 3 (2009).

323. This position is eloquently discussed, with copious examples, in Boeck's article. Ibid., 293–295.

324. *Adam of Bremen,* bk. 2, 22 (19).

325. *The Povest' vremennykh let,* 155:26–28.

326. Obolensky argues that the appointment may have been agreed upon as part of the 1046 treaty, though there is no evidence for this. The patriarch

of Constantinople did later recognize Ilarion. Obolensky, "Byzantium, Kiev and Moscow," 142.

Conclusion

1. Frederick J. Teggart, *Rome and China: A Study of Correlations in Historical Events* (Berkeley: University of California Press, 1939), 74.
2. Pethahiah of Regensburg, *Travels of Rabbi Petachia of Ratisbon*, trans. A. Benisch (London: Trubner, 1856), 3.
3. Such studies are present in other languages, but do not necessarily take into account Rus' as part of Europe. Two such recent Russian studies are I. A. Gagin, "Diplomatiia Volzhskoi Bulgarii v X-pervoi treti XIII vekov" (PhD diss., Saint Petersburg University, 1997); and Tatiana Kostiuchenko, "The Union of Black Klobuks: The Turkic Tribes in Rus', X–XIII c." (PhD diss., Oriental Institute of the National Aacademy of Science, 2005) (in Ukrainian). Also, in a recent collection of articles there are several French articles on Rusian trade, including, I. Konovalova, "Les Rus sur les voies de commerce de l'Europe orientale d'après les sources arabo-persanes," in *Les centres proto-urbains russes entre Scandinavie, Byzance et Orient*, ed. M. Kazanski, A. Nercessian, and C. Zuckerman (Paris: Éditions P. Lethielleux, 2000); and M. Espéronnier, "Villes et commerce: La Khazarie et la Bulgarie de la Volga, d'après les textes arabes et persans des IXe et Xe siècles," in *Les centres proto-urbains russes entre Scandinavie, Byzance et Orient*, ed. M. Kazanski, A. Nercessian, and C. Zuckerman (Paris: Éditions P. Lethielleux, 2000).
4. The work of Z. J. Kosztolnyik exemplifies this trend in English. Z. J. Kosztolnyik, *Five Eleventh Century Hungarian Kings: Their Policies and Relations with Rome* (New York: Columbia University Press, 1981); Kosztolnyik, *From Coloman the Learned to Bela III (1095–1196): Hungarian Domestic Policies and Their Impact upon Foreign Affairs* (New York: Columbia University Press, 1987); and Kosztolnyik, *Hungary under the Early Árpáds, 890s to 1063* (Boulder, Colo.: East European Monographs, 2002).
5. There is a variety of Russian examples of such work from the Soviet period, though few were translated into English. The best-known is perhaps M. N. Tikhomirov, *The Towns of Ancient Rus*, trans. Y. Sdobnikov (Moscow: Foreign Language Publishing House, 1959).
6. Ukrainian scholars have the best reason for doing this type of work—attempting to create their own identity separate from that of the Russian Empire or Soviet Union. The classic work, and the best-known now due to the modern reprinting, is Mykhailo Hrushevsky, *History of Ukraine-Rus'*,

ed. Andrzej Poppe and Frank E. Sysyn, trans. Marta Skorupsky, vol. 1 (Edmonton: Canadian Institute of Ukrainian Studies Press, 1997).

7. The fine work of Nora Berend is only one such example. Nora Berend, *At the Gate of Christendom: Jews, Muslims, and "Pagans" in Medieval Hungary, c. 1000–c. 1300* (Cambridge: Cambridge University Press, 2001).

Bibliography

Primary Sources

Abel, D. Ottone, ed. *Ortliebi Zwifaltensis chronicon.* In Monumenta Germaniae Historica Scriptores, vol. 10, edited by George Pertz. Hannover: Impensis Bibliopolii Avlici Hahniani, 1852.

Adam of Bremen: History of the Archbishops of Hamburg-Bremen. Translated by Francis J. Tschan. New York: Columbia University Press, 1959.

Adamus Bremensis. *Adami gesta Hammaburgensis ecclesiae pontificum.* Edited by J. M. Lappenberg. Scriptores rerum germanicarum in usum scholarum ex Monumentis Germaniae historicis recusi. Hannover: Impensis Biblipolii Hahniani, 1876.

"Addition Decima: Leges Portorii c.a. 906." In Monumenta Germaniae Historica. Leges, vol. 3. Hannover: Impensis Bibliopolii Avlici Hahniani, 1863.

Albertus Standensis. *Chronicon Alberti, abbatis Stadensis.* Helmstadt: J. Lucius, 1587.

The Alexiad of Anna Comnena. Translated by E. R. A. Sewter. New York: Penguin Books, 1969.

Alfred the Great. Translated by Simon Keynes and Michael Lapidge. New York: Penguin, 1983.

The Anglo-Saxon Chronicle. Translated by M. J. Swanton. London: J. M. Dent, 1996.

"Annales Posonienses." In *Sciptores rerum Hungaricarum,* edited by Emerus Szentpetery, 119–128. Budapest: Academia Litter. Hungarica atque Societate Hist. Hungarica, 1937.

"Annales Quedlinburgenses." In Monumenta Germaniae Historica Scriptores, vol. 3, edited by George Pertz. Hannover: Impensis Bibliopolii Avlici Hahniani, 1839.

The Annals of St-Bertin. Translated by Janet L. Nelson. Vol. 1 of Ninth-Century Histories. New York: Manchester University Press, 1991.

Athanasius, P., ed. *Documenta pontificum Romanorum historiam Ucrainae illustrantia (1075–1953)*. Vol. 1 (1075–1700). Rome: P. P. Basiliani, 1953.

Bauer, Albert, and Reinhold Rau, eds. *Fontes ad historiam aevi Saxonici illustrandam: Widukindi res gestae Saxonicae; Adalberti continuato Reginonis; Liudprandi opera*. Darmstadt: Wissenschaftliche Buchgesellschaft, 1971.

Beck, H. G., ed. *Ioannis Scylitzae synopsis historiarum*. Berlin: Walter de Gruyter, 1973.

Benjamin of Tudela. *The Itinerary of Benjamin of Tudela*. Translated by Masa'ot shel Tabi Benjamin. Cold Spring, N.Y.: NightinGale Resources, 2005.

Bernard of Clairvaux. *Opera*. 8 vols. Rome: Editiones Cistercienses, 1957.

Bethmann, L., ed. *Donizonis vita Mathildis*. In Monumenta Germaniae Historica Scriptores, vol. 12, edited by George Pertz. Hannover: Impensis Bibliopolii Avlici Hahniani, 1861.

Bielowski, August, ed. *Monumenta Poloniae Historica*. Vol. 1. Paris: Mouton, 1960.

"Boguphali II episcopi Posnaniensis Chronicon Poloniae, cum continuatione Basconis custodis Posnaniensis." In *Monumenta Poloniae Historica,* edited by August Bielowski, 467–600. Paris: Mouton, 1961.

Bruno of Querfurt. "List Brunona do Henryka II, ok. 1008." In *Monumenta Poloniae Historica,* 223–228. Lwow: Nakladem Wlasnym, 1864.

Bryennios, Nicephorus. *Histoire*. In Corpus Fontium Historiae Byzantinae, vol. 9, edited by P. Gautier. Brussels: Byzantion, 1975.

Byzance et la France médiévale; manuscrits à peintures du IIe au XVIe siècle. Paris: Bibliothèque nationale, 1958.

Cecaumenus. *Strategikon*. Edited by B. Wassiliewsky and V. Jernstedt. Saint Petersburg: Imperatorskaia Akademiia Nauk, 1896.

Choniates, Nicetas. *O City of Byzantium: Annals of Niketas Choniates*. Translated by H. Magoulias. Detroit: Wayne State University Press, 1984.

Chronica monasterii Casinensis. Edited by Hartmut Hoffmann. Vol. 34 of Monumenta Germaniae Historica. Hannover: Impensis Bibliopolii Hahniani, 1980.

"Chronica Polono-Silesiaci: Loci ad Petrum spectantes." In *Monumenta Poloniae Historica: Nova series,* edited by Marian Plezia, 31–33. Cracow: Subsidio Ministerii Scholarum Superiorum et Studiorum, 1951.

"Chronici Hungarici." In *Sciptores rerum Hungaricarum,* edited by Emerus Szentpetery, 217–506. Budapest: Academia Litter. Hungarica atque Societate Hist. Hungarica, 1937.

The Chronicle of the Slavs by Helmold, Priest of Bosau. Translated by Francis J. Tschan. New York: Columbia University Press, 1935.

"Chronicon: Vindocinense seu de Aquaria." In *Chroniques des églises D'Anjou*, edited by Paul Marchegay and Émile Mabille, 153–178. Paris: Libraire de la société de l'histoire de France, 1869.

Clarius. *Chronique de Sant-Pierre-le-vif de sens, diter de Clarius*. Edited by Robert-Henri Bautier and Monique Gilles. Paris: Centre national de la recherche scientifique, 1979.

Conrad, Klaus, ed. *Pommersches Urkundenbuch*. Vol. 1. Cologne: Böhlau Verlag, 1970.

"Cosmae chronicon Boemorum cum continuatoribus." In *Fontes rerum Bohemicarum*, edited by Jos. Emler. Prague: Nákladem Musea Království Ceského, 1874.

Cross, Samuel Hazzard, and Olgerd P. Sherbowitz-Wetzor, eds., transls., *The Russian Primary Chronicle*. Cambridge, Mass.: Mediaeval Academy of America, 1953.

D'Aguilers, Raymond. *Historia Francorum qui ceperunt Iherusalem*. Translated by John Hugh Hill and Laurita L. Hill. Philadelphia: American Philosophical Society, 1968.

De administrando imperio / Constantine Porphyrogenitus. Translated by R. J. H. Jenkins. Washington D.C.: Dumbarton Oaks Center for Byzantine Studies, 1967.

Dercesnyi, Dezso, ed. *The Hungarian Illuminated Chronicle: Chronica de gestis Hungarorum*. Budapest: Corvina Press, 1969.

Dlugosz, Jan. *Annales seu cronicae incliti regni Poloniae*. Vols. 1–4. Warsaw: Panstwowe Wydawnictwo Naukowe, 1964.

Dvornik, Francis. *Les légendes de Constantin et de Méthode vues de Byzance*. Prague: Orbis, 1933.

Eustathios of Thessaloniki. *The Capture of Thessaloniki*. Translated by J. R. Melville Jones. Canberra: Australian Association for Byzantine Studies, 1988.

Fejér, Georgii, ed. *Codex diplomaticus Hungariae, ecclesiasticus ac civilis*. Vol. 1. Buda: Regiae Universitatis Ungaricae, 1829.

Friedrich, Gustavus, ed. *Codex Diplomaticus et Epistolaris Regni Bohemiae*. Vol. 1. Prague: Topos, 1904.

Frutolf of Michelsburg. *Chronica*. Edited by F.-J. Schmale and I. Schmale-Ott. Darmstadt: Ausgewählte Quellen zur deutschen Geschiste des Mittelalters, 1972.

Fulcher of Chartres. *A History of the Expedition to Jerusalem, 1095–1127*. Translated by Frances Rita Ryan. Knoxville: University of Tennessee Press, 1969.

Gallus Anonymous. *Gesta principum Polonorum: The Deeds of the Princes of the Poles.* Translated by Paul W. Knoll and Frank Schaer. New York: Central European University Press, 2003.

Geoffrey of Villehardouin. "The Conquest of Constantinople." In *Chronicles of the Crusades,* edited by M. R. B. Shaw, 9–162. Baltimore: Penguin, 1963.

Gerbert of Aurillac. *The Letters of Gerbert with His Papal Privileges as Sylvester II.* Translated by Harriet Pratt Lattin. New York: Columbia University Press, 1961.

Gregory of Tours. *History of the Franks.* Vol. 2. Oxford: Clarendon Press, 1927.

Grumel, V., ed. *Les régestes des actes du patriarcat de Constantinople.* Vol. 1 of Les actes des Patriarches. Rome: Socii Assumptionistae Chalcedonenses, 1936.

The Hagiography of Kievan Rus'. Translated by Paul Hollingsworth. Vol. 2 of Harvard Library of Early Ukrainian Literature. Cambridge, Mass.: Harvard University Press, 1992.

Hasse, V. Cl. Lud. Frid., ed. *Lamberti Hersfeldensis Annales.* In Monumenta Germaniae Historica Scriptores, vol. 5, edited by George Pertz. Hannover: Impensis Bibliopolii Hahniani, 1844.

Hausmann, Friedrich, ed. *Monumenta Germaniae Historica: Diplomatum regum et imperatorum Germaniae.* Vol. 9. Vienna: Hermann Bohlaus Nachf, 1969.

Henricus Lettus. *The Chronicle of Henry of Livonia.* Translated by James A. Brundage. Records of Western Civilization. New York: Columbia University Press, 2003.

Historia Norvegiae. Translated by Peter Fisher. Edited by Inger Ekrem and Lars Boje Mortensen. Copenhagen: Museum Tusculanum Press, 2003.

The Homilies of Photius Patriarch of Constantinople. Translated by Cyril Mango. Cambridge, Mass.: Harvard University Press, 1958.

ibn Chardadbeh. "Book of Roads and Government." In *Bibliotheca geographorum arabicorum* Vol. 1, edited by M. J. de Goeje, 1–208. Lugduni-Batavorum: E. J. Brill, 1927.

Ilarion. *Slovo o zakone i blagodati Ilariona.* Edited by A. M. Moldovan. Kiev: Naukova Dumka, 1984.

Ipat'evskaia letopis'. Vol. 2 of *Polnoe sobranie russkikh letopisei.* Moscow: Iazyki slavianskoi kul'tury, 2001.

John Scylitzes. *Ioannis Scylitzae synopsis historiarum.* Edited by Ioannes Thurn. Corpus fontium historiae Byzantinae. Berolini: De Gruyter, 1973.

Jónsson, Finnur. *Fagrskinna, Nóregs kononga tal.* Copenhagen: S. L. Mollers Bogtrykkeri, 1902–1903.

"Kanonicheskie otvety mitropolita Ioanna II." *Russkaia istoricheskaia biblioteka* 6 (1908): 1–20.

Karwasin'ska, Hedvigis, ed. *Monumenta Poloniae Historica: Nova series,* vol. 4; *S. Adalberti Pragensis episcopi et martyris vita prior.* Warsaw: Polska Akademia Umiejetnosci, 1962.

"Khozhenie Daniila, igumena Russkoi zemli." In *Kniga khozhenii: Zapiski russkikh puteshestvennikov XI–XV vv.,* 27–80. Moscow: Sovetskaia Rossiia, 1984.

Kinnamos, John. *Deeds of John and Manuel Comnenus.* Translated by Charles M. Brand. New York: Columbia University Press, 1976.

Knytlinga Saga: The History of the Kings of Denmark. Translated by Hermann Pálsson and Paul Edwards. Odense: Odense University Press, 1986.

Komroff, Manuel, ed. *Contemporaries of Marco Polo, Consisting of the Travel Records to the Eastern Parts of the World of William of Rubruck, the Journey of Pian de Carpini, the Journal of Friar Odoric and the Oriental Travels of Rabbi Benjamin of Tudela.* New York: Boni and Liveright, 1928.

Krause, Victor, ed. *Monumenta Germaniae Historica: Capitularia regum Francorum.* Vol. 2. Hanover: Impensis Bibliopolii, 1897.

Lappenberg, I. M., ed. *Annales Stadenses auctore M. Alberto.* In Monumenta Germaniae Historica Scriptores, vol. 16, edited by George Pertz. Hannover: Impensis Bibliopolii Avlici Hahniani, 1859.

Lavrent'evskaia letopis'. Vol. 1 of *Polnoe sobranie russkikh letopisei.* Moscow: Iazyki slavianskoi kul'tury, 2001.

Leo Grammaticus. *Chronographia.* Edited by I. Bekker. Vol. 47 of Corpus Scriptorum Historiae Byzantinae. Bonn: Impensis Ed. Weberi, 1842.

Leo the Deacon. *The History of Leo the Deacon: Byzantine Military Expansion in the Tenth Century.* Translated by Alice-Mary Talbot and Denis F. Sullivan. Washington, D.C.: Dumbarton Oaks Research Library and Collection, 2005.

———. *Lev Diakon. Istoriia.* Translated by M. M. Korylenko. Edited by G. G. Litavrin. Moscow: Nauka, 1988.

Leo VI. *Tactica.* Budapest: Typis Regiae Universitatis Scientarum Budapestinensis, 1917.

Letopisnyi sbornik, imenuemyi: Patriarshei ili Nikonovskoi letopis'iu. Vol. 9 of *Polnoe sobranie russkikh letopisei.* Moscow: Iazyki russkoi kul'tury, 2000.

Letopis' po voskresenskomu spisku. Vol. 7 of *Polnoe sobranie russkikh letopisei.* Moscow: Iazyki slavianskoi kul'tury, 2001.

Liudprand of Cremona. *The Complete Works of Liudprand of Cremona.* Translated by Paolo Squatriti. Washington, D.C.: Catholic University of America Press, 2007.

——. *Liudprandi Opera.* Edited by Joseph Becker. Scriptores rerum Germanicarum. Hannover: Impensis Bibliopolii Hahniani, 1915.

The Livonian Rhymed Chronicle. Translated by Jerry C. Smith and William L. Urban. 2nd ed. Chicago: Lithuanian Research and Studies Center, 2001.

Miklosich, F., ed. *Codice Suprasliensi.* Monumenta Linguae Palaeoslovenicae. Vindobonae: Carl Gerold's Sohn, 1851.

Miklosich, Fr., and Ios. Müller, eds. *Acta Patriarchatus Constantinopolitani.* Vol. 2. Vindobonae: Carolus Gerold, 1862.

"Mnich Sázavsky." In *Fontes rerum Bohemicarum,* edited by Jos. Emler. Prague: Nákladem Musea Království Ceského, 1874.

Monumenta Germaniae historiae: Diplomatum regum et imperatorum Germaniae. Vol. 6, *Heinrici IV: Diplomata.* Weimar: Hermann Bohlaus Nachfolger, 1953.

Morozov, T. S., ed. *Izbornik velikago kniazia Sviatoslava Iaroslavicha 1073 goda.* Vol. 3 of Monumenta Linguae Slavicae Dialecti Veteris. Wiesbaden: Otto Harrassowitz, 1965.

"Nicolai I. Papae Epistolae." In *Monumenta Germanica historiae epistolarum,* edited by Ernestus Perels, 257–690. Berolini: Apud Weidmannos, 1925.

The Nikonian Chronicle: From the Beginning to the Year 1132. Translated by Serge A. Zenkovsky and Betty Jean Zenkovsky. Edited by Serge A. Zenkovsky. Princeton, N.J.: Kingston Press, 1984.

Novgorodskaia chetvertaia letopis'. Vol. 4, part 1, of *Polnoe sobranie russkikh letopisei.* Moscow: Iazyki slavianskoi kul'tury, 2000.

Novgorodskaia pervaia letopis': Starshego i mladshego izvodov. Vol. 3 of *Polnoe sobranie russkikh letopisei.* Moscow: Iazyki slavianskoi kul'tury, 2000.

Ostrowski, Donald, ed. *The Povest' vremennykh let: An Interlinear Collation and Paradosis.* 3 vols. Cambridge, Mass.: Harvard Ukrainian Research Institute, 2003.

Othlo. "Ex Libro Visionum." In Monumenta Germanica historiae Scriptores, vol. 11, edited by George Pertz, 378–387. Hannover: Impensis Bibliopolii Hahniani, 1854.

Otto, Bishop of Freising. *The Two Cities: A Chronicle of Universal History to the Year 1146 A.D.* Translated by Charles Christopher Mierow. New York: Octagon Books, 1966.

Ottonian Germany: The "Chronicon" of Thietmar of Merseburg. Translated by David A. Warner. Manchester: Manchester University Press, 2001.

The Paterik of the Kievan Caves Monastery. Translated by Muriel Heppell. Cambridge, Mass.: Harvard University Press, 1989.

Pertz, George, ed. *Annales Augustani.* In Monumenta Germaniae Historica Scriptores, vol. 3, edited by George Pertz. Hannover: Impensis Bibliopolii Avlici Hahniani, 1839.

———, ed. *Annales Magdeburgensis.* In Monumenta Germaniae Historica Scriptores, vol. 16, edited by George Pertz. Hannover: Impensis Bibliopolii Avlici Hahniani, 1859.

———, ed. *Annales Sancti Disibodi.* In Monumenta Germaniae Historica Scriptores, vol. 17, edited by George Pertz. Hannover: Impensis Bibliopolii Avlici Hahniani, 1861.

———, ed. *Annalista Saxo.* In Monumenta Germaniae Historica Scriptores, vol. 6, edited by George Pertz. Hannover: Impensis Bibliopolii Avlici Hahniani, 1844.

———, ed. *Bernoldi Chronicon.* In Monumenta Germaniae Historica Scriptores, vol. 5, edited by George Pertz. Hannover: Impensis Bibliopolii Avlici Hahniani, 1844.

———, ed. *Bertholdi Annales.* In Monumenta Germaniae Historica Scriptores, vol. 5, edited by George Pertz. Hannover: Impensis Bibliopolii Avlici Hahniani, 1844.

———, ed. *Bruno de Bello Saxonico.* In Monumenta Germaniae Historica Scriptores, vol. 5, edited by George Pertz. Hannover: Impensis Bibliopolii Avlici Hahniani, 1844.

———, ed. *Capitularia regum Francorum.* In Monumenta Germaniae Historica Legum, vol. 1, edited by George Pertz. Hannover: Impensis Bibliopolii Avlici Hahniani, 1835.

———, ed. *Cosmae Chronica Boemorum.* In Monumenta Germaniae Historica Scriptores, vol. 9, edited by George Pertz. Hannover: Impensis Bibliopolii Avlici Hahniani, 1851.

———, ed. *Ekkehardi Chronicon.* In Monumenta Germaniae Historica Scriptores, vol. 6, edited by George Pertz. Hannover: Impensis Bibliopolii Avlici Hahniani, 1844.

———, ed. *Lamberti Hersfeldensis Annales.* Hanover: Impensis Bibliopolii Hahniani, 1843.

Pethahiah of Regensburg. *Travels of Rabbi Petachia of Ratisbon.* Translated by A. Benisch. London: Trubner, 1856.

Photius. *The Homilies of Photius Patriarch of Constantinople.* Edited by Cyril Mango. Cambridge, Mass.: Harvard University Press, 1958.

———. *Photii patriarchae Constantinopolitani epistulae et amphilochia.* Edited by B. Laourdas. Vol. 1. Leipzig: Teubner Verlagsgesellschaft, 1983.

Pravda russkaia. Edited by B. D. Grekov. Moscow: Izdatel'stvo akademii nauk SSSR, 1947.

Pritsak, Omeljan. *The Old Rus' Kievan and Galician-Volhynian Chronicles: The Ostroz'kyj (Xlebnikov) and cetvertyns'kyj (Pogodin) Codices.* Cambridge, Mass.: Harvard University Press, 1990.

Prou, Maurice, ed. *Recueil des actes de Philippe I-er, roi de France (1059–1108).* Paris: Imprimerie nationale, 1908.

Psellus, Michael. *Fourteen Byzantine Rulers: The Chronographia of Michael Psellus.* Translated by E. R. A. Sewter. New York: Penguin Books, 1966.

———. *The History of Psellus.* Edited by Constantine Sathas. London: Methuen, 1899.

Pskovskie letopisi. Vol. 5 of *Polnoe sobranie russkikh letopisei.* Moscow: Iazyki russkoi kul'tury, 2000.

The Register of Pope Gregory VII, 1073–1085. Translated by H. E. J. Cowdrey. Oxford: Oxford University Press, 2002.

Reiske, I. I., ed. *De cerimoniis aulae Byzantinae.* Vol. 9 of Corpus Scriptorum Historiae Byzantinae, edited by B. G. Niebuhr. Bonn: Impensis Ed. Weberi, 1829.

The Rhodian Sea-Law. Edited and translated by Walter Ashburner. Oxford: Clarendon Press, 1909.

Robert of Clari. *Conquete de Constantinople.* Translated by M. A. Zaborova. Moscow: Nauka, 1986.

Rogozhskii letopisets / Tverskoi sbornik. Vol. 15 of *Polnoe sobranie russkikh letopisei.* Moscow: Iazyki slavianskoi kul'tury, 2000.

Sauerland, H. U., and A. Haselhoff, eds. *Der Psalter Ezbischof Egberts von Trier: Codex Gertrudianus, in cividale.* Trier: Selbstverlag der Gesellschaft für nützliche forschungen, 1901.

Saxo Grammaticus. *Danorum Regum Heroumque Historia Books X–XVI: The Text of the First Edition with Translation and Commentary in Three Volumes.* Translated by Eric Christiansen. Vol. 1: Books X, XI, XII and XIII. Oxford: B.A.R., 1980.

———. *Gesta Danorum: The History of the Danes.* Translated by Peter Fisher. Edited by Hilda Ellis Davidson. Totowa, N.J.: Rowman and Littlefield, 1979.

———. *Saxonis Grammatici gesta Danorum.* Strassburg: K. J. Trubner, 1886.

Sedulius Scottus. *On Christian Rulers and the Poems.* Translated by Edward Gerard Doyle. Binghamton, UK: Medieval and Renaissance Texts and Studies, 1983.

Sermons and Rhetoric of Kievan Rus'. Translated by Simon Franklin. Harvard Library of Early Ukrainian Literature. Cambridge, Mass.: Harvard University Press, 1991.

Shchaveleva, N. I., *Drevniaia Rus' v "Pol'skoi Istorii" Iana Dlugosha: Tekst, perevod, kommentarii.* Edited by A. V. Nazarenko. Moscow: Pamiatniki Istoricheskoi Mysli, 2004.

———. *"Velikaia khronika" o Pol'she, Rusi i ikh sosediakh XI–XIII vv.* Moscow: Izdatel'stvo Moskovskogo universiteta, 1987.

Société de Géographie. *Recueil de voyages et de mémoires publié par la Société de Géographie.* Vol. 4. Paris: Impr. Royale, 1839.

Sogur Danakonunga 1. Sogubrot af Fornkononungum 2. Knytlinga Saga. Copenhagen, 1919–1925.

Sturluson, Snorri. *Heimskringla: History of the Kings of Norway.* Translated by Lee M. Hollander. Austin: University of Texas Press, 1964.

———. *Heimskringla edr Noregs konunga-Sögor.* Edited by Gerhard Schøning. 6 vols. Havniae: Typis Augusti Friederici Stenii, 1777–1826.

Tatishchev, V. N. *Istoriia Rossiiskaia.* Vols. 1–3. Moscow: Akademii Nauk SSSR, 1963.

Theodoricus Monachus. *Historiae de antiquitate regum Norwagiensum.* Translated by David and Ian McDougall. London: Viking Society for Northern Research, 1998.

———. "Theodrici monachi historia de antiquitate regum Norwagiensium." In *Monumenta Historica Norvegiae*, edited by Gustav Storm, 1–68. Kristiania: A. W. Brøgger, 1880.

Theophanes continuatus. *Theophanes continuatus: Chronographia.* Edited by Immanuel Bekker. Bonn: Weber, 1838.

Theophilus. *De Diversis Artibus: The Various Arts.* Translated by C. R. Dodwell. London: Thomas Nelson and Sons, 1961.

Thietmar of Merseburg. "Die Chronik des Bischofs Thietmar von Merseburg." In Monumenta Germaniae Historica Scriptores rerum Germanicarum, Nova series, vol. 9, edited by Robert Holtzmann, 3–533. Berlin: Weidmannsche Buchandlung, 1935.

Tschan, Francis J., ed. *Saint Bernward of Hildesheim.* Vol. 2, *His Works of Art.* South Bend, Ind.: University of Notre Dame, 1951.

Unger, C. R., ed. *Flateyjarbók.* Vol. 3. Christiania: P. T. Mallings, 1868.

Urban II. B. *Urbani II pontificis Romani epistolae, diplomata, sermones.* Edited by J. P. Migne. Patrologiae Cursus Completus. Paris: Garnier fratres, 1881.

"Vita Mariani," in *Acta Sanctorum*, vol. 4. February, 1894.

Walram Bishop of Naumburg. *Liber de unitate ecclesiae conservanda.* Scriptores rerum Germanicarum. Hannover: Impensis Bibliopolii Hahniani, 1883.

White, Despina Stratoudaki. *Patriarch Photius of Constantinople: His Life, Scholarly Contributions and Correspondence Together with a Translation of Fifty-Two of His Letters.* Brookline, Mass.: Holy Cross Orthodox Press, 1981.

White, Despina Stratoudaki, and Joseph R. Berrigan Jr. *The Patriarch and the Prince: The Letter of Patriarch Photios of Constantinople to Khan Boris of Bulgaria.* Brookline, Mass.: Holy Cross Orthodox Press, 1982.

Wilhelm. "Wilhelmi abbatis genealogia regum Danorum." In *Scriptores minores historiae danicae medii aevi,* edited by M. C. L. Getz, 145–194. Copenhagen, 1917.

William of Tyre. *A History of Deeds Done beyond the Sea.* Translated by Emily Atwater Babcock and A. C. Krey. 2 vols. New York: Columbia University Press, 1943.

Zonaras, John. *Epitome historiarum.* Vol. 4. Lipsiae: B. G. Teubneri, 1871.

Secondary Sources

Aalst, V. D. van, and K. N. Ciggaar, eds. *Byzantium and the Low Countries in the Tenth Century: Aspects of Art and History in the Ottonian Era.* Hernen: A. A. Brediusstichting, 1985.

Abu-Lughod, Janet L. *Before European Hegemony: The World System, A.D. 1250–1350.* New York: Oxford University Press, 1989.

Alekseev, M. P. "Anglo-saxonskaia parallel' k Poucheniu Vladimira Mono-makha." *Trudy otdela drevne-russkoi literatury* 2 (1935): 39–80.

Aleshkovskii, M. Kh. *Povest' vremennykh let: Sud'ba literaturnogo proizvede-niia v dreveni Rusi.* Moscow: Nauka, 1971.

Althoff, Gerd. *Otto III.* Translated by Phyllis G. Jestice. University Park: Pennsyl-vania State University Press, 2003.

Amundsen, Darrell W., and Carol Jean Diers. "The Age of Menarche in Medieval Europe." *Human Biology* 45 (1973): 363–369.

Angold, Michael. "Belle Époque or Crisis (1025–1118)." In *The Cambridge History of the Byzantine Empire, c. 500–1492,* edited by Jonathan Shepard, 583–626. Cambridge: Cambridge University Press, 2009.

———. *The Byzantine Empire, 1025–1204.* New York: Longman, 1997.

Ashley, Kathleen, and Véronique Plesch. "The Cultural Processes of 'Appropriation.'" *Journal of Medieval and Early Modern Studies* 31, no. 1 (2002): 1–16.

Ashtor, E. *A Social and Economic History of the Near East in the Middle Ages.* Berkeley: University of California Press, 1976.

Bachrach, Bernard S. "On the Origins of William the Conqueror's Horse Transports." *Technology and Culture* 26, no. 3 (1985): 505–531.

Backman, Clifford R. *The Worlds of Medieval Europe*. Oxford: Oxford University Press, 2003.

Bak, János M. "Roles and Functions of Queens in Árpádian and Angevin Hungary (1000–1386 A.D.)." In *Medieval Queenship*, edited by John Carmi Parsons, 13–24. Gloucestershire: Sutton, 1994.

Baker, Derek. "'A Nursery of Saints': St. Margaret of Scotland Reconsidered." In *Medieval Women*, edited by Derek Baker, 119–142. Oxford: Basil Blackwell for the Ecclesiastical History Society, 1978.

Balzer, Oswald. *Genealogia Piastów*. Cracow: Nakladem Akademii Umiejetnosci, 1895.

Bariev, Riza. *Volzhskie bulgary: Istoriia i kul'tura*. Saint Petersburg: online at http://fstanitsa.ru/his_barievl_3.shtml, 1999.

Bartlett, Robert. *The Making of Europe: Conquest, Colonization and Cultural Change, 950–1350*. Princeton, N.J.: Princeton University Press, 1993.

Baumgarten, N. de. "Cunegonde d'Orlamunde." *Orientalia Christiana* 20, no. 66 (1930): 22–28.

———. "Généalogies et mariages Occidentaux des Rurikides Russes du X-e au XIII-e siècle." *Orientalia Christiana* 9, no. 25 (1927): 5–95.

———. "Pervaia vetv' kniazei Galitskikh." *Letopis' istoriko-rodoslovnago obshchestva v Moskve* 4 (1908): 1–30.

———. "Pribyslava de Russie." *Orientalia Christiana* 20, no. 3 (1930): 156–161.

———. *Saint Vladimir et la conversion de la Russie*. Rome: Pontifical Institute of Oriental Studies, 1932.

———. "Sofiia russkaia, koroleva datskaia, a zatem landgrafinia tiuringenskaia." *Seminarium Kondakovianum* 4 (1931): 95–104.

Bautier, Robert-Henri. "Anne de Kiev, reine de France, et la politique royale au XI-e siècle, étude critique de la documentation." *Revue des études Slaves* 57, no. 4 (1985): 539–564.

———. *The Economic Development of Medieval Europe*. Translated by Heather Karolyi. New York: Harcourt Brace Jovanovich, 1971.

———. "Henri Ier, l'empire et l'Anjou, 1043–1056." *Revue Belge de philologie et d'histoire* 25 (1947): 87–110.

Benson, Robert L. "Political *Renovatio*: Two Models from Roman Antiquity." In *Renaissance and Renewal in the Twelfth Century*, edited by Robert L. Benson and Giles Constable. Cambridge, Mass.: Harvard University Press, 1982.

Berend, Nora. *At the Gate of Christendom: Jews, Muslims, and "Pagans" in Medieval Hungary, c. 1000–c. 1300*. Cambridge: Cambridge University Press, 2001.

———. "Hungary, 'the Gate of Christendom.'" In *Medieval Frontiers: Concepts and Practices,* edited by David Abulafia and Nora Berend, 195–216. Burlington, Vt.: Ashgate, 2002.

Bernhardt, John W. *Itinerant Kingship and Royal Monasteries in Early Medieval Germany, c. 936–1075.* Cambridge: Cambridge University Press, 1993.

Beskow, Per. "Byzantine Influence in the Conversion of the Baltic Region?" In *The Cross Goes North: Processes of Conversion in Northern Europe, AD 300–1300,* edited by Martin Carver, 15–27. York, UK: York Medieval Press, 2003.

Bloch, Herbert. "Monte Cassino, Byzantium, and the West in the Earlier Middle Ages." *Dumbarton Oaks Papers* 3 (1946): 163–224.

———. "The New Fascination with Ancient Rome." In *Renaissance and Renewal in the Twelfth Century,* edited by Robert L. Benson and Giles Constable, 615–636. Cambridge, Mass.: Harvard University Press, 1982.

Blomqvist, Ragnar, and Anders W. Mårtensson. "Vardagsliv i Lerhyddor." In *Archaeologica Lendensia: Investigationes de antiquitatibus urbis Lundae,* edited by Ragnar Blomqvist and Anders W. Mårtensson. Lund: Kulturhistoriska Museet, 1961.

Boeck, Elena. "Simulating the Hippodrome: The Performance of Power in Kiev's St. Sophia." *Art Bulletin* 41, no. 3 (2009): 283–301

Bogomoletz, Wladimir V. "Anna of Kiev: An Enigmatic Capetian Queen of the Eleventh Century: A Reassessment of Biographical Sources." *French History* 19 (2005): 299–323.

Bouchard, Constance B. "Consanguinity and Noble Marriages in the Tenth and Eleventh Centuries." *Speculum* 56, no. 2 (1981): 268–287.

———. "Family Structure and Family Consciousness among the Aristocracy in the Ninth to Eleventh Centuries." *Francia* 14 (1986): 639–658.

———. "The Migration of Women's Names in the Upper Nobility, Ninth–Twelfth Centuries." *Medieval Prosopography* 9, no. 2 (1988): 1–20.

———. "Patterns of Women's Names in Royal Lineages, Ninth–Eleventh Centuries." *Medieval Prosopography* 9, no. 1 (1988): 1–32.

Brown, Elizabeth A. R. "The Tyranny of a Construct: Feudalism and Historians of Medieval Europe." *American Historical Review* 79, no. 4 (1974): 1063–1088.

Brown, Peter. "Eastern and Western Christendom in Late Antiquity: A Parting of the Ways." In *The Orthodox Churches and the West,* edited by Derek Baker, 1–24. Oxford: Basil Blackwell, 1976.

Brown, Peter Robert Lamont. *The Rise of Western Christendom: Triumph and Diversity, AD 200–1000.* 2nd ed. Malden, Mass.: Blackwell, 2003.

Browning, Robert. *Byzantium and Bulgaria: A Comparative Study across the Early Medieval Frontier.* Berkeley: University of California, 1975.

Brutzkus, J. "Trade with Eastern Europe, 800–1200." *Economic History Review* 13, nos. 1–2 (1943): 31–41.

Butler, Francis. *Enlightener of Rusʹ: The Image of Vladimir Sviatoslavich across the Centuries.* Bloomington, Ind.: Slavica, 2002.

———. "The Representation of Oral Culture in the *Vita Constantini.*" *Slavic and East European Journal* 39, no. 3 (1995): 367–384.

———. "Wenceslas: The Saint and His Name in Kievan Rus." *Slavic and East European Journal* 48, no. 1 (2004): 63–78.

Callmer, Johan. "The Archeology of Kiev ca A.D. 500–1000: A Survey." In *Les Pays du Nord et Byzance (Scandinavie et Byzance): Actes du colloque nordique et international de byzantinologie,* edited by Rudolf Zeitler. Uppsala: Almqvist and Wiksell, 1981.

Charvat, Petr. "Bohemia, Moravia and Long-Distance Trade in the 10th–11th Centuries." *Quaestiones Medii Aevi Novae* 5 (2000): 255–266.

Chaume, M. *Les origines du duché de Bourgogne.* Vol. 1. Dijon: Librarie E. Rebourseau, 1925.

Chibnall, Marjorie. *The Empress Matilda: Queen Consort, Queen Mother and Lady of the English.* Cambridge, Mass.: Blackwell, 1992.

Christiansen, Eric. *The Norsemen in the Viking Age.* Oxford: Oxford University Press, 2002.

———. *The Northern Crusades.* New York: Penguin, 1997.

Ciggaar, Krijnie N. "Byzantine Marginalia to the Norman Conquest." *Anglo-Norman Studies* 9 (1986): 43–63.

———. "Denmark and Byzantium from 1184 to 1212." *Mediaeval Scandinavia* 13 (2000): 118–143.

———. "The Empress Theophano (972–991): Political and Cultural Implications of Her Presence in Western Europe for the Low Countries, in Particular for the County of Holland." In *Byzantium and the Low Countries in the Tenth Century: Aspects of Art and History in the Ottonian Era,* edited by V. D. van Aalst and K. N. Ciggaar, 33–76. Hernen: A. A. Brediusstichting, 1985.

———. "England and Byzantium on the Eve of the Norman Conquest (The Reign of Edward the Confessor)." *Anglo-Norman Studies* 5 (1982).

———. "Theophano: An Empress Reconsidered." In *The Empress Theophano: Byzantium and the West at the Turn of the First Millennium,* edited by Adalbert Davids, 49–63. Cambridge: Cambridge University Press, 1995.

———. *Western Travellers to Constantinople: The West and Byzantium, 962–1204; Cultural and Political Relations.* Leiden: Brill, 1996.

Ciggaar, Krignie N., and Jos. M. M. Hermans. "Byzantium and the West in the Tenth Century: Some Introductory Notes." In *Byzantium and the Low Countries in the Tenth Century: Aspects of Art and History in the Ottonian Era,* edited by V. D. van Aalst and K. N. Ciggaar, 1–12. Hernen: A. A. Brediusstichting, 1985.

Claussen, M. A. *The Reform of the Frankish Church: Chrodegang of Metz and the* Regula canonicorum *in the Eighth Century.* Cambridge: Cambridge University Press, 2004.

Colucci, Michele. "The Image of Western Christianity in the Culture of Kievan Rus'." *Harvard Ukrainian Studies* 12–13 (1988–1989): 576–586.

Constable, Giles. "The Second Crusade as Seen by Contemporaries." *Traditio* 9 (1953): 213–280.

Conte, Francis. *The Slavs.* New York: Columbia University Press, 1995.

Cowdrey, H. E. J. *Pope Gregory VII, 1073–1085.* Oxford: Clarendon Press, 1998.

Cross, Samuel Hazzard. "Medieval Russian Contacts with the West." *Speculum* 10, no. 2 (April 1935).

———. "Yaroslav the Wise in Norse Tradition." *Speculum* 4, no. 2 (1929): 177–197.

Curta, Florin. *The Making of the Slavs: History and Archeology of the Lower Danube Region, c. 500–700.* Cambridge: Cambridge University Press, 2001.

Cutler, Anthony. "Byzantine Art and the North: Meditations on the Notion of Influence." In *Byzantium: Identity, Image, Influence; XIX International Congress of Byzantine Studies, University of Copenhagen, 18–24 August, 1996,* edited by Karsten Fledelius, 169–182. Copenhagen: Eventus, 1996.

———. "Garda, Kallunge, and the Byzantine Tradition on Gotland." *Art Bulletin* 51, no. 3 (1969): 257–266.

———. "Misapprehension and Misgivings: Byzantine Art and the West in the Twelfth and Thirteenth Centuries." In *Byzantium, Italy and the North: Papers on Cultural Relations,* 474–509. London: Pindar Press, 2000.

———. "The Sculpture and Sources of 'Byzantios.'" In *Byzantium, Italy and the North, Papers on Cultural Relations,* 431–454. London: Pindar Press, 2000.

Darden, Bill J. "Who Were the Sclaveni and Where Did They Come From?" *Byzantinische Forschungen* 28 (2004): 133–158.

Darkevich, V. P. "Proizvedeniia zapadnogo khudozhestvennogo remesla v vostochnoi evrope (X–XIV vv.)." *Arkheologiia SSSR* E1–57 (1966).

———. *Puteshestvie v drevniuiu Riazan': Zapiski arkheologa.* Riazan' Novoe vremia, 1993.

———. *Putiami srednevekovykh masterov,* Iz istorii mirovoi kul'tury. Moscow: Nauka, 1972.

Darkevich, V. P., and I. I. Edomakha. "Pamiatnik zapadnoevropesiskoi torevtiki XII veka." *Sovestskaia Arkheologia* 3 (1964): 247–255.

Davidan, O. I. "K voprosu o proiskhozhdenii i datirovke rannikh grebenok staroi ladogi." *Arkheologicheskii Sbornik* 10 (1968): 54–63.

———. "Bronzoliteinoe delo v Ladoge." *Arkheologicheskii Sbornik* 21 (1980): 59–67.

———. "Vesovye gir'ki Staroi Ladogi." *Arkheologicheskii sbornik* 28 (1987): 119–123.

Davids, Adalbert, ed. *The Empress Theophano: Byzantium and the West at the Turn of the First Millennium.* Cambridge: Cambridge University Press, 1995.

———. "Marriage Negotiations between Byzantium and the West and the Name of Theophano in Byzantium (Eighth to Tenth Centuries)." In *The Empress Theophano: Byzantium and the West at the Turn of the Millennium,* edited by Adalbert Davids, 99–120. Cambridge: Cambridge University Press, 1995.

Davies, Norman. *God's Playground: A History of Poland in Two Volumes.* Vol. 1, *The Origins to 1795.* Oxford: Oxford University Press, 2005.

Demus, Otto. *Byzantine Art and the West.* New York: New York University Press, 1970.

———. "Vorbildqualität und Lehrfunktion der byzantinischen Kunst." In *Stil und Überlieferung in der Kunst des Abendlandes,* 92–98. Berlin: Verlag Gebr Mann, 1967.

Dhondt, Jean. "Sept femmes et un trio de rois." *Contributions a l'histoire économique et sociale* 3 (1964–1965): 36–70.

Dimnik, Martin. *The Dynasty of Chernigov, 1054–1146.* Toronto: Pontifical Institute of Mediaeval Studies, 1994.

———. *The Dynasty of Chernigov, 1146–1246.* Cambridge: Cambridge University Press, 2003.

———. "The 'Testament' of Iaroslav 'The Wise': A Re-Examination." *Canadian Slavonic Papers* 29, no. 4 (1987): 369–386.

Dölger, Von Franz. "Wer war Theophano?" *Historisches Jahrbuch* 69 (1949): 646–658.

Drboglav, D. A. *Zagadki latinskikh kleim na mechakh IX–XIV vekov: Klassifikatsiia, datirovka i chtenie nadpisei.* Moscow: Izdatel'stvo Moskovskogo universiteta, 1984.

Duby, Georges. *The Early Growth of the European Economy: Warriors and Peasants from the Seventh to the Twelfth Century.* Ithaca, N.Y.: Cornell University Press, 1973.

———. "Le mariage dans la société du Haut Moyen Âge." *Il matrimonio nella societa altomedievale* 24 (1977): 13–42.

———. "Marriage in Early Medieval Society." In *Love and Marriage in the Middle Ages,* edited by Georges Duby, 3–21. Cambridge: Polity Press, 1994.

———. "Towards a History of Women in France and Spain." In *Love and Marriage in the Middle Ages,* edited by Georges Duby, 95–104. Cambridge: Polity Press, 1994.

Duczko, Wladislaw. "Viking Sweden and Byzantium: An Archeologist's Version." In *Byzantium: Identity, Image, Influence; XIX International Congress of Byzantine Studies, University of Copenhagen, 18–24 August, 1996,* edited by Karsten Fledelius, 193–200. Copenhagen: Eventus, 1996.

Dunbabin, Jean. *France in the Making, 843–1180.* Oxford: Oxford University Press, 1985.

———. "What's in a Name? Phillip, King of France." *Speculum* 68, no. 4 (1993): 949–968.

Dunlop, Eileen. *Queen Margaret of Scotland.* Edinburgh: National Museums of Scotland, 2005.

Dvornik, Francis. *Byzantine Missions among the Slavs.* New Brunswick, N.J.: Rutgers University Press, 1970.

———. *The Slavs in European History and Civilization.* New Brunswick, N.J.: Rutgers University Press, 1962.

Dzhakson, T. N. "Ingigerd, zhena kniazia Iaroslava mudrogo v izobrazhenii 'Priadi ob eimunde.'" In *Vostochnaia evropa v drevnosti i srednevekov'e,* edited by V. T. Pashuto, 14. Moscow: RAN, 1994.

Eastmond, Antony. "An Intentional Error? Imperial Art and 'Mis'-Interpretation under Andronikos I Komnenos." *Art Bulletin* 76, no. 3 (1994): 502–510.

Edwards, Carolyn. "Dynastic Sanctity in Two Early Medieval Women's *Lives.*" In *Medieval Family Roles: A Book of Essays,* edited by Cathy Jorgensen Itnyre, 3–20. New York: Garland, 1996.

Ericsson, K. "The Earliest Conversion of the Rus' to Christianity." *Slavonic and East European Review* 44, no. 102 (1966): 98–121.

Espéronnier, M. "Villes et commerce: La Khazarie et la Bulgarie de la Volga, d'après les textes arabes et persans des IXe et Xe siècles." In *Les centres proto-urbains russes entre Scandinavie, Byzance et Orient,* edited by M. Kazanski, A. Nercessian, and C. Zuckerman, 409–424. Paris: Éditions P. Lethielleux, 2000.

Featherstone, Jeffrey. "Ol'ga's Visit to Constantinople." *Harvard Ukrainian Studies* 14, nos. 3–4 (1990): 293–312.

Fine, John V. A., Jr. *The Early Medieval Balkans: A Critical Survey from the Sixth to the Late Twelfth Century.* Ann Arbor: University of Michigan Press, 1983.

———. "A Fresh Look at Bulgaria under Tsar Peter I (927–969)." *Byzantine Studies/Études Byzantines* 5, nos. 1–2 (1978): 88–95.

———. *The Late Medieval Balkans: A Critical Survey from the Late Twelfth Century to the Ottoman Conquest.* Ann Arbor: University of Michigan Press, 1987.

Fledelius, Karsten. "Royal Scandinavian Travellers to Byzantium: The Vision of Byzantium in Danish and Norwegian Historiography of the Early 13th Century—and in the Danish Historical Drama of the Early 19th Century." In *Byzantium: Identity, Image, Influence; XIX International Congress of Byzantine Studies, University of Copenhagen, 18–24 August, 1996,* edited by Karsten Fledelius, 212–219. Copenhagen: Eventus, 1996.

Fomin, A. V. "Drevnerusskie denezhno-monetniie rynki v 70–80 godakh X v." In *Drevneishiie gosudarstva Vostochnoi Evropy—Materialy i issledovaniia, 1992–1993 gody,* 63–73. Moscow: 1995.

Font, Márta. "Missions, Conversions, and Power Legitimization in East Central Europe at the Turn of the First Millenium." In *East Central and Eastern Europe in the Early Middle Ages,* edited by Florin Curta, 283–296. Ann Arbor: University of Michigan Press, 2008.

———. "Old-Russian Principalities and Their Nomadic Neighbours: Stereotypes of Chronicles and Diplomatic Practices of the Princes." *Acta Orientalia Academiae Scientiarum Hungaricae* 58, no. 3 (2005): 267–276.

Franklin, Simon. "The Empire of the Rhomaioi as Viewed from Kievan Russia: Aspects of Byzantino-Russian Cultural Relations." In *Byzantium—Rus'—Russia: Studies in the Translation of Christian Culture,* 507–537. Burlington, Vt.: Ashgate/Variorum, 2002.

———. *Writing, Society and Culture in Early Rus, c. 950–1300.* Cambridge: Cambridge University Press, 2002.

Frazer, Margaret English. "Church Doors and the Gates of Paradise: Byzantine Bronze Doors in Italy." *Dumbarton Oaks Papers* 27 (1973): 145–162.

Freccero, Carla. "Marguerite de Navarre and the Politics of Maternal Sovereignty." In *Women and Sovereignty,* edited by Louise Olga Fradenburg, 132–149. Edinburgh: Edinburgh University Press, 1992.

Freidson, Marion F. "A Study of Medieval Queenship: Capetian France, 987–1234." PhD diss., University of Chicago, 1964.

Fry, Peter Somerset, and Fiona Somerset Fry. *The History of Scotland.* New York: Barnes and Noble, 1982.

Fuglesang, Signe Horn. "A Critical Survey of Theories on Byzantine Influence in Scandinavia." In *Byzantium: Identity, Image, Influence; XIX International Congress of Byzantine Studies, University of Copenhagen, 18–24 August, 1996,* edited by Karsten Fledelius, 137–168. Copenhagen: Eventus, 1996.

Fulton, Rachel. *From Judgement to Passion: Devotion to Christ and the Virgin Mary, 800–1200.* New York: Columbia University Press, 2002.

Gagin, I. A. "Diplomatiia Volzhskoi Bulgarii v X-pervoi treti XIII vekov." PhD diss., Saint Petersburg University, 1997.

Gallén, J. "Vem var Valdemar den stores drottning Sofia?" *Historisk Tidskrift för Finland* 61 (1976): 273–288.

Garipzanov, Ildar. *"David imperator augustus, gratia Dei rex:* Communication and Propaganda in Carolingian Royal Iconography." In *Monotheistic Kingship: The Medieval Variants,* edited by Aziz Al-Azmeh and János M. Bak. Budapest: Central European University, 2004.

Gautier, Paul. "Le typikon de la Théotokos Kécharitôménè." *Revue des études Byzantines* 43 (1985): 5–165.

Geary, Patrick J. "Barbarians and Ethnicity." In *Late Antiquity: A Guide to the Postclassical World,* edited by G. W. Bowersock, Peter Brown, and Oleg Grabar, 107–129. Cambridge, Mass.: Harvard University Press, 1999.

Georgieva, Saška, "The Byzantine Princesses in Bulgaria," in *Byzantino-Bulgarica IX,* ed. N. Evtimova. Sofia: Editions de L'Academie Bulgare des Sciences, 1995.

Gimbutas, Marija. "Ancient Slavic Religion: A Synopsis." In *To Honor Roman Jakobson: Essays on the Occasion of His Seventieth Birthday* 1 (1967): 738–759.

Goetz, Hans-Werner. "Constructing the Past: Religious Dimensions and Historical Consciousness in Adam of Bremen's *Gesta Hamburgensis ecclesiae pontificum.*" In *The Making of Christian Myths in the Periphery of Latin Christendom (c. 1000–1300),* edited by Lars Boje Mortensen, 17–51. Copenhagen: Museum Tusculanum Press, University of Copenhagen, 2006.

Golb, Norman, and Omeljan Pritsak. *Khazarian Hebrew Documents of the Tenth Century.* Ithaca, N.Y.: Cornell University Press, 1982.

Golovko, A. B. *Drevniaia Rus' i Pol'sha v politicheskikh vzaimo-otnosheniiakh X-pervoi treti XIII vv.* Kiev: Naukova Dumka, 1988.

Grabar, André. "Pénétration Byzantine en islande et en Scandinavie." *Cahiers Archéologiques* 13 (1962): 296–301.

de Gray Birch, Walter. "Index of the Styles and Titles of English Sovereigns," *Report of the First Annual Meeting of the Index Society* (London, [n.p.], 1879): 4–72.

Grekov, B. D. *Kievskaia Rus'.* Moscow: Uchebno-pedagogicheskii izdatel'stvo, 1949.

Grierson, Philip. *Byzantine Coins.* Berkeley: University of California Press, 1982.

———. "Harold Hardrada and Byzantine Coin Types in Denmark." *Byzantinische Forschungen* 1 (1966): 124–138.

Gullbekk, Svein H. "Coinage and Monetary Economies." In *The Viking World,* edited by Stefan Brink in collaboration with Neil Price, 159–169. London: Routledge, 2008.

Gupalo, K. N. *Podol v drevnem Kieve.* Kiev: Naukova Dumka, 1982.

Györffy, György. *King Saint Stephen of Hungary.* New York: Columbia University Press, 1994.

Haastrup, Ulla. "Byzantine Elements in Frescoes in Zealand from the Middle of the 12th Century." In *Les Pays du Nord et Byzance (Scandinavie et Byzance): Actes due colloque Nordique et international de Byzantinologie,* edited by Rudolf Zeitler, 315–322. Uppsala: Almqvist and Wiksell, 1981.

Hammer, Carl I. *A Large-Scale Slave Society of the Early Middle Ages: Slaves and Their Families in Early Medieval Bavaria.* Burlington, Vt.: Ashgate, 2002.

Hanak, Walter K. "Saint Procopius, the Sázava Monastery, and the Byzantine-Slavonic Legacy: Some Reconsiderations." In *Byzantina et Slavica Cracoviensie III: Byzantium and East Central Europe,* edited by Günter Prinzing and Maciej Salamon, with the assistance of Paul Stephenson, 71–80. Cracow: Jagiellonian University, 2001.

Harris, Anthea. *Byzantium Britain and the West: The Archeology of Cultural Identity, AD 400–650.* Charleston, S.C.: Tempus, 2003.

Hellie, Richard. "Late Medieval and Early Modern Russian Civilization and Modern Neuroscience." In *Cultural Identity in a Multicultural State: Muscovy, 1359–1584,* edited by A. M. Kleimola and G. D. Lenhoff, 146–165. Moscow: ITS-Garant, 1997.

———. *Slavery in Russia, 1450–1725.* Chicago: University of Chicago Press, 1982.

Hendy, M. F. "Michael IV and Harold Hardrada." *Numismatic Chronicle* 10 (1970): 187–197.

Herrin, Judith. "Theophano: Considerations on the Education of a Byzantine Princess." In *The Empress Theophano: Byzantium and the West at the Turn of the First Millennium,* edited by Adalbert Davids, 64–85. Cambridge: Cambridge University Press, 1995.

Heyd, W. *Histoire du commerce du Levant.* Vol. 2. Leipzig: O. Harrassowitz, 1886.

Hilsdale, Cecily. "Diplomacy by Design: Rhetorical Strategies of the Byzantine Gift." PhD diss., University of Chicago, 2003.

———. "The Social Life of the Byzantine Gift: The Royal Crown of Hungary Re-Invented" *Art History* 31:5 (2008): 603–631.

———. "Constructing a Byzantine 'Augusta:' A Greek Book for a French Bride." *The Art Bulletin* 87:3 (2005): 458–83.

Holmes, Catherine. *Basil II and the Governance of Empire (976–1025).* Oxford: Oxford University Press, 2005.

———. "Basil II and the Government of Empire (976–1025)." DPhil diss., University of Oxford, 1999.

Holweck, F. G. *A Biographical Dictionary of the Saints.* St. Louis: B. Herder, 1924.

Honigmann, Ernest. "Studies in Slavic Church History." *Byzantion* 17 (1944–1945): 128–182.

Houben, Hubert. *Roger II of Sicily: A Ruler between East and West.* Translated by Graham A. Loud and Diane Milburn. Cambridge: Cambridge University Press, 2002.

Howard-Johnston, James. "Byzantium and Its Neighbors." In *The Oxford Handbook of Byzantine Studies,* edited by Elizabeth Jeffreys with John Haldon and Robin Cormack, 939–956. Oxford: Oxford University Press, 2009.

Hrushevsky, Mykhailo. *History of Ukraine-Rus'.* Translated by Marta Skorupsky. Edited by Andrzej Poppe and Frank E. Sysyn. Vol. 1. Edmonton: Canadian Institute of Ukrainian Studies Press, 1997.

Hunneycutt, Lois. "Female Succession and the Language of Power in the Writings of Twelfth-Century Churchmen." In *Medieval Queenship,* edited by John Carmi Parsons, 189–202. Gloucestershire: Sutton, 1994.

———. "The Idea of the Perfect Princess: The Life of Saint Margaret in the Reign of Matilda II, 1100–1118." *Anglo-Norman Studies* 12 (1989): 81–98.

Ianin, V. L., ed. *Aktovye pechati Drevnei Rusi X–XV vv.* Moscow: Nauka, 1970.

———, ed. *Arkheologiia Novgoroda: Ukazatel' literatury, 1981–1990 gg.; Dopolneniia k ukazateliu za 1917–1980 gg.* Moscow: 1992.

———. *Denezhno-vesovye sistemy russkogo srednevekoviia: Domongolskii period.* Moscow: Moskovskogo universiteta, 1956.

———. "Nakhodka drevnerusskikh vislykh pechatei v Sigtune (Shvetsiia)." In *Vostochnaia evropa v drevnosti i srednevekov'e: X cheteniia k 80-letiiu chlena-korrespondenta AN SSSR Vladimira Terent'evicha Pashuto,* edited by E. A. Mel'nikova, 139–141. Moscow: RAN, 1998.

———. "Pechati Feofano Muzalon." *Numizmatika i sfragistika* 2 (1965): 76–90.

———. "Russkaia kniaginia Olisava-Gertruda i ee syn Iaropolk." *Numizma-tika i epigrafika* 4 (1963): 142–164.

Ingham, Norman W. "Has a Missing Daughter of Iaroslav Mudry Been Found?" *Russian History* 25, no. 3 (1998): 231–270.

———. "The Litany of Saints in 'Molitva Sv. Troicĕ.'" In *Studies Presented to Professor Roman Jakobson by His Students,* 121–136. Cambridge, Mass.: Slavica, 1968.

———. "The Martyred Prince and the Question of Slavic Cultural Continuity in the Early Middle Ages." In *Medieval Russian Culture,* edited by Henrik Birnbaum and Michael S. Flier. Berkeley: University of California Press, 1984.

———. "A Slavist's View of Agatha, Wife of Edward the Exile, as a Possible Daughter of Yaroslav the Wise." *New England Historical and Genealogical Register* 152, no. 606 (1998): 217–223.

———. "The Sovereign as Martyr, East and West." *Slavic and East European Journal* 17, no. 1 (1973): 1–17.

Ioannisyan, Oleg M. "Archeological Evidence for the Development and Urbanization of Kiev from the 8th to the 14th Centuries." In *From the Baltic to the Black Sea: Studies in Medieval Archeology,* edited by David Austin and Leslie Alcock, 285–312. London: Unwin Hyman, 1990.

Ivakin', I. M. *Kniaz' Vladimir Monomakh i ego pouchenie.* Moscow: Univer-sitetskaia tipografia, 1901.

Ivanov, Sergey A. "Kogda v Kieve poiavilsia pervyi khristianskii khram?" *Slaviane i ikh sosedi* 11 (2004): 9–18.

———. "Religious Missions." In *The Cambridge History of the Byzantine Empire, c. 500–1492,* edited by Jonathan Shepard, 305–332. Cambridge: Cambridge University Press, 2009.

Jakobson, Roman. "The Beginnings of National Self-Determination in Europe." *Review of Politics* 7, no. 1 (1945): 29–42.

Jetté, René. "Is the Mystery of the Origin of Agatha, Wife of Edward the Exile, Finally Solved?" *New England Historical and Genealogical Register* 150, no. 600 (1996): 417–432.

Johnson, Edgar N. "The German Crusade on the Baltic." In *A History of the Crusades,* edited by Kenneth M. Sutton et al., 2:545–585. Madison: University of Wisconsin Press, 1969–1989.

Jónsdóttir, Selma. *An 11th Century Byzantine Last Judgement in Iceland.* Reykjavík: Almenna Bókafélagið, 1959.

Kaiser, Daniel H. "The Economy of Kievan Rus': Evidence from the *Pravda Rus'kaia.*" In *Ukrainian Economic History: Interpretive Essays,* edited by

I. S. Koropeckyj, 37–57. Cambridge, Mass.: Harvard University Press, 2001.

———. *The Growth of the Law in Medieval Russia.* Princeton, N.J.: Princeton University Press, 1980.

Kaldellis, Anthony. *Hellenism in Byzantium: The Transformations of Greek Identity and the Reception of the Classical Tradition.* Cambridge: Cambridge University Press, 2007.

Karamzin, N. M. *Istoriia gosudarstva Rossiiskogo.* Vol. 2. Moscow: Kniga, 1988.

Karger, M. K. *Arkheologicheskie issledovaniia drevnego Kieva: Otchety i materialy, 1938–1947 gg.* Kiev: Akademii nauk Ukr. SSR, 1951.

———. *Drevnii Kiev: Ocherki po istorii material'noi kul'tury drevnerusskogo goroda.* Leningrad: Akademii nauk SSSR, 1958–1961.

Karras, Ruth Mazo. *Slavery and Society in Medieval Scandinavia.* New Haven, Conn.: Yale University Press, 1988.

Kashtanov, S. M. "Byla li Oda Shtadenskaia zhenoi velikogo kniazia Sviatoslava Iaroslavicha?" In *Vostochnaia Evropa v drevnosti i srednevekov'e,* edited by V. T. Pashuto, 15–19. Moscow: RAN, 1994.

Kazhdan, Alexander P. "The notion of Byzantine diplomacy." In *Byzantine Diplomacy: Papers from the Twenty-Fourth Spring Symposium of Byzantine Studies, Cambridge, March 1990,* edited by Jonathon Shepard and Simon Franklin, 3–24. Brookfield, Vt.: Variorum, 1990.

———, ed. *The Oxford Dictionary of Byzantium.* Vols. 2–3. Oxford: Oxford University Press, 1991.

———. "Rus'-Byzantine Princely Marriages in the Eleventh and Twelfth Centuries." *Harvard Ukrainian Studies* 12–13 (1988–1989): 414–429.

———. "Vizantiiskii podatnoi sborshchik na beregakh kimmeriiskogo bospora v kontse XII v." *Problemy obshchestvenno-politicheskoi istorii Rossii i slavianskikh stran; Sbornik statei k 70-letiiu akademika M. N. Tikhomirova* (1963): 93–101.

Kazhdan, Alexander P. and Ann Wharton Epstein. *Change in Byzantine Culture in the Eleventh and Twelfth Centuries.* Berkeley: University of California Press, 1985.

Kholodilin, A. N. "Avtografy Anny Iaroslavny—koroleva Frantsii." *Russkaia Rech',* no. 2 (1985): 109–113.

Khrustalev, D. G. *Razyskaniia o Efreme Pereiaslavslom.* Saint Petersburg: Evraziia, 2002.

Kilievich, S. R. *Detinets Kieva IX-pervoi poloveny XIII vekov: Po materialam arkheologicheskikh issledovanii.* Kiev: Naukova Dumka, 1982.

Kirpichnikov, A. N. "Drevnerusskoe oruzhie: Vypusk pervyi, mechi i sabli IX–XIII vv." *Arkheologiia SSSR* E1, no. 36 (1966): 5–181.

Kirpichnikov, A. N., Lena Thålin-Bergman, and Ingmar Jansson. "A New Analysis of Viking-Age Swords from the Collection of the Statens Historiska Musser, Stockholm, Sweden." *Russian History/Histoire Russe* 28, nos. 1–4 (2001): 221–244.

Kitzinger, Ernst. "The Arts as Aspects of a Renaissance." In *Renaissance and Renewal in the Twelfth Century,* edited by Robert L. Benson, and Giles Constable, 637–670. Cambridge, Mass.: Harvard University Press, 1982.

———. "The Byzantine Contribution to Western Art of the Twelfth and Thirteenth Centuries." In *The Art of Byzantium and the Medieval West: Selected Studies,* edited by W. Eugene Kleinbauer, 357–388. Bloomington: Indiana University Press, 1976.

Klasson, Christofer. "The Byzantine Heritage in Sweden." *Byzantium and the North: Acta Byzantina Fennica* 1 (1985): 69–75.

Knoll, Paul. "Economic and Political Institutions on the Polish-German Frontier in the Middle Ages." In *Medieval Frontier Societies,* edited by Robert Bartlett and Angus MacKay, 151–176. Oxford: Clarendon Press, 1989.

Koehler, Wilhelm. "Byzantine Art in the West." *Dumbarton Oaks Papers* 1 (1941): 61–87.

Kolchina, B. A., and V. L. Ianin, eds. *Arkheologicheskoe izuchenie Novgoroda: Sbornik statei.* Moscow: Nauka, 1978.

Kollman, Nancy Shields. "Collateral Succession in Kievan Rus'." *Harvard Ukrainian Studies* 14, nos. 3–4 (1990): 377–387.

Komech, A. I. *Drevnerusskoe zodchestvo kontsa X-nachala XII v.: Vizantiiskoe nasledie i stanovlenie samostoiatel'noi traditsii.* Edited by V. L. Ianin. Moskva: Nauka, 1987.

Konovalova, I. "Les Rus sur les voies de commerce de l'Europe orientale d'après les sources arabo-persanes." In *Les centres proto-urbains russes entre Scandinavie, Byzance et Orient,* edited by M. Kazanski, A. Nercessian, and C. Zuckerman, 395–408. Paris: Éditions P. Lethielleux, 2000.

Korpela, Jukka. *Prince, Saint and Apostle: Prince Vladimir Svyatoslavic of Kiev, His Posthumous Life, and the Religious Legitimization of the Russian Great Power.* Wiesbaden: Harassowitz, 2001.

Kostiuchenko, T. Iu. "Soiuz chernykh klobukov (Tiurkskoe ob'edinenie na Rusi v XI–XIII v.v.)." PhD diss., Oriental Institute of National Academy of Science, 2005.

Kosztolnyik, Z. J. *Five Eleventh Century Hungarian Kings: Their Policies and Relations with Rome.* New York: Columbia University Press, 1981.

———. *From Coloman the Learned to Bela III (1095–1196): Hungarian Domestic Policies and Their Impact upon Foreign Affairs.* New York: Columbia University Press, 1987.

———. *Hungary under the Early Árpáds, 890s to 1063.* Boulder, Colo.: East European Monographs, 2002.

Kotliar, N. F. *Diplomatiia iuzhnoi Rusi.* Saint Petersburg: Aleteiia, 2003.

———. "Stranstvuiushchie dvory galitskikh kniazei." In *Vostochnaia evropa v drevnosti i srednevekov'e.* Moscow: Institut vseobshchei istorii RAN, 2008, 110–115.

Kovalev, Roman K. "Mint Output in Tenth-Century Bukhārā: A Case Study of Dirham Production and Monetary Circulation in Northern Europe." *Russian History/Histoire Russe* 28, nos. 1–4 (2001): 245–271.

Kromann, Anne, and Jørgen Steen Jensen. "Byzantine Inspired Nordic Coinage from the 11th Century." In *Byzantium: Identity, Image, Influence; XIX International Congress of Byzantine Studies, University of Copenhagen, 18–24 August, 1996,* edited by Karsten Fledelius, 183. Copenhagen: Eventus, 1996.

Laiou, Angeliki E., ed. *The Economic History of Byzantium: From the Seventh through the Fifteenth Century.* 3 vols. Washington, D.C.: Dumbarton Oaks Research Library and Collection, 2002.

———. "Exchange and Trade: Seventh–Twelfth Centuries." In *The Economic History of Byzantium: From the Seventh through the Fifteenth Century,* edited by Angeliki E. Laiou, 697–770. Washington, D.C.: Dumbarton Oaks Research Library and Collection, 2002.

Lascaratos, John, and S. Marketos. "The Penalty of Blinding during Byzantine Times: Medical Remarks." *Documenta opthalmologica* 81, no. 1 (1992): 133–144.

Leib, Bernard. *Rome, Kiev et Byzance à la fin du XIe siècle.* Paris: Auguste Picard, 1924.

Levin, Eve. "The Role and Status of Women in Medieval Novgorod." PhD diss., Indiana University, 1983.

———. *Sex and Society in the World of the Orthodox Slavs, 900–1700.* Ithaca, N.Y.: Cornell University Press, 1989.

Lewis, Andrew W. *Royal Succession in Capetian France: Studies on Familial Order and the State.* Cambridge, Mass.: Harvard University Press, 1981.

Lewis, Archibald R. *The Northern Seas: Shipping and Commerce in Northern Europe, a.d. 300–1100.* Princeton, N.J.: Princeton University Press, 1958.

Leyser, Karl. "Ends and Means in Liudprand of Cremona." In *Byzantium and the West, c. 850–c. 1200: Proceedings of the XVIII Spring Symposium of*

Byzantine Studies, edited by J. D. Howard-Johnston, 119–144. Amsterdam: Verlag Adolf M. Hakkert, 1988.

———. *Medieval Germany and Its Neighbours, 900–1250.* London: Hambledon Press, 1982.

———. "The Tenth Century in Byzantine-Western Relationships." In *Relations between East and West in the Middle Ages,* edited by Derek Baker. Edinburgh: Edinburgh University Press, 1973.

———. "'Theophanu divina gratia imperatrix augusta': Western and Eastern Emperorship in the Later Tenth Century." In *The Empress Theophano: Byzantium and the West at the Turn of the First Millennium,* edited by Adalbert Davids, 1–27. Cambridge: Cambridge University Press, 1995.

Likhachev, D. S., and N. V. Ponyrko, eds. *Epistoliarnoe nasledie Drevnei Rusi XI–XIII: Issledovaniia, teksty, perevody.* Saint Petersburg: Nauka, 1992.

Limonov, Iu. A. "Etnicheskii i geograficheski 'spravochnik' cheloveka drevnei rusi (IX–XIII v.v.)." In *Vostochnaia evropa v drevnosti i srednevekov'e,* edited by V. T. Pashuto, 21–22. Moscow: RAN, 1994.

Lindkvist, Thomas. "The Emergence of Sweden." In *The Viking World,* edited by Stefan Brink in collaboration with Neil Price, 668–674. London: Routledge, 2008.

Litvina, A. F., and F. B. Uspenskii. "'Monastyr' Sv. Simeona v Kieve: K istorii russko-nemetskikh sviazei XI v." *Slaviane i ikh sosediakh* 12 (2008): 276–284.

———. "Var'irovanie rodovogo imeni na russkoi pochve: Ob odnom iz sposobov imianarecheniia v dinastii Riurikovichei." *Imenoslov* (2003): 136–183.

———. *Vybor imeni u russkikh kniazei v X–XVI vv.* Moscow: Indrik, 2006.

Loparev, Kh. "Vizantiiskaiia pechat' s imenem russkoi kniagini." *Vizantiiskii Vremennik* 1, no. 1 (1894): 159–166.

Lopez, Robert Sabatino. "The Dollar of the Middle Ages." *Journal of Economic History* 11, no. 3 (1951): 209–234.

Loseva, O. V. *Russkie mesiatseslovy.* Moscow: Pamiatniki istoricheskoi mysli, 2001.

Lotter, Friedrich. "The Crusading Idea and the Conquest of the Region East of the Elbe." In *Medieval Frontier Societies,* edited by Robert Bartlett and Angus MacKay, 267–306. Oxford: Clarendon Press, 1989.

Lowden, John. "The Luxury Book as Diplomatic Gift." In *Byzantine Diplomacy: Papers from the Twenty-Fourth Spring Symposium of Byzantine Studies, Cambridge, March 1990,* edited by Jonathan Shepard and Simon Franklin, 249–262. Brookfield, Vt.: Variorum, 1990.

L'vova, Z. A. "Stekliannye busy staroi ladogi." *Arkheologicheskii sbornik* 10 (1968): 64–94.

———. "Stekliannye busy Staroi Ladogi: Chast II. Proiskhozhdenie bus." *Arkheologicheskii sbornik* 12 (1970): 89–111.

———. "K voprosu o prichinakh pronikhoveniia stekliannykh bus X–nachala XI veka v severnye raiony vostochnoi evropy." *Arkheologicheskii sbornik* 18 (1977): 106–109.

Macrides, Ruth. "Dynastic Marriages and Political Kinship." In *Byzantine Diplomacy: Papers from the Twenty-Fourth Spring Symposium of Byzantine Studies, Cambridge, March 1990,* edited by Jonathan Shepard and Simon Franklin, 263–280. Brookfield, Vt.: Variorum, 1990.

Magdalino, Paul. "The Empire of the Komnenoi (1118–1204)." In *The Cambridge History of the Byzantine Empire, c. 500–1492,* edited by Jonathan Shepard, 627–663. Cambridge: Cambridge University Press, 2009.

———. "The Medieval Empire (780–1204)." In *The Oxford History of Byzantium,* edited by Cyril Mango, 169–213. Oxford: Oxford University Press, 2002.

Maiorov, A. V. *Galitsko-Volynskaia Rus': Ocherki sotsial'no-politicheskikh otnoshenii v domongol'skii period.* Saint Petersburg: Universitetskaia kniga, 2001.

Majeska, George. "Patriarch Photius and the Conversion of Rus'." *Russian History/Histoire Russe* 32, nos. 3–4 (2005): 413–418.

Makarov, N. "Traders in the Forest: The Northern Periphery of Rus' in the Medieval Trade Network." In *Pre-Modern Russia and Its World: Essays in Honor of Thomas S. Noonan,* edited by Kathryn L. Reyerson, Theofanis G. Stavrou, and James D. Tracy, 115–133. Wiesbaden: Harrassowitz, 2006.

Malingoudi, Jana. *Die russisch-byzantinischen Verträge des 10. Jahrhunderts aus diplomatischer Sicht.* Thessaloniki: Vanias 1994.

Malinin, V. A. *Rus' i zapad.* Kaluga: N. Bochkarevoi, 2000.

Malmer, Brita. "The Byzantine Empire and the Monetary History of Scandinavia during the 10th and 11th Century A.D." In *Les pays du nord et Byzance (Scandinavie et Byzance): Actes du colloque Nordique et international de Byzantinologie,* edited by Rudolf Zeitler, 125–130. Uppsala: Almqvist and Wiksell, 1981.

———. "Some Observations on the Importation of Byzantine Coins to Scandinavia in the Tenth and Eleventh Centuries and the Scandinavian Response." *Russian History/Histoire Russe* 28, nos. 1–4 (2001): 295–302.

Martin, Janet. "Coins, Commerce, and the Conceptualization of Kievan Rus'." In *Pre-Modern Russia and Its World: Essays in Honor of Thomas S.*

Noonan, edited by Kathryn L. Reyerson, Theofanis G. Stavrou, and James D. Tracy, 161–172. Wiesbaden: Harrassowitz, 2006.

———. *Medieval Russia, 980–1584.* Cambridge: Cambridge University Press, 2nd Ed. 2007.

———. *Treasure of the Land of Darkness: The Fur Trade and Its Significance for Medieval Russia.* Cambridge: Cambridge University Press, 1986.

Martin, Therese. "The Art of a Reigning Queen as Dynastic Propaganda in Twelfth-Century Spain." *Speculum* 80, no. 4 (2005): 1134–1171.

Mateos, Juan. *Le typicon de la grande église.* Vols. 165–166 of Orientalia Christiana Analecta. Rome: Pont. Institutum Orientalium Studiorum, 1962.

Mauri, Carmen. "Chronica Petri comitis Poloniae." In *Monumenta Poloniae Historica: Nova Series,* edited by Marian Plezia, 1–30. Cracow: Subsidio Ministerii Scholarum Superiorum et Studiorum, 1951.

Mavrodin, V. V. *Obrazovanie drevnerusskogo gosudarstva.* Leningrad: Leningradskogo universiteta, 1945.

McCormick, Michael. "Byzantium's Role in the Formation of Early Medieval Civilization: Approaches and Problems." *Illinois Classical Studies* 12, no. 2 (1987): 207–220.

———. *Origins of the European Economy: Communications and Commerce,* a.d. *300–900.* Cambridge: Cambridge University Press, 2001.

Medieval Russian Laws. Translated by George Vernadsky. New York: Oxford University Press, 1947.

Mel'nikova, E. A. "Put' kak strukturnaia osnova mental'noi karti sostavitelia 'povesti vremennykh let.'" In *Vostochnaia evropa v drevnosti i srednevekov'e,* 150–156. Moscow: Institut vseobshchei istorii RAN, 2008.

Meyendorff, John. *Byzantium and the Rise of Russia: A Study of Byzantino-Russian Relations in the Fourteenth Century.* Cambridge: Cambridge University Press, 1981.

Mezentsev, Volodymyr I. "The Territorial and Demographic Development of Medieval Kiev and Other Major Cities of Rus': A Comparative Analysis Based on Recent Archeological Research." *Russian Review* 48, no. 2 (1989): 145–170.

Minasian, R. S. "Chetyre gruppy nozhei Vostochnoi Evropy epokhi rannego srednevekov'ia: K voprosu o poiavlenii slavianskikh form v lesnoi zone," *Arkheologicheskii Sbornik* 21 (1980): 68–74.

Morrisson, Cécile. *Catalogue des monnaies byzantines de la bibliothèque nationale.* Vol. 2. Paris: Bibliothèque nationale, 1970.

Moshin, V. V. "Russkie na Afone i russko-vizantiiskie otnosheniia v XI–XII vv." *Byzantinoslavica* 9 (1947–1948): 55–85.

Nazarenko, A. V. *Drevniaia Rus' na mezhdunarodnykh putiakh: Mezhdist-siplinarnye ocherki kul'turnykh, torgovykh, politicheskikh sviazei IX–XII vekov.* Moscow: Iazyki russkoi kul'tury, 2001.

———. "Kievskaia kniagina—vnuka papy L'va IX (1049–1054): Imperatora Genrikha III (1039–1056); Novye dannye o vneshnei politike Rusi v 70-kh gg. XI v." In *Vostochnaia Evropa v drevnosti i srednevekov'e,* edited by V. T. Pashuto, 26–29. Moscow: RAN, 1994.

———. "Mitropolii iaroslavichei vo vtoroi polovine XI veka." In *Drevniaia Rus' i Slaviane,* 207–245. Moscow: RAN, 2009.

———. "Proiskhozhdeniie drevnerusskogo denezhno-vesevogo scheta." In *Drevneishiie gosudarstva Vostochnoi Evropy 1994 g. Novoye v numizma-tike,* 5–79. Moscow: Nauka, 1996.

———. "Rus' i Germaniia v IX–X vv." In *Drevneishie gosudarstva Vostochnoi Evropy: Materialy i issledovaniia—1991 god,* 5–138. Moscow: Nauka, 1994.

———. "'Zelo nepodobno pravovernym': Mezhkonfessional'nye braki na rusi v XI–XII vekakh." In *Drevniaia Rus' i Slaviane,* 269–283. Moscow: RAN, 2009.

Nesbitt, John. "Sigillography." In *The Oxford Handbook of Byzantine Studies,* edited by Elizabeth Jeffreys with John Haldon and Robin Cormack, 150–156. Oxford: Oxford University Press, 2009.

Nesbitt, John, and Nicolas Oikonomidès, eds. *Catalogue of Byzantine Seals at Dumbarton Oaks and in the Fogg Museum of Art.* 5 vols. Washington, D.C.: Dumbarton Oaks Research Library and Collection, 1991–2005.

Nicol, D. M. "The Byzantine View of Western Europe." In *Byzantium: Its Ecclesiastical History and Relations with the Western World,* 315–339. London: Variorum Reprints, 1972.

Nightingale, Pamela. "The Evolution of Weight-Standards and the Creation of New Monetary and Commercial Links in Northern Europe from the Tenth Century to the Twelfth Century," *Economic History Review* 38, no. 2 (1985): 192–209.

Noonan, T. S. "The Flourishing of Kiev's International and Domestic Trade, ca. 1100–ca.1240." In *Ukrainian Economic History: Interpretive Essays,* edited by I. S. Koropeckyj, 102–146. Cambridge, Mass.: Harvard University Press, 2001.

———. *The Islamic World, Russia and the Vikings, 750–900: The Numismatic Evidence.* Brookfield, Vt.: Ashgate, 1998.

———. "Medieval Islamic Copper Coins from European Russia and Surrounding Regions: The Use of the Fals in Early Islamic Trade with Eastern Europe." *Journal of the American Oriental Society* 94, no. 4 (1974): 448–453.

——. "Medieval Russia, the Mongols, and the West: Novgorod's Relations with the Baltic, 1100–1350." *Mediaeval Studies* 37 (1975): 316–339.

——. *The Millennium of Russia's First Perestroika: The Origins of a Kievan Glass Industry under Prince Vladimir.* Washington, D.C.: Wilson Center, Kennan Institute for Advanced Russian Studies, 1989.

——. "Technology Transfer between Byzantium and Eastern Europe: A Case Study of the Glass Industry in Early Russia." In *The Medieval Mediterannean: Cross-Cultural Contacts,* edited by M. J. Chiet and K. L. Reyerson, 105–111. St. Cloud, Minn.: North Star Press of St. Cloud, 1988.

——. "When Did Rus Merchants First Visit Khorezm and Baghdad?" *Archivum Eurasiae Medii Aevi* 7 (1987): 213–220.

——. "Why Dirhams First Reached Russia: The Role of Arab-Khazar Relations in the Development of the Earliest Islamic Trade with Eastern Europe." *Archivum Eurasiae Medii Aevi* 4 (1984): 151–282.

——. "Why the Vikings First Came to Russia." In *The Islamic World, Russia and the Vikings, 750–900: The Numismatic Evidence,* 321–348. Brookfield, Vt.: Ashgate, 1998.

Nordhagen, Per Jonas. "Byzantium and the West." In *Les Pays du Nord et Byzance (Scandinavie et Byzance): Actes du colloque nordique et international de byzantinologie,* edited by Rudolf Zeitler. Uppsala: Almqvist and Wiksell, 1981.

Nordstrom, Byron J., ed. *Dictionary of Scandinavian History.* Westport, Conn.: Greenwood Press, 1985.

Nosov, Evgeny N. "The Problem of the Emergence of Early Urban Centres in Northern Russia." In *Cultural Transformations and Interactions in Eastern Europe,* edited by John Chapman and Pavel Dolukhanov, 236–256. Brookfield, Vt.: Aldershot, 1993.

Novoseltsev, A. P., and V. T. Pashuto. "Vneshniaia torgovlia drevnei Rusi do serediny XIII." *Istoriia SSSR* 3 (1967): 81–108.

Obolensky, Dimitri. *The Byzantine Commonwealth: Eastern Europe 500–1453.* London: Weidenfeld and Nicolson, 1971.

——. "Byzantine Frontier Zones and Cultural Exchanges." In *Actes du XIVe congrès international des études Byzantines,* 303–314. Bucharest: Editura Academiei Republicii Socialiste România, 1974.

——. *The Byzantine Inheritance of Eastern Europe.* London: Variorum Reprints, 1982.

——. "Byzantium and Russia in the Late Middle Ages." In *Byzantium and the Slavs: Collected Studies,* edited by Dimitri Obolensky, 248–275. London: Variorum Reprints, 1971.

————. "Byzantium, Kiev and Moscow: A Study in Ecclesiastical Relations."
In *Byzantium and the Slavs: Collected Studies,* edited by Dimitri Obolensky, 23–78. London: Variorum Reprints, 1971.

Ohnsorge, Werner. "Otto I. und Byzanz." In *Konstantinopel und der Okzident,* 208–226. Darmstadt: Wissenschaftliche Buchgesellschaft, 1966.

————. *Das Zweikaiserproblem im früheren Mittelalter.* Hildesheim: Verlags-
buchhandlung, 1947.

Oikonomidès, Nicolas. *A Collection of Dated Byzantine Lead Seals.* Washington, D.C.: Dumbarton Oaks Research Library and Collection, 1986.

Ostrogorsky, George. *History of the Byzantine State.* Translated by Joan
Hussey. Rev. ed. New Brunswick, N.J.: Rutgers University Press, 1969.

————. "Vizantiia: Kievskaia kniaginia Ol'ga." In *To Honor Roman Jakobson:
Essays on the Occasion of His Seventieth Birthday* 2 (1967): 1458–1473.

Ostrowski, Donald. "The Account of Volodimer's Conversion in the *Povest'
vremennykh let:* A Chiasmus of Stories." *Harvard Ukrainian Studies* 28,
nos. 1–4 (2006 [2009]): 567–580.

————. *Muscovy and the Mongols: Cross-Cultural Influences on the Steppe
Frontier, 1304–1589.* Cambridge: Cambridge University Press, 1998.

Paris, Louis. "Roger II, XLIVe eveque de Chalons, sa vieet sa mission en
Russie," in *La Chronique de Champagne* [1837], 2:89–99.

Parsons, John Carmi. "Family, Sex, and Power: The Rhythms of Medieval
Queenship." In *Medieval Queenship,* edited by John Carmi Parsons, 1–12.
Gloucestershire: Sutton, 1994.

————. "Mothers, Daughters, Marriage, Power: Some Plantagenet Evidence,
1150–1500." In *Medieval Queenship,* edited by John Carmi Parsons,
63–78. Gloucestershire: Sutton, 1994.

Pashuto, V. T. *Vneshniaia politika Drevnei Rusi.* Moscow: Nauka, 1968.

Pashuto, V. T., and A. P. Novosel'tsev. "Vneshnaia torgovykh sviazei Drevnei
Rusi." *Istoriia SSSR* 1 (1967).

Pchelov, E. V. *Genealogiia drevnerusskikh kniazei.* Moscow: Rossiiskii
gosudarstvennyi gumanitarnyi universitet, 2001.

————. "Pol'skaia kniagina—Mariia Dobronega Vladimirovna." In *Vostochnaia Evropa v drevnosti i srednevekov'e,* edited by V. T. Pashuto, 31–33.
Moscow: RAN, 1994.

Perkhavko, V. B. "Kievo-Pecherskii paterik o torgovle sol'iu v drevnei rusi." In
Vostochnaia evropa v drevnosti i srednevekov'e, edited by V. T. Pashuto.
Moscow: Akademii nauk SSSR, 1990, 105–109.

————. *Torgovyi mir srednevekovoi Rusi.* Moskva: Academia, 2006.

————. "Zarozhdenie kupchestva na Rusi." In *Vostochnaia evropa v drevnosti i
srednevekov'e: X Cheteniia k 80–letiiu chlena-korrespondenta AN SSSR*

Vladimira Terent'evicha Pashuto. Edited by E. A. Mel'nikova. Moscow: RAN, 1998.

Petrukhin, V. Ia. "Pokhod Olega na Tsar'grad: K problem istochnikov letopisnogo rasskaza." In *Slaviane i ikh sosedi: Grecheskii i slavianskii mir v srednie veka i rannee novoe vremia,* 15–16. Moscow: Institut slavianovedeniia i balkanistiki RAN, 1994.

Picchio, Riccardo. "From Boris to Volodimer: Some Remarks on the Emergence of Proto-Orthodox Slavdom." *Harvard Ukrainian Studies* 12–13 (1988–1989): 200–213.

Pikio, Rikardo. *Provoslavnoto slavianstvo i starob'lgarkata kultura traditsiia.* Sofia: Sv. Kliment Okhridski, 1993.

Piskorski, Jan M. "Medieval Colonization in East Central Europe." In *The Germans and the East,* edited by Charles Ingrao and Franz A. J. Szabo, 27–36. West Lafayette, Ind.: Purdue University Press, 2008.

Poluboiarinova, M. D. *Rus' i Volzhskaia Bolgariia v X–XV vv.* Moscow: Nauka, 1993.

Poppe, Andrzej V. "Feofano Novgorodskaia." *Novgorodskii istoricheskii sbornik* 6, no. 16 (1997): 102–120.

———. "The Political Background to the Baptism of Rus': Byzantine-Russian Relations between 986–989." In *The Rise of Christian Russia,* 197–244. London: Variorum, 1982.

———. *The Rise of Christian Russia.* London: Variorum Reprints, 1982.

———. "Russkie mitropolii konstantinopol'skoi patriarkhii v XI stoletii." *Vizantiiskii vremennik* 28 (1968): 95–104.

Potin, V. M. *Drevniaia Rus' i evropeiskie gosudarstva v X–XIII vv.: Istoriko-numismaticheskii ocherk.* Leningrad: Sovetskii Khudozhnik, 1968.

Poulet, André. "Capetian Women and the Regency: The Genesis of a Vocation." In *Medieval Queenship,* edited by John Carmi Parsons, 93–116. Gloucestershire: Sutton, 1994.

Priselkov, M. D. *Ocherki po tserkovno-politicheskoi istorii Kievskoi Rusi X–XII vv.* Saint Petersburg: M. M. Stasiuloevicha, 1913.

Pritsak, Omeljan. *The Origin of Rus'.* Vol. 1, *Old Scandinavian Sources Other Than Sagas.* Cambridge, Mass.: Harvard Ukrainian Research Institute, 1981.

———. *The Origins of the Old Rus' Weights and Monetary Systems: Two Studies in Western Eurasian Metrology and Numismatics in the Seventh to Eleventh Centuries.* Cambridge, Mass.: Harvard Ukrainian Research Institute, 1998.

———. *When and Where was Ol'ga Baptized?* Cambridge, Mass.: Harvard Ukrainian Studies Fund, 1987.

Pushkareva, Natalia L. *Chastnaia zhizn' russkoi zhenshchiny: Nevesta, zhena, liubovnitsa (X-nachalo XIX v.)*. Moscow: Ladomir, 1997.

———. *Women in Russian History: From the Tenth to the Twentieth Century*. Translated by Eve Levin. Armonk, N.Y.: M. E. Sharpe, 1997.

———. *Zhenshchiny Drevnei Rusi*. Moscow: Mysl', 1989.

Putsko, V. G. "Kamennyi relief iz kievskikh nakhodok." *Sovestskaia Arkheologia* 2 (1981): 223–232.

Rabinowitz, L. *Jewish Merchant Adventurers: A Study of the Radanites*. London: Edward Goldston, 1948.

Radke, Christian. "Money, Port and Ships from a Schleswig Point of View." In *Connected by the Sea: Proceedings of the Tenth International Symposium on Boat and Ship Archeology, Roskilde 2003*, edited by Lucy Blue, Fred Hocker, and Anton Englert, 147–151. Oxford: Oxbow Books, 2006.

Raffensperger, Christian. "Dynastic Marriage in Action: How Two Rusian Princesses Changed Scandinavia." In *Imenoslov: Istoricheskaia semantika imeni*, 187–199. Moscow: Indrik, 2009.

———. "Evpraksia Vsevolodovna between East and West." *Russian History/Histoire Russe* 30, no. 1–2 (2003): 23–34.

———. "Rusian Influence on European Onomastic Traditions." In *Imenoslov: Istoricheskaia semantika imeni*, 116–134. Moscow: Indrik, 2007.

Rapov, O. M. "Vneshniaia politika Vladimira Velikogo posle ofitsial'nogo priniatiia rus'iu khristianstva." In *Vostochnaia Evropa v drevnosti i srednevekov'e*, edited by V. T. Pashuto, 33–36. Moscow: RAN, 1994.

Raumer, Georg Wilhelm von. *Historiche Charten und Stammtafeln zu den Regesta Historiae Brandenburgesis*. Berlin: Trowitzsch und Sohn, 1837.

Reisman, Edward. "Determinants of Collective Identity in Rus', 988–1505." PhD diss., University of Chicago, 1987.

Reuter, Timothy. *Germany in the Early Middle Ages, c. 800–1056*. London: Longman, 1991.

Reynolds, Susan. *Fiefs and Vassals: The Medieval Evidence Reinterpreted*. Oxford: Oxford University Press, 1994.

Robinson, Fred C. "Medieval, the Middle Ages." *Speculum* 59, no. 4 (1984): 745–756.

Robinson, I. S. *Henry IV of Germany, 1056–1106*. Cambridge: Cambridge University Press, 1999.

———. *The Papacy, 1073–1198: Continuity and Innovation*. Cambridge: Cambridge University Press, 1990.

Roesdahl, Else. *Viking Age Denmark*. Translated by Susan Margeson and Kirsten Williams. London: British Museum Publications, 1982.

——. *The Vikings*. London: Penguin, 1991.

Rozanov, S. P. "Evfimiia Vladimirovna i Boris Kolomanovich: Iz evropeiskoi politiki XII v." *Izvestiia Akademii Nauk SSSR* 8 (1930): 585–599.

——. "Evpraksiia-Adel'geida Vsevolodovna, (1071–1109)." *Izvestiia Akademii Nauk SSSR* 8, ser. 7 (1929).

Rozhdestvenskaia, T. V. "Dogovory Rusi s Vizantiei X v. v strukture letopisnogo povestvovaniia." In *Vostochnaia evropa v drevnosti i srednevekov'e: X Cheteniia k 80-letiiu chlena-korrespondenta AN SSSR Vladimira Terent'evicha Pashuto*, edited by E. A. Mel'nikova. Moscow: RAN, 1998.

Runciman, Steven. *A History of the Crusades*. Vol. 1. New York: Penguin, 1951.

——. *A History of the Crusades*. Vol. 2. Cambridge: Cambridge University Press, 1962.

——. *A History of the First Bulgarian Empire*. London: G. Bell and Sons, 1930.

Russell, Josiah. *Medieval Regions and Their Cities*. Bloomington: Indiana University Press, 1972.

Rybakov, B. A., ed. *Keramika i steklo drevnei Tmutarakani*. Moscow: Akademii nauk SSSR, 1963.

——. *Remeslo Drevnei Rusi*. Moscow: Akademii Nauk SSSR, 1948.

Rydzevskaia, E. A. "Drevniaia Rus' i Skandinaviia v IX–XIV vv.: Materialy i issledovaniia." *Drevneishie gosudarstva na territorii SSSR* (1978): 8–236.

Sakharov, A. N. *Diplomatiia Sviatoslava*. Moscow: Mezhdunarodnye otnosheniia, 1982.

Samsonowicz, Henryk. "The City and the Trade Route in the Early Middle Ages." In *Central and Eastern Europe in the Middle Ages: A Cultural History,* edited by Piotr Górecki and Nancy van Deusen, 20–29. London: Tauris, 2009.

Sawyer, Birgit, and Peter Sawyer. *Medieval Scandinavia: From Conversion to Reformation, circa 800–1500*. Minneapolis: University of Minnesota Press, 1993.

Sawyer, Peter. *Kings and Vikings: Scandinavia and Europe, ad 700–1100.* London: Methuen, 1982.

Schmid, Karl. "The Structure of the Nobility in the Earlier Middle Ages." In *The Medieval Nobility: Studies on the Ruling Classes of France and Germany from the Sixth to the Twelfth Century,* edited by Timothy Reuter, 37–60. Amsterdam: North-Holland, 1979.

Schramm, Percy Ernst. "Der Titel 'Servu Jesu Christi' Kaiser Ottos III." *Byzantinische Zeitschrift* 30 (1930).

Sevcenko, Ihor. *Byzantium and the Slavs: In Letters and Culture.* Cambridge, Mass.: Harvard Ukrainian Research Institute, 1991.

Shahîd, Irfan. *Rome and the Arabs: A Prolegomenon to the Study of Byzantium and the Arabs.* Washington, D.C.: Dumbarton Oaks Research Library and Collection, 1984.

Shakhmatov, A. A. *Razyskaniia o russkikh letopisiakh.* Moscow: Akademicheskii Proekt, 2001. Reprint of the 1908 edition.

Shchalova, Iu. L. "Nekotorye materialy k istorii russko-vizantiiskikh otnoshenii v xi–xii vv." *Vizantiiskii vremennik* 19 (1961): 60–75.

Shchapov, Ia. N. *Gosudarstvo i tserkov': Drevnei Rusi X–XIII vv.* Moscow: Nauka, 1989.

———. *State and Church in Early Russia: 10th–13th Centuries.* Translated by Vic Schneierson. New Rochelle, N.Y.: Aristide D. Caratzas, 1993.

Shchaveleva, N. I. *Drevniaia Rus' v "Pol'skoi Istorii" Iana Dlugosha: Tekst, perevod, kommentarii.* Edited by A. V. Nazarenko. Moscow: Pamiatniki Istoricheskoi Mysli, 2004.

———. "Kniaz' Iaropolk Iziaslavich i khristianskaia tserkov' XI v." In *Vostochnaia Evropa v drevnosti i srednevekov'e: X cheteniia k 80-letiiu chlena-korrespondenta AN SSSR Vladimira Terent'evicha Pashuto,* edited by E. A. Mel'nikova, 132–136. Moscow: RAN, 1998.

———. "Pol'ki—zheny russkkh kniazei (XI—seredina XIII v.)." *Drevneishie gosudarstva na territorii SSSR* (1989): 50–57.

Sheehan, Michael M. "Choice of Marriage Partner in the Middle Ages: Development and Mode of Application of a Theory of Marriage." In *Marriage, Family, and Law in Medieval Europe: Collected Studies,* edited by James K. Farge, 87–117. Toronto: University of Toronto Press, 1997.

Shepard, Jonathan. "Byzantine Diplomacy, A.D. 800–1204: Means and Ends." In *Byzantine Diplomacy: Papers from the Twenty-Fourth Spring Symposium of Byzantine Studies, Cambridge, March 1990,* edited by Jonathon Shepard and Simon Franklin, 41–72. Brookfield, Vt.: Variorum, 1990.

———. "Byzantium and Russia in the Eleventh Century: A Study in Political and Ecclesiastical Relations." PhD diss., University of Oxford, 1973.

———. "Conversions and Regimes Compared: The Rus' and the Poles, ca. 1000." In *East Central and Eastern Europe in the Early Middle Ages,* edited by Florin Curta, 254–286. Ann Arbor: University of Michigan Press, 2008.

———. "A Marriage Too Far? Maria Lekapena and Peter of Bulgaria." In *The Empress Theophano: Byzantium and the West at the Turn of the Millennium,* edited by Adalbert Davids, 121–149. Cambridge: Cambridge University Press, 1995.

———. "Some Remarks on the Sources for the Conversion of Rus'." In *Le origini e lo sviluppo della Cristianità Slavo-Bizantina,* edited by S. W. Swierkosz-Lenart, 59–96. Rome: Nella Sede Dell'istituto Palazzo Borromini, 1992.

———. "Western Approaches (900–1025)." In *The Cambridge History of the Byzantine Empire, c. 500–1492,* edited by Jonathan Shepard, 537–559. Cambridge: Cambridge University Press, 2009.

———. "Why Did the Russians Attack Byzantium in 1043?" *Byzantinische-Neugriechische Jahrbücher* 22 (1985): 147–212.

Shepard, Jonathan, and Simon Franklin. *The Emergence of Rus, 750–1200.* Longman History of Russia. New York: Longman, 1996.

Shtakel'berg, Iu. I. "Glinianye diski iz Staroi Ladogi." *Arkehologicheskii sbornik* 4 (1962): 109–115.

Shusharin, V. P. *Sovremenaia burzhuaznaia istoriografiia Drevnei Rusi.* Moscow: Nauka, 1964.

Sindbæk, Søren Michael. "Local and Long-Distance Exchange." In *The Viking World,* edited by Stefan Brink in collaboration with Neil Price, 150–158. London: Routledge, 2008.

Skovgaard-Petersen, Inge. "Queenship in Medieval Denmark." In *Medieval Queenship,* edited by John Carmi Parsons, 25–42. Gloucestershire: Sutton, 1994.

Smolka, Stanislaw. *Mieszko Stary i jego wiek.* Warsaw: Geberthnera i wolfa, 1881.

Sokolov, P. L. *Russkii arkhierei iz Vizantii i pravo ego naznacheniia do nachala XV veka.* Kiev: I. I. Chokolov, 1913.

Sorokin, Petr. "Staraya Ladoga: A Seaport in Medieval Russia." In *Connected by the Sea: Proceedings of the Tenth International Symposium on Boat and Ship Archeology, Roskilde 2003,* edited by Lucy Blue, Fred Hocker, and Anton Englert, 157–162. Oxford: Oxbow Books, 2006.

Sotnikova, M. P., ed. *Drevneishie russkie monety X–XI vekov: Katalog i issledovanie.* Moscow: Banki i birzhi, 1995.

Southern, R. W. *The Making of the Middle Ages.* New Haven, Conn.: Yale University Press, 1974.

Stafford, Pauline. "The Portrayal of Royal Women in England, Mid-Tenth to Mid-Twelfth Centuries." In *Medieval Queenship,* edited by John Carmi Parsons, 143–168. Gloucestershire: Sutton, 1994.

———. *Queen Emma and Queen Edith: Queenship and Women's Power in Eleventh-Century England.* Malden, Mass.: Blackwell, 1997.

———. *Queens, Concubines, and Dowagers: The King's Wife in the Early Middle Ages.* Athens, Ga.: University of Georgia Press, 1983.

Stephenson, Paul. "Balkan Borderlands (1018–1204)." In *The Cambridge History of the Byzantine Empire, c. 500–1492,* edited by Jonathan Shepard, 664–691. Cambridge: Cambridge University Press, 2009.

———. *Byzantium's Balkan Frontier: A Political Study of the Northern Balkans, 900–1204.* Cambridge: Cambridge University Press, 2000.

Sullivan, Richard E. "Khan Boris and the Conversion of Bulgaria: A Case Study of the Impact of Christianity on a Barbarian Society." *Studies in Medieval and Renaissance History* 3 (1966): 53–140.

Sunderland, Elizabeth. *Five Euphemias: Women in Medieval Scotland, 1200–1420.* New York: St. Martin's Press, 1999.

Sverdlov, M. B. "Rus' i evropeiskie gosudarstva." In *Sovetskaia istoriografiia Kievskoi Rusi,* edited by V. V. Mavrodin, 177–189. Leningrad: Nauka, 1978.

Tachiaos, Anthony-Emil N. "The Greek Metropolitans of Kievan Rus': An Evaluation of Their Spiritual and Cultural Activity." *Harvard Ukrainian Studies* 12–13 (1988–1989): 430–445.

Teggart, Frederick J. *Rome and China: A Study of Correlations in Historical Events.* Berkeley: University of California Press, 1939.

Thomas, Alastair H., and Stewart P. Oakley. *Historical Dictionary of Denmark.* Lanham, Md.: Scarecrow Press, 1998.

Thomsen, Vilhelm. *The Relations between Ancient Russia and Scandinavia and the Origin of the Russian State.* New York: Burt Franklin, 1877.

Thomson, Francis J. "The Bulgarian Contribution of the Reception of Byzantine Culture in Kievan Rus': The Myths and the Enigma." In *The Reception of Byzantine Culture in Mediaeval Russia,* 214–261. Brookfield, Vt.: Ashgate, 1999.

———. "The Intellectual Silence of Early Russia." In *The Reception of Byzantine Culture in Medaeval Russia,* ix–xxii. Brookfield, Vt.: Ashgate, 1999.

Tikhomirov, M. N. *Drevnerusskie goroda.* Moscow: Politicheskaia Literatura, 1956.

———. *The Towns of Ancient Rus.* Translated by Y Sdobnikov. Moscow: Foreign Language Publishing House, 1959.

Tolochko, Aleksei. *"Istoriia Rossiiskaia" Vasiliia Tatishcheva: Istochniki i izvestiia.* Kiev: Kritika, 2005.

Tolochko, P. P., ed. *Arkheologicheskie issledovaniia Kieva, 1978–1983 gg.: Sbornik nauchnykh trudov.* Kiev: Naukova Dumka, 1985.

———, ed. *Chernigov i ego okruga v IX–XIII vv.: Sbornik nauchnykh trudov.* Kiev: Naukova Dumka, 1988.

———. *Kochevye narody stepei i Kievskaia Rus'.* Kiev: Abris, 1999.

UIlman, Walter. *A Short History of the Papacy in the Middle Ages.* London: Methuen, 1972.

Urban, William L. *The Baltic Crusade.* Chicago: Lithuanian Research and Studies Center, 1994.

———. *The Livonian Crusade.* Washington, D.C.: University Press of America, 1981.

———. *The Prussian Crusade.* Lanham, Md.: University of America, 1980.

———. *The Samogitian Crusade.* Chicago: Lithuanian Research and Studies Center, 1989.

Urbańczyk, Przemysław. "The Politics of Conversion in North Central Europe." In *The Cross Goes North: Processes of Conversion in Northern Europe, ad 300–1300,* edited by Martin Carver, 15–27. York, UK: York Medieval Press, 2003.

Uspenskii, F. B. *Imia i vlast': Vybor imeni kak instrument dinasticheskoi bor'by v srednevekovoi skandinavii.* Moscow: Iazyki russkoi kul'tury, 2001.

Uspensky, F. "Notes sur l'histoire des études Byzantines en Russie." *Byzantinische Zeitschrift* 2 (1925): 1–53.

Vasil'evskii, V. "Drevniaia torgovlia Kieva s Regensburgom." *Zhurnal' ministerstva narodnago prosveshcheniia* (1888): 121–150.

Vasil'evskii, V. G. *Trudy.* Vols. 1–2. Saint Petersburg: Izdanie Imperatorskoi Akademii Nauk, 1908.

Vasiliev, A. A. "Hugh Capet of France and Byzantium." *Dumbarton Oaks Papers* 6 (1951): 227–251.

———. *The Russian Attack on Constantinople.* Cambridge, Mass.: Harvard University Press, 1946.

Vasmer, Max. *Russisches etymologisches Wörterbuch.* Heidelberg: Carl Winter, 1953.

Vavrinek, V., and Bohumila Zasterova. "Byzantium's Role in the Formation of Great Moravian Culture." *ByzantinoSlavica* 43, no. 2 (1982): 161–188.

Vernadsky, George. *Kievan Russia.* New Haven, Conn: Yale University Press, 1948.

Vincenz, A. de. "West Slavic Elements in the Literary Language of Kievan Rus'." *Harvard Ukrainian Studies* 12–13 (1988–1989): 262–275.

Vlasto, A. P. *The Entry of the Slavs into Christendom.* Cambridge: Cambridge University Press, 1970.

von Falkenhausen, Vera. "I Diplomi Rei Re Normanni in Lingua Greca." In *Documenti Medievali Greci e Latini: Studi Comparativi,* edited by Giuseppe De Gregorio e Otto Kresten, 253–308. Spoleto: Centro Italiano di Studi Sull'alto Medioevo, 1998.

Voyce, Arthur. *The Art and Architecture of Medieval Russia.* Norman: University of Oklahoma Press, 1977.

Wall, Valerie. "Queen Margaret of Scotland (1070–1093): Burying the Past, Enshrining the Future." In *Queens and Queenship in Medieval Europe: Proceedings of a Conference Held at King's College London, April 1995,* edited by Anne J. Duggan. Woodbridge: Boydell Press, 1997.

Wasilewski, T., ed. *Slownik Starozlnosci Slowianskich.* Vol. 4. Warsaw: Polskiej Akademii Nauk, 1970.

Werner, Karl Ferdinand. "Kingdom and Principality in Twelfth-Century France." In *The Medieval Nobility: Studies on the Ruling Classes of France and Germany from the Sixth to the Twelfth Century,* edited by Timothy Reuter, 243–290. Amsterdam: North-Holland, 1979.

Wertner, Mór. *Az Árpádok családi története.* Nagy-Becskereken, 1892.

Whittow, Mark. *The Making of Byzantium, 600–1025.* Berkeley: University of California Press, 1996.

———. "The Middle Byzantine Economy." In *The Cambridge History of the Byzantine Empire, c. 500–1492,* edited by Jonathan Shepard, 465–492. Cambridge: Cambridge University Press, 2009.

Williams, Edward V. *The Bells of Russia: History and Technology.* Princeton, N.J.: Princeton University Press, 1985.

Wilson, Alan. *St. Margaret, Queen of Scotland.* Edinburgh: John Donald, 1993.

Wolf, Armin. "Reigning Queens in Medieval Europe: When, Where, and Why." In *Medieval Queenship,* edited by John Carmi Parsons, 169–188. Gloucestershire: Sutton, 1994.

Wolff, Robert Lee. "The Three Romes: The Migration of an Ideology and the Making of an Autocrat." *Daedalus* 88, no. 2 (1959): 291–311.

Wozniak, Frank Edward, Jr. "The Nature of Byzantine Foreign Policy toward Kievan Russia in the First Half of the Tenth Century: A Reassessment." PhD diss., Stanford University, 1973.

Zaitseva, Irina E. "Metal Ornaments in the Rural Sites of Northern Russia: Long Distance Trade or Local Metalwork?" In *Centre, Region, Periphery: Medieval Europe: Basel 2002,* vol. 3, edited by Guido Helmig et al. Hertingen: Folio Verlag Dr. G. Wesselkamp 2002.

Zakharov, Sergey. "Beloozero Town: An Urban Centre on the Periphery." In *Centre, Region, Periphery: Medieval Europe—Basel 2002,* vol. 3, edited by Guido Helmig et al. Hertingen: Folio Verlag Dr. G. Wesselkamp 2002.

Zernov, Nicholas. "Vladimir and the Origin of the Russian Church." *Slavonic and East European Review* 28 (1949–1950): 123–138.

Živković, Tibor. "The Earliest Cult of Saints in Ragusa." In *Forging Unity: The South Slavs between East and West—550–1150,* 147–156. Belgrade: Institute of History, 2008.

Zotov, R. V. *O Chernigovskikh kniaz'iakh po Liubetskomu sinodiku v tatarskoe vremia.* Saint Petersburg: Tipografiia brat'ev Panteleevykh, 1892.

Acknowledgments

This project began a decade ago as a master's seminar paper for Richard Hellie at the University of Chicago. Since then I have had help from innumerable people, far too many to list all of them, for which I apologize.

At the University of Chicago, Sheila Fitzpatrick had enough confidence in me to assist me with research funding and graciously assisted on a project nearly one thousand years outside of her own interests. Walter Kaegi was, and remains, an invaluable advisor. His bibliographic memory has provided me with more footnotes than I can count. In addition he provided me with an early publication that allowed me to get some of my own ideas in print, ideas that have since evolved into the Byzantine Ideal included here. Finally, Richard Hellie was an amazing mentor who always had a minute, or an hour, to spend working through drafts, questions, and general problems. I am deeply saddened that he did not get the chance to see this book in print, but I hope that he would approve.

There are a number of people who have given advice and feedback on this project over its long history, too many to name all of them. That said, I would like to thank a few personally, including Edward Cohn for being a friend as well as a critic; Francis Butler for taking in a young scholar and walking him through multiple conferences; Brian and Elena Boeck for their mentoring and words of wisdom on both history and art history (even if I don't always listen); Janet Martin for being a gracious advisor who always had a word of encouragement; Norman Ingham for allowing a historian into his literature class and proceeding to educate me on much more than literature. As I say, there are too many people who have added to this project to name individually, but corporately I would like to thank the members of the Early Slavic Studies Association, who have all, at one time or another, helped and advised me on my work. And, of course, the editorial staff at Harvard University Press, who helped turn this manuscript into a book.

My colleagues at Wittenberg University deserve an enormous vote of thanks as well. They are wonderful colleagues who provide a supportive environment on good and bad days both. Many of them have participated in this project, and so I would like to thank the entire History Department: Thomas Taylor, Molly Wood, Tammy Proctor, Amy Livingstone, Scott Rosenberg, Tanya Maus, Dar Brooks Hedstrom, and Joe O'Connor. They provided the sanity and encouragement to help get this project done. At Wittenberg as well, I have had two exceptional student assistants, Ruby Daily and Adam Matthews, who helped with various portions of the book.

Additionally, there are a number of granting institutions that have helped to fund the research that underlies this work, particularly the University of Chicago, University of Nebraska, and Wittenberg University, which have provided the bulk of the support for putting this project together. The administration and library staffs at those institutions have been incredibly supportive, especially June Farris and Sandra Levy at the University of Chicago, who (even for an alumnus) can find anything, anywhere, anytime; and Doug Lehman at Wittenberg University, who doesn't have everything, but can always get it fast.

Finally, I would like to thank my wife, Cara, for taking a chance on me even when I decided to give up a budding career and go back to school. I appreciate the support more than I can ever say.

Index

Harvard University Press is a member of Green Press Initiative
(greenpressinitiative.org), a nonprofit organization working to
help publishers and printers increase their use of recycled paper
and decrease their use of fiber derived from endangered forests.
This book was printed on recycled paper containing 30%
post-consumer waste and processed chlorine free.